W9-BBN-124

NOV 1988

RECEIVED
OHIO DOMINICAN
COLLEGE LIBRARY
COLUMBUS, OHIO
43219

A History and Philosophy
of the
Social Sciences

A History and Philosophy
of the
Social Sciences

PETER T. MANICAS

Basil Blackwell

300.9
M 278 R
1987

Copyright © Peter T. Manicas 1987
First published 1987
Basil Blackwell Ltd
108 Cowley Road, Oxford OX4 1JF, UK

Basil Blackwell Inc.
432 Park Avenue South, Suite 1503
New York, NY 10016, USA

All rights reserved. Except for the quotation of short passages for the purposes of criticism and review, no part of this publication may be reproduced, stored in a retrieval system, or transmitted, in any form or by any means, electronic, mechanical, photocopying, recording or otherwise, without the prior permission of the publisher.

Except in the United States of America, this book is sold subject to the condition that it shall not, by way of trade or otherwise, be lent, re-sold, hired out, or otherwise circulated without the publisher's prior consent in any form of binding or cover other than that in which it is published and without a similar condition including this condition being imposed on the subsequent purchaser.

British Library Cataloguing in Publication Data

Manicas, Peter T.
A history and philosophy of the social sciences.
1. Social sciences—Philosophy
2. Social sciences—History
I. Title
300'.1   H61

ISBN 0–631–15258–X

Library of Congress Cataloging in Publication Data

Manicas, Peter T.
A history and philosophy of the social sciences.

Bibliography: p.
Includes index.
1. Social sciences—History.   2. Social sciences—Philosophy.   I. Title.
H51.M37   1987   300'.9   86–17525

ISBN 0–631–15258–X

Typeset in 10 on 12pt Times New Roman
by The Word Factory, Tonbridge, Kent
Printed in Great Britain by T J Press, Padstow

Contents

127576

Acknowledgements

This book is embarrassingly ambitious, and I would not have attempted it except for a great deal of good luck in my teaching situations – Queens College, the New School for Social Research, and, intermittently over the years, the Political Science Department at the University of Hawaii. The immediate opportunity to do the book derived from an offer from Deane Neubauer, Dean of the Social Sciences at the University of Hawaii. He asked me to run a seminar for his Division which would endeavour to integrate the history and philosophy of the social sciences. I brought together many years of teaching various aspects of these subjects, constructed a course, and gave it in the spring of 1985. The book is the result of this. So my first debt is to Deane Neubauer. The group which he encouraged to come to this seminar included some excellent graduate students and a number of faculty members as well. I must mention five who were particularly kind: Jack Bilmes and Brian Hallett, who read parts of the manuscript, Tom Maretski, Magid Tehranian, and Alan Howard.

My second debt is to Queens College, but especially to its President, Saul B. Cohen, now doing other important work, for the sabbatical during which most of the book was written. Queens gave me the time, Neal Milner and the Political Science Department at Hawaii gave me the space. The word processor was Larry Meacham's idea, and a good one indeed. My last debt to Hawaii is to Manfred Henningsen, gadfly *par excellence*, who carefully read the entire manuscript, keeping me from some egregious errors of conception, fact, and syntax. Very special thanks are due to him.

But 20 years of mostly undergraduate teaching at Queens College was the precondition. I was lucky there to have chaired the program in Contemporary Civilization for many years, a series of courses which went the way of all good things, but which for me was an invaluable education. But I also have had the chance to do an extraordinary amount of team-teaching at Queens, first in an adult seminar in the methodology of the social sciences in the very exciting Queens ACE program, guided for many years by its Dean, Ernest Schwarcz. Over the years, I shared this course with some distinguished social scientists, including Raymond Franklin, Charles Smith, Burton Zwiebach and Solomon Resnik. More recently, I had the chance to chair the Honors Seminar in the social sciences. This is also an expensive course since four faculty are in the room at the same time; but it provided an opportunity to learn, for students and teachers alike, which these days is all too rare. In this seminar, I have had as co-faculty Paul Avrich, Tito Gerassi, Alem Habtu, Ed Hansen, Albert Levinson, Milt Mankoff, Lenny Markovitz, Carl Riskin, Mark Rosenblum, Eugene Sachs, Alice Sardell, Dean Savage, Paul Secord, Mariam Slater, Bill Tabb, Ron Waterbury, Alan Wolfe, Mike Wresnik, and the others already named. Bill Tabb and I recently did a course on socialism, and last year Tito Gerassi and I gave a course in the new Queens College Master of Arts and Liberal Studies program. All these people have been my teachers over the years, and there is no way to measure my debt to them.

One final piece of good fortune must be mentioned. For a number of years, there has been at Queens College what has come to be called 'the Monday Group'. This group meets for lunch and discussion, stimulated by a presentation given sometimes by a Queens' person, sometimes by a visitor. Not only have I had the chance to present my ideas to this group, but every occasion has been one which has convinced me that knowledge is indeed a social product. In addition, then, to most of those already mentioned, regular participants to the Monday Group include Barry Commoner, Ralph Della Cava, Kim Edel, Matt Edel, Bob Factor, Mike Harrington, Mike Krasner, Ron Lawson, Marvin Leiner, Harry Levine, Ruth Milkman, Charles Molesworth, Len Rodberg, Frank Rosengarten, Samona Sheppard, and Dave Sprintzen.

Nevertheless, despite the excellent opportunities, my fight to get straight as to what realism is has depended on persistent attacks from my dear friends in the Philosophy Department: Ralph Sleeper, Alan Rosenberg, Gene Fontinell, and Jack Noone. Now that John McDermott has gone to greener pastures, they have had to suffer the full impact of my stubbornness.

I am grateful, finally to Basil Blackwell for permission to use, in chapters 13 and 14, materials which originally appeared in *The Journal for the Theory of Social Behavior* and portions of material in chapters 9 and 14 which appeared in *Psychology: Designing the Discipline* (Basil Blackwell, 1986).

Author's Note

Where reference is made to an edition of a work first published some years earlier, the date in the reference is the date of the edition. The bibliography gives full details of that edition as well as the date of original publication. A few works alluded to by name and date only do not appear in the bibliography – these dates are intended as 'pointers' only.

Part I

The Critical Ideas

Introduction

This book is a history of the social sciences, but it is meant to contribute to the current discussion in the philosophy of the social sciences. As a history, it looks at the past from a particular vantage point; but since I cannot imagine how one escapes this, I do it unapologetically. I look at the past from the point of view of the current debate in the philosophy of science, in particular with an eye toward taking seriously the hypothesis that the very idea of science is contestable.

Now the idea that the very notion of science is contestable may seem innocent enough, especially as regards the notion of a social or human science. But it is critical to notice that there was, for a very long time, a very stable notion of 'science', and that this very stable idea of science has been the point of departure taken for granted by all parties to the more recent debates over the nature of social science – both 'naturalistic' defenders of the idea of a social science and promoters of the several 'anti-naturalistic' alternatives. Moreover, it is only very recently that radically different understandings of the nature of science have become serious alternatives. This means that we can now reconsider the history of ideas about 'science' in the light of the possibility that the relatively stable view of science, familiar in all the textbooks, stems from misconceptions going back into history, not merely from the period immediately preceding this one, the heyday of the 'philosopher/physicists' of the late nineteenth century, but perhaps from the very beginnings of modern science in the West. That is, we can consider the possibility that the practices of the modern sciences which emerged in the sixteenth and seventeenth centuries were *in*correctly characterized and that for various historical reasons, this remained unrecognized in the more refined and sophisticated 'philosophies' of science which subsequently came to be articulated.

But since the present shape of the modern social sciences dates only from the turn of the century – or so I shall argue – we can consider the further possibility that for good historical reasons, the social sciences have been constituted in terms of an untenable conception of what a proper science is. The upshot is the possibility of a thoroughgoing revolution in the received ideas of science, natural and social. It allows us to ask whether there is a huge gap between the ideology of science and practices in the physical sciences, and whether, more disastrously, the social sciences have been ideologically constituted in the sense that they were based on *false* beliefs about what the physical sciences are.

The argument of the present book has three parts. Part I is a selective history of ideas which has two related aims. First, I try to identify the often unclear conceptions of the distinguishing features of 'science' as they affect the competing visions about the nature and province of a human science or sciences. Thus I begin with an account of the first critical division, the eighteenth-century divorce of 'science' from 'philosophy', the development of 'theory of knowledge' and the critical idea, shared by British empiricists and Kant, that whatever there may be that lies beyond experience cannot belong to the domain of 'science'. I then show in subsequent chapters how these notions, along with ideas about 'causality', 'lawfulness', and 'explanation' drive alternative conceptions of human science.

I also try to show how different substantive 'political' conclusions, part product of the theorist's reflections on what we now call 'modernity' entered into these different visions. Speaking broadly, and recognizing notable exceptions – for example, Comte and his French legacy – positivist theories tended toward epistemological, methodological, and political individualism. After the French Revolution, they tended also toward racism, sexism, and anti-egalitarianism. The anti-positivists, including here Rousseau, Montesquieu, Herder, Hegel, and Marx were each in their own ways 'radical'.

The historical account of part I attempts to be contextualist regarding the contestable assumptions and categories. This allows me to reconnect in a more historically apt way what are usually thought of as *separate* histories, of 'philosophy', of 'science', of 'history', of 'political thought', and so on. Moreover, I try to show that it is not the case that the whole 'development' represents some sort of 'progressive' emancipation of the 'disciplines' from a 'pre-scientific' and confused past. Figures not usually juxtaposed thus become part of the story I want to tell – for example, Herder, Ranke, Hegel, Schmoller, Menger, and Max Weber; neoclassical political economy, Pareto and Durkheim; J. S. Mill, Spencer, Helmholtz, Wundt, and Mach.

In part I, I do nothing more than hint at the pertinent 'sociology' of the struggles over the 'knowledges' which constitute the materials from which the modern social sciences were constituted. I try to keep in mind the fundamental conditions – capitalism, the French and Industrial Revolutions, the emergence of the modern state, the nation-state, and the 'social problem'. Part II is a more serious effort along these lines. I argue that for historically specific reasons, the by now familiar practices and disciplinary divisions in the human sciences were constituted in the 20 or 30 years which span the turn of the nineteenth century, and I argue that this occurred in the United States. Put in other terms, if, as social scientists, we were to imagine ourselves transported to Oxford, the Sorbonne, or Harvard in, say, 1870, we would find almost nothing familiar. There would be no 'departments' of 'sociology' or 'psychology'; the research practices of the faculties and the modes of graduate instruction of those institutions would be for the most part alien. But we would find *very little* which is *not* familiar if we were to make a similar visit to *any* 'department' in *any* American university in 1925.

If I am correct, then, the practices which define what may be called 'mainstream' social science, including psychology, were largely settled in this period and in the past 50 years or so, these practices have changed surprisingly little. This is not to say that there have been no dissenters in the academies of America, nor is it to say that such 'Americanized' social science fully conquered the older European traditions. All through this period there have been a number of competing conceptions of the human sciences. This fact points to the way that this book is most seriously incomplete, for I make no effort to complete the history of these struggles in the period following World War I. It is clear that even a selective review of this history would demand a book at least as large as the present one. Consider merely the literature on the Frankfurt school or the complicated debates of French structuralism since World War II. Instead, I turn, in part III, to an effort to clarify an alternative which arises from my reflection on the debates of the past 30 years or so. Critical to this, in my view, is the critique of empiricism (chapter 13), not merely as an untenable philosophy of the human sciences, but as a philosophy of *any* science. It will be clear from part I, I hope, how developments in the eighteenth century and then in last two decades of the nineteenth century made the victory of 'empiricism' in the twentieth century such an easy one, even though, as in the philosophy of Helmholtz, there were 'realist' alternatives which fully acknowledged the Kantian (and Humean) critique of 'metaphysics'. Critical in regard to an alternative realist human science is the context and program of Marx and Engels. I argue that a crucial failure in their philosophy, fully explainable, is the absence of a clear and adequate theory of science. On the other hand, I think that it is only very recent developments which have made a fully coherent 'realist' alternative plausible. The philosophy of social science offered in chapters 13 and 14, then, is an attempt to assimilate the recent debate, in both the philosophy of natural science and as regards the competing conceptions of the possibility of a human science, and to provide a comprehensive sketch of such an alternative. This account draws on a variety of recent and much better developed sources. Its goal is synoptic. It is, accordingly, but a sketch or perhaps a sketch of a sketch, meant to provoke and enlarge the recent debate in philosophy of the psychology and philosophy of the social sciences.

1

Science and Philosophy

More or less systematic inquiry into the human condition surely dates to antiquity. The social sciences, complete with the now familiar disciplinary divisions, emerge in a recognizably modern form no earlier than the end of the nineteenth century. In between is 'modern science', from Copernicus to Newton. It is at least here that we must begin if we are to make sense of the career of the social sciences.

The revolutionary transformation of ideas which represents the beginnings of modern science is, of course, a topic which is much discussed. Although debate continues, there are some facts which are both critical and uncontended. There is, first, the quite literal replacement of the 'old universe' by a 'new universe', the result of the revolutions initiated by Copernicus and Descartes. With Copernicus, the neatly ordered hierarchy of beings leading from humankind to the heavenly spheres to God was shattered. Not only were we not at the center, but in the new, infinite universe there was no need even for our sun to be at the center of anything. Giordano Bruno, who as Randall wrote, 'really *felt* the infinity of the universe', became, in consequence, an early martyr of the new science. The next step, not as dramatic as the one inspired by Copernicus, and thus not usually emphasized, was the reintroduction of the ancient doctrine of atomism, the *bête noire* of Plato and Aristotle and of the complicated tradition which had followed them. Once Copernicanism had destroyed the earth's uniqueness, abolished the terrestial–celestial distinction, and provoked the idea that the universe was infinite, the atomist's infinite void became a natural place for Copernicus's solar system, and for many others as well. With this, then, came the idea, promoted by Descartes, that 'all change in the corpuscular universe resulted from a succession of free corpuscular motions punctuated by intercorpuscular collisions' (Kuhn, 1957, p. 238).

There followed a struggle to construct an entirely new 'general conceptual scheme' (Harré, 1964). In the 'new philosophy' – 'the corpuscular philosophy' – 'form' and *'telos'* gave way to the search for those mathematical laws which governed the mechanical motions and interactions of corpuscles. The program had two large parts. In addition to the problem of discovering these laws, there was the question of their application to explain 'the rich flux of sensory experience', perhaps even, as in Hobbes, to develop a 'social physics', a new science of society. If the newly discovered laws of nature applied to the new cosmology and to the new physics – to 'natural philosophy' – should they not apply as well to 'moral philosophy'? The upshot, again familiar enough, was the Age of Reason, the idea that 'the great object of human endeavor was to discover what in every field was natural and reasonable, and to brush aside the accretions of irrational tradition that Reason and Nature might the more easily be free to display its harmonious order' (Randall, 1940, p. 276). It is impossible to overestimate the importance of these ideas – as subsequent chapters will try to show. Having noted these important general facts, this chapter turns to a theme which, though in one sense obvious enough, is not usually developed. By the end of the eighteenth century, as each began to acquire an important new sense, 'science' was divorced from 'philosophy'. Especially crucial here was the rejection of 'metaphysics', and along with this, the idea of epistemology as providing a necessary 'foundation' for the newly conceived 'science'.

THE MEANING OF 'SCIENCE'

What we call 'science' was, of course, part of a much older tradition in which *epistemé, scientia, Wissen,* was all of a piece. Rational inquiry, the use of reason and 'experience', the development of 'theory' and argument, were ways to knowledge. Such knowledge could be of God as well as Nature, of the good as well as the cosmos, of the *polis* as much as the *psyche.* In the medieval university, 'philosophy' had embraced a family of 'disciplines'. Mathematics and astronomy were identified as parts of 'natural philosophy'. This contrasted to 'moral philosophy' and 'theology'. 'Natural theology' was the 'philosophical' part of theology, distinguished from the rest of 'philosophy' by its subject – not its methods. In crucially relevant respects, these were much like those of physics or astronomy.

Wightman notes that 'the actual words "natural science" in the sense of "inquiry by reason alone into all things in the natural kingdom of God" were first used by Thomas Hobbes in *Leviathan,*' but he also points out that 'natural philosophy' continued to be the preferred term throughout the seventeenth and eighteenth centuries (in Smith, 1980,

p. 12). Adam Smith, like others, used the terms 'philosophy', 'arts', and 'science' very nearly indiscriminately, and the word 'scientist' did not, if Wightman is correct, exist before 1839.

By the time of Newton (1642–1727), and in large part because of his work, one could distinguish within 'natural philosophy' a subdivision termed 'experimental philosophy'. Put briefly, natural philosophy was conceived as the effort to grasp the fundamental explanatory principles of nature. Its 'hypotheses' were conjectural, speculative, unprovable; but they were designedly explanatory. They ranged from what we would now straightforwardly call 'metaphysical' to what to us looks a great deal more 'scientific'. In the former category fell the 'Aristotelian' explanations, in terms of 'substantial forms' or 'occult powers' – for example, the loadstone's powers of 'sympathy', its 'craving of strength and company', or its 'fellow feeling' (Manicas, 1965). At the opposite end were versions of the 'corpuscular' hypotheses in the variant versions of Boyle and the Cartesians. 'Experimental philosophy', by contrast, eschewed such hypotheses, 'whether metaphysical or physical, whether of occult qualities or mechanical'. 'In this philosophy particular propositions are inferred from the phenomena, and afterwards rendered general by induction' (Newton, 1934, p. 371).

It is clear that at issue here is a fundamental contrast, which to speak anachronistically, takes us into the Popperian problem of demarcating 'science' and 'philosophy', a problem which requires a conceptualization of both. It is less obvious, but perhaps as important, that between Descartes *Discours de la méthode* (1637) and Hume's *Treatise* (1739), there was a remarkable shift in the understanding of what Newton and the new 'experimental philosophers' were up to. I want to argue, first, that while both Newton and Locke (along with Boyle and others) held to a *realist* theory of natural science, at least by the time we get to Hume, Newton was read as holding to what must be called a *positivist* theory of science. I then turn to the idea of epistemology as an autonomous discipline.

Since 'positivist' will be such an important concept in later debates, I mean to be precise in restricting its meaning here. Let us call a philosophy (of science) positivist if it holds that a scientific explanation must thoroughly eschew appeal to what is in principle beyond experience. It is in this sense an empirical philosophy. All the self-named positivists of the nineteenth and twentieth centuries were positivists in this sense, but so too are a host of 'empiricists' of various stripes, including Kant and his followers. For them knowledge is restricted to the realm of phenomena – the Greek word, it is worth noting, for what appears. As I will employ the term positivism here, it will *not* be concerned with *how* 'experience' is constituted, a fundamental point of dispute between Kantians and nineteenth-century positivists, from Mill to Mach. By contrast, a realist holds that a valid scientific explanation can appeal to the in principle non-observable.

REALISM AND TRANSDICTION

Historians of science agree, as I. B. Cohen has said of the seventeenth and eighteenth centuries, that 'a basic "corpuscular postulate" underlay all scientific thought in that age.' That is, 'the "new science" or "new philosophy" which Newton called "experimental philosophy" was simply a "corpuscular philosophy"' (Cohen, 1956, p. 145). This committed all its proponents – Gassendi, Locke, Boyle, and Newton – to the real existence of atoms which were not perceivable. Moreover, none of these writers 'regarded atomism as a speculative or metaphysical system, but as an inductively confirmable theory basic to their new experimental philosophy' (Mandelbaum, 1964, p. 1). More generally, then, none of these writers denied the legitimacy of what we may call, following Mandelbaum, 'transdiction', or inference from 'experience' to what is in principle beyond experience. This is not, we must emphasize, merely the so-called 'problem of induction', discovered by Hume. The issue is not merely whether we can infer from what is observed to what is not observed, from the past to the future, say, but whether we can infer from what is observed to what is unobser*able*, and in principle un-observable.

It is not hard to see what happened. To defend a realist theory of science (in the foregoing restricted, but broad sense), one needs to defend *epistemological* realism. But once epistemology is conceived as an autonomous inquiry which provides the *foundation* for knowledge – and thus of science, one cannot *assume* science, neither 'psychology' nor 'physics' as part of one's epistemology. One can try to show, as Hume did, that a foundation for science can be found *in* experience, and that one does not need to go beyond it to have science; or one can argue, as Kant did, that the conditions for the possibility of science can be reached by transcendental argument. The first alternative, 'empiricism', in its many modern varieties – empirical realism, phenomenalism, pragmatism – eschews the *need for* retrodiction. Science proceeds without it. The second argues, in effect, that while knowledge must be restricted to the realm of the 'empirical', empiricists cannot account for science, that on their grounds, science is not possible. Kantians give the mind constitutive ordering powers, acknowledge existence 'beyond experience', but hold that as 'thing-in-itself', it is unknowable – the province of metaphysics, not 'science'. These two epistemologies have been the substantial competitors now for about 250 years – with implications regarding the understanding of science which have been nothing short of disastrous. It is not merely that our philosophy of science is bad – so much the worse for the philosophers! It is rather that, as I shall argue, the very genesis and articulation of a scientific psychology and of social science has been powerfully distorted by a series of ideas which follow from this initial misconception. But it is not the purpose of the present chapter to show this, nor to defend its alternative. Here we need only see how it came to be that realistic philosophies of science lost their persuasiveness.

FOUNDATIONIST EPISTEMOLOGY

In his search for foundations for the new philosophy, Descartes had made an onslaught on the naive realism of ordinary common sense; but in contrast to ancient skepticism, there was a double-barrelled shift, first, from the problem of discriminating 'appearance' and 'reality' to the problem of 'inner' and 'outer', and second, from the idea that one needed non-question-begging criteria for truth to the idea that an inquiry into 'mental' entities and processes could provide a way to get at truth itself. 'Thoughts', 'sensations', 'ideas', 'impressions', were firmly housed in 'the mind' and were disconnected from what was not in the mind. Once this had occurred, the problem of truth took on a new, individualist cast. For these writers, there was no serious doubt about the existence of 'the external world' or of 'other minds'. The problem was how we come to *know* what is *not* in the individual mind. This problem, shared by so-called 'rationalists' and 'empiricists' is the modern problem of knowledge, the problem of seeing how an individual's ideas can be an accurate 'representation' of 'nature'. Yet, because for Descartes and for Locke, inquiry into the mental processes of the individual could satisfy this demand, neither Descartes nor Locke were 'epistemologists' in the modern sense. For them, explanation of belief was at the same a justification of belief (Rorty, 1979, pp. 139ff.). While they disagreed on what inquiry into the mind would yield, they agreed that the problem of knowledge could be solved by the *science of mind* itself. Viewed from the point of view of twentieth-century philosophy, this represents, of course, a 'confusion' of psychology and epistemology. One might equally hold that the putative confusion represents an early, if crude, version of a naturalized epistemology, and thus a denial of the distinction between epistemology and psychology (Quine, 1969). But it is perhaps more critical to notice that the alternative sciences of the mind of 'rationalists' and 'empiricists' were all instances of *epistemological* individualisms, of the idea that nothing *social* needs to enter into questions regarding the truth of belief, that truth is a relation determined by a solitary subject standing in relation to an independent reality.[1]

A second critical assumption, also shared by all the parties, was the older idea that 'science' was demonstrable knowledge, neither 'opinion' nor 'probability'. The difference between 'knowledge' and 'opinion' was not a matter of degree, but of kind. It was an absolute difference. Until Hume, at least, knowledge of 'matters of fact' was, if it was to be called knowledge, certain. Indeed, the failure of *this* program, common to traditional philosophy, *and* to Descartes, Newton, and Locke – a failure which prompted the work of Kant – was not the failure of a realist *ontology*, even though this is the standard view, but the failure of *the quest for certainty*. That is, Hume's 'sceptical' critique of the positions of those who preceded him left a redefinition of scientific knowledge – as but probable, but it *also and for no good reason* undermined the non-Platonic ontological realism of Newton and the Newtonians. Thereafter, 'realism' will be either 'empirical' – Kant and a host of contemporary neo-positivists – or it will be Platonic – the idea that knowledge is of subsistent 'universals'. 'Empiricism' will be contrasted to 'rationalism', with 'rationalists' as holdouts for the certainty not yielded by 'empirical science'. This is obviously a highly complicated story highly telescoped in the foregoing paragraphs, and I mean, in what follows, to fill in but a small piece of it, concentrating on aspects which have not been given sufficient attention, in particular, on the roles of Locke and Newton.

LOCKE AND THE 'EMPIRICISTS'

Descartes, of course, had savaged the idea of 'sensible knowledge' and had 'saved' science with his famous doctrine of innate ideas. He offered, as well, an anti-Aristotelian metaphysics of three 'substances' – God, matter, and mind. Both of these characteristic Cartesian doctrines were, of course, challenged by Locke, who despite his best intentions, contributed decisively to the shift from realism. We can distinguish three aspects of this contribution. First, Locke attacked both Descartes and the entire Scholastic tradition with his repudiation of substance. For Locke, as for later 'empiricists', it was an unintelligible notion. But as Harré and Mandelbaum both show, this repudiation of substance was not a repudiation of 'body' or of what, to quote Harré, 'Locke dis-

---

[1] I suggest below how Herder, Marx, and Helmholtz challenged these individualist assumptions. Drawing on their views and recent materials, I make the effort in chapters 13 and 14 to sketch a coherent alternative.

ingenuously calls "the common notion of substance"'. Locke had a vigorous conception of *matter*. Indeed, he seems to have accepted Galileo's quasi-definition of it, 'as bounded, and as having this or that shape; as being large or small in relation to other things, and in some specific place at any given time; as being in motion or at rest; as touching or not touching some other body; and as being one in number, or few, or many' (quoted from Galileo by Harré, 1964, p. 85). For Locke, as for Galileo and Newton, matter and atoms were real, having real physical properties and causal powers. The text here quoted from Galileo begins his account of the distinction between primary and secondary qualities. This distinction, held by Boyle and other defenders of the corpuscular philosophy, gives rise to the second problem which contributed to the new understanding of Newtonian science.

It is frequently, but mistakenly, believed that Locke held that colors, tastes, and so on are not ideas, but are secondary qualities – a belief undoubtedly encouraged by carelessness in Locke's own use of key terms. If so, then, it is easy to suppose that the distinction between primary and secondary qualities is made *in experience*. But then it is easy to argue that the distinction cannot be sustained, and in any case, is unnecessary. *Epistemologically speaking,* this shows that the corpuscular philosophy, construed as holding to the real existence of material atoms, cannot be sustained.

As Berkeley was to argue, in our experience there are only ideas, what Hume called 'impressions', paradigmatically – sensations of color, warmth, resistance, and so on. Primary ideas are inseparable from secondary ideas, and there is as much variability in the latter as in the former. Moreover, and here I continue to follow Harré's crisp account, if, as *per* Berkeley, only 'ideas' are *known* to exist, then even if we admit groups of ideas of primary properties to a special status, matter, as required by Newtonian science, still could not be sustained. As Berkeley argued, 'the very being of an idea implies passiveness and inertness'. Accordingly, 'it is impossible for an idea to be the cause of anything'; *a fortiori,* ideas of primary qualities cannot be the cause of anything. The doctrine that our sensations 'are the effects of powers resulting from the configuration, number, motion and size of corpuscles must certainly be false' (Berkeley, *Principles,* pt. I, XXV; cf. Harré, 1964, p. 116).

It must be emphasized here that Berkeley's critique of matter as *unnecessary* for science, calls for a very different notion of what science is. There is regularity in our experience, no doubt, but on this view, 'the laws of nature' are not postulates about unobservables or about the connections of these *to* experience. As Berkeley said, 'the set of rules, or established methods, wherein the Mind we depend on excites in us the ideas of Sense, are called *the laws of nature*; and these we learn by experience, which teaches us that such and such ideas are attended with such and such other ideas, in the ordinary course of things' (*Principles,* pt. I, XXX). As Harré points out, 'on this view the purpose of the laws of nature cannot be, among other things, to assist in understanding but can only be for the prediction of the sensations we are likely to experience following upon the occurrence of some other sensations' (Harré, 1964, p. 116). The next step, easily taken by Hume, was to subject the idea of causality to critique. Arguing that 'there are no ideas which occur in metaphysics more obscure and uncertain than those of *power, force, energy* or *necessary connection*', Hume contended that 'when we look about us toward external objects and consider the operation of causes, we are never able, in a single instance, to discover any power or necessary connection. . . . We only find, that the one does actually, in fact, follow the other' (Hume, 1955, section V, pt. I).[2]

Some philosophers, including, of course, Berkeley, had said that 'everything is full of God'; but, insists Hume, 'I cannot perceive any force in the arguments on which this theory is founded.' Indeed, as regards human knowledge and its limits – and thus the limits of science – Hume pressed a theme already found in Locke, the third and final difficulty in the Lockean effort to develop the implications of the new corpuscular philosophy.

As Harré writes, it is quite clear that Locke believed that modifications of matter can cause us to have perceptions, yet not only does he nowhere claim to know how this happens, but worse, he suggests that this knowledge will be *forever inaccessible,* as if, remarks Harré, 'some kind of categorical disparity separates the collocations of primary qualities that are the objective counterparts of secondary qualities and the secondary qualities in perception' (Harré, 1964, p. 103). That is, while the primary/secondary distinction is not made in experience at all, but is rather to be drawn on how our ideas are caused, we can, in Locke's view, acquire knowledge *only* of the *primary* properties of bodies, for to each of them, there is a *perceptual* counterpart – a real 'resemblance'. The secondary properties – that is, 'the powers of several combinations of those primary ones' – stand in a quite mysterious relation to our ideas of warmth, color, and so on (see Mandelbaum, 1964, pp. 21 and 27 esp.; Harré, 1964, esp. p. 103). This is a lingering Cartesianism as regards both the strict definition of knowledge and the relation of 'bodies' and 'ideas'. Unable to see how we could ever have *certain* knowledge of the power of matter to cause perceptions in us, Locke despairs. This lingering Cartesianism will have monumental effects on the history of what came to be called 'psychology'. For the present, however, we can

[2] For a contemporary critique of Hume's claims in this regard, see Harré and Madden, 1975, chapter 3.

note that Hume made a *principle* of Locke's reluctance to infer causal mechanisms for the secondary qualities. By this means he 'solved' the mind/body problem and *at the same time* thoroughly 'operationalized' science. Thus:

> We are ignorant, it is true, of the manner in which bodies operate on each other. Their force or energy is entirely incomprehensible. But are we not equally ignorant of the manner or force by which a mind, even the Supreme Mind, operates, either on itself or on body? (Hume, 1955, VII, pt. I)

The upshot is not skepticism, but as Randall says, 'a radical empiricism' and an 'experimental pragmatism' (Randall, 1962, p. 629). Put in other terms, Hume's skepticism is what Burnyeat calls – in honor of Montaigne – a 'country gentleman's skepticism', a skepticism not about the existence of an 'external world' or the reality of space and time, but a skepticism about *any* 'theory' which is not logically implicated in experience. That which is not is 'metaphysical', pure and simple. Thus, in good pragmatic fashion, 'dogma' is eschewed, including 'any scientific pronouncement about, for example, the underlying physical structure which makes warm things warm, any theory about the real nature of heat, perhaps even the assertion or belief that there is such a thing as the real nature of heat about which a theory could in principle be given' (Burnyeat, 1984, p. 231). Hume thus concluded the empiricist understanding of the new philosophy which had been ambiguously begun with Locke. Yet it is not likely that without the authority of Newton, this could have been accomplished as easily as it was, if at all. Indeed, the methodological dicta of Newton were crucial.

NEWTON'S 'PHILOSOPHY OF SCIENCE'

Newton surely saw himself to be siding with those who, 'rejecting substantial forms and occult qualities, have endeavored to subject the phenomena of nature to the laws of mathematics' (Newton, 1934, preface, p. 1). What has been less clear is whether Newton's philosophy of science was realist or positivist.

The place to begin, following Mandelbaum, is with the famous dictum *hypothesis non fingo* offered in the General Scholium and added by Newton in the second edition of the *Principia* – *after* it had been charged that his notion of universal gravitation had reintroduced 'occult qualities'. The translation of this dictum has been debated – between 'I feign no hypotheses' and 'I frame no hypotheses – and his use of 'hypothesis' is not unequivocal (Hanson, 1970), although it is clear that its use in the context of the Scholium was special. It is glossed in a letter to Cotes and in the sentences which follow in the Scholium. Both are worth quoting. First, the sentences which follow in the Scholium:

> . . . Whatever is not deduced from the phenomena is to be called an hypothesis; and hypotheses, whether metaphysical or physical have no place in experimental philosophy. . . .

And the gloss of this in the letter to Cotes:

> . . . As in geometry the word hypothesis is not taken in so large a sense as to include the Axiomes and Postulates, so in Experimental philosophy it is not taken in so large a sense as to include the first principles or Axiomes which I call the laws of motion. These principles are deduced from Phaenomena and made general by Induction. . . . The word Hypothesis is here used by me to signify only such a Proposition as is not a Phaenomenon nor deduced from any Phaenomenon but assumed or supposed without any experimental proof.

Hypotheses in this restricted sense are explanatory and indeed are so *because* they give the causes of the phenomenon. But they are not legitimately part of experimental philosophy, regardless of whether they are otherwise legitimate for 'philosophy'. They are not legitimately to be offered in experimental philosophy because they are neither observational nor 'deduced' from what is.

But what does 'deduced' mean here, and what is the role of 'induction'? It seems clear that Newton, not without precedent, then as now, uses 'deduce' to mean 'infer' where indeed, the inference is going from the concrete and particular to the abstract. Such inference, best called 'abstraction', is what Aristotle in *Posterior Analytics* called *epagogé* – and of course, it is indispensable, not only to science but to thinking itself.[3] The text partially quoted above continues as follows:

> . . . for whatever is not deduced from the phenomena is to be called an hypothesis; and hypotheses, whether metaphysical or physical, whether of occult qualities or mechanical, have no place in experimental philosophy. In this philosophy particular propositions are inferred from the phenomena, and thereafter rendered

[3] The word 'induction', of course, covers a multitude of kinds of inferences, but it is pure anachronism to hold that prior to Hume(?) it referred to any sort of non-demonstrative inference. *Epagogé*, misleadingly translated 'induction' was certain for Aristotle, the way one arrived at 'first principles' by which one 'demonstrated' other propositions. 'Deduce', of course, is a common synonym for 'infer', and at this time, we are still a long way from the extensionalist conception of 'deduction'. The idea that 'inference' is either 'deductive' or 'inductive', where the criteria of validity for both are modelled on the extensionalist criteria of modern deductive logic, has in this century done untold damage, as we shall see. See chapters 9 and 14.

general by induction. Thus it was that the impenetrability, the mobility, and the impulsive force of bodies, and of the laws of motion and of gravitation were discovered. (Newton, 1934, p. 371)

The proposition 'All bodies are impenetrable' is arrived at in two steps or stages. In the first step, a property is abstracted and is seen to be true of all the observed cases and false of none of them. We establish 'by sensation' that all the bodies which we handle are impenetrable and that none are not. This is the 'deduced from phenomena' or 'inferred from the phenomena' of the foregoing. But then, we *further* infer that bodies *not* known to us 'by experiments' are impenetrable. This is 'by induction', and it is justified by the third of Newton's 'Rules of Reasoning in Philosophy'. Indeed, in Newton's view we can do this, as well, for bodies which in principle are not knowable 'by experiments' – in particular, the atoms themselves. That is, 'transdiction' is a legitimate mode of inference.

As Mandelbaum argues, this is made quite clear by the Third Rule, a rule often underplayed in accounts of Newton's methodology and philosophy of science. It runs as follows:

> *The qualities of bodies, which admit neither of intensification nor remission of degrees, and which are found to belong to all bodies within the reach of our experiments, are to be esteemed the universal qualities of all bodies whatsoever.*
>
> For since the qualities of bodies are only known to us by experiments, we are to hold for universal all such as universally agree with experiments. . . . We know other way know the extension of bodies than by our senses, nor do we reach these in all bodies; but because we perceive extension in all that are sensible, therefore we ascribe it universally to all others also. That abundance of bodies are hard, we learn by experience; and because the hardness of the whole arises from the hardness of the parts, we therefore justly infer the hardness of the undivided particles not only of the bodies we feel but of all others. (Cited in Mandelbaum, 1964, pp. 81–2)

The text continues with a similar treatment of impenetrability, mobility, and inertia. For Newton, then, 'this is the foundation of all philosophy'.

The text shows that Newton held that retrodiction is legitimate, whatever problems there may be in using his Rule III. Moreover, and not unrelated, both Harré and Mandelbaum point out that 'universality' and 'invariance' are invoked in applying it, and that this raises interpretative difficulties. (See Harré, 1964, p. 104–8; Mandelbaum, 1964, esp. pp. 75–88.) In particular, while for Newton, gravitation is arrived at 'inductively', it is *not* taken via Rule III to be a primary property of matter on a par with, for example, impenetrability, inertia, and so on. We need not settle here why Newton was so convinced that it could not be so treated,[4] but it is essential to note that if it *could* be so treated, the requirement that it be explained could be dropped. Newton did *not* try to explain inertia – that *was* a essential property of matter. In his second letter to Bentley, he says:

> You sometimes speak of Gravity as essential and inherent to Matter. Pray do not ascribe this notion to me; for the Cause of Gravity is what I do not pretend to know, and therefore would take more time to consider it. (Quoted by Harré, 1964, p. 107)[5]

Newton offered highly speculative, though mechanical, accounts of gravitation in terms of the ether and it is quite clear that he was never satisfied with the way he had left things in this regard. We can guess why. If gravitation was not a primary property, it had to be explained, but as *hypothesis non fingo* makes clear – it could not be explained by means of appeal to an occult property.

SOME CONCLUSIONS

At this point, a number of important conclusions can be drawn. First, Newton distinguished his explanations from those of 'philosophers' who appealed to occult powers by restricting his explanatory principles to what could be 'inferred from phenomena' in the foregoing clear, but not always recognized, sense. It is this, of course, that allows us call his philosophy 'empirical'. Second, this was no positivism, for the very good reason that the same rights of inference which allowed Newton to say

---

[4] Harré argues that for Newton, gravitational action is not invariant in the sense that it admits of intensification and remission of degree and that this is the decisive fact in terms of Newton's reasoning. Newton writes:

> It is inconceivable, that inanimate brute Matter should, without the Mediation of something else, which is not material, operate upon, and affect other Matter without mutual Contact, as it must be, if Gravitation in the sense of Epicurus, be essential and inherent in it. . . . Gravity must be caused by an Agent acting constantly according to certain Laws; but whether this Agent be material or immaterial I have left to the consideration of my Readers. (Quoted by Harré, 1964, p. 108)

Harré says that the key word here is 'constantly'. If the action is constant, we have Newtonian invariance, and the 'Agent' is then a primary property of matter (1964).

[5] This text is often quoted as evidence that Newton held to a positivist theory of science, but as seems clear enough, Newton is not saying that the question 'What explains gravity?' is unintelligible, nor indeed, that it is not a cause in the sense that there is some mechanism which produces the effects which the inverse square law represents.

that the laws of motion were universal, *also* allowed him to infer, as part of *experimental* philosophy, that there were material atoms and that, like the macro-objects of sensible experience, they too answered to the laws of motion. That is, Newton's 'empiricism' was not Humean, because for him transdiction was a legitimate mode of inference.

Third, Newton's Rule III serves to justify the distinction between primary and secondary qualities in a way that is perfectly consistent with the new science of mechanics (Mandelbaum, 1964, pp. 84f.; Harré, 1964, pp. 104f.). Nothing in Newton's inquiries, unfortunately, helped towards ameliorating Locke's skepticism regarding improvement in our understanding of the secondary qualities. The 'resolution' of these difficulties, by Berkeley and Hume, transformed what might have been a 'psychological' problem into an assumption of 'epistemology' – with disastrous consequences for both. Fourth, 'the corpuscular philosophy' is not a 'philosophy' but a scientific theory, as Harré says, 'a general conceptual system'. Accordingly, its acceptability is a matter for science – not some autonomous 'philosophy'. Berkeley did not grasp that (Newtonian) matter was a *theoretical* (scientific) concept, even if, as Harré says, 'its main features were drawn from the perceivable properties of such stuffs as cheese and water'. Its justification, however, did not consist in the *impossible* task of showing 'that perceptual experience forces the primary properties of matter upon us, but in its power to unify and underwrite the laws of the superficial relations of phenomena' (Harré, 1964, pp. 117f. See also Mandelbaum, 1964, pp. 27f., 116f., 234ff.). That is, the postulation of 'matter' as 'underlying' and as causally effacious was to be justified, if at all, not by arguments drawn from 'philosophy', but by arguments drawn from science, realistically understood.[6] To be sure, the distinctions we draw between 'science', 'metaphysics', and 'epistemology' were not distinctions available to early modern philosophers and that is why, to us, their writings seem to be a jumble of ideas, 'metaphysical', 'scientific', and 'epistemological'.

Berkeley was perhaps the first modern 'philosopher' in that he tried to circumscribe the limits of the science of his day, a task brought to self-conscious completion by Kant. This has left us with two questions, where before there was only one. We have the distinctly philosophical problem of justifying what we call science – the problem of epistemology – and we have the straightforward scientific problem of justifying particular scientific theories – an effort which, at least in the physical sciences, has proceeded *independently* of the success or failure of the first enterprise. As we shall see, not only were the social sciences not so

---

[6] Of course, the Galilean concept of matter turned out to be inadequate to *physics*. But that was determined on scientific, nor 'philosophical', grounds. For some discussion, see Harré, 1970.

lucky, but this also explains the large gap between the actuality of scientific practice and twentieth-century 'philosophy of science'. The idea that 'philosophy' could legislate the 'limits' of 'science', was part of this story. On the one hand, it encouraged nineteenth-century 'scientism', the idea that Newtonian 'science', confusedly comprehended, provided the model for a science of *anything*; on the other, it encouraged the system-building of the Idealist philosophers. The nineteenth-century scientific philosophies were, of course, positivisms, exactly because science was 'empirical' in the special sense given to that word by the British 'empiricists' and by Kant. Accordingly, they were also anti-metaphysical.[7] The Idealists, by contrast, were happy to legislate to 'science' by showing how, on epistemological grounds, 'science' was but part of an inclusive 'philosophy' which was unabashedly 'metaphysical'. In subsequent chapters, I try to show how these ideas figured in the struggle to articulate a human science. But before concluding this chapter it may be useful to establish that the legacy of late eighteenth-century accounts of the new science was confusing. To do this, we will look briefly at a little-read text by Adam Smith.[8] Since he had considerable influence as the founder of modern 'economics', a topic which constitutes part of the chapter to follow, the text is nearly ideal for this purpose.

REALISM AND EMPIRICISM IN ADAM SMITH

'Philosophy', writes Smith, 'is the science of the connecting principles of nature' (1980, p. 45). Nature 'abounds' in events 'which appear solitary'. Philosophy, then, 'by representing the invisible chains which bind together all these disjointed objects, endeavors to introduce order into this chaos of jarring and discordant appearances'. 'Philosophy, therefore, may be regarded as one of those arts which address themselves to the imagination' (1980, pp. 45f.).

Raphael and Skinner (Smith, 1980, general introduction, p. 18)

---

[7] Worth noticing here is the fact that 'scientific materialisms', with the exception of the burst of German materialisms in the mid-nineteenth century, are largely seventeenth- and eighteenth-century phenomena, *before* 'science' became 'empirical' in the sense of the British empiricists and Kant. Consider here Hobbes (1650), La Mettrie (1748), Baron d'Holbach (1770), and a number of French Enlightenment writers who were inconsistently materialist, drawing from Locke *and* Hume. These include Diderot, Cabanis, and Destutt de Tracy, writers who were critical influences on Comte. See below, chapter 4.

[8] The text is 'The History of Astronomy', one of three essays which Smith wrote, probably sometime before 1758, evidently as part of a much larger, but incomplete, project whose general title was 'The Principles which lead and direct Philosophical Inquiries'. Published finally in 1795, along with some other 'philosophical' essays, the history is called by Schumpeter (1954) 'the pearl of the collection'.

argue, rightly, that Smith is here making use of Hume's *Treatise,* but in particular, that Smith thinks that science is but an 'enlargement of commonsense belief' as that was analysed by Hume. Closely following the section of the *Treatise* entitled, 'Of the connexion or association of ideas' (I, i), Smith puts emphasis on the role of 'imagination'. In both ordinary experience and in 'philosophy', it works to 'bind together' the phenomenal chaos, 'representing the invisible chains' and thereby introducing order into what otherwise is disorder. Smith's account occurs early in the *History.* It is followed by a review of the efforts of mankind, from 'the first stages of society' to the present, to make intelligible 'celestial appearances', 'the most universal objects of the curiosity of mankind' (1980, p. 53).

Smith concludes with an account of Newton's system. He finds that its 'parts are all more strictly connected together, than those of any other philosophical hypotheses' (1980, p. 104). His system 'now prevails over all opposition' and 'his principles, it must be acknowledged, have a degree of firmness and solidity that we should in vain look for in any other system' (1980).

What is striking about Smith's account of this 'firmness and solidity', which indeed 'the most skeptical cannot avoid feeling', is Smith's emphasis on the power of the system to connect so very much that would otherwise be 'disjointed'. He writes:

[Newton's principles] not only connect together most perfectly all the phaenomena of the Heavens . . . but those also which the persevering industry and more perfect instruments of later Astronomers have made known to us; have been either easily explained by the application of his principles, or have been explained in consequence of more laborious and accurate calculations from these principles. (Smith, 1980, p. 105)

But – and this is crucial – we cannot be misled here into supposing that Smith understood this the way Newton did. There is no question but that the unifying power of Newton's system comes from the central notion of gravitation, but this is exactly because we readily understand it to be a universal and real force acting between *all* bodies. Yet it was not true, as Smith believed, that 'the gravity of matter is, of all its qualities, after its inertness, that which is most familiar to us' (p. 104).

That what goes up comes down is indeed 'familiar', but on Newton's theory, these are but the *effects* of gravity; and, as both he and his critics understood full well, gravity was, itself, the most theoretical and problematic of properties. How, indeed, could such a 'force' act across millions of miles of empty space? For Newton, gravity was not an essential property of matter (a 'primary quality'), and therefore, it needed an explanation; yet try as he might, he could not offer one. If gravitation was a physical property, a cause, then what was the mechanism? Newton agreed with Leibniz and his other critics, that gravity, regarded as 'action at a distance' was unintelligible; but Smith seems to think that it is not only intelligible but 'familiar'. The implications of these difficulties and the differences in the two views should not be missed. It was exactly the non-empirical character of universal gravitation that led critics of Newton to say that it was an 'occult power', that it functioned in Newton's explanatory system in just the same way as the occult powers of the Aristotelians! It was just this which led Newton to try desperately to separate the purely mathematical representation of 'forces' from consideration of their 'physical causes and seats'. It was a neat trick on Smith's part to admit that the great merit of Newton's synthesis was its great power to unify *and* to think of the *gravity of matter* as a 'quality' which is 'most familiar to us'.

But Smith pulls in the direction of Hume with the remark that follows. He says:

> And even we, while we have been endeavoring to represent all philosophical systems as mere inventions of the imagination, to connect together the otherwise disjointed and discordant phaenomena of nature, have insensibly been drawn in, to make use of language expressing the connecting principles of this one, *as if they were real chains which Nature makes uses of to bind together her several operations.* (Smith, 1980, p. 105; my emphasis)

It is, we may take it, a 'natural mistake', fully on a par with the 'vulgar' belief in the matter of bodies, to believe that gravity is a real force of real matter 'binding together' the 'several operations of Nature'. But if it is a mistake, it would seem to have been one that was not recognized as such by Newton. Indeed, Smith's concluding sentence in this remarkable account looks for all the world to be an emphatic Newtonian realism:

> Can we wonder, then, that [Newton's system] should have gained the general and complete approbation of mankind, and that it should now be considered, not as an attempt to connect in the imagination the phaenomena of the Heavens, but as the greatest discovery that ever was made by man, the discovery of an immense chain of the most important and sublime truths, all closely connected together, by one capital fact, of the reality of which we have daily experience. (p. 105)

How are we to understand this? Surely, even given that Smith is correct in believing that scientific theory is a creation of the 'imagination', the issue here is whether Newton was a realist in his understanding of scientific theory or a positivist, whether the explanation of 'phaenomena of nature' *essentially* involves discovery of the 'forces' of nature, that is, of the theoretized *causes* of phenomena, or whether science is restricted to establishing the *relations* of phenomena. Like so many after him, Smith seems to believe that this is no difference at all.

Hume had insisted in the *Treatise* (1978) that, 'tis natural for men, in their common and careless way of thinking, to imagine they perceive a connexion betwixt such objects as they have constantly found united together' (bk. I, IV, 3). The false philosophers 'have sufficient force of genius to free them from the vulgar error, that there is a natural and perceivable connexion betwixt the several sensible qualities and actions of matter, but not sufficient to keep them from ever seeking for this connexion in matter, or causes' (1978). Hume's 'true philosophy' approached 'nearer to the sentiments of the vulgar' because it offered, in terms of 'custom' and 'imagination', a satisfactory account of 'common-sense belief'. While 'all belief of matter of fact or real existence is derived merely from some object present to the memory or senses and a customary conjunction between that and some other object' (*Inquiry*, V, I), our *belief* that there is some power or agency apart from mind and 'belonging to causes' is 'as unavoidable as to feel the passion of love, when we receive benefits; or hatred when we meet with injuries' (V, I). Since for Smith, science is but an 'enlargement of commonsense belief' as analyzed by Hume, it is easy to explain the lapse into the realist language of the vulgar when talking about the remarkable achievement of Newtonian science. In reality, gravitation is no 'real chain' connecting 'so very much that would otherwise be 'disjointed'. Like vulgar talk about material bodies causing in us impressions, gravitation is nothing other than an observed invariance – what goes up comes down. Just as Hume had explained the vulgar and false belief that there is a witness-able connection 'betwixt the several qualities and actions of matter', it is easy to explain the false belief that gravity is a real causal power.

I have said enough here, I hope, to reveal a fundamental problem in the historical understanding of the idea of modern science. Subsequent chapters, can pursue the history of this problem as it bears on the career of the social sciences. The next chapter looks first at the origin of the idea of social science. In modern times, this is the origin in the idea of a 'science of the commonwealth'. The foundations of this idea, not to be pursued here, are found in late medieval thought (Skinner, 1978); but we need to go back at least to the sixteenth century, to before Newton's synthesis of the new physics and the new problems which it engendered.

2

Of the Commonwealth

The materials from which were wrought the emerging science of politics, the first of the modern human sciences, are themselves the result of an extremely complex series of conjunctures and tendencies rooted in the late medieval period. Yet it is possible to identify three elements of this complex which were crucial. The first and most obvious is the new physics, of which something was said in the last chapter. The second is the development of the whole series of new relations, opportunities, and problems which we call capitalism. Both of these have been widely noted in the literature, and except where it seems necessary, they will not be pursued in any detail in what follows. The third element, not usually acknowledged, is the emergence of the modern state, of which at least something needs to be said here. It is these three developments, taken together, which help us to comprehend the development of thought from Machiavelli to Bodin to Hobbes and thence to the idea of a 'science of government'.

SOCIETY AND THE STATE

The ideas of 'the state' and of 'society' are modern ideas; they did not become pertinent to inquiry before the seventeenth century. I say, 'pertinent to inquiry', because it would be wrong to say that either of them acquired their modern senses as early as that. This required a further shift, in the nineteenth century, with the emergence of the idea of a 'nation' in its modern sense. It was only then that the idea of 'a society' as 'a community, nation or broad grouping of people having common traditions, institutions and collective activities and interests' came into use. And with that, the idea of a nation-state, in its modern sense, also became possible. While it is clear that these ideas were constructions, the question of whether they are sustainable constructions may be passed over here. At this point we need only notice that in the sixteenth and seventeenth centuries, the 'unity' of 'society' was constructed otherwise.[1]

Similarly, prior to the sixteenth century, the study of 'politics' was still very much rooted in the framework of the *polis,* from which, of course, the word comes. The words 'citizen', 'civil society', 'republic', and a great many others derive from the Latin (Roman) equivalents of Greek terms, now familiarly interchanged in the vocabularies of European languages. But while the *words* continue, the concepts have undergone a radical transformation. Indeed, I want to suggest that this transformation *attended* the emergence of the idea of society and the state, and that both were part of the process of the development of the modern European State. Thus, if we are to grasp the by now long forgotten framing assumptions of 'modern' political science, we must make the effort to get some sort of handle on this complex story. The effort here is hopelessly oversimplified, but it may nonetheless serve its primary purpose.

In 1500, Europe comprised some 500 more or less independent political units answering to a variety of descriptions: duchies, grand and not so grand, principalities, republics, kingdoms, and empires, real and not so real. Through conquest, rebellion, secession, treaties, assassinations, intermarriages, purchases, 'the extinction of palatine independences, the consolidation of expired fiefs, and the falling of feudal inheritances', the states of Europe emerged. As Oakeshott remarks, 'the history of modern Europe is the history of Poland only a little more so' (Oakeshott, 1975, p. 186).

At some point in the sixteenth century, the word 'state' (and its equivalents) began to be employed to refer to the institutional apparatus surrounding the ruler (Hexter, 1973) and thence, though confusedly, to the new conglomeration of human beings who, as in older 'empires', shared little other than a common monarch – 'king' is related etymologically to 'kin' – and a common 'bureaucracy', civil and military. The ambiguity in the word 'state' remains with us: the state as the 'government' – itself a new word – and the state as the association of 'citizens'. Three points of difference between the new 'states' and older large-scale organizations may be noted.

First, the new states had 'governments' which, through increased differentiation and coordination, became increasingly capable of exer-

---

[1] This problem is discussed in chapter 4.

cising control over members of the association (Finer, 1975). Second, governments became increasingly concerned to maintain their 'autonomy' not only versus competing organizations of similar types – other 'states' – but as regards other organizations within the territory. The idea of 'the monopoly of legitimate coercive force' thence arises.

Machiavelli was no doubt prophetic in noticing that the dialectic of aggrandizement, once set in motion, immensely accelerated the process of state-formation, a process only now coming to a close. It is fair to say that the imperative to acquire offensive and defensive strength in the face of competitive aggrandizement became the primary imperative of politics. This process was related to the disintegration of Western feudalism and the development of a commodity economy, though the story is far too complex to tell here.[2] The 'states-system', the outcome of this, may be said to be visible by the time of the treaty of Westphalia in 1648.

Third, and related to the foregoing, with the development of the idea of government and the attendant separation of 'civil society' and the state, the problem of legitimation arose in new forms. The modern concept of 'sovereignty' is a sign of this (Manicas, 1986).

As Oakeshott writes, 'everything in this state . . . was vaguely familar, but nothing was recognizably the same'. The effort to comprehend this 'ramshackle construction', was – and is – difficult. It depended upon 'several well-worn analogies' – 'family' was an early one, 'organism' somewhat later. An idea, of Roman origin, emerged and became critical. *Societas* originally was an *alliance,* a voluntary coming together, usually for some purpose. When it was generalized, later, as *societas generis humani,* the word 'social', as Arendt has pointed out, began to acquire 'the general meaning of a fundamental human condition' (Arendt, 1958, p. 24). Oakeshott, who distinguishes between *societas* and *universitas,* of which more later, holds that *societas* was used to refer to the whole of the human race, as above, and sometimes, to refer to a *civitas,* or *regnum.*

This is Oakeshott's characterization of *societas*:

---

[2] Machiavelli's *Discourses,* bk. I, chapter 6, provides the classic argument. Machiavelli distinguishes between a politics of expansion, Rome, and a politics of preservation, Sparta. In the modern era, he argues, Sparta is no longer possible; hence one must choose for Rome. See my 'Montesquieu and the Eighteenth Century Vision of the State' for a brief account of this in the context of Montesquieu's discussion of 'peaceful republics'. For an account of the relation to the emergence of the 'absolutist' state and feudalism, see Perry Anderson, 1974. Anderson notices, but does not develop, the idea that the absolutist state, never 'an arbiter between the aristocracy and the bourgeoisie' was, in critical ways, a solution to the problem Machiavelli had foreseen. See also Anthony Giddens, 1985.

The idea of *societas* is that of agents who, by choice or circumstance, are related to one another so as to compose an identifiable association of some sort. The tie which joins them, and in respect of which each recognizes himself to be *socius,* is not that of an engagement or enterprise to pursue a common substantive purpose or to promote a common interest, but of loyalty to one another, the conditions of which may achieve the formality denoted by the kindred word 'legality'. Juristically, *societas* was understood to be the product of a pact or agreement, not to act in concert but to acknowledge the authority of certain conditions of acting. (1975, p. 201)

The contrast to the traditional view is dramatic. As Aristotle had argued, and Aquinas after him, a *polis* (*republica*) was not 'merely the sharing of a locality for the purpose of preventing mutual injury and exchanging goods', but a 'community' (*koinonia*) of 'households and clans' (*oikias kai genesi*) in 'living well' (*Politics,* 1280b30). Bodin sees the difference very clearly. Writing in 1576, he had said:

> ... Ancient writers have called Common weals (*Républiques*), Societies of men assembled to live well and happily together. Which as it may serve for a description of a Citie, so can it not stand for a true definition of a CommonWeale. (Bodin, 1962, p. 3)

For Bodin, an entity could be a Commonwealth even if its members did not live 'happily, as they understand it', and even if it were badly governed. Moreover, as individuals pursue 'many ends', so, too, do commonwealths (p. 7). For Bodin, then, 'all assemblies of men lawfully joined together, whether they be Families, Colleges, Universities, or Commonweals, are kept together, and preserved by the mutual duties of commanding and obeying' (p. 17). Indeed, a Commonwealth is constituted when citizens are 'governed by a puissant sovereign of one or many rulers: albeit that they differ in lawes, language, customes, religions, and diversity of nations' (p. 49).

Missing, evidently, is the idea that a polity is 'natural', a natural 'community' in which a shared *ethos* derives from a common *ethnos* and serves natural ends. On the modern view, as Oakeshott notes, even where accidental circumstances are responsible for bringing a group together, a *societas* is preserved and maintained by the voluntary acts of obedience to the rules (or rulers) which 'govern' it. A series of over-simplifications, each contributing to our understanding of this complex phenomena, all highlight aspects of the emergence of society as a framing notion: 'individualism', 'bourgeois capitalism', the disintegration of 'community', and as Arendt has it, the supercession of the 'social' for the 'political'. As she says, almost paraphrasing Bodin and Hobbes:

> Society is the form in which the fact of mutual dependence for the sake of life and nothing else assumes public significance and where the activities connected with sheer survival are permitted to appear in public. (Arendt, 1958, p. 46)

And where,

> when it first entered the public realm, assumed the disguise of an organization of property owners who, instead of claiming access to the public realm because of their wealth, demanded protection from it for the accumulation of more wealth. (1958, p. 68)

Where, finally, the only thing which people have in common is 'the government' and, paradoxically, their *private* interests!

The ideas are familiar enough. We find them in 'state of nature' theory, of course, but as the example from Bodin suggests, they precede it. They also postdate it. Indeed, *societas* is a dominant background assumption of a host of thinkers stretching from Bodin to the present, including figures who, as Oakeshott rightly says, perhaps share little else. Thus we can count, among the many, Hobbes, Locke, Algernon Sidney, Burke, Kant, Paine, Helvetius, Constant, the authors of the Federalist Papers, Bentham, James, and J. S. Mill. Indeed, one can include what may fairly be called the entire 'liberal tradition' of political thought.

But it was Hobbes, that recalcitrant liberal, who really put the whole business in motion.

HOBBES'S SOCIAL PHYSICS

Not only did Hobbes (*Leviathan*, 1651) articulate a version of *societas*, show how it *required* the concept of the state, and give 'individualism' a point of departure, but he did this with a firm consciousness of the methods and analogies of the new physics. Yet, as Randall notes, 'the only immediate effect of Hobbes's pioneer enterprise was to engender a swarm of horrified refutations'. Remembered primarily for his description of 'the natural condition of mankind' as a 'war of all against all' (*bellum omnium contra omnes*) and as having provided what turned out to be the most influential line of argument in justifying obedience to 'the sovereign'. Hobbes explicitly conceived his project as a Galilean 'composition' from 'simple motions' in the '*more geometrico*' fashion more formally realized by his younger contemporary Spinoza (cf. *Ethics*,

1677). In a provocative text,[3] Hobbes wrote:

> Geometry is demonstrable, for the lines and figures from which we
> reason are drawn and described by ourselves; and civil philosophy
> is demonstrable, because we make the commonwealth ourselves.
> (Quoted in Randall, 1962, p. 554, from Hobbes, 'Six Lessons to
> the Professors of the Mathematics')

A purer expression of a voluntarism in social theory will be harder to
find, but just as important, there has never been a deeper analysis of the
behavioral principles of *capitalist* society than the one provided by
Hobbes's *Leviathan*.

After an examination of 'the Thoughts of Man' – the context makes it
clear that Hobbes is unselfconsciously using 'man' in its generic sense –
he turns, in chapter 10, to an account of 'Power, Worth, Dignity,
Honour, *and* Worthiness'. 'The power *of a Man*', he writes, 'is his
present means, to obtain some future apparent Good.' 'Natural power,
is the eminence of the Faculties of Body, or Mind.' It is that edge of
superiority which this individual or that, 'naturally has'. But as he later
makes perfectly clear, this edge is not so very great:

> Nature has made men so equall . . . that though there bee found
> one man sometimes manifestly stronger in body, or of quicker
> mind than another; yet when all is reckoned together, the differ-
> ence between man and man is not so considerable, as that one man
> can thereupon claim to himselfe any benefit, to which another may
> not pretend, as well as he. (chapter XIII)

Hobbes was not alone in this observation, a striking, though forgotten
fact of Enlightenment thought, undermined, perhaps, by the consequences of the French Revolution – the first revolution of modernity
and the signal of the end of the Enlightenment. Moreover, as Okin
(1979) writes, Hobbes is explicit in including *women* in this argument for
equality.

Of course, there are inequalities in society, and individuals *do* lay
claim to benefits therefrom. But such inequalities stem from 'Instrumental Power', power acquired by whatever eminence of 'natural

---

[3] The text is provocative, since, while it is a pure case of voluntarism, it suggests the
somewhat later view of Vico (1668–1744) – and indeed, Peter Winch's argument in *The
Idea of a Social Science*. That is, for Hobbes, to say that 'we make the commonwealth
ourselves' is to say that we deliberately and consciously make it. While this is surely false,
it never occurred to Hobbes, as it did to Vico, that because 'we make the commonwealth',
human science needs to have a different method from physical science. Hobbes's
voluntarism had influence, but Vico's idea had almost no impact, for better or worse, until
the latter part of the nineteenth century, with the writings of Dilthey and others (see
below, chapter 7). For this reason, Vico, who surely deserves a place in any account of the
history of the social sciences, is omitted here, if reluctantly.

power' a person may have, *and*, significantly, 'by fortune'. 'Riches, Reputation, Friends, and the secret working of God, which men call Good Luck' are 'means and instruments' to acquire greater power (chapter X). But he is less convincing on the question of male dominance in society, arguing that 'for the most part Common-wealths have been erected by the Fathers, not the Mothers of families' (chapter XX).

Moreover, and remarkably, 'The *Value,* or WORTH of man, is as of all other things, his Price; that is to say, so much as would be given for the use of his Power' (chapter XX). It is not, therefore, 'absolute', but is dependent on the need and judgment of another. In a move extra-ordinary for its elegance, Hobbes stripped the veneer of conventional wisdom about 'the Value of a man' of all of its 'superstition' and replaced it with a straightforward market logic. As Macpherson has argued, there is, for Hobbes, a market in power – 'as of all other things'. Accordingly, 'to Value a man at a high rate, is to *Honour* him; . . . to obey, is to Honour; because no man obeyes them, whom they think have no power to help, or hurt them.' And do not, insists Hobbes, confuse the Value of man, his worth, with *either* Worthiness *or* Merit or Desert. Worthiness is 'FITTNESS or *aptitude*', and 'Merit, praesup-poseth a right, and that thing deserved is due by promise'. It depends on a contract, a central theme of the argument of the *Leviathan*. Thus, you may *think* that you are valuable, but if little attention is paid to you, you are not. You may *think* that your skills entitle you to Wealth, but you *deserve just* what you have contracted for. It is hardly surprising that Hobbes generated a swarm of horrified refutations.

But where there is a sovereign, 'a common power to keep them all in awe', there is at least 'peace'. Indeed, the idea of 'the natural condition of mankind', analytically a condition of war, is a brilliant piece of theorizing which is a *logical construction,* derived via abstraction from Hobbes's keen observations of the social transformation of England in process at exactly the time of the English civil wars.

Hobbes sets out the premises of his 'social physics', his ingenious analogue of atomism in society. The first we have already noted. It is the approximate natural equality of mankind. But 'from this equality of ability, ariseth equality of hope in the attaining of our Ends'. The idea that if people recognized their natural equality, there would be equality of hope is a revolutionary idea, but it seems *also* to suppose that people see themselves as *social* equals – a bizarre assumption in Hobbes's England and one that reveals dramatically the near absence in Hobbes's theory of an understanding of the constraining power of social structure. This fact is of some importance, not merely as regards the assessment of Hobbes's effort, but because, as seems plain, an entire tradition shared in the 'methodological individualism' that Hobbes took for granted.

Also, there is a motivational postulate: 'a generall inclination of all mankind, a perpetuall and restless desire of Power after power, that ceaseth only in death' (chapter XI). This psychological postulate, however, also has an important structural dimension, specifically, the assumption that there is a *market in power*. Indeed, while it is surely true that Hobbes and those who followed him believed that social explanation was, in effect, *applied psychology,* Hobbes, like them, found it impossible to entirely preclude social structural factors. That there is a market in power is clear:

> ... the cause of this, is not alwayes that man hopes for a more intensive delight, than he has already attained to; or that he cannot be content with a moderate power: but because he cannot assure the power and means to live well, which he hath present, without the acquisition of more. (chapter XI)

Considered psychologically, there may be those 'content with moderate power', but they cannot drop out of the competition lest, *even by standing still,* they lose what they have. They compete, not because it is 'human nature', but because where there is a market in power, there is no other option.

Competition is one of the 'causes of quarrell', and there are two others, 'Diffidence and Glory'. 'The first, maketh men invade for Gain; the second, for Safety; and the third, for Reputation' (chapter XIII). Given these premises, then, in the condition where there is no Law, and for Hobbes, there is no Law where there is no Sovereign, 'the life of man', in his memorable phrase, is 'solitary, poore, nasty, brutish, and short'.

The account is theoretical and counter-factual. It is not quasi-anthropological, but analytic and deductive; and the rationality assumption, overlooking here some internal problems in Hobbes's scheme, is crucial. People are rational enough to arrive at 'precepts or general Rules' – the 'Laws of Nature' – but they are rational enough to know *as well* that in the *absence* of law in the strict sense – prescriptions carrying enforceable sanctions – there is no assurance that others will abide by them. It would be in our interest to live by the Laws of Reason, but unless each can be sure that the other will, *rational self-interest will lead to war.* It is thus that a rational individual *would* choose to live under law, *would* choose to convert the treacherous competition of the construction of the 'natural condition' into a 'peaceful' competition in which inequalities will result, but where one can, at least, define one's own 'interests', live 'freely', and have security in one's person and property – a brilliant analysis *and* defense of *societas.*

It is striking that for all of Hobbes's emphasis on the idea of war, he seems to lack utterly a concern for war in its main sense, that is, as violent conflict not between the members of some polity – civil war – but between polities. Of course, he was writing in the midst of the English civil wars, as noted; but as Machiavelli had so prophetically seen, imperialist wars of state-building and colonization had, by the time of Hobbes, become the dominant imperative of states. Indeed, it is of some importance, as we shall see, that after Machiavelli, *no* theorist in the 'liberal tradition' of social science put war at the center of his analysis. Once 'the state' and 'society' have been discovered, it is as if nothing that happens in 'society' is affected either by war or by mobilization for war.[4]

Nevertheless, Hobbes's performance was remarkable – even if, equally remarkably, on the present view, it is not acknowledged that versions of his views still underpin a vast amount of current social science – that, to put it simply, *societas remains, unspoken, in the background of much contemporary social science.* This lack of acknowledgement is due, in part at least, to the fact that we overlook the pertinence in Hobbes of the competitive model which he used to join premises regarding 'human nature' to 'politics'. The idea of the competitive market is the explanatory linchpin not only of modern economics, but of much modern politics as well. In part, we fail to acknowledge our Hobbesian premises because Hobbes is wrongly seen as some sort of extreme anti-liberal. In fact, in many ways, he was the *founder* of liberal social theory. To be sure, no subsequent liberal choose to defend his Leviathan – a legitimated absolutism – but his methodology, his premises, and his arguments are thoroughly liberal. Thus, Hobbes may well be the first great theorist to *define* freedom in liberal terms as 'the absence of Opposition' (chapter XXI) and to argue that law – the *only* pertinent 'impediment' – *defined* the 'civil condition', the condition which allows people to live together privately.

But indeed, the idea that *societas* could be a framing concept for the new kind of political order had a significant role to play in the very definition of the science of politics. In a word, it promoted the idea that the science of politics was the *science of government.*

THE SCIENCE OF GOVERNMENT

With the concept of *societas, political science could take 'society' for granted.* There were 'private persons', each possessing 'property', and

---

[4] Comte held that there were but 'two possible active aims' of 'a social system', either conquest or production: 'The military aim characterized the ancient, while the industrial aim characterizes the modern, system.' A 'peaceful republic' was a *civitas cupitidas.* This is, I believe, a fairly common assumption, even though it would seem to be so thoroughly taken for granted that it goes unnoticed.

there were rules which bound them. These effectively reduced to the taken-for-granted assumptions of a market society. Occupation, class, status, religion, race, even gender, could be ignored with regard to the main concerns of the science of government. And after Mill, as we shall see, 'the economy', as the special concern of 'economists', could be excluded as well. Political science could proceed with the description and analysis of 'constitutions' and of executive, legislative, and judicial practice, with facts about 'laws' and 'branches of government', and with processes affecting the formation of 'public policy' *within* government.

Moreover, as was just suggested, from the key idea that 'society' precedes the state and may be conceived independently of it followed a series of additional consequences: political power is the power of the state – and it is the only power; the problem of power, accordingly, is the problem of the best *form* of state; freedom is freedom from interference *by* the state, except, of course, insofar as the state exists to preserve 'the rules of the game'; justice is substantially a procedural issue, a matter of articulating 'rights' and establishing machinery whereby these can be preserved and protected.[5]

This did not happen all at once, of course, nor were the practitioners of the new science of politics always able to keep cleanly to the research program – reality had a way of obtruding itself. Nonetheless, even a quick survey of Joseph Priestley's *An Essay on the First Principles of Government* (1768), Bentham's *Fragment on Government* (1776), *The Federalist Papers* (1787), James Mill's *Essay on Government* (1823), and J. S. Mill's *Considerations on Representative Government* (1861) will confirm that in the 'liberal' tradition the 'science of politics' had early on become the science of government.

AN ALTERNATIVE CONCEPTION

There were eighteenth-century writers who had alternative conceptions of the science of politics. Outstanding here are Rousseau and Montesquieu – as Hegel and then Durkheim both recognized. No writer has been as difficult to understand, perhaps, as Rousseau, and I do not here pretend to give an adequate account of his thought. Yet a key point, germane to the present problem, bears emphasis. For, if political science was to be the science of government, then in Rousseau's view, it would be the science of the *il*legitimate state. Since for him the sovereign remained

---

[5] Nineteenth-century Marxists saw that the 'state' did not hold exclusive power in society, but they fell into the complementary mistake of holding that its power was entirely derivative. The state as 'instrument of the ruling class' assumes the separation of 'state' and 'civil society' just as much as does the liberal theory of the state. A consequence of this, of course, has been the near absence, until recently, of a Marxist theory of the state.

the whole people united by the contract, 'government' was merely magistracy. Its power was exclusively executive, 'particular acts, which are not with the province of law'. Law is the sole province of the sovereign, whose power and right is 'inalienable'. Because Rousseau was a *radical* democrat – Comte refers to him, rightly, as the founder of 'the anarchical school' – for 'government' was a purely technical consideration, of little real importance; in the legitimate state, it would take care of itself. Of course, as J. B. Noone has pointed out, Rousseau 'manages to obscure this point completely with his digressions on the internal structures of governments and on the conditions appropriate to each form', writing in these sections as if he agreed with that tradition that held that governments made law (Noone, 1980, p. 59). Indeed, while the idea that *democracy* is a *form of government* – an idea that has been taken for granted now for about 200 years by political science – would have been anathema to Rousseau, it is quite plain that it is a further consequence of the definition of political science as the science of government. Not incidentally, the assumption that democracy is a form of government rather than a form of association or 'constitution', is an assumption that has well served the *enemies* of democracy – as that had been understood from Aristotle to Madison. For those who still thought in terms of 'republics' the size of Athens, Venice, or Holland, 'democracy' meant rule *by* 'the people' (the *demos*), not rule *of* or *for* the people. It meant what we oddly call 'direct democracy'. Since the late eighteenth century, the idea that 'the people' should themselves make the rules which 'govern' their lives has been a key feature of the *ideology* of the modern state, ideology exactly because, as the writers of the eighteenth century acknowledged, 'representative government' is *not* 'democracy'. Indeed, while 'representative government', in the era of the modern state, came to be thought of as a *form* of democracy, its entire novelty was exactly that it could avoid the problems of democratic rule, but especially the problem that Aristotle had identified and which had been the focus of Madison's brilliant *Federalist* #10, the problem of rule by the poor in the interests of the poor.[6] Of course, in the era of states, it has been easy to dismiss that older concept, and since World War I at least, it has been easy to make fun of Rousseau, to accuse him of incoherence, or worse, to transform him into a precursor of fascism!

With Montesquieu we are on less contentious ground. Far more the 'political scientist', far less extreme in his political sympathies, his *L'esprit des lois* (1748) is a far clearer and better example of an alternative conception of political science. Randall puts the point neatly:

[6] For an account of the specific class fears of America's leading elites, see Gordon Wood, 1969. For a more general theoretical account, see my 'The Foreclosure of Democracy in America'.

... Unlike the other pioneer social scientists of the eighteenth century, he did not conceive [the science of society] as a social physics on the Newtonian model. Rather, such a science should be a natural history of human societies, based not on the geometric method but on the method of naturalists like Buffon or Linnaeus: the patient investigation of the facts, the careful classification of types of society, the exact study of their careers and their relations to their environment, bringing to light general principles. (Randall, 1962)

Durkheim was basically correct in contending, against widespread criticism, that the famous tripartite classification of *gouvernements* as 'monarchies', 'despotisms', or 'republics' was both 'truthful' and 'penetrating'. And Durkheim was further correct in arguing that this was not a classification of governments if by that one means 'political regimes'. Montesquieu's 'vision was far wider'. 'As he describes them the three types of society differ not only in the number of rulers and in the administration of public affairs, but in their entire nature' (Durkheim, 1960, p. 25). This confusion in language is symptomatic of a main point of this section. It is wrong to say that Montesquieu offered a classification of governments as we use that term, and it is misleading to say that he gave us a classification of societies – the language used by Randall (above) and Durkheim. Strictly speaking, it was neither. It was a classification of human associations conceived as *social wholes,* politically constituted societies, if you will. Critically, these were complex interconnected wholes, the product of complex causal determinants.

It was thus that geography had to be considered: 'despotisms' thrive on broad plains (*Spirit,* bk. XVII, 6). And climate: 'The law of Mohammed, which prohibits the drinking of wine, is . . . fitted to the climate of Arabia' (bk. XIV, 10). It was thus also that the size of the polity was important: 'It is natural for a republic to have only a small territory; otherwise it cannot long subsist' (bk. VIII, 16). But law stands 'in relation' not only to these, but to all aspects of life, 'to the religion of the inhabitants, to their inclinations, riches, numbers, commerce, manners, and customs'. Montesquieu's interest was in all these relations, and it is 'these together [which] constitute what I call the Spirit of Laws' (bk. I, 3). Indeed, 'I have not separated the political from the civil institutions, as I do not pretend to treat of laws, but of their spirit' (bk. I, 3).

As I have argued elsewhere (1981), Montesquieu's effort – because he was sensitive to the causal complexities which determine the character of civilizations and polities – is an extraordinarily illuminating account of the political world of his time – a world undergoing remarkable transition. For Montesquieu, 'republics' were the manageably sized historical paradigms of Athens and Sparta; 'monarchies' were paradigmatically those kingdoms which developed from the roots of Western feudalism, complete with a relatively autonomous aristocracy and '*parlements*'. 'Despotisms' were empires, the Ottoman or Russian, conglomerates of many different linguistic and religious groups, all under the military domination of a Caesar and a retinue of lieutenants loyal to him. But because this world was in such a remarkable condition of transition, Montesquieu's brilliant classification was made anachronistic within 40 years of its publication. After Montesquieu, and except for Rousseau, the models of ancient republics lose their force, and monarchies, Montesquieu's clear preference, are deemed equivalent to despotisms, exactly because of the ideology of the 'sovereign people'.

The Americans will have much to do with this. Having fought a successful war of independence, they will give the world the idea of a sovereign people, a 'nation', with the right of 'self-determination'. And, after a period of experimentation with 'confederation, they will arrive at an utterly novel solution to the problem of the modern state, even more novel than the English State' – that 'republic disguised in the form of a monarchy' (*Spirit,* XIII, 15), which they tried so hard to emulate. Rejecting completely Montesquieu's admonitions on the precariousness of 'peaceful republics' – even in confederation, they will manage all the same to appropriate from his confusing account of 'political liberty' (in bk. XI) what was needed in the new circumstances. The French will not have such an easy time of it. The revolt of the nobility will issue in a violent revolution in which king and aristocracy will give way to a series of 'republican' efforts at constituting 'the modern state'. The consequences of these events go well beyond the rejection of Montesquieu's theory of the good state by the *philosophes*. Nevertheless, it is important to notice that as these views so quickly became anachronisms, his notion of a unified 'political science' all but fell on deaf ears. As I argue in chapters 4 and 5, 'positive philosophy', in the hands of Comte *and* German Idealist philosophy of history are further consequences of these remarkable events. But we need first to return to the period from which we have just come, to identify the emergence from 'politics' of 'political economy' – the human science which first secures the idea of social *laws* and which, accordingly, is rightly taken to be the first of the genuinely scientific human sciences.

3

The Emergence of
Political Economy

The last chapter argued that the concept of *societas* underpinned thinking about politics in the modern era. But the idea that 'civil society' was
defined by rules which allowed persons to pursue their self-defined
interests, to live together privately and in peace, was – and is – in
continual tension with another, contradictory, but nonetheless closely
related, idea. Oakeshott finds it in the medieval concept of *universitas*,
the idea of the state not as a maker of rules, but as the manager of an
enterprise. On this view, the membership is a corporation, organized in
respect to some common purpose. The idea is evident in the writings of
the so-called Cameralists, the late seventeenth- and eighteenth-century
German theorists of the 'enlightened state', in the writings of the French
Physiocrats and in the post-Napoleonic period in St Simon and Comte,
among others. It was not a dominant idea in the British thought of the
period, probably because of the earlier beginnings and fuller development of market capitalism in England. But it is there, nonetheless.
Indeed, it is in the background of early 'political economy', as the
phrase suggests. That is, 'political economy', originally, was the *politics
of acquiring wealth*; this is reflected in the full title of Adam Smith's
great work, *An Inquiry into the Nature and Causes of the Wealth of
Nations*.

In this chapter, an attempt is made to account for the emergence of
political economy as the science we now call 'economics'. As it turns
out, this process was not separate from the one we looked at in the
previous chapter. The idea that the science of politics was the science
of government involved the freeing of the 'economy' from politics.
Developing capitalism was the key element here. When capitalist relations
were once free from the dead weight of the old society – a task taken on
at some point by the new governments of the modern state – it was

possible also to free political economy from politics – a process clearly
evident by the time of J.S. Mill's *Unsettled Questions on Political
Economy* (1829), as we shall see. However, this process was completed
only in the last stages of the nineteenth century, the era of *laissez-faire
and* of the so-called 'marginalist revolution'. But we ought to begin at
the beginning.

The so-called 'Cameralists', mainly professors and administrators of
public enterprises in Germany, from Seckendorff (1626–92) to Justi
(1720–71) to Schlozer (1733–1817), Quesnay (1694–1774), and the
'Physiocrats' provided variant versions of the idea of the state as an
enterprise. As Oakeshott writes, the Cameralists 'turned a collection of
well-used expedients into an administrative machine' (Oakeshott, 1975,
p. 300). Composed of boards, commissions, ministers, directors, inspec-
tors, agronomists, and assorted other technicians and managers, the
Cameralists, like the *philosophes,* 'had little use for *parlementaires'*, and
'judicial offices occupied an inconspicuous place in this scheme' (1975,
p. 300). To refer to this as 'enlightenment despotism' is both misleading,
and perhaps misses the main point. It is misleading because, as Krieger
has noted, 'eighteenth century man was relatively indifferent to the idea
of political absolutism per se' (Krieger, 1975, p. 27). And it misses the
main point since, as suggested, it has always been at least a tacit
assumption of the ruling classes of the modern state that government
had a responsibility defined in terms of the 'welfare' of its subject
population and thus had a role in organizing and managing the 'corporation' of members. What this role was has varied, of course; also,
whether 'parliaments' were effective instruments, whether 'rule of law'
prevailed, and what constituted the realm of the private. Finally, *laissez-
faire* capitalism, never fully realized in any case, is very much more the
exception than the rule. It is thus that *societas* and *universitas* have been
uneasy partners in the modern state. And it is thus that the policies of
politicians and political economists have varied.

QUESNAY AND THE LAWS OF NATURE

As Krieger points out, there is some irony in the fact that, as a literal
idea, 'enlightened despotism' was espoused by the French Physiocrats
only during a brief period between the 1760s and 1770s. The irony is that
these same Physiocrats are remembered as advocates – among the very
first – of *laissez-faire!* But Quesnay and the Physiocrats had made a
discovery of some importance: it was the obligation of the rulers of the
state to 'procure the whole sum of happiness and enjoyments possible
for humanity' (quoted in Krieger, 1975, p. 50). To do this, of course,

rulers had to think of the state as a corporate enterprise directed at achieving the greatest amount of wealth possible. Getting the job done called for an active state. But the policies of this state had to be based on an understanding of 'the laws of nature'. Indeed, it was thus that 'despotism' was justified *and* that it was thought that the market should be left to work its logic.

'Physio-cracy', literally 'rule of nature', defined physical law as 'the regulated (*règle*) course of all physical events which is evidently the most advantageous to mankind'. Moral law was 'the rule (*règle*) of every human action conforming to the physical order evidently most advantageous to mankind'. Together, they constitute 'the natural laws', which are both immutable and the best possible ones (*les meilleures possibles*). Indeed, 'All social facts are linked together in the bonds of eternal, immutable, ineluctable, inevitable laws, which individuals and governments would obey if they were once known to them' (quoted in Randall, 1962, p. 963, from Dupont de Nemours, *Maximes du Docteur Quesnay*). The problem of public policy was to discover what these natural laws were. Quesnay found the answer in the unfettered productive efforts of free 'farmers' rationally exploiting the technological and commercial opportunities available to them. His famous *Tableau Économique* (1758 or 1759), in many ways a brilliant theoretical synthesis, offered a highly abstract income flow schema, which linked expenditures and products between social classes.

Like Adam Smith and those who followed him, Quesnay first identified the main economic actors. He did this, as did Smith, in terms of the common experience of his day. There were, then, the landowners: *la classe des proprietaires,* or significantly, the *class souveraign* or *class distributive.* This class contributed the necessary *avances,* or capital, which bought the means of production and the means to sustain life while awaiting the product. The second group was the *classe productive,* the farmer/entrepreneurs engaged in active agriculture. The third group, *le class stérile,* included all those not engaged 'productively'. Expenditures on rents, servants, clothing, 'commercial costs', even manufactured commodities are to be included here. That this classification reveals a space- and time-bound theoretical bias is evident. For Quesnay, *labor on land* was the *sole* source of 'surplus value', and all expenditures came from it alone. Quesnay attempted to demonstrate this by showing a flow of expenditures which depended on the specific roles performed by the respective 'classes'.

The *Tableau* was a great simplification of what, in the real world, is a complex set of processes, and one can hardly minimize the importance of Quesnay's effort. First, he put to work the analytic kernel of 'natural law' and, as is well-known, drew the appropriate policy conclusions – *laissez-faire* and a single tax on the income from land. Second, the

Tableau shows the interdependence of the individuals engaged in the transactions. Quesnay, a physician who wrote a three-volume work on physiology entitled *Essai physique sur l'économie animale* (1747), conceived of an economy as a *system,* governed by principles. Third, and following on this, he may well have been the first 'to convey an explicit conception of the nature of economic equilibrium' (Schumpeter, 1954, p. 242), a critical step in what, eventually, will allow political economy to *escape* from history. Finally, as Schumpeter points out, the *Tableau* opened great possibilities for some econometrics, a fact of which Quesnay was not unaware.

'State-tistics', data about the 'state' – but especially its 'economy' – dates, it seems, from the early seventeenth century, with the real beginnings of the early modern state. A good manager, after all, has to know what he is managing. Herman Conring (1606–81), a German professor, is usually given credit, says Schumpeter, for having been the first to lecture on a 'purely descriptive presentation of facts relevant to public administration'. The word 'statistics', was evidently first used by Gottfried Achenwald (1719–72). In England, meanwhile, William Petty (1623–87) and Charles Davenant (1656–1714) were developing 'political arithmetic', 'the art of reasoning by figures upon things relating to government' (Schumpeter, 1954, p. 210). Quesnay, seeing the possibilities provoked by his theory, 'troubled himself about statistical data and actually tried to estimate the values of annual output and other aggregates' (p. 243), an idea of enormous importance, realized – if we may here be generous – only in this century. Adam Smith, it is worth noticing, had 'no great faith in political arithmetick' (Smith, 1976, bk. IV, ch. v, p. 534), but like Quesnay, he had and used a notion of 'natural law' which was most important to his project.

ADAM SMITH AND NATURAL LAW

The Wealth of Nations is a very large book. Most of it is not read by anyone today – not even historians of economics. From their point of view, the heart of it is in books I and II, excluding the rich illustrations, about 10 per cent of the entire effort.

The key distinction occurs in book I, chapter vii, where Smith distinguishes between the natural and the real price of commodities. The natural price represents precisely what the commodity is worth. The real price may be above, below, or the same as the natural price. While different 'accidents' have effects on prices, the prices of all commodities are 'continually gravitating' towards the natural price. This is, then, as Schumpeter points out (1954, p. 112), a perfect example of the *analytic* kernel of natural law, a unique sequence determined by a social process, where, at the same time, a *ceteris paribus* clause allows that the 'natural' may not, in fact, occur. The idea is found in all classical writers on political economy, including Marx, and as his inclusion here suggests, the ideological content was profoundly various, from the crude harmonism of Bastiat to the revolutionary socialism of Marx. For Bastiat, for example, unconditional *laissez-faire* promised unqualified Human Glory; though it is too often forgotten, Smith was much less sanguine, and Marx, of course, sought to demystify 'the natural' as *the alienated,* and thereby to restore the control of institutions to man.[1] But the analytic kernel requires some further development.

It seems that Edward West, in his 1815 *Essay on the Application of Capital to Land,* was the first to use the word 'tend' to refer to the process caught by Smith's metaphoric (?) 'continually gravitating'. But, significantly, this was given a *realist* interpretation by West and Ricardo – as indeed, it was by Smith also. That is, as Richard Whately said later (1832), a tendency is 'the existence of a cause which, if operating unimpeded, would produce [some constant] result' (quoted from Brown, 1984, p. 134). In this sense, then, 'The earth, or any other body moving round a centre, has a tendency to fly off at a tangent; i.e., the centrifugal force operates in that direction, although it is controlled by the centripetal' (1984, p. 134). Whately also made clear what later positivist writers obscure, that this sense of 'tendency' is not to be confused with another in which the word 'is understood to mean "the existence of such a state of things that that result *may be expected to take place*"' (1984, p. 134). Put in contemporary language, a tendency in this latter sense is a reliable pattern; in the former sense it is an actual or existing state of something which, *if not prevented,* will produce some constant result. It is, if you will, *a causal power of the system.* In this sense, a tendency may *never* actually be realized, because, obviously, it is *always* possible for there to be *other causes* operating which prevent *its* realization. In such cases, something *else* results. The tendency is real, but its outcome, when impeded, is not *manifest.* It is because of inertia *and* gravitation that planetary motion is elliptical and *never* rectilinear. Although the classicists were either fuzzy or mistaken regarding the locus of the causal powers determining natural price, they were clear enough that they were the basis of the 'laws' which they tried to articulate. Ricardo, for example, says:

In speaking, then, of the exchangeable value of commodities, or the power of purchasing possessed by any one commodity, I mean

---

[1] There are several senses of 'natural' in Smith and the literature of the period. For Marx, the division of labor, money, the forms of property, and the resulting inequalities *appear* as 'natural', not as *human products.* This is the cause of the fundamental alienation of man. Social realities are real, but *conventional* – though not for this reason, the voluntary or deliberate creations of persons. See chapter 13.

always that power which it would possess if not disturbed by any temporary or accidental cause, and which is its natural price. (Ricardo, 1962, chapter IV, p. 51)

There are surely some evident analogies here to Newtonian mechanics, and it can hardly be denied, I think, that the classicists were attempting to identify the *causes* of patterns in 'the economy' and that the methodological assumptions made regarding the understanding of these processes as tendencies realistically understood are not *outré*. An important shift in this regard will take place, though it is not clear exactly when it occurs. J. S. Mill, for example, offers a most confusing account which is probably *inconsistent,* and indeed, it may well be that the ability of writers to hold simultaneously to both a realist *and* a positivist (i.e., Humean) view of a causality is what stands in the way both of locating this shift and, today, seeing that it is an important one.[2] We saw in chapter 1 that the understanding of Newtonian gravitation was alternatively realist and positivist, and that Smith managed, in his own way, to hold to both.

We next need to look at some other problems which may have been inspired by illicit analogy to – and confusion over – the Newtonian scheme of atoms and forces. Fundamental here is the social atomism of political economy, already alluded to in our account of Hobbes and the liberal tradition of political science.

THE DERIVATION AND EXPLANATION OF 'COMMERCIAL SOCIETY'

Smith's social atomism is perfectly clear in book I of *The Wealth of Nations.* Newton's Rule III (above) allowed inference from what was invariably true of observed bodies to all others, observed and unobservable. Now Smith not only lacked the concept of social structure, but presumably it was as obvious to him as it is to us that there are *only* individuals. Accordingly, what was there to investigate *except* individuals and their actions?

Smith looked, and he 'induced'. He sharpened the functional categories of common sense and tried to find principles that would explain the acts

[2] A. R. Ryan makes a heroic effort to save Mill from inconsistency on this in chapter IV of his *John Stuart Mill.* Mill certainly held to a Humean constant conjunction concept of causality, and I think that Peter Geach is correct in arguing that 'Mill is, in fact, pushed by the facts . . . into saying "All laws of causation, in consequence of their liability to be counteracted require to be stated in words affirmative of tendencies only."' But 'to talk of "what would failing interference happen . . ." is to abandon the Humian position' (quoted by Ryan, pp. 62, 65, from Anscombe and Geach, 1961). See also Anschutz, 1953. I consider Mill's later thoughts on causality below, in discussing his criticism of Comte. For discussion of the current literature on this central problem, see below, chapter 12.

of these individuals, characterized in terms of their roles in 'production' and 'exchange'. From this point of view, it made absolutely no difference whether a consumer was rich or poor, whether a worker lacked tools and land and why, or whether he was Irish or the descendant of royalty! Moreover, at the bottom of his account, he put principles of 'human nature' – psychological principles. Two stand out. One was the very famous principle of 'self-love: It is not from the benevolence of the butcher, the brewer, or the baker, that we expect our dinner, but from their regard to their own interest' (bk. I, ii). But of course, Smith did not consistently ignore the non-psychological, since, as in Hobbes, this principle was operative *only* by virtue of a structural principle – the same market arrangements which had been in the background of Hobbes's account. Not only were the good effects of exchange the unintended consequences of this taken-for-granted structural principle, but the principle was motivational *only* by virtue of this. If I want to eat, have no benefactor, and live in a competitive market society, 'self-love' is *necessary*.

A second principle was the equally famous 'propensity [of human nature] to truck, barter and exchange one thing for another' (bk. I, ch. i). This was put forward to explain the transition from the 'early and rude state of society' to 'commercial society', 'improved' *because* of the development of the division of labor. The propensity to truck and barter presumably generates the division of labor, but it seems that the principle assumes, as before, a market arrangement of some sort. That would explain the feeling one gets that for Smith, a division of labor *requires* the existence of markets.

Smith's effort is bold. *From this one principle,* he will 'explain' not only the occupational division of labor in society, but in turn, the transition to a money economy, and thence to 'the accumulation of stock and the appropriation of land,' and with this, inequality in society and, finally, that 'improvement' which his England had realized so prominently.

Originally, there was no division of labor, and presumably individuals, or at least families, lived autarchically. But, given the 'propensity to truck and barter', the division of labor arises as the unintended consequence – 'necessary, though very slow and gradual' (bk. II, ch. i). He tells us, moreover, that a consequence of this is the development by different individuals of different talents – inequality of ability: 'The difference of natural talents in different men is, in reality, much less than we are aware of', and the differences we see are not 'so much the cause, as the effect of the division of labor' (bk. I, ch. ii). Following Locke, he then argues that, in the absence of money, 'improvement' would be restricted to what is possible through barter, and he suggests that this limitation would be severe. But he does not follow Locke's argument as regards the origin of money. He does not argue, as Locke did, that infinite acquisition was the *motive* for the introduction of money, nor that, prior to the institution of the state, people *consented* – even tacitly – to its use as a medium of exchange. (Locke, 1967, II, v.) For Smith, it seems that money has a telic utility, so that the movement from the use, first, of some commonly desirable commodity, to metals, and finally, with the institution of the state, to money in the strict sense, was inevitable. It had been important to Locke, that the use of money did *not* presuppose the state, since, unlike Hobbes, he wanted the right to accumulation to be a *natural* right – not dependent on the conventions of law.

Moreover, Locke seems to have felt a need to explain (and justify) *private property,* whereas Smith does not. Indeed, so far as I can tell, Locke has provided the *only argument,* which *both* explains *and* justifies private property. The other famous argument, in Rousseau's remarkable 'Discourse on Inequality' explains it, but it also condemns it – as a conspiracy of the rich!

Locke had argued that individuals had a *right* 'to appropriate from the common store' to satisfy their needs, and that money, introduced in the state of nature, made possible acquisition beyond immediate *use.* Money did not 'spoil', and, of greater significance, such appropriation was not – *in a market society* – prejudicial to the interests or well-being of those who, because nothing was left to appropriate freely, *could* not appropriate freely. Indeed, in a truly remarkable passage, Locke insisted:

> To which let me add, that he who appropriates land to himself by his labour, does not lessen but increase the common stock of mankind. For the provisions serving to the support of humane life, produced by one acre of inclosed and cultivated land, are (to speak much within compasse) ten times more, than those, which are yeilded [sic] by an acre of Land, of equal richnesse, lyeing wast in common. And therefor he, that encloses Land and has a greater plenty of the conveniencys of life from ten acres, than he could have from an hundred left to Nature, may truly be said, to give ninety acres to Mankind. (Locke, 1967, bk. I, V)

This is certainly the first effort to provide the landless with words of praise for the landed, as indeed, it is the primary – and enduring – rationale for capitalist development! Just as some landless laborer may be thankful for the 'gift' of commodities produced on the land of the enterprising, so the poor of the world can be thankful for the enterprise of General Motors. As Macpherson has noted, the 'argument' plainly assumes that there are those without land who *need* its products, and that they can somehow earn the money to buy them. Moreover, as landless (and capital-less), they *must* earn this money as wage-workers. All this is assumed by Locke as part of his 'argument'.

But Smith does worse. For him, private property is a datum – which means that as far as his inquiry is concerned – 'political economy?' – it does not need to be explained. Finally, with less sophistication than Locke, who saw that money and private property *had* to generate social inequalities, Smith assigns the blame – if such is to be assigned – to the division of labor. Thus,

> ... After the division of labor has once thoroughly taken place, it is but a very small part of the [necessaries, conveniences, and amusements of human life] with which a man's own labor can supply him. The far greater part of them he must derive from the labour of other people, and he must be either rich or poor according to the quantity of that labor which he can command, or which he can afford to purchase. (Smith, 1976, I, V)

It is clear that, looked at from one point of view, at any given time, most people have some money by which labor can be commanded, if that means, as it does here, that money can buy the *product* of labor. But it is by no means clear that most people have money to *purchase* labor – power – the distinctly capitalist relationship. Once this difference is obscured – as it is in Smith – capitalism can be defined as 'free enterprise' – and capitalists can rest easy.

It is a remarkable fact, nonetheless, that Smith came close to an analysis which could have been used as a critique of capitalism. As noted, Smith was no simple-minded Harmonist of the (later) Bastiat (1850)/Henry Carey (1851) variety, and as Donald Winch has demonstrated, there were, for Smith, losses along with the gains of 'commercial society', not least the violence that it does to the humanity of 'those who live by labour'. Moreover, his analytic machinery, pushed in the right places, could also serve critics of capitalism. It is not much of a step, for example, to start treating the holders of 'stock' in the same way that Smith treated landlords.[3]

'INVISIBLE HAND' EXPLANATIONS

But to return to Smith's 'explanation' of the division of labor and all that follows from it. His account is a clear example of what Nozick has called – with deference to Smith – an 'invisible hand explanation' (Nozick,

[3] For discussion, see Ronald Meek, 1977, 'Smith and Marx', and Schumpeter, 1954, pp. 190f.

1974, p. 18). Since this is such an important kind of explanation for social science generally, it will be well to pause and examine its logic – and its limitations. Invisible hand explanations

> show how some overall pattern or design, which one would have thought had to be produced by an individual's or group's success-ful attempt to realize the pattern, instead was produced and maintained by a process that in no way had the overall pattern or design 'in mind'. (Nozick, 1974, p. 18)

Locke's 'explanation' of money is *not* an invisible hand explanation even if, for him, there were unintended consequences, such as the subsequent social inequality. Money was consented to *in order to* overcome the obstacles of barter, which it succeeded in doing. Smith's explanation of the division of labor, on the other hand, was an invisible hand expla-nation, since the division was *not* intended by *anybody* to make possible the great 'improvements' which (in fact) resulted. It was the con-sequence of the propensity to truck and barter, making it not only an invisible hand explanation but, for Nozick, a 'fundamental' one as well. It explains 'the political' in terms of 'the non-political' – for Nozick the most satisfactory kind of explanation (Nozick, 1974, p. 6). Moreover, such explanations can be 'illuminating' even if they are not 'correct', which means roughly that though what is to be explained *could have happened* the way it was 'explained', *it did not.*

Yet one may reasonably request the sense in which an incorrect explanation is illuminating? While Nozick leaves us to do some guessing here, one might argue, plausibly, that since it is not possible to know how something *really* came about, seeing how it *could have* come about is illuminating. It is not clear whether this is how Smith saw what he was doing or, for that matter, how some more recent attempts at funda-mental invisible hand explanations see the matter. Consider here one or two of the examples cited by Nozick: Hernstein's account of genetic factors in a society's class stratification patterns and the Austrian theory of the trade cycle. It will be clear that for many people at least, the 'illumination' will be limited – especially if we know that it is quite *unlikely* that the proferred explanation is correct. Indeed, a realist understanding of explanation, as we shall see, would insist that *no* explanation is provided unless we can show that the proferred expla-nation is correct. If we are unable to do that, then we have reached the *limits* of science! More radically, of course, one might reject realism altogether here and say that it doesn't matter if the explanation is *correct*: all 'explanations' are *fictions* in any case. We need to return to this, but as noted in chapter 1, it is not impossible that Smith had something like this in mind. One should notice here, finally, that the relation of such 'explanations' to justification is unclear. The 'contract' arguments of classical 'state of nature theory' were justificatory but were *not* invisible hand explanations. Hobbes and Locke had the state come into existence *voluntarily*, through the cooperating wills of the members. Were Smith's arguments justificatory? It has appeared so to many.

ADAM SMITH'S ACCOUNT OF NATURAL PRICE

Smith defined the goals of book I of his inquiry as providing an account of 'the rules which men naturally observe in exchanging [goods] either for money or for one another' (bk. I, ch. iv). He broke this down into three particular questions:

> First, what is the real measure of this exchangeable value; or, wherein consists the real price of commodities.
> Second, what are the different parts of which this real price is composed or made up.
> And, lastly, what are the different circumstances which sometimes raise some or all these different parts of one price, and sometimes sink them below their natural or ordinary rate. (Smith, bk. I, ch. iv)

Given a market society in which there is an accumulation of stock and in which all land is owned, Smith's answers to his first and second questions are unequivocal (despite considerable dispute over this in the literature). He writes:

> When the price of any commodity is neither more nor less than what is sufficient to pay the rent of the land, the wages of the labour, and the profits of the stock employed in raising, preparing, and bringing it to market, according to their natural rates, the commodity is then sold for what may be called its natural price. (bk. I, ch. vii)

Each of these 'components' has a 'natural rate', which is to say that there is a tendency defined by the laws governing their price. Roughly, the natural wage rate is subsistence, where subsistence may be defined relatively, as a function of what we might call 'standard of living'. Of course, this makes the natural rate of wages *unexplained in economic terms*. The profit rate is dependent on the wage rate (and rises with a decrease in it), but it cannot fall below what is 'sufficient to compensate the ordinary losses to which every employment of stock is exposed' (bk. I, ch. ix), which, of course, means that *it cannot be given a wholly economic explanation*. The rate of rent 'is naturally the highest which the tenant can afford to pay in the actual circumstances of the land' and is 'naturally a monopoly price' (bk. I, ch. xi). One might add here that rate of rent requires a *political explanation*!

It is hardly necessary to say that this is anything but elegant. Indeed, it is hardly apparent that Smith has explained *anything*. He has given us a program for explanation, but *the program seems to take us right out of considerations of the market*. The point here is not to be critical of Smith, who seems to have recognized some limits to the explanatory capacities of *this portion of his inquiry*. Indeed, it was just this, it seems, which so upset all those who, beginning with Ricardo, *were* critical of him.

Many have held that Smith's theory is inconsistent, that he waffles between a cost-of-production theory of value and a labor theory of value. More recent writers, having the advantage of the marginalist 'revolution', have accused Smith and all those concerned with the problem of 'value' of being 'metaphysicians', arguing roughly that it is a superfluous concept, with no scientific validity. But Smith was consistent. The labor-quantity theory of value *as a theory of price* holds, for Smith, only in the special case in which there is no 'accumulation of stock' or 'appropriation of land'. Improvements in the productivity of labor would not have altered this since, presumably, the existence of the market in commodities (there is no market in land or labor) would still have equalized labor costs. But this 'original state of things . . . could not last'. Once land is appropriated and stock has accumulated, rent and profit enter as factors in cost and hence in price.

As noted, this makes the key facts institutional 'givens', not to be explained by the theory. *But of course, it was nowhere written down what it was that this 'science', anymore than any other, was supposed to explain.* Indeed, just the reverse is true. Once institutionalized as a science, its practitioners and teachers, sharing in the aims and techniques of forebears, can know what it is that defines their 'science'. But we are now witnessing incipient institutionalization. Smith's role is crucial, because he left an ambiguous legacy. If we read the *Wealth* from the point of view of *subsequent* development, it is easy to say with Schumpeter, that 'Books I and II – respectively about 24 and 14 per cent of the whole – also overflowing with illustrative fact, present the essentials of A. Smith's analytic schema' (Schumpeter, p. 187). This means that well over 60 per cent of his effort – the comparative, almost Weberian, account of book III, the indictment of mercantilism in book IV, the primarily historical account of public finance in book V, and the treatment of 'the four stages' – all fall out as *merely* of historical interest. Moreover, judged from the same perspective, Smith emerges as *analytically* confused. Surely, so the implicit argument goes, if 'economics' is an autonomous science, there must be some law or set of laws which determines *price*. Ricardo, for all his over-simplification, at least made the effort to overcome Smith's fumbling.

There were good reasons, of course, for Smith's choices as regards what needed explanation and what did not, and, as important, there were good reasons why it was *the theory of price* which came to form the center of analytic economics. As any adequate sociology of knowledge acknowledges, scientific 'interests', as all others, have explanations. In this case, we need only notice that these reasons were both 'intellectual' – the conceptual materials available – and political – the interests and needs of the business classes which quickly came to political and intellectual hegemony.

When Smith published his work, 'political economy' referred to 'the art or practical science of managing the resources of nations, so as to increase its material wealth' (*The Oxford English Dictionary*). That is why the full title of his book is *An Inquiry into the Nature and Causes of the Wealth of Nations,* and why the 60 per cent of 'merely historical interest' was so important to Smith. Smith conceived his project *holistically* and as substantially *practical,* not analytic. Indeed, if Adam Smith has any legitimate successor, it is not Ricardo or James Mill, or McCulloch or Nassau Senior. One does better here with Sismondi – perhaps even, as I shall later suggest, with Schmoller or Max Weber! We might credit Ricardo's *Principles of Political Economy and Taxation* (1817), rather than Smith's work, as the real springboard for the discipline of modern economics. Yet, it was J. S. Mill who provided the explicit rationale. In 1829, when Mill was writing his essay 'On the Definition of Political Economy; and the Method of Investigation proper to it', neither the subject-matter nor the methods or aims were settled. Mill meant to straighten things out. It is fair to say – and important – that he but *half* succeeded. After Mill, it is at least possible to say what political economy *is*: an abstract and restricted science which treats of the laws which regulate the production, accumulation, and distribution of commodities. But despite nominal support for Mill regarding the *limits* of political economy, so conceived, Mill's altogether sound views in this regard seem to have been largely ignored.

HOW MILL SETTLED THE UNSETTLED QUESTIONS
IN POLITICAL ECONOMY

Mill begins with a lengthy critique of the idea, familiar since James Steuart (1767), that political economy is an art or practical science. For Mill, it was neither. It was for him a *pure* science: 'Science takes cognizance of a phenomena, and endeavors to discover its law; art proposes to itself an end, and looks out for means to effect it' (Mill, 1974, p. 124). Which is not to say that its laws could not be employed practically: 'Political Economy does not of itself make a nation rich; but whoever would be qualified to judge of the means of making a nation rich, must first be a political economist' (1974, p. 124).

Secondly, Mill argues that political economy is a 'moral or psychological science' – what the Germans, following him, will call *Geisteswissenschaft*. A crucial implication was this: 'The production of the objects which constitute wealth, are the subject matter both of Political Economy and of almost all the physical sciences'; thus both physical and mental laws are involved. Political economy, however, is concerned *only with* the pertinent laws 'of the human mind' (p. 132). And we must identify these from the larger set of such laws.

There are, he says, 'laws of human nature' which 'appertain to man as a mere individual'. They 'form a part of the subject of pure mental philosophy' (p. 134). There are other 'principles of human nature which are peculiarly connected with the ideas and feelings generated in man by living in a state of society'. These laws 'form the subject of a branch of science which may be aptly designated from the title of *social economy*; somewhat less happily by that of *speculative politics,* or the *science* of politics . . .' (p. 135).

Mill's view of the matter is patently 'psychologistic'. It isn't that the word 'sociology' has not yet been invented, but that, from Mill's point of view, an understanding of human nature is *sufficient* for the science of man. What then of political economy? It is, he says, 'not the science of speculative politics, but a branch of that science' (p. 137).

It may be identified as follows:

> It does not treat of the whole of man's nature as modified by the social state, nor of the whole conduct of man in society. It is concerned with him solely as a being who desires to possess wealth, and who is capable of judging of the comparative efficacy of means for that end. (p. 137)

This means that political economy is 'essentially an abstract science, and its method [is] the method *a priori*' (p. 143). This should not be misunderstood, however. Mill means that political economy is not a Baconian science in which 'an *experimentum crucis* may always be attained' (p. 147). Rather, it proceeds by 'hypotheses', from 'assumed premises', 'strictly analogous to those which, under the name of definitions, are the foundation of the other abstract sciences'. Thus,

> Geometry presupposes an arbitrary definition of a line, 'that which has length but not breadth'. Just in the same manner does Political Economy presuppose an arbitrary definition of man, as a being

who invariably does that by which he may obtain the greatest amount of necessaries, conveniences, and luxuries, with the smallest amount of labor . . . (p. 144)

It is for this reason that 'the conclusions of Political Economy . . . like those of geometry, are only true, as the common phrase is, *in the abstract*' (p. 144).

We must remember, of course, that, for Mill, geometry, like mechanics, was an *empirical* science – if abstract. Given this, Mill has provided an illuminating and influential new definition of political economy. But there was a large problem, to which Mill was extremely sensitive. It was how to go from 'abstract truths', to 'the facts in the concrete, clothed in all the complexity with which nature has surrounded them' (p. 148). Once 'applied to a particular case', there are 'disturbing causes', of which some at least belong to some *other science*. When this is the case, 'the mere political economist . . . will fail' (p. 151). It is thus absolutely crucial to see that, for Mill, *political economy could not be a predictive science,* and indeed that, *taken by itself,* it was not even explanatory! For Mill, the political economist – as any scientist of the abstract – stands to the 'practical philosopher', the legislator, as, for example, the geographer to the practical navigator, 'telling him the latitude and longitude of all sorts of places, but not how to find whereabouts he himself is sailing' (p. 155). The 'practical philosopher' has the problem of joining the results of the abstract sciences with a host of 'facts' gleaned by experience.

He must analyse the existing state of society into its elements, not dropping and losing any of them by the way. After referring to the experience of individual man to learn the law of each of these elements, that is, to learn what are its natural effects and how much of the effect follows from so much of the cause, there remains the operation of synthesis; to put all these effects together, and, from what they are separately, to collect what would be the effect of all the causes acting at once. (p. 159)

Mill published the foregoing essay in 1844, along with four others, under the title *Essays on Some Unsettled Questions of Political Economy.* I have suggested that he did settle *some* of the unsettled questions; in particular, he made it clear that political economy proceeded from principles of human nature, that it was abstract and deductive, and significantly, that it had an autonomous subject-matter – the laws of 'the economy'. But it was not, on his view, to be an imperial discipline, swallowing up politics and moral philosophy. While legislators needed the advice of political economists, the political economist, by himself, was *incapable* of providing explanations or predictions except where the 'disturbing causes', which were not part of his discipline, could be ignored without detriment. This last seems obvious enough. Yet evidence suggests that, by the 1880s or perhaps even earlier, the idea was lost. Economic imperialism was attended by the imperialism of the economists.

4

Progress:
The Laws of Development

It is hardly an exaggeration to say that, without noticeable exception, nineteenth-century thought was preoccupied with the idea of progress. It provided the explicit point of departure for the 'Positive Philosophy' of August Comte (1798–1857), the 'synthetic' and evolutionary philosophy of Herbert Spencer (1820–1903), and the 'dialectics' of Hegel. Marx and Engels were committed to it. J. S. Mill acknowledged a debt to 'the Saint Simonians' for giving him a new understanding of progress. It is the leading theme of the 'social evolutionists' – for example, Bachofen, Lubbock, and Tyler – and the pseudo-Darwinists – for example, W. G. Sumner and von Bernhardi. The socialist Schaeffle, Lester Ward, in his 'dynamic' sociology, and a host of lesser lights held to the idea as a fundamental premise of their inquiries.

This chapter takes up a piece of this, concentrating on the antecedents of the idea, and then on Comte and his critic, Mill, on Herbert Spencer, and, finally, on the social evolutionists. I hope to show that these 'naturalistic philosophies' of progress bequeathed a sizeable burden to social science, both in terms of explicit apologetics – for example, racism – and as regards the tasks of social science. The idea of a 'generalizing', 'functionalist', deterministic and ahistorical social science owes much to the naturalist philosophies of progress.

THE ANTECEDENTS OF THE NINETEENTH-CENTURY PHILOSOPHIES OF PROGRESS

When Locke asserted (in ch. V of the *2nd Treatise*) that 'in the beginning all the World was *America'*, his intention was to provide a basis for his argument that there was a natural right to private property.

But whether intended or not, he also suggested that European society *started* out from a society like the American, that it had somehow *developed* or evolved from such a condition. Meek is correct in noting that the discovery of the peoples of America, so *remote,* in a way so *surprising* 'was bound to offer a challenge to many of the prevailing ideas about religion, government, and social organization' (Meek, 1976, p. 38). But the mere discovery of un-citified (my preference for 'uncivilized') America was not sufficient to provoke the idea that human civilizations had developed from some primitive beginning, since Europeans could have seen Americans as having degenerated from some more neutral beginning, like that described in Genesis, or to have been blighted by some punishment from God, as for example, in the Book of Mormon. As we know, Genesis can be read in a variety of ways as regards this problem. Of course, the idea of progress was already in the air, and one would like to say that our common *humanity* was patent. If so, development was the 'natural' explanation. This is not all wrong, I am sure. As already noted, Hobbes, Leibniz, Buffon, Condorcet, and many Enlightenment writers accepted the unity *and natural* equality – sameness – of humankind; and it was not only Rousseau who held that differences were 'artificial' – merely 'conventional' and/or 'accidental', due to differences in, for example, climate.[1] The idea of a branching tree with a common root would then be an adequate metaphor. But, Enlightenment attacks on traditional religious grounds for universalism had some other unintended effects. Thus, David Brion Davis writes:'Insofar as the Enlightenment divorced anthropology and comparative anatomy from theological assumptions, it opened the way for theories of racial inferiority' (Davis, 1966, p. 446). But matters were not even that simple, since a good deal of the nineteenth-century argument was over *which* racialist theory was to be preferred: genetic or environmental racism. Moreover, as Davis has argued in another book, the doctrine of progress was used to defend the 'inevitability' of slavery and to resist abolition. It was not that these 'progressive' writers did not condemn slavery. It was rather than, on their view, the process of emancipation could not be hastened without drastic consequences: every stage in development depended on previous stages which were causally necessary. The more 'scientific' our understanding of the origin and nature of mankind the easier it seems to have become to defend racism and 'natural' inequality. While it is not possible to pursue this fundamental

[1] There were, of course, Enlightenment thinkers who did not hold this view. Hume and Kant stand out as defenders of genetic racism. The defense rests on a polygenic theory of human origins, a theory rooted in pre-Adamite sixteenth-century Spanish missionary thought. Rightly or wrongly, Montesquieu was a source for subsequent environmental racism. I owe this reference to an important work in progress by Madeleine and Lenn Goodman.

theme here, nineteenth-century defenses of inequality and racism are inconceivable without the contributions of 'science'.[2]

By the time we get to the mid-eighteenth century, there is a substantial 'theory' of progress. Now widely recognized as a key document in the history of the eighteenth-century notion of progress is the second of a pair of speeches given by Turgot in July and December of 1750 at the Sorbonne and entitled 'A philosophical review of the successive advances of the human mind'. This document contains the germ, at least, of Comte's later (1830) famous 'Law of the Three Stages', the linchpin of his 'positive philosophy'. And by the late 1750s, as Meek has argued, Turgot, Quesnay, Helvetius, and Goguet in France and Adam Smith, Sir John Dalrymple, and Lord Kames in Scotland *all* had a version of what Meek refers to as 'the four stages theory', the idea that there are four 'conditions' in the development of mankind, from 'living by hunting animals and feeding on the spontaneous fruits of the earth', to 'the condition of peoples living as shephards, or the pastoral', to 'the agricultural', to the fourth and last, 'the commercial' (Meek, 1976).

More generally, Meek is quite correct to conclude that by 1780, 'a new way of looking at society and its history' had emerged (p. 174). This new view assumed 'a great guiding principle or set of principles'. These could provide the analytic structure for the dramatically increased flow of information coming to Europe from everywhere on the globe. Indeed, it is not too much to say that this new view is the point of departure for all the nineteenth-century theories of progress, the evolutionary, the dialectic, and the rest. In all of them, as Mandelbaum (1971) has suggested, history becomes an *immanent process,* governed by a principle or principles. Change is not merely change, since it has a direction. 'Development', of course, is a loaded word, a word which does not necessarily connote 'progress', although, plainly, *from this time on,* it did. The 'later stages' are 'higher' and therefore 'better' than the earlier. Moreover, once the principles were in hand, not only could we understand 'mankind's advance from savagery to civilization', but we could foresee the future of mankind as well.

---

[2] As far as I know, this point has not, as yet, been carefully documented, but the work of the Goodmans will remedy this. They show, for example, how the complex of associations between warm climate and fecundity led to sexual stereotyping, and thence to out-and-out racism. Early anatomical 'studies' reinforced vague mythology and generated a whole series of new myths, based on 'science'. For example, O. Dapper, a Dutch observer writing in 1688, noted that in Hottentot women 'the lining of the body appears to be loose so that in certain places, part of dangles out'. Wilhem ten Rhyne, writing in 1686 described 'finger shaped appendages, always double hanging down from the private parts' of African women. What is more startling than this fanciful anatomy is the fact that John R. Baker, in a book entitled *Race,* published by Oxford University Press in 1974, endorses this. For the relation between slavery and progress, see David Brion Davis, *Slavery and Human Progress,* especially part II.

This future was surely bright. Mandelbaum's summary of the Enlightenment can serve us here:

> If superstition, that monstrous offspring of ignorance, could be overcome, then a growth in experience; in science, and in technology, would of itself produce a harmony of the actual and the ideal. . . . The men of the enlightenment saw no grounds for doubting that enlightenment was ushering in a new age. Mankind could henceforth make more rapid progress toward the ideal. (Mandelbaum, 1971, p. 52)

THE POSITIVE PHILOSOPHY OF AUGUST COMTE

Comte was an heir of the French Enlightenment, but between Turgot and Montesquieu, on the one hand, and Comte's *Cours de Philosophie Positive* (1830–42), on the other, came the French Revolution and Henri Saint-Simon. The former is critical, since not only did it bury Rousseau and Montesquieu, but it seriously raised the question as to whether one could have both progress and order, in many ways the fundamental divide of nineteenth-century social thought. St Simon's connection to Comte – the 'adopted son' who later referred to the 'father' as a 'depraved juggler' – is important to note, not to engage the question of which of the two was the 'original' thinker, but to emphasize that the amalgam which constituted 'positive' philosophy included what are sometimes thought to be conflicting strains and traditions. Comte defended industrial capitalism and St Simon, the 'utopian socialist', was, perhaps, the first 'positivist' social theorist.[3]

In a late work, Comte noted that 'positivism consists essentially of a philosophy and a polity', and that 'these can never be dissevered' (*Système de Politique Positive,* in Lenzer, 1975, p. 317). But in addition, as already noted, the 'philosophy' is a complicated amalgam, and it will pay us first to clarify its elements, some severable, some not. They have various roots and have left various marks – or none at all.

Everything hangs on the famous three laws, as chapter I of book I of the *Cours* says:

> In order to understand the true value and character of the Positive Philosophy, we must take a brief general view of the progressive course of the human mind, regarded as a whole. . . . The law is this: – that each of our leading conceptions – each branch of our knowledge passes through three different theoretical conditions:

[3] Two books by Frank E. Manuel are here indispensable. See his *The New World of Henri Saint Simon*, 1956, and *The Prophets of Paris*, 1962.

the Theological or fictitious; the Metaphysical or abstract; and the Scientific, or Positive. . . .

   In the theological state, the human mind, seeking the essential nature of beings, the first and final causes . . . of all effects, – in short, Absolute knowledge, supposes all phenomena to be produced by the immediate action of supernatural beings.

   In the metaphysical state, which is only a modification of the first, the mind supposes, instead of supernatural beings, abstract forces . . . inherent in all things, and capable of producing all phenomena. . . .

   In the final, positive state, the mind has given over the vain search after Absolute notions, the origin and destination of the universe, and the causes of phenomena, and applies itself to the study of their laws, – that is, their invariable relations of succession and resemblance. (Comte, 1875, vol. I, p. 2)

I will return to Comte's characterization of the 'positive state' and look at what else he has to say about it. The full text provides, as we shall see, a wonderful summary of what will become *the* dominant view in the 'philosophy of science' – until today. But we need, first, to be clear about what the 'Law' is about, and to see how Comte has connected it to substantive history.

As he says, it is about 'knowledge', but he means by this, 'methods of philosophizing', or *ways of thinking*. But even this is misleading insofar as, in Comte's view, people think in this way or that *by virtue of* a 'general mind' – what we might call the *Weltanschauung* of a period and place. There are, he says, 'epochs of the mind of the race' (p. 3). For Comte, 'mind' is social, and the law of the three stages or states is 'sociological'. The idea that mind is social is itself a powerful idea, in one sense familiar enough and in another an idea that is still not taken very seriously. It means not just that the people of different 'epochs' have different beliefs, but that there are different 'forms' of consciousness, or 'understanding'. Comte is, indeed, a sociological Kant. As we shall see, the idea that mind is social is found contemporaneously in German Idealism, where its Kantian roots are plain, and later in Wundt and his French contemporary Durkheim. It has important implications as regards 'psychology' and the latter's *absence* from Comte's famous 'hierarchy of the positive sciences'.

Secondly, as Manuel notes, Comte had 'the extraordinary insight that as mankind advanced, the earlier stages of consciousness would not be completely sloughed off and forgotten forever' (Manuel, 1962, p. 282). They remain, to use a different language, part of the collective unconscious of the race. Third, Comte postulates that 'the different kinds of knowledge have passed stages of progress at different rates, and have not therefore arrived at the same time' (Comte, 1875, p. 5). Astronomy arrived first, then physics. 'Physiology' has just recently become a science, and 'social physics' – sociology – was, according to Comte, just then liberating itself.

The first stage was long and itself underwent many transformations. All this is detailed in the chapters of the *Cours* on 'Social Dynamics' – the 'theory of the natural progress of human society'. But it is the second, the metaphysical, 'transitory stage', which is of special interest to us here. It dates from the 'political degradation of the spiritual power'. It is called by Comte, depending on whether he is talking about its 'political' or 'philosophical' dimension, 'the revolutionary philosophy' and the 'critical', or 'negative', philosophy. Hobbes is 'the father of the revolutionary philosophy' (1875, vol. II, p. 291), and 'the political school of the negative doctrine is usually supposed to be represented by Rousseau', though for Comte, 'we must not overlook the participation in it of the political sect of the Economists' (p. 299).

But 'the social system' which was brought forward by the 'negative', 'metaphysical' philosophy and which was marked by the French Revolution, while itself transitionary, cannot take humanity further. Indeed, 'the preponderance still maintained by the negative tendency constitutes the greatest obstacle to the progress of civilization and even to the abolition of the old system' ('Plan of the Scientific Operations Necessary for Reorganizing Society' (1822), in Lenzer, 1975, p. 9). The reason is clear:

> The only way of ending this stormy situation, of staying the anarchy that day by day invades society – in a word, of reducing the crisis to a simple moral movement – consists in inducing the civilized nations [the others still linger in the theological stage] to abandon the negative and adopt an organic attitude. (1975, p. 10)

From the point of view of the negative philosophers, whether the 'anarchical school of Rousseau' *or* the 'Economists', 'government . . . is represented as a natural enemy encamped in the midst of our social system against which society seeks to fortify itself' (p. 13). 'Unlimited liberty of conscience', the doctrine of the 'sovereignty of each individual reason' and, collectively, of 'the people', promotes 'complete anarchy'. What is required and what positive philosophy can supply is 'Order and Progress'.

By placing order on 'the firmest possible foundation – that is, on the doctrine of the invariability of the laws of nature' (in Lenzer, 1975, p. 341), order is reconciled with progress. More than that, 'progress . . .

is, in its essence identical with order, and may be looked on as order made manifest' (1975, p. 342). Social physics provides the knowledge – those in possession of it must make the decisions. Echoing St Simon: 'In the system to be constituted, the spiritual power will be confided to the hands of the savants, while the temporal power will belong to heads of industrial works' (Lenzer, 1975, pp. 25f.). Indeed, because 'Positivists stand forward now as the party of construction', 'enabled to satisfy the poor and, at the same time, to restore the confidence of the rich', positivism is 'the only doctrine which can preserve Western Europe from some serious attempt to bring communism into practical operation' (*System,* 1851, in Lenzer, 1975, p. 357).

This brief overview is enough to suggest, I hope, that there is considerable systemic power in the thought of Comte and some genuine historical insight, an assessment offered by none other than J. S. Mill. It also shows that the first self-conscious 'positivist' social scientist was *anti-metaphysical, anti-democratic, anti-revolutionary.* Indeed, he was these *because* he thought he was 'scientific'. In the next chapter, I will counterpose this collocation of ideas in Comte with the tradition of Hegel and of Marx and Engels, hoping thereby to enhance the intelligibility of both. In many ways, the twentieth-century ideological present is the product of this conflict – and accommodation.

COMTE'S PHILOSOPHY OF SCIENCE

We need now to examine more closely what Comte meant by 'science', an idea which was by no means settled at the time Comte was writing. After that we can turn to some important specific questions in his theory of society. It will be best to begin by re-quoting, this time in full, Comte's characterization of 'the positive state' of knowledge.

In the final, the positive state, the mind has given over the vain search for Absolute notions . . . and the causes of phenomena, and applies itself to the study of their laws, – that is, their invariable relations of succession and resemblance. Reasoning and observation, duly combined, are the means of this knowledge. What is now understood when we speak of an explanation of facts is simply the establishment of a connection betwen single phenomena and some general facts, the number of which continually diminishes with the progress of science. (Comte, 1875, vol. I, p. 2)

This is a succinct summary of a philosophy of science, each piece of which calls for some comment.

There is first of all the positivism, the restriction of the knowable to phenomena – to the empirical, to what is *in* experience. This strain had been present in French philosophy in, for example, Condillac, and perhaps especially in the anti-metaphysical 'ideologues'. The word 'ideology' (now so abused) was, as Boas remarks, 'invented by Destutt de Tracy (1754–1836) to denote that study which was to supplant metaphysics' (Boas, 194, p. 24). Boas quotes an incisive text of Destutt's phenomenalist program:

> In treating general ideas [Destutt] says, a good method is to decompose them, 'to examine the elementary ideas from which they are extracted and to go back to the first facts, to the simple perceptions, to the sensations from which they emanate, if one could reach that point'. (Boas, 1924, p. 25)

Familiar here, of course, is the 'reductionist' program of Hume, but more startling perhaps is the language, which sounds like that of Carnap. Merely substitute 'protocols' for 'first facts'.

Second, having 'given over the vain search' for the *causes* of phenomena – not merely the first and final causes, but all causes, inquiry is to be directed at the study of the *laws of phenomena,* of 'their invariable relations of succession and resemblance'. This is straightforward Hume, of course, but comprehended after Kant. The causes of phenomena are unknowable – metaphysical. Laws concern only relations of phenomena.

Third, Comte is no 'empiricist' if by empiricism one means that the construction of theory is irrelevant to science. 'Observation' is the foundation of knowledge, to be sure, but it must be 'duly combined' with 'reasoning': 'No real observation of any kind of phenomena is possible, except in as far as it is first directed, and finally interpreted, by some theory' (Comte, 1875, vol. II, p. 80). Of course, Comte is an empiricist in that he is a positivist *and* insofar as he denies, à la Kant, that there is *a priori* synthetic knowledge (cf. his most interesting account of mathematics, in Comte, 1875, vol. I, bk. I).

Fourth, explanation is what we would call 'hypothetico-deductive', the subsumption of 'single phenomena' under 'general facts'. Again, we should note his choice of words: 'general facts', the term later appropriated by Russell to satisfy the double need of an austere empiricism *and* the possibility of science: knowledge of law.

Finally, Comte sees scientific knowledge as a unity, increasingly systematizable as the sciences progress. Some writers, noticing this, have said that he anticipates the 'unity of science' movement of twentieth-century positivism. But this is not the case. Indeed, although each of the items already identified does have a clear analog in twentieth-century positivist or neo-positivist philosophy of science (item four, above, is neo-positivist), Comte's views on the 'hierarchy of the sciences', the first attempt to systematize the modern sciences, are emphatically *not* those of the twentieth-century unity of science movement. Against that view, Comte held that the sciences were *stratified* and *non-reducible*. Before pausing over this important aspect of Comte's philosophy of science, two more general aspects of his view of the sciences should be introduced.

Comte thought of science as Aristotle did, as the theoretical effort of 'satisfying the craving of our understanding' (vol. I, p. 16). Moreover, he was sensitive to a shift which was taking place in this regard. It was, he said, 'an error of our time', that science was regarded 'chiefly as a basis of Art' (p. 16). This put the cart before the horse. While 'the arts flow from science', 'the neglect of science must destroy the consequent arts' (p. 17). Indeed, 'some of the most important arts are derived from speculations pursued during long ages of purely scientific intention' (p. 17). Second, and directly pertinent to his ideas of the hierarchy, he offers a distinction which we have already encountered in the 1829 essay on political economy by J. S. Mill. While it is not clear where the distinction originated, it had, as we shall see, a long history. For Comte there are 'two classes' of science:

> The abstract or general, which have for their object the discovery of the laws which regulate phenomena in all conceivable cases; and the concrete, particular, or descriptive . . . whose function is to apply these laws to the actual history of existing beings. (p. 18)

Physiology and chemistry are abstract; zoology and mineralogy are concrete. The idea is essential to his conception of the hierarchy, since 'the actual histories of existing beings' are 'governed' by the abstract laws discovered in *all* the abstract sciences. Thus we have

> . . . Five fundamental Sciences in successive dependence, – Astronomy, Physics, Chemistry, Physiology, and finally, Social Physics. The first considers the most general, simple, abstract, and remote phenomena known to us, and those which affect all others without being affected by them. The last considers the most particular, compound, concrete phenomena, and those which are the most interesting to Man. (vol. I, p. 23)

The key word is 'dependence', glossed by the relation of what is capable of being affected but not affecting. Put in other terms, we might say that abstract laws of the 'lower' determine the 'higher', but not conversely, since at each 'level' there are *new* laws pertinent at that 'level' and, accordingly, at each succeeding level. While we cannot pursue the point here – we will return to it in chapter 13 – Comte's notion of stratification is *incompatible* with his Humean conception of law. That is, once 'phenomena' are construed as causal outcomes of abstract laws at different levels, laws *cannot* be relations of phenomena. This problem, as we shall see, surfaces time and time again in nineteenth-century 'philosophy of science'. Mill, Spencer, Engels, and Max Weber each make efforts, albeit unsuccessfully, to get it right.

Comte's theory of stratification fits into his larger scheme of the three stages. Positive science has been achieved in Astronomy and Physics, but not yet in Social Physics. It is thus that we are as yet unable to 'explain' social phenomena.

It is absolutely clear that Comte was no reductionist, as is evident in his critique of Cabanis. Cabanis, a straightforward materialist, had argued that 'a positive character' could be given to social science 'by treating it simply as a direct consequence of physiology' ('Plan . . .', in Lenzer, 1975, p. 61). Comte insisted, however, that 'the collective phenomena of the human race, as well as individual phenomena, must ultimately be traced to the special nature of its organization'. That is, although beavers are 'social', there is a 'demarcation', not crucial to beaver activity, but essential as regards human activity, between physiological determinants and social determinants. 'Thus', he writes, 'several distinguished physiologists have given an exaggerated importance to characteristics of race as explaining political phenomena.' No egalitarian, Comte could nevertheless not agree to genetic racism. Moreover, 'the condition of human civilization in each generation directly depends only on that of the preceding, and directly produces only that of the following generation' (1975, p. 62). These are decisive considerations for both a historical and a holistic social science. Unfortunately, Comte got the former wrong and persuaded no one as regards the latter.

But it is a serious mistake, in any case, to hold that Comte initiated the modern idea of sociology as a science, if by 'sociology' one means a science *distinct* from some other social sciences and distinct from history. It was for just these reasons that he names Aristotle and Montesquieu as precursors of his 'sociology'.

COMTE'S VISION OF 'SOCIOLOGY'

A metaphor frequently found in the writings of St Simon and Herder and already current in late eighteenth-century thought was also used by Comte. The 'organic', as Manuel suggests, 'implied an attack on the eighteenth century philosophers because their encyclopedia had chopped up knowledge into discrete components instead of integrating it' (Manuel, 1956, p. 131). The metaphor was dangerous, for, while 'unity' required that 'parts' or 'elements' be constituents of a 'whole', 'organic' in these writers did not *necessarily* connote that the unity was substantial, as it is in an organism. Nor was it necessary that the relations of elements be 'functional' as in an organism. Comte seems, indeed, to have preferred the neutral – and more general – term 'system'. He may have been among the first to use it in reference to 'society' as a replacement for the metaphoric 'organism'. He wrote:

> It is, in fact, true that wherever there is any system whatever, a certain interconnection must exist. The purely mechanical phenomena of astronomy offer the first suggestion of it. . . . But the relation becomes closer and more marked in proportion to the complexity and diminished generality of the phenomena. . . . The idea must therefore be scientifically preponderant in social physics, even more than in biology, where it is so decisively recognized by the best order of students. (1875, vol. II, p. 67)

Comte turned his analysis directly against the 'science of government' theorists. As he said, 'the existing political philosophy supposes the absence of any such interconnection among the aspects of society' (p. 67). For Comte, 'there can be no scientific study of society . . . if it is separated into portions, and its divisions are studied apart' (p. 67). The 'metaphysicians' say that 'we should always . . . proceed from the simple to the compound', but 'the reverse method is necessary in the study of Man and Society; Man and Society as a whole being better known to us, and more accessible subjects of study, than the parts which constitute them' (p. 68). Separating the 'parts' for study distorts them precisely because they are what they are *by virtue of* their relations. A similar point, of course, is later made by Hegel – who also acknowledges an indebtedness to Montesquieu.

But Comte did not escape the dangers of his metaphors. Organisms and societies are usefully construed to be 'systems', but instead of freeing the study of society from the connotations associated with *organisms,* 'system' came to be inexorably associated with 'organism'. Indeed, although it is not clear whether Comte held that society was a substantial unity, there is little doubt that he went headfirst for a scientifically gratuitous – and optimistic – *functionalism.*[4] Thus,

> . . . there must always be a spontaneous harmony between the whole and the parts of a social system, the elements of which must inevitably be, sooner or later, combined in a mode entirely conformable to their nature.

---

[4] The issue of functionalism in social science is discussed in chapter 8.

Indeed,

> this consolidated whole must be always connected, by its nature,
> with the corresponding state of the integral development of
> humanity, considered in all its aspects . . .: and the only object of
> any political system whatever . . . is to regulate the spontaneous
> expansion so best to direct it towards its determinate end. (p. 65)

Comte thus ties the whole package together with a unilinear, progressive, and *deterministic* conception of social change. And with this, he
has kept his promise, since he has built 'a social science that will satisfy
the twofold intellectual need of modern societies' for 'order and progress'.

And, let us emphasize, this view is profoundly conservative – more
conservative in many ways than that of the 'theologians' whom he
criticized. Boas observes:

> Comtism has been called 'inverted Catholicism'. As a matter of
> fact, it is not at all inverted. It is Catholicism of the Bonald-
> Maistre type expressed in more or less secular terms. The supremacy
> of the spiritual powers, the belief in tradition the inequality of
> individuals, sexes, and ages, the social irreducibility of the family
> are all in 'Legislation Primitive'. That Bonald and Maistre found a
> pretended sanction for their ideas in the teaching of the Church
> corroborated by observation, whereas Comte found his verifi-
> cation for them in pretended observation alone, is an accident of
> biographical importance only. (Boas, 1924, pp. 292f.)

Indeed, the important lesson of positive philosophy is 'resignation'.
Now quoting Comte:

> True resignation, that is, a disposition to endure necessary evils
> steadfastly and without any hope of compensation therefore, can
> result only from a profound feeling for the invariable laws that
> govern the variety of natural phenomena. (Quoted from *Cours*,
> IV, by Marcuse, 1954, p. 345)

Because they are 'embodied in the entire system of social concepts'
Comte established on 'unshakeable foundations the twofold notion of
order and progress' (in Andreski, 1974, p. 148). Unshaken, perhaps? –
or at least as far as the ideological struggle over social change has
progressed date. But unshakeable? In the present book, disembodying
that 'system', separating the sense from the non-sense, is a main aim.

WHAT IS THE NATURE OF A LAW OF PROGRESS?

I have featured Comte in this chapter for reasons which I hope are clear. Nor are we quite finished with him. I want now to use his famous three laws as a foil for Mill, who subjected them to close scrutiny in his *Logic* (1843). This gives us a nifty way of addressing the general question of what a law of progress would look like.

Like everyone else in the nineteenth century, Mill accepted the idea of the inevitability of progress, but he was by no means uncritical of Comte's version of it. Mill was working on his *Logic* when he read the later volumes of Comte's *Cours*. He seems to have been persuaded to accept Comte's radical idea that 'there is progressive change, both in the character of the human race and in their outward circumstances' (*Logic*, bk. VI, ch. X, sec. 3). But Mill was dissatisfied with what he took to be the key idea of Comte's program. This was:

> by a study and analysis of the general facts of history, to discover . . . the law of progress; which law, once ascertained must . . . enable us to predict future events, just as after a few terms of an infinite regress in algebra we are able to predict the rest of the series to any number we please. (*Ibid.*)

Now if Comte's law was *a law*, it had, at the very least, to be 'invariant', and therefore, as Comte said, 'there is a necessarily identical development of all humanity' (in Andrewski, 1974, p. 190). Societies which are, for example, in the 'theological stage' will pass to the 'metaphysical', and so forth. In this sense, then, the law was not merely an empirical generalization to the effect that all societies so far observed have *in fact* passed through these stages. Comte admitted that in this trajectory of humanity, there were 'variables' – differences in climate, geography, and relations to other societies – and he did not deny that these figured in development. But in his view, these were subordinated to the fundamental law of change (Comte, 1875, vol. II, pp. 58–62). For Mill, this wouldn't do.

Mill distinguished between what he called 'laws of nature' and 'empirical laws'. As noted in chapter 3, Mill contributed significantly to the confusion over the status of 'laws of nature', and we will now see how.

Like Comte, Mill was a good Humean. Acordingly, he saw 'laws' as constant conjunctions, relations of 'resemblance and succession'. As Mill said, in the by now familiar language, questions about 'the ultimate or ontological cause of anything', or about the 'ultimate mode of production of phenomena, and . . . every question regarding the nature of "Things in themselves"' may be left to the 'schools of metaphysics'

(*Logic,* bk. III, ch. V). A law is an 'invariance'. Some laws, however, give us confidence to predict, and some do not. Mill writes:

> Scientific inquirers give the name of Empirical laws to those uniformities which observation and experience has shown to exist, but on which they hesitate to rely on cases varying much from those which have been actually observed, for want of any reason why such a law should exist. It is implied, therefore, that in the notion of an empirical law, that it is not an ultimate law. (ch. XVI, p. 338)

What is an 'ultimate law'? To get at this, we must grasp that, for Mill, as for Comte, explanation was derivation, either the 'resolution' of a law into other laws or its 'subsumption' by a more general law (cf. ch. XII, pp. 305–10). 'Ultimate laws', then, are unexplained explainers, as it were. Derivative laws are 'resolved' into ultimate laws and are thereby explained by them. Kepler's laws, in Mill's view, are 'derivative'. Yet we have enormous predictive confidence in them. But this is somewhat of a special case, and the reason is clear. 'A derivative law which results wholly from the operation of some one cause [one law] will be as universally true as the laws of the cause itself' (p. 340). Mill seems to have in mind that only (?) one 'ultimate law', the 'Inverse Square law' is involved here (actually, the principle of inertia is also required). Given the facts about the masses of the pertinent bodies and their distances – which, says Mill, could have been otherwise – we explain the Keplerian laws. Moreover, if these 'facts' about the masses and so on had been different, Kepler's laws, which are not 'ultimate', would have been different (p. 340).

By contrast, a derivative law could be the result of 'a collocation of causes', and then we are without predictive confidence:

> ... Since we are entirely ignorant, in case of its depending on collocation, what the collocation is, we are not safe in extending the law beyond the limits of time and space in which we have actual experience of its truth. Since within these limits the law has always been found true, we have evidence that the collocations, whatever they are, on which it depends, do really exist within these limits. But knowing of no rule or principle to which the collocations themselves conform, we cannot conclude that because a collocation is proved to exist within certain limits of space and time, it will exist beyond those limits. (p. 341)

Such laws are 'empirical laws', not laws of nature. The difference is not that empirical laws are not true regularities or uniformities, because, like the laws of nature, they are. Given some true regularity, it may be *merely* an empirical law, the result of collocation, or a law of nature, an ultimate law. Because a collocation is an accidental coming together of causes not reducible to 'principle' (law), prediction is risky. We can never be confident that the non-lawfully generated collocation will continue to hold beyond the space/time region in which it has been observed to hold.

It is perfectly clear that Mill was wise to acknowledge a distinction between 'mere' empirical generalizations and laws of nature, but it is hardly clear that his account will suffice. Although this is a piece of business for later, the reader might ponder the following: are there any *empirical* uniformities which are not 'collocations'? Can't a law of nature be explained? But if so, why is it then 'ultimate'? *Everything* in the world might have been otherwise, not merely the particular masses of the sun and the planets.

In any case, it is easy to see how Mill could use his analysis to undermine Comte's laws. He writes:

> The succession of states of the human mind and of human society cannot have an independent law of its own; it must depend upon the psychological and ethological laws which govern the circumstances on men and of men on circumstances. (p. 597)

That is, empirical uniformities about the succession of states of the human mind and society cannot be 'ultimate'. This is because the patterns are at least in part the result of a non-lawful collocation, specifically, particular combinations of 'psychological and ethological laws' governing 'the circumstances on men and of men on circumstances'. The issue between Comte and Mill, we should emphasize, is not whether there are *social* laws, either in addition to or instead of Mill's 'psychological and ethological laws'. For if there are social laws, this only compounds the collocation. The issue is whether there are *historical laws,* laws governing *the course of history.* Mill wisely denied that there were. The question of whether there are social laws, laws governing events in society, which are not merely empirical generalizations, was first raised, as I indicated in chapter 3, by the classical political economists.[5]

Mill's line of argument, effective against Comte, did not, however, touch Herbert Spencer who also believed that there were laws of progress. What follows hardly does justice to Spencer's encyclopedic efforts to define, classify, and unify the sciences. I concentrate only on

---

[5] The laws determining natural price are social laws, realistically understood, as Ricardo perhaps was the first to see clearly. Neither Ricardo nor Marx provide laws of history. It is a common error, fostered by Marxists, to hold that Marx was Comtean in providing laws of history. See chapter 6.

his 'law of evolution', here again attempting to separate the sense from the non-sense.

In all things, Spencer argued, there was but a single law of development: 'There is a change from an incoherent homogeneity to a coherent heterogeneity, accompanying the dissipation of motion and the integration of matter' (1862, p. 325). This 'law of evolution' was grounded inductively, and it held for 'each order of existence considered as a separate order'. But indeed,

> ... the induction as so far presented falls short of that completeness which it gains when we contemplate the several orders of existence as forming a natural whole. While we think of Evolution as divided into astronomic, geologic, biologic, psychologic, sociologic, &c., it may seem to some extent a coincidence that the same law of metamorphosis holds throughout all its divisions. But when we recognize these divisions, as mere conventional groupings, made to facilitate the arrangement and acquisition of knowledge ... we see at once that there are not several kinds of Evolution having traits in common, but one evolution going on everywhere after the same manner. (p. 490)

Spencer has discerned a very genuine problem – although it is not usually acknowledged as such. If there is but one 'nature' and many different sciences, each probing different aspects or 'orders' (strata), what is the relation of these sciences to each other? Indeed, it is important to notice that the problem arises even within a 'science' – when we have different theories whose relation to one another is perplexing.

Thus, in this century, we can ask, what is the relation of quantum mechanics to statistical mechanics or to special relativity?[6] Similarly, the chemist defines the subject-matter of inquiry as 'chemical phenomena', but surely it is not denied that these are *also physical* phenomena. Yet chemistry is not physics. The biologist is in a similar situation. Unless we want to say that the coherence of science requires that there is but one science and one super-theory, that, eventually, biology and chemistry and the different, not necessarily consistent theories in these sciences will *disappear,* we have the problem of seeing how the reality being probed by different theories and by different sciences, is *one* reality.

Spencer's solution was bold: one nature, one process. Each of the 'divisions' are *merely* conventions, with no standing in reality. They are but *our* ways to acquire knowledge, convenient and, because of the severe limits of our knowing capacities, perhaps even necessary. Each of

---

[6] For discussion, see chapter 12.

these 'divisions', then, articulate that *one* process as we discern it in the 'orders' which our conventions 'facilitate'.

As is plain, Comte's and Spencer's 'laws' were of different types. Comte wanted to argue from history that progressive 'stages' could be discerned, and that one could infer from this an invariance which was lawful. Spencer, by contrast, found 'by induction', an *abstract principle,* which for him 'governed' every possible system, from astral to cellular, from psychological to cultural.

Spencer seems to have been aware that his one 'law of evolution' was incredibly abstract and that if it were to have scientific status, there would have to be concrete mecanisms which instantiated it. Moreover, he seems to have been aware that these mechanisms could be of very different sorts, from elementary mechanical systems of forces and atoms to the far more complex mechanisms of chemical transformation and so on. Even so, he did his cause enormous disservice with his confidence in the progressive character of all change and with his relentless drive for unity. In one of his earliest papers on the topic of the law of evolution, he saw the movement from homogeneity to heterogeneity in terms of 'the multiplication of effects':

> This multiplication of effects, which is displayed in every event of today, has been going on from the beginning; and is true of the grandest phenomena of the universe as the most insignificant. . . . Throughout creation there must have gone on, and must still go on, a never ceasing transformation of the homogeneous to the heterogeneous.

But the vacuousness of the idea is manifest when he applies it to social change. Thus,

> As soon as a combination of men acquires permanence, there begin actions and reactions between the community and each member of it, such that either affects the other in nature. The control exercised by the aggregate over its units [by means of 'the super-organic structure of society'], tends ever to mould their activities and sentiments and ideas into congruity with social requirements; and these activities, sentiments and ideas, as far they are changed by changing circumstances, tend to re-mould the society into congruity with themselves. (Spencer, 1901: 'Progress: its law and cause' (1857), p. 38)

Why the movement from homogeneity to heterogeneity should issue in a *functional harmony* is not clear, although the language of 'adaptation' was by then already fundamental to 'evolutionists' – regardless of their stripes. But Spencer's most famous formulation, from the influential book of 1850 which bears the Comtean title *Social Statics,* shows how fundamental it was for Spencer's social science:

> Progress . . . is not an accident, but a necessity. Instead of Civiliz-
> ation being artificial it is a part of nature; all of a piece with the
> development of an embryo or the unfolding of a flower. The
> modifications mankind have undergone, and are still undergoing,
> result from a law underlying the whole organic creation. . . . As
> surely as the tree becomes bulky when it stands alone, and slender
> if one of a group . . . as surely as there is any meaning in such terms
> as habit, custom, practice; so surely must the human faculties be
> moulded into complete fitness for a social state; so surely must evil
> and immorality disappear; so surely must man become perfect.
> (Spencer, 1897, p. 32)

Not only has Spencer's idea of one nature, one process become a
monistic naturalism in which agency has disappeared altogether – raising the hackles of William James, among others, but 'the law underlying
the whole organic creation' now seems to be 'survival of the fittest':
functionalism with a vengeance.

The memorable phrase 'survival of the fittest' was of course Spencer's,
not Darwin's. We can round out this chapter on the laws of progress
with a brief summary of the relation of Darwin to the nineteenth-
century development of the social sciences.

EVOLUTIONARY BIOLOGY AND PROGRESS

As Mandelbaum writes, it is probably as a result of Darwin's monumental *Origin of Species* (1859) that 'evolutionism became firmly in-
trenched as a way of looking at all aspects of the world' (1971, p. 47).
But, as Mandelbaum notes, it would be a serious error to suppose that
the views so far discussed either needed Darwin or were influenced by
his work. Comte's publications preceded Darwin's by some 30 years or
more; Spencer had set out is main ideas in his *Social Statics* of 1850. At
about this time, a number of writers who could reasonably be called
'social evolutionists' were putting forward important ideas which were
neither Darwinian nor Comtean/Spencerian. All agreed that progress
was inevitable.

These writers include Henry Maine (*Ancient Law,* 1861), J. J.
Bachofen (*Das Mutterecht,* 1861), John Ferguson McLennan (*Primitive Marriage,* 1865), Lewis H. Morgan (*Systems of Consanguinity and
Affinity,* 1871), and *Ancient Society,* 1877), E. B. Tylor (*Researches into
the Early History of Mankind,* 1865 and *Primitive Culture,* 1871), and
John Lubbock (*Pre-Historic Times,* 1865). All of them, as well as others
who might be mentioned, were influenced by biology, but not so much

by its substantive claims or theories as by its method and metaphors. Mandelbaum writes:

> Even for those who did not regard social evolution as part of single evolutionary process, and even when its truth was not taken to be a corrollary of Darwin, it was widely believed that the only scientifically correct way of understanding man's history was through the use of comparative methods, in which societies were seen as representing stages in human development. (1971, p. 95)

The issue here is not whether a mechanism like natural selection was operating in society or between societies – the view, for example, of American pseudo-Darwinists or of Germans such as Bernhardi. In contrast to these writers, the foregoing authors had little or no interest in providing an all-encompassing *explanation* of social evolution. Rather, they argued that because human history was a long social evolution, one should adopt appropriate methods. In particular, they regarded the comparative method as essential. This idea had already been advanced by Comte, who in the *Cours* had argued that the 'Historical method,' – 'the only basis on which the system of political logic can rest' – was essentially a comparative method (Comte, 1875, I, pp. 84–8). Although by mid-century this notion was very much in the air, we may suppose that the writers named above were not unaware of Comte's views on the subject.

There was, however, an enormous problem which seems not to have been noticed by any of these writers. Let us ask first what evolution means. Does it mean that there is some *invariable sequence* from, say, micro-organisms (primitive societies) to complex organisms (civilizations), or does it refer to a sum of successive changes in which patterns can be discerned? It is clear that Comte, Spencer, and the social evolutionists thought of it in the first way. Our account of Mill suggests that he saw it in the second way.

In asking about the evidence favoring biological evolution construed the first way, we must note that it is all indirect. It is of two sorts. First, there is an enormous body of material from comparative studies: comparative anatomy, physiology, embryology, and so on. Second, we have considerable understanding, if still incomplete, of the *mechanisms* of biological evolution. Beginning with Darwin, we have 'natural selection', and by now we have theories about a variety of other sorts of mechanisms which are presumed to be at work. But, of course, all this evidence is also evidence for the second interpretation of evolution, an interpretation which demands far less in the way of evidence. Accordingly, it is hard to see why we should opt for the first over the second.

Turning now to social evolution, the evidence is again indirect; but in contrast to the situation as regards biological evolution, the evidence is radically incomplete – indeed, it is almost non-existent! Where there are no written records, there is but archaeology. One might insist that such is not the case; for, after all, in addition to archaeology and written records, we have the 'living laboratories' of less 'advanced' societies. Yet a moment's consideration will show that these are pertinent only if we assume that the practices of 'less advanced' peoples are practices that characterized societies which are chronologically earlier in the 'evolution' of modern Western societies. But this is to assume, with Comte, that there is a 'necessarily identical development' of all humanity. It is to assume 'evolution' in the first and strongest sense.

It is hard to know how much damage has turned on this relatively simple point. Of course, societies change, and of course, present societies, as Comte rightly insisted, are the products of their pasts. But this does not entail an immanent unidirectional process of development. *A fortiori,* it does not mean that the process is progressive. Quite the contrary; it entails that we need history, the analysis of the concrete and particular transformations which constitute the history of some society.[7] Unfortunately, in the absence of written records, this history cannot be written. 'Anthropology', a term that came into general use only at mid-century, got off to very bad start in supposing that it could.

One final point should be made as regards the relation of Darwin to the idea of social evolution. As Mandelbaum shows, Darwin explicitly affirmed that the mechanism of natural selection did not 'necessarily include progressive development'. As he said, 'it only takes advantage of such variations as arise and are beneficial to each creature under its conditions of life' (quoted by Mandelbaum, 1971, p. 83). As a scientific idea, it is wholly neutral with respect to 'progress'. Conditions could 'worsen' or 'improve', and a creature's adaptation could be for better or for worse, however one chooses to define these terms. Nevertheless, the modes of speech which Darwin employed, especially, 'lower' versus 'higher', along with many of his similes and examples, show, as Mandelbaum says, that 'he thought of evolution as a single process of development which not only had a single source but grew in a definite direction – a direction which constituted an advance over earlier growth' (1971, p. 84). No one in the nineteenth century could quite free themselves from the idea of progress so defined. Nor has our century.

---

[7] There are still people who believe that Darwin explained the evolution of species. He provided one mechanism, natural selection. Had we, then, pertinent information as regards the organism/environment relations, we would have a start in reconstructing the course of this 'evolution'. This information is not and will not become available. Moreover, what did occur as the causal outcome of the mechanism of selection, could have occurred otherwise; there was no invariable sequence which *had* to occur. See Hull, 1974; Levins and Lewontin, 1985. As I argue in chapter 13, there is a perfect analogy to historical explanation when the evolution of the species is rightly understood.

5

The German Conception of History: Herder or Hegel?

In the eighteenth century, Vico, isolated in Naples, and Rousseau, 'citizen of Geneva' in the heart of Paris, had offered radical alternatives to what we generally and rightly take to be the Enlightenment conception of man and society. At almost the same time, Montesquieu, naturalist of societies, had offered a holistic understanding of human associations which up to his time seemed possible. In French and English thought, these beginnings came to a dead end. But there is a German pre–French Revolutionary writer who now needs to be brought into the picture. In many ways, he will be in the background of the next three chapters, since he influenced, directly or indirectly, Hegel and Marx, von Humboldt and Ranke – indeed, what is not misleadingly called 'the German conception of history'.

Johann Gottfried Herder (1744–1803), son of a Pietist schoolmaster, was a young student at Königsberg when the young Kant was giving courses in physical geography, astronomy, and Wolffian philosophy. It was Kant, it seems, who gave Herder his copy of Rousseau's *Émile* – as a corrective to Hume – and it was Kant, it seems, who inspired Herder to read Montesquieu's *L'esprit des lois* and Buffon's *Histoire naturelle*. There is some irony in this, since it was in reflection especially on the ideas of Rousseau and Montesquieu that Herder developed those seminal ideas which the elder Kant was to find so repugnant. But if it is difficult to identify the influences on Herder,[1] it is even more difficult to

---

[1] At one point, Herder called Rousseau 'a colossus among all authors of the century' and called Leibniz 'the greatest man Germany ever possessed'. Herder was close to Goethe, and he admired Spinoza and Kant – the latter as his teacher of geography, physics, and astronomy, not as the author of the famous three critiques. The elder Kant, as we shall see, was a severe critic of Herder's maturing thought and did as much as anyone, perhaps, to bury it by distortion (Wells, 1959). The mystical Hamann was also Herder's teacher, but it seems that although Herder was always a religious man, 'he

characterize his legacy which, it is fair to say, is as ambiguous as it is extensive.

Known as a figure in the history of German literature and philology, an influence on the Grimm brothers, Goethe, and the writers of the *Sturm und Drang,* as a religious thinker, and 'hardly at all as a sociologist' (Wells, 1959, p. 9), Herder's thought represented a decided, but ambiguous, alternative sociology, in some ways at the root of both Weber's and Marx's thinking. Known also as 'one of the leaders of the Romantic revolt against classicism, rationalism, and faith in the omnipotence of scientific method', as Berlin rightly says, he was, 'no less than Goethe', 'fascinated and influenced by the findings of the sciences'. Like Goethe, he thought that 'false general inferences were often drawn from them' (Berlin, 1976, p. 146). Known also as the 'founder of German Nationalism' and as 'the Copernicus of history' (Cassirer's appellation), his defense of 'nation' was anti-statist, and his conception of history left marks on many, although it was not promoted by *anybody.* Thus, while he is held to have been a nationalist, a determinist, a historicist, and a bad metaphysician, it seems clear that his immediate successors, horrified by the Terror, wounded by the military humiliation of Germany, and galled by the Restoration, misrepresented him as they exploited his complex and many-dimensional writings.

In what follows I focus on Herder's original fusion of religious metaphysics and naturalism, the fundamental tension in his complicated thought. I want to suggest that Herder diagnosed correctly the 'false inferences' drawn from misunderstood 'science', but that through no fault of his own, his reconstitution was inherently unstable, leading in two opposing directions at once. There is a sense in which Hegel and Marx, Ranke and Weber, are not fully intelligible without reference to Herder.

HERDER'S PROJECT FOR THE HUMAN SCIENCES

Wells tells us that 'quite early in his career Herder expressed a desire to be "the Newton of history"' and that his diary of 1769 is 'full of suggestions and plans for a "universal history of civilization"' (Wells, 1959, p. 14). His ironically entitled *Auch eine Philosophie der Geschichte* (*Yet Another Philosophy of History*), 1774, and his major work,

---

remained impervious to Hamann's mysticism' (Clark, 1955, p. 3). In addition to the 'Berlin program' for the development of the German language and literature, which included Nicolai, Lessing, and Moses Mendelssohn among others, Lord Shaftesbury's *Characteristicks of Men, Manners, Opinions, Times* should perhaps be included among the critical influences on Herder. Herder did read Vico, but not before his own ideas had been firmly set out.

the four-volume *Ideen zur Philosophie der Geschichte der Menschheit* (*Ideas for a Philosophy of the History of Mankind*), 1784–91, are his main attempts to realize his ambition. But we ought first to emphasize that 'philosophy of history' did not *yet* have a settled meaning, that, as noted, 'science' and 'philosophy' could still be used interchangeably. Herder emphatically rejected the abstract 'philosophies of history' of Turgot, Condorcet, Voltaire, and Kant, albeit not because he rejected the project of a scientific history, but because these 'philosophers' were merely propagandists:

> Those who have thus far taken it upon themselves to explain the centuries of progress, have mostly cherished the notion that it must lead to ever increasing happiness. In support of this they have embroidered or invented facts, played down or suppressed facts that belie it . . . taken words for works, enlightenment for happiness, and so invented the figment of 'the general progressive improvement of the world'. (Quoted by Berlin, 1976, p. 191)

Only later will 'philosophy of history' become the *non*-scientific or *un*scientific – metaphysical – effort to comprehend history. In Herder's view, to be the Newton of history would be to synthesize the currently available scientific knowledge about the causes of the course of history, to put history, an all-encompassing human science, on a scientific footing. As Barnard has noted, Herder assured us that 'in embarking on his *Ideen* . . . he did so not as a theologian following in Bossuet's steps but from the point of view of the social scientist' (1965, pp. 112f.). But what was this 'social science?' From our perspective, its central terms reside in two vocabularies, that of 'science' and that of pre-Kantian metaphysics. It will be useful to discuss his position in terms of three related topics: Herder's rejection of the abstract for the particular; his view that explanation in history is 'causal' explanation, albeit in a sense that remains unclear; and his effort to reconcile 'chance, destiny and divinity' in history.

THE ABSTRACT AND THE CONCRETE

Leibniz had offered the principle of the identity of indiscernibles, holding that no two 'things' were the same; that they were necessarily different – for example, in not being in the same place at the same time. Similarity is not identity, and, for Herder, it may be the most seemingly unimportant difference which makes *all* the difference. Herder knew, of course, that what logicians call 'terms' are all abstractions – 'monarchy',

'Christian', 'savage', and so on – and he knew also that they are as unavoidable as they are dangerous. Words are indeed poor markers for the particularity of the concrete. It was a rationalist prejudice to celebrate the attainment of abstraction as knowledge – indeed, as the best and only kind of knowledge. That was precisely the problem with the 'laws' and 'principles' of the 'philosophers of history,' for these writers drained from the real concrete all that made it real. This was the case even with Montesquieu, who had himself wisely protested against '*les grands simplificateurs*'. Yet what was his famous trichotomy but

> Three wretched generalizations! . . . the history of all times and peoples, whose succession forms the great, living work of God, reduced to ruins, divided neatly into three heaps, even though it does not lack noble and worthy material. Oh, Montesquieu!. (Herder, 1969, p. 217)

'. . . the concrete is to us not merely the main concern but the *conditio sine qua non*' (1969, p. 102). Thus,

> The Greeks spoke with practical application, each word found its place; and in the best times, when men scarcely spoke through words at all but through deeds, custom, example and a thousand different kinds of influence. . . . We speak about a hundred social classes, period, human species, in order to avoid speaking about each of them individually. Our wisdom is so delicate and insubstantial; it is volatile abstraction which evaporates with having been put to use. Theirs on the contrary, was and remained civic wisdom, a matter of concrete human substance, full of sap and nourishment. (1969, p. 204)

The concrete provided the link between 'theory' and practice. To break this, was to fly to 'the clouds and fog of universal truth'. But Herder's commitment to the concrete did not entail the impossibility of causal explanation, nor that what happens was not subject to law. But this too had to be seen concretely.

LAW AND CAUSALITY IN HERDER

Everyone agrees that Herder rejected the Humean account of causality as constant conjunction, but there is real difficulty in seeing exactly what he put in its place. F. M. Barnard suggests that it is substantially an Aristotelian conception. But, given the genuine problem of discerning Aristotle's conception and distinguishing it from its various interpretations, neo-Platonic, Christian, and naturalistic, to say this raises as many questions as it answers.[2]

This much seems clear: first, that Herder believed that causes are productive, that they 'bring about' their effects. Second, he believed that 'things' have 'inherent powers'. Both ideas are anti-Humean and 'Aristotelian' – as indeed, they are at the root of the ordinary sense of causality. Herder writes:

> Whenever we observe a power (*Kraft*) in operation, it is inherent in some organ and in harmony with it. For power as such is not open to investigation, at least not by our senses. It only exists for these by its manifestations in and through material forms which, if we may trust the analogy pervading nature as a whole, have been fashioned to meet its particular requirements. Seeds *in posse* . . . are not evident to our eyes; all that we observe . . . are acting organic powers. (1969, p. 272)

This is a striking 'realist' formulation, putting aside for the moment the evident functionalist, teleological elements. Herder acknowledges with the 'empiricists' that *Kräfte* are not knowable, 'at least not by our senses'; but, despite his declared distrust of metaphysics, it is quite clear that *Kräfte* constitute the indispensable underpinning of his own 'empirical' view. The idea was, as Barnard says, 'the unifying principle of is philosophy of organism' (Barnard, 1965, p. 52).

There are two aspects of this. First, there are, as it were, natural unities conceived in persistent interaction (1965, p. 46). Second, these are conceived processively, as in a continuous state of change or 'becoming'. Now both these ideas can be given a plausible naturalistic and wholly descriptive reading: acorns, after all, are natural unities, and they become oaks, not squirrels or pieces of quartz. There need be no assumption here of the neo-Platonic Aristotelianism which the Galileans worked so hard to expunge. Even so, it is moot how far the idea is generalizable. Herder was not timid, arguing ultimately that individuals and *Volk* – defined as linguistic communities (see below) – have an inherent 'organic' character which makes them what they are, distinguishes them from others, and is a 'force' in their 'becoming'. A *Volk*, like an individual, has a particular and unique 'character' or 'spirit'. In individuals and groups, it is something which is realized causally, but once in existence, it is itself a causal force.

We can see how these ideas are applied to history. The *Ideen* begins with an account of the place of human life, the earth. This is because, as Montesquieu said, 'the climate' – that is, the natural environments of

[2] Cf. Manicas (1965), Elizabeth Anscombe and Peter Geach (1961), and William Wallace (1972).

The Critical Ideas

humankind – have effects on people and their civilizations: 'The constitution of their body, their way of life, the nature of work and play . . .
indeed their whole mentality are climatic' (Herder, 1969, p. 285). Thus,
Herder concludes, 'the history of human civilization is in great measure
zoological and geographical' (quoted by Wells, 1959, p. 29). But, despite
the reading of Herder by Kant and a host of his critics, this was neither a
'reductive' naturalism nor a positivist regularity determinism of, for
example, the Comtean variety. 'Climate promotes, but it does not
compel, a given course of development' (Herder, 1969, p. 291). The
'forces' which operate in history are multivarious and include, critically,
'the genetic'. As Herder writes:

> The genetic force (*Kraft*) is the mother of all creations on earth,
> to which the climate can only contribute, favorably or unfavor-
> ably. . . . But whatever the climatic influence, every human being,
> every animal, every plant has a climate of its own; for each absorbs
> and adapts to external influences in its own organic manner.
> (Quoted by Barnard, 1965, p. 120)

Natural entities, by virtue of what they are, have 'ecological spaces'
which are causally pertinent to their 'becoming'. What happens is the
product of a *transaction* between the 'genetic force' embodied in the
individual and particular environmental factors. And this is true also of
persons and of *Volk*. More specifically, by virtue of the *human* nature, it
is clear that in Herder's view psychosocial forces are also at work in
(biography and) history.
    Much in Herder sounds 'evolutionary', but he was no Darwinian.
Humans are a distinct natural kind, 'created' like all others. But
Herder's first humans are more like those of Rousseau than those of
Genesis. They are migratory primitives, in many ways like lower animals,
if profoundly different. With Condorcet and Rousseau as his foils, he
argues that mind and human anatomy are interdependent, and that
'speech alone awakens slumbering reason', clearly implying here, as in
other places, that while lower animals have minds, 'mind' *as speech* is a
unique inherent power. In his provocative essay 'The Origin of Language'
(1770), he writes: 'language has its origin in our animal nature'; but
whereas all animals 'give expression to their sensations', none 'has as
much as the beginnings of a human language properly so-called' (in
Herder, 1969, p. 124). His reasons for saying this are not clear. But,
however that may be, he argues that speech is a power which depends
on its 'organ', the human brain, which itself is somehow dependent on
the human 'upright stance'; crucially, it is a power 'formed by experience', 'fashioned by [a *Volk*'s] organization and mode of life'. In a

remarkable text, he writes that 'human reason [*Vernunft der Mensch*][3] is the creation of *humans*' (Herder, 1969, p. 264). Accordingly,

[the] human essence – *Humanität* – is not ready made, yet it is potentially realizable. And this is true of a New Zealand cannibal no less than of a Fenelon . . . for all are creatures of one and the same species. (1969, p. 266)

Indeed, it is just because humans are environmentally flexible – not restricted to a narrow ecological space – and because 'the human being has to learn everything' that there is such great variety in humans and human civilizations, each with its own special and idiosyncratic character. Language and tradition, then, are 'inherited', giving continuity to the changing history of each *Volk*:

This is the invisible, hidden medium that links minds through ideas, hearts through inclinations and impulses, the senses through impressions and forms, civil society through laws and institutions, generations through examples, modes of living and education. (Quoted by Barnard, 1965, p. 117)[4]

Moreover, and remarkably, Herder strikes an astounding anti-essentialist note:

No-one would . . . expect that the rose should become a lily, or the dog a wolf in another climate. Nature has made distinct genera, and prefers that they should perish rather than change so radically. But the rose can degenerate and the dog can acquire certain wolf-like characteristics. This lies in the nature of the historical process. . . . Climate is a chaos of heterogeneous elements, and hence acts in various ways. Gradually these diverse environmental elements penetrate the inner nature of a being, and bring about changes in its genetic and acquired characteristics. Its genetic force, to be sure, offers resistance. . . . But as it is not independent of the heterogeneous external factors, it must accommodate itself to these in due course. (Herder, 1969, p. 193)

Herder thereby explains the differences between Laplanders and their civilization and the inhabitants of Polynesia and theirs, between

---

[3] German, of course, has both *Mann* and the generic *Mensche*. I have taken the liberty of altering translations, where appropriate, to reflect this.

[4] The capacity of 'tradition' is by no means an unmixed blessing:

Is there any ridiculous idea the mind can frame that has not been actually made sacred by hereditary traditions in one place or another . . . From the means chosen by the Creator, that our species should be educated only by our species, nothing else was possible. Follies had to be inherited as well as the treasures of wisdom. (Quoted by Wells, 1959, pp. 59f.)

Mongolians and Europeans. Having a common origin, each, in transaction with its 'climate' has created 'a human world', a concrete realization of our shared *Humanität*. Contrary to Hume, Kant, and so many of their intellectual heirs, Herder denies the usefulness of the term 'race':

> . . . there are neither four or five races, nor exclusive varieties, on this earth. Complexions run into each other . . . *in toto* they are, in the final analysis, but different shades of the same great picture which extends through all ages and all parts of the earth. Their study, therefore, properly forms no part of biology or systematic natural history but belongs rather to the anthropological history of man. (Herder, 1969, p. 284)

Accordingly, 'to trace this human essence in its manifold expressions, in social intercourse, in politics, in scientific and artistic pursuits is the true function of social philosophy' (1969, p. 271).

It is of some importance that, as Herder's alternative for a human science was buried, by empiricists, so too was his anti-racism. The two were not unrelated insofar as the rejection of 'metaphysics' in favor of 'observables' and the collapse of 'causes' in favor of 'correlations' encouraged racialist ideology. In another place, as above, Herder makes his point in distinctly 'metaphysical' and anti-empiricistic terms:

> This elusive double creature [humans] can be modified in a thousand ways and almost has to be . . . [but this] does not rule out that, within the ever-changing husk, the same kernel of human substance and happiness can, and in all probability does, remain virtually the same. (Herder, 1969, p. 215)[5]

'CHANCE, DESTINY, AND DIVINITY'

But perhaps the clearest place to see the difference between Herder's project for a human science and the empiricist alternative is in regard to the question of human agency and its relation to causality and to natural law. It is easy to argue that Herder failed in his attempt to reconcile 'freedom' and 'determinism', 'chance and Providence', or that he was just plain inconsistent. But if we are to understand the subsequent struggle to articulate a human science, it is critical to see that Herder

---

[5] Indeed, as already suggested, and as I argue in chapter 11, with the realization at the end of the nineteenth century of the social sciences as autonomous empirical 'disciplines', racism will have vigorous 'scientific' support. Chapter 14 tries to show how sexism and racism enter into characteristic contemporary 'empiricistic' explanations.

stood absolutely between a Kantian anti-naturalism and a positivistic – post-Humean – naturalism.

It is clear that he believed that law governed all creation, and that mankind was part of this:

> If there be a God in nature, the same God is in history too. For man is a part of creation, and in his wildest extravagances and passions must obey laws. . . . Is it to be supposed that man, with his powers, changes and passions is above these bonds of nature? (Quoted by Wells, 1959, p. 41)

On the other hand, he also believed that humans are free, and that there is a radical contingency in history. But the two ideas are not inconsistent if by 'freedom' one does not mean absolute freedom – freedom from the constraints of natural law – and if contingency in history is meant to deny merely that there are historical laws.

Herder's view of freedom was *not* Kantian and demanded only what seems obvious, that humans do choose between alternatives. He wrote:

> The animal is a slave, bent down to the ground . . . and its mind, not quite ripened into reason, must follow the base promptings of its instincts. . . . [The human] is the first of nature's creatures to be set free; he stands upright. He can explore possibilities and choose between alternatives. (Quoted by Wells, 1959, p. 37)

This capacity, Aristotelian *proairesis,* is radically different from the Kantian 'autonomous' will, which when operating freely, acts in the 'noumenal' world as 'a pure moral will'. For Herder, human choices are fully part of nature and are not 'uncaused'. But the capacity to deliberate and thence to consciously choose was sufficient for Herder's Aristotelian and naturalistic notion of agency. Motivated to clearly demarcate 'science' and to make room for God, Freedom, and Immortality, Kant's obliteration of this older view has had immeasurable consequences for the idea of a human science. Since Kant, it has seemed that we have but two choices; either natural law does not apply to the will (or to history) or it does. Either one denies the possibility of a social science, or one denies the reality of freedom. G. A. Wells has done us the service of reviewing the response to Herder's *Ideen*. He has shown that Herder was widely misrepresented by Kant, who in effect employed his own (newly found) categories in his critical account. In these terms, of course, Herder had to be read as a naturalistic determinist. As Wells notes, Herder's Kantian critics 'cannot conceive that Herder, who denies that man's will is free, can grant any efficacy to human intiative' (Wells, 1959, pp. 259f.).[6]

---

[6] Cf. Hayden White's tantalizing remarks in his *Metahistory,* pp. 72ff.

Since deliberative actions, springing from self-chosen ends, are part of 'the causal chain', Herder insisted also on the contingency of history. What we do makes a difference in history. Nevertheless, Herder insisted that *because* the causal chain 'is twisted and tangled a thousand times', there is no way to discern the lawfulness of historical change, if such there be. He waffled on this last possibility. In *Yet Another Philosophy of History,* his Copernican task was to argue that it was the 'civilized' European's illusion that he was at the center of things. The Eurocentric 'philosophers of history' were deluded in believing that all history was merely a means in the gradual preparation of the 'enlightened' civilization which makes 'savages all over the world . . . ripe for conversion as they grow fonder of our brandy and our luxuries' (Herder, 1969, p. 206).[7]

In this text, he clearly implies that there is 'a chain of an almighty and omniscient goodness', and thus that history is lawful; but because the chain is 'twisted and tangled a thousand times', our place in the chain is unknown, and we cannot be made 'aware of the end to which the chain is finally attached' (Herder, 1969, p. 215). At other times, he speaks of 'fate' more radically: 'Chance, destiny and divinity affect both the whole and the details' (Herder, 1969, p. 194). 'A thousand-fold contingency is evident in the simplest thing', and historical events have 'an unbound course' (quoted by Spitz, 1955, p. 465). In either case, it is not within our finite human competence to discover the lawfulness of historical change – if such exists.

---

[7] Herder is as brilliant a critic of Enlightenment Eurocentrism as one is likely to find. I cannot resist offering one or two texts. The line quoted continues:

Savages all over the world will become ripe for conversion as they grow fonder of our brandy and our luxuries; they will soon approach our culture and become, so help me God, good, strong and happy men, just like us!

Trade and popery, how .much you have already contributed to this great undertaking! Spaniards, Jesuits and Dutchmen: all you philanthropic, disinterested, noble and virtuous nations!

'Our system of trade!' This all-embracing, refined scientific system of ours, what do we really mean by it? how wretched were the Spartans to use their helots for field work, how barbaric the Romans to imprison their slaves in dungeons! In our Europe slavery has been abolished, because it has been actually established that slaves are far more costly and far less productive than free men. Nonetheless this did not prevent our raiding three other continents for slaves, trading in them, banishing them to silvermines and sugar plantations. But then, they are not European, not Christian! What is more, we get silver, precious stones, spices, sugar and – secret diseases, in return. For the sake of international trade, mutual brotherly assistance, and the common interests of all countries, therefore, let us forge ahead!

'System of trade!' The magnitude and uniqueness of the enterprise is manifest. Three continents are devastated, yet policed by us; we in turn are depopulated, emasculated and debauched as a result. . . . The old name 'shephard' has been changed into 'monopolist': Mammon is the god we all serve. (Herder, 1969, pp. 206, 209)

To this point I have argued that Herder's conception of humanity, society, and history can be understood as a variation of a plausible scientific naturalism. Of course, his metaphors suggest a dynamic nature, infused with life and spontaneity – in the face of mechanical materialism, a re-animated Leibnizian concept of nature. The new science, did not, on his view, entail the matter was inert, any more than it required that causality had to be reduced to constant conjunction. Between his view and that of the mechanical materialists (of which, more later), it is hard not to side with Herder. Nevertheless, there is, in Herder's thought, another side. This comes out in the many passages which speak of 'the passage of God in nature', and in explicit assertions bearing testimony to Herder's religious impulse. For example, 'everywhere the great analogy of nature led to the truths of religion which I could suppress only with difficulty' (quoted by Spitz, 1955, pp. 469f.). It is, however, his central idea, *Kraft*, which gives us our greatest interpretative difficulties.

I have offered a realist and naturalistic understanding of Herder's concept of *Kraft*, a version of a Lockean 'power'. Such a view, of course, is consistent with a religious naturalism, so that, as Barnard writes, *Kraft* was 'the basic concept of his theological cosmology': 'In *Kraft* he saw both the First Cause and the continuous energizing power of "becoming", which he identified with existence. *Kraft*, therefore, embodied for Herder the continuous manifestation of God' (Barnard, 1965, pp. 120f.). But this has also been read more mystically. Thus, Berlin writes that *Kräfte* were 'the mysterious, dynamic, purpose-seeking forces, the interplay of which constitutes all growth and movement' (Berlin, 1976, p. 204).

Herder ambitiously attempted to establish a new direction for inquiry. Yet commentators would seem to be correct in maintaining that there are layers or strands of his thought which cannot be pressed into the service of this or that subsequent philosophy. As Manfred Henningsen has remarked, the *Kraft*-language belongs to the German intellectual ecology and surfaces in various forms in a wide range of writers: Jacob Boehme, Fichte, Humboldt, Goethe, Hegel, the Romantics, and even in Engels and Helmholtz.

At the same time Berlin would appear to be right in noting that Herder's assertion that 'we live in a world which we ourselves create' will be 'inflated into extravagant metaphysical shapes by Fichte, Schelling, Hegel and the Idealist Movement in philosophy' (Berlin, 1976, p. 204). For the more religious-minded, a vibrant metaphysics of cosmic abstractions would result. For the more naturalistically minded, Herder was merely suggestive. Indeed, as Berlin also notes, the idea that we make our own world is also 'at the source of the profoundest sociological insights of Marx' (1976, p. 204). But the 'real scientists' – the positivists?

– could hardly take him seriously. Surely, 'science' could not be constructed from such materials?

EXPRESSIONISM, POPULISM, AND PLURALISM

However that may be, we must return to three ideas identified by Berlin
as 'expressionism', 'populism', and 'pluralism', ideas which are perhaps
the most original in Herder's rich thought, but have only been touched
on in the foregoing. The first left a definite and clear mark on Hegel
and Marx, as we shall see; the second was distorted by Hegel and the
philosophers and historians of the state who followed Hegel and Ranke;
and the third was thoroughly buried by the philosophers of progress,
German, French, and English.

Berlin defines 'expressionism' thus:

> The doctrine that human activity in general, and art in particular,
> expresses the entire personality of the individual or the group . . .
> expressionism claims that all the works of men are above all voices
> speaking, are not objects detached from their makers, are part of a
> living process of communication between persons and not in-
> dependently existing entities, beautiful or ugly, interesting or
> boring, upon which external observers may direct the cool and
> dispassionate gaze with which scientists . . . look on nature. (Berlin,
> 1976, p. 153)

A great deal is contained in this: Herder's passion for the novel and the
concrete particularity of persons and cultures; and, when this is combined with the idea that the concrete forms of humanity are social
constructions, the idea, shared by Marx and Dilthey, that the objects of
knowledge of the human sciences are human products, requiring, as will
be argued below, a hermeneutic epistemology. It is within this framework of ideas that Herder's 'populism' and 'pluralism' must be seen.

'Populism' is an apt word for Herder's idea, not just because the other
choice, 'nationalism' is worse, but because 'the terms *nation,* nation,
and *nazione* evoked loftier associations than the words *peuple,* people,
or *populo*' (Meinecke, 1970, p. 23). Herder's *Volk were* 'the lowly, the
common, and the members of the mass', and it was *their* language,
songs, and stories which he had in his mind. Descriptively, Herder
generalized Montesquieu's *L'esprit des lois* into the idea that such a
Volk creates its special experience, its particular world. Moreover,
insofar as it is the genuine expression of its particularity, it has value – a
value that is *equal* to any other. It is in this sense, accordingly, that

invocations of *Nationalgeist* (or its alternatives, *Geist des Volkes, Seele des Volkes, Geist der Nation, Genius des Volkes, Nationalcharakter*) are best located. 'Each nation', he writes, 'has a center of gravity' (quoted by Spitz, 1955, p. 459). Each has it is own 'spirit', its own 'genius', its own 'character'.

As before, then, to comprehend a nation is to grasp its special *Geist* and thence to seek its explanation. But this is no 'nationalism' as usually understood since, for Herder, *the state destroys the nation*. While Herder seems to have coined the word *Nationalismus* (nationalism) and to have believed that language defines a 'natural' community of persons, his vision was anarchist and cosmopolitan, the world as a plurality of such communities having no *need* for sovereign authorities. He admitted that preservation of the community was essential. He thus was, if you will, a linguistic patriot, insisting on the purity of language and the preciousness of folksongs, stories, and the like. It was through this belief that he stimulated comparative philology and the efforts of the brothers Grimm. But he also denied vociferously, as against Machiavelli, that the preservation of the 'nation' required centralized authority – the state. As Barnard writes,

> Not war, but peace, Herder maintained, was the natural dis-
> position of unoppressed humanity. War was the result of oppres-
> sion. . . . The institution of central political power, therefore, was
> not the beginning but the collapse of politics. (Barnard, 1965,
> p. 62)

States were organizations of force, 'machines', instrumentalities of oppression. Striking a Rousseauian notes, he writes: 'the state can give us many ingenious contrivances; unfortunately, it can also deprive us of something far more essential; our own selves' (p. 310).

Herder's vision is quite the opposite of those of Fichte or Hegel. It is also a striking fact that Marx failed utterly to notice the immense emancipatory potential of the social-psychological phenomena which Herder had unearthed. The concept of class seems to have blinded Marx to seeing the pertinence of 'nation'.

Herder's 'pluralism' follows. Not only does he value the unique character of a 'nation', but, as part of his rejection of the Eurocentric philosophies of progress, he insists that there is no objective human ideal or ideal of society, and that each *Volk* is valuable in its own right. The nineteenth century, of course, would have none of this, and in the positivism of the twentieth century, it took a paradoxical form, in that even imperialism could be rationalized, not as in the eighteenth and nineteenth centuries, in the name of the ideal society as defined by the 'civilized' nations of Western Europe, but in the name of 'moderniz-ation' or 'development' – masked as scientific neutrality.

HEGEL'S PHILOSOPHY OF HISTORY

Herder was ambiguously a social scientist. By contrast, Hegel (1770–1831) is the very paradigm of a philosopher: rationalist, system-builder, learned sage. Herder left no schools, though he left a legacy – which, of course, Hegel drew on. Hegel left 'the Hegelians', 'young' and not young, from whom Marx drew. But it is not just for that reason that Hegel must be considered in a history of the social sciences. His mark extends well beyond his influence on Marx. His thought is a key element in the background of *all* German social science, a fact of some import-ance as we shall see. In particular, it may be but a slight exaggeration to say that Hegel's concept of the state is, by now, part of the background of almost *all* 'social science'.

It would be as unwise as, I hope, unnecessary to attempt a sketch of Hegel's philosophy – unwise, because it cannot be sketched without doing considerable violence to it, and unnecessary, because from the point of view of the history of the social sciences, we need focus on only one or two key, if difficult, ideas in Hegel's rich thought. These include his concept of the state, 'dialectic', and especially the contrast between an 'idealist' theory of history and a 'materialist' theory.

As was suggested above, the Industrial and French Revolutions were both decisive events for Comte, as they were for Hegel and Marx. The Romantics – Novalis, Fichte, the Schlegels, and Schleiermacher – moved from applause to denunciation. The French Revolution pro-voked Hegel to believe that 'the History of the World is none other than the progress of the consciousness of Freedom' (Hegel, 1956, p. 19).[8] It was Hegel's intention to show this, both 'empirically' and 'demon-stratively'.

In the 1830/31 lectures which have come down to us as *The Philos-ophy of History,* Hegel tells us that 'the only thought which Philosophy brings with it to the contemplation of History, is the simple conception of *Reason*; that Reason is the Sovereign of the World; that the history of the World, therefore, presents us with a rational process' (Hegel, 1956, p. 9). In philosophy, this is no 'hypothesis', since, he insists, it is demonstrable, the task of his *Science of Logic.* But in the domain of history, it remains a hypothesis, subject to the test of the evidence of

---

[8] Hegel may well have traversed the same route as those mentioned. See his *Philos-ophy of Right,* para. 5.

history. Hegel intends, in *The Philosophy of History,* to 'proceed historically – empirically', recognizing, of course, that even the so-called 'impartial' historian 'is by no means passive as regards the exercise of his thinking powers', that he too 'brings his categories with him' (1956, p. 11).

We need not review Hegel's substantive effort to confirm his 'hypothesis'. It is essential, though, that we identify the key features of his argument. They are set out in the Introduction to *The Philosophy of History.*

First of all, Hegel wants, like Herder, to explain history, 'to depict the passions of mankind, the genius, the active powers, that play their part on the great stage' (p. 3). This was a task affirmed by Anaxagoras, but rejected by Christian theodicies. Still, almost quoting Herder, he asks: 'if it be allowed that Providence manifests itself in [animals, plants, and isolated occurrences – miracles] why not also in Universal History?' (p. 15). Explaining history is 'a Theodicaea' (p. 15), just as Leibniz had suggested.

Second, for Hegel, 'the motive power' of what happens in history is 'the need, instinct, inclination, and passion of man' (p. 22). He writes: 'I wish to assert my personality in connection with some conception of mine: I wish to be satisfied by its execution' (p. 22). The idea, plainly, is Hegel's original version of 'expressionism' and the root of the doctrine of alienation of Marx. The text continues: 'if I am to exert myself for any object, it must in some way or other be my object. . . . This is the absolute right of personal existence – to find itself satisfied in its activity and labor' (p. 22). In the present context, as regards explanation in history, I should emphasize only that Hegel's point is that it is individual intentions which are the 'spring' of action, and individual 'labor' and 'activities' which are the *material* of history. For Hegel, as for Marx, *individuals* make history.

But they do not make it as they choose to make it. That is because – and this is our third point – there are *unintended consequences of all our acts.* This fundamental idea, which is found in Mandeville and others before Hegel, becomes in Hegel 'the cunning of Reason'. He says:

> In history an additional result is commonly produced by human actions beyond that which they aim at and obtain. . . . They gratify their own interests; but something further is accomplished, latent in the actions in question, though not present to their consciousness, and not included in their design. (p. 27)

There are two aspects of this. First, in their effort to 'develop themselves and their aims in accordance with their natural tendencies', human beings 'built up the edifice of a human society; thus fortifying a position of Right and Order *against themselves'* (p. 27). Hegel here stands smack between Rousseau and Marx. For Rousseau, humans are born free, but everywhere live in chains; for Marx, human history *begins* at just the point where individuals collectively control the conditions of their lives. Second, the *telos* of history is not the *object* of individual action. For Hegel, Providence works by means of the unintended consequences of our acts. Historical change goes on 'behind the backs of persons'.

Fourth, while individuals provide the 'energy' for historical process, 'in the history of the world, the *Individuals* we have to do with are *Peoples*; totalities that are States' (p. 14).

HEGEL'S THEORY OF THE STATE

We must be careful here. The 'peoples' are and are not Herder's *Völker*. The center of Herder's conception is repeated by Hegel. The *Volk* is the 'nation' which has a common language, and we can speak of 'the spirit of a people', a *Volksgeist*. Each *Volk,* moreover has 'a peculiar National Genius', whose spirit is 'concretely manifested, expresses every aspect of its consciousness and will – the whole cycle of its realization. Its religion, its polity, its ethics, its legislature, and even its science, art, and mechanical skill, all bear its stamp' (p. 64). Moreover, this is empirical: 'That such or such a specific quality constitutes the peculiar genius of a people, is the element which must be derived from experience, and historically proved' (p. 64).

But this is *not* Herder, since Hegel is speaking not merely of a *Volk,* but of a *Volk that is politically organized.* Hegel is talking about a nation-state, the historical realization of the condition for the possibility of 'freedom':

> It is only by a Constitution that the abstraction – the State – attains life and reality; but this involves a distinction between those who command and those who obey. . . . [But] a State is an individual totality, of which you cannot select any particular side, although a supremely important one, such as its political constitution; and deliberate and decide respecting that isolated form. Not only is that constitution most intimately connected with and dependent on those other spiritual forces; but the form of the entire moral and intellectual individuality . . . is only a step in the development of the grand Whole. (pp. 43f., 46)

If anything, this sounds more like Montesquieu, except that by 1830, the fictitious idea of a nation-state – not present in Montesquieu – has come to have *experienced reality*. The 'nation' is now not a *de facto* linguistic community, but an 'imagined community', *defined politically*. As a unity *fictitiously* bound by language and culture, 'the nation' can have a Will which the State expresses; the laws of such a State can be legitimated as the expression of such 'a people'.

It is surely clear that no 'state' was (or is) a 'nation', however easily the two ideas may seem to combine. Hegel's 'Germany' certainly wasn't, since it did not then exist as a state; nor was 'England' – Great Britain? – or for that matter, 'The United States' or Spain or France, the best candidates then available. In all these states, *nothing* was really common except their 'constitution', as Hegel himself almost admits.[9] They were all 'unnatural enlargements' in Herder's sense, 'patched-up contraptions, fragile machines, appropriately called "state machines"' (Herder, 1969, p. 324). All were made up of extensive minorities – linguistic, ethnic, and religious – united by 'one sceptre'. In none of them was there, as Hegel aimed to have it, 'the true unity of the general and the particular'. Indeed, Hegel acknowledged that in addition to 'the independence of the nation [*not* State] as an individuality against other nations' (1956, p. 448), the true unity of the general and particular required solution of the 'monstrous inconsistency' in which 'the ultimate decision is the prerogative of the monarch' (p. 448). In his view, the French Revolution had dramatically raised the problem of the locus of 'sovereignty': 'this collision, this nodus, this problem is that with which history is now occupied, and whose solution it has to work out in the future' (p. 452).

In direct reference to Montesquieu, Hegel sees clearly what Montesquieu had seen but dimly, that the era of the ancient republic was over, and that therefore it could offer no solutions:

> If by 'sovereignty of the people' is understood a republican form of government, or to speak more more specifically . . . a democracy . . . we can longer speak of such a notion in the face of the Idea of the state in its full development. (Hegel, 1952, para. 279)

The state involves a distinction 'between those who command and those who obey', the machinery of 'government', 'the judiciary and the

[9] One might argue, as Avineri does, that 'it is precisely in the modern state that Hegel sees ethnic-linguistic ties as unnecessary' (1972, p. 45). Even if this be granted, however, it is quite clear that as *imagined*, the nation functions critically, not merely in Hegel, but in *all* modern political thinking about the state. The easy shift between 'state' and 'nation' attests to this, not to mention the power of appeals to defend the nation, by 'leaders' of the National Security State. Avineri's account, although stimulating, seems often to be too much motivated to put Hegel into the liberal tradition of political thought. There are, of course, liberal elements, especially the clear division between 'civil society' and 'the state'. It is just because we are now all 'Hegelians' when we think of the 'state' that confusion is so rampant (cf. Avineri's epilogue).

90 *The Critical Ideas*

police'. Failing to see that the Americans had indeed solved the problem, Hegel opted for a reactionary solution.[10] The famous paragraph 279 of his *Philosophy of Right* just cited struggles with the idea of 'the sovereignty of the people' and its antithesis, 'the sovereignty existing in the monarch'. Hegel insists that 'the sovereignty of the people is one of the confused notions based on the wild idea of the "people"', and he concludes finally that, 'taken without its monarch and the articulation of the whole which is the indispensable and direct concomitant of monarchy, the people is a formless mass and no longer a state.' The *nation* is actual, even if 'the people' are 'a formless mass'. Both are given *concrete reality by the organization of the state.* The state, ultimately, is sovereign. It will be well to pause here, if only briefly, to hint at what seems to have happened in the 80 years between Montesquieu and Hegel.

THE STATE AND THE NATION

There are two aspects to be considered. First, there is understanding how it came to be that 'the imagined community' came to have a *lived reality* sufficient to cooperate in the reconstitution of the sociological problem of 'legitimacy'. This is the shift from Herder's *Volk* to Hegel's *Nation*. Second, there is the shift in the concepts of 'republic' and of 'democracy', the shift from the sovereignty of 'the people' to the sovereignty of 'the nation'.

In *The Imagined Community,* Benedict Anderson has offered an extremely plausible account of what is plainly a complex phenomenon. Here, I can only sketch some of the key elements, leaving out much and foregoing extended gloss altogether. Anderson argues that there were three ideas, which, having 'lost their axiomatic grip' on consciousness, made possible the phenomenon of nationalism. First, there was the incapacity of the great 'sodalities of Christendom, The Ummah Islam, and the rest' to sustain the view that 'a particular script language offered privileged access to ontological truth' (Anderson, 1983, p. 40). The secularization of knowledge challenged the invisible community of the saved and made room for the earthly community of 'citizens'. The second change was the collapse of the belief that 'the dynastic realm' was the natural order of things. The dynast was inadequate as a center

[10] As Avineri says, Hegel may have been the first political theorist 'to confront the realities of the modern age' (1968, p. 239), but it is important to see that it is in terms of Montesquieu's suddenly anachronistic categories that his analysis is couched. This explains, in part, his 'reactionary' defense of monarchy. Hegel fails to see that the Americans proved that monarchy is not necessary *in a modern state*. In my 'The Foreclosure of Democracy in America', I have argued that America did solve Hegel's problem, but European writers, with eyes on the French Revolution, have always missed this.

for the 'extended' community of the state, and after James I, or earlier, 'divine right' was undetermined by *societas* (see above, chapter 2). Third, impelled by science and rationalized capitalism, there was a remarkable shift in the perception of time, from 'simultaneity-along-time' to 'homogeneous, empty time' (1983, p. 30). This makes it possible for each of the 240 million 'Americans' who now live in the United States to conceive of themselves as engaged in 'steady, anonymous, simultaneous activity'; each are characters in a large novel in which events, atomistically reported in the daily newspaper, are 'performed at the same clocked, calendrical time' (p. 31).

But the more proximate cause was print-capitalism, the printed word as a commodity. This impelled a 'revolutionary vernacularizing', which 'made it possible for rapidly growing numbers of people to think about themselves, and to relate themselves to others, in profoundly new ways' (p. 40). When print-capitalism joined with Protestantism, cheap popular editions created new reading publics, making Latin arcane, both because of its subject-matter and because of its status as text. Finally, administrative vernaculars, in existence before print-capitalism, became with print-capitalism the usual and accepted instruments of administrative centralization.

But the 'fatality of human linguistic diversity', coupled with the foregoing, was crucial. 'Mutual incomprehensibility was historically of only slight importance until capitalism and print created monoglot reading publics' (p. 46). The print-languages laid a basis for 'national consciousness' in three ways: first, 'they created unified fields of exchange and communication below Latin and above the spoken vernaculars'. Variety in the countless French, English, or Spanish dialects which made it difficult, even impossible, for one group to understand another in conversation, was now overcome via print (p. 47). Herder's *Volk* became aware of the thousands or millions of others who shared exclusively a written language, 'the embryo of the nationally imagined community' (p. 47). Second, print-capitalism brought a fixity to language, stabilizing across time and space the ensemble of fellow-readers. Finally, a language of power was created. High German, the King's English, and so on became the *official* languages. With these changes, then, the possibility of a new form of 'community' was created.

The independence movements of the New World were the dramatic catalyst. The American nation, invented during the struggle of the thirteen colonies for independence, was followed by the unfurling of the Revolutionary Tri-colors across Europe, by Toussaint L'Ouverture's creation of the second independent republic in the New World, and then, of course, by the liberation movements against the Spanish and

Portuguese American empires. Anderson neatly summarizes what followed:

> Out of the American welter came these imagined realities; nation-states, republic institutions, common citizenships, popular sovereignty, national flags and anthems, etc. and the liquidation of their conceptual opposites: dynastic empires, monarchical institutions, absolutisms, subjecthoods, inherited nobilities, serfdoms, ghettos, and so forth. (Anderson, 1983, p. 78)[11]

The model or blueprint, once created, was irresistible, and the process accelerated as it was confirmed by the emergence of each new 'nation' in the new plurality of 'nations'.

IMPLICATIONS OF HEGEL'S VIEW

The idea, then, that 'in the history of the world, the *Individuals* we have to do with are *Peoples*; totalities that are States', has a clear meaning and a number of important implications. For Hegel, it is only in and between *states* that *world* history takes place. Pre-state peoples are only on the margin of world history, ultimately subject to the acts of those entities which, by virtue of their size and organization, are capable of affecting the processes of world history. Hegel thus recaptures the perception of Machiavelli, that achieving offensive and defensive strength, which is possible only through 'unity', is the fundamental fact of modern history. But he goes well beyond Machiavelli. For, whereas Machiavelli lacked a clear idea of the state, not to mention the nation-state, Hegel has both. Moreover, Hegel's particular view of the state as a substantial unity existing in a competitive arena of *other* states has dramatic implications.

Hegel assents to the idea held by Locke and the liberal tradition that it is the state's function to protect property and the private interests of the members of 'civil society'; but, *contra* that tradition, *because* the state is a substantial unity and the locus of contingent individual life, war transcends 'the finite' and calls on us to sustain unity once threatened. As Taylor writes, war is 'the moment of truth' (Taylor, 1975, p. 448):

> It is the moment wherein the substance of the state – i.e., its absolute power against everything individual and particular, against life, property, and their rights, even against societies and associ-

---

[11] Cf. Giddens, 1985, whose otherwise excellent account minimizes the American experience.

ations – makes the nullity of these finite things an accomplished fact and brings it home to consciousness. (Hegel, 1952, para. 323)

A further implication of Hegel's view is that only individuals who are *leaders of states* are capable of influencing history so construed. As Hegel writes, 'what special course of action . . . is good or not, is determined, as regards the ordinary contingencies of private life, by the laws and customs of a State. . . . Each individual has his position' (1956, p. 29). Private morality is defined by 'society'. But, 'it is quite otherwise with the comprehensive relations that History has to do with. In this sphere are presented those momentous collisions between existing, acknowledged duties, laws, and rights.' These involve 'a general principle of a different order from that on which depends the permanence of a people or a State'.

This powerfully suggestive Machiavellian text shows also why it is that 'Historical men – *World-Historical Individuals*' are Hegel's focus. 'Historical men . . . are those in whose aims such a general principle lies' (p. 29). Hegel's first example is Caesar, his second is Alexander the Great, and his third is Napoleon. The idea that history *equals* political history *equals* narratives of the choices and decisions of leaders of states owes much to this Hegelian notion. But, more than this, Hegel may well have been the first to have seen that modern wars involve *everyone* in the state, and for this reason, that, while the decision to make war will be made by leaders of states, it will have to be made in the name of the state conceived as a substantial unity. Thenceforth, *Staatsräson* has a new meaning. The 'leader' of a 'nation' is not bound by the morality which governs the relations of his 'people', since it is his task to secure them *as a people*. The National Security State was, of course, the consequence.

As already suggested, Herder's metaphorical organism has become for Hegel, a definite metaphysical entity, a substantive unity. But this means as well that we can think of it as 'unfolding' in the strictest sense of that word. We have here true *immanence,* which we didn't with Herder's 'genetic forces'. The idea seems to have become almost common property, not only of Hegel, but of Fichte and Schelling before him and of Savigny, leader of the Historical School of Jurisprudence and Hegel's colleague at the newly formed University of Berlin. (See Wells, 1959, pp. 196ff., and Berlin, 1976, p. 198)

Hegel recurs to this idea in many places, but a clear statement may be offered from his *Philosophy of Right*:

The fundamental characteristic of the state as a political entity is the substantial unity, i.e., ideality, of its moments. . . . Much the same thing as this ideality of its moments in the state occurs with life in the physical organism. Life is present in every cell. There is only one life in all the cells and nothing withstands it. Separated from that life every cell dies. This is the same as the ideality of every single class, power, and Corporation. (Hegel, 1952, sec. 276, with its addition; cf. Mandelbaum, 1971, p. 184)

Organisms surely are substantial unities, and life is present in every cell. But, just as surely, the state is not a substantial unity and the *persons* who live *in* states can live without state. On the other hand, it is important to notice, as Mandelbaum does, that here, as in the *Philosophy of History,* there is an empirical component which ought not to be overlooked.

Hegel conceived of the state as an integrated system of institutions, rather than, as Hobbes and the tradition which followed him had seen it, an aggregation or aggregations of individuals acting in consort to satisfy individual interests. His view, though rooted in different metaphors, and grounded in an entirely different ontology, is very similar to the one held by Comte. It is important to see this, since it will play a very big part in explaining the ease with which American structural-functionalism can incorporate these two traditions.

But individuals effectively drop out. As noted, 'the cunning of Reason' allows Hegel to utterly discount the pertinence of individual goals and motivations for action. The larger design gets satisfied by the unintended consequences of individual actions by people acting within the institutional orders which are connected organically. In the last analysis, each person has a 'position' in an utterly *role-determined* system. Even world-historical individuals, by virtue of their position, are merely role-players in the drama of world history.

Finally, then, Hegel sees *empirically* that there is progress and that, as I noted at the beginning of the chapter, 'the history of the World is none other than the progress of the consciousness of freedom'. Hegel's view was no naive Eurocentrism – even if it was a Eurocentrism. The *telos* of history was not 'happiness' – to be purchased by our 'brandy and luxuries', but the *consciousness* of freedom, a consciousness which, for Hegel, would be realized in and through the state. It is not inappropriate to note here that the empirical Tocqueville had said much the same thing. In his new preface to *Democracy in America,* written in 1848 amid revolutionary upheavals in all of Europe, he reported that his book 'was written fifteen years ago with a mind constantly preoccupied with a single thought: the thought of the approaching and irresistible spread of democracy throughout the world'. That neither Hegel nor Tocqueville were democrats, either in Aristotle's sense or Rousseau's, tells us more about the words 'democracy' and 'freedom' than about their respective philosophies. Empirically, both may have been on to something, however much the *politics of the nation-state,* which they both took so thoroughly for granted, seems empirically to be leading us straight to nuclear holocaust. Yet Hegel would resist this conclusion, insisting that the evidence is not yet all in.

THE PHILOSOPHY OF HISTORY
AND THE SCIENCE OF HISTORY

I have emphasized that Hegel's *Philosophy of History* is meant to be an *empirical* argument in favor of his 'hypothesis', but it will not pay us to try to refute it empirically, either by critically examining his effort to trace the progress of the consciousness of freedom from the civilizations of the Chinese, the Indians, Persians, Greeks, and so on, or to point to twentieth-century genocide and the build-up of nuclear arms. For Hegel did not intend his account in *The Philosophy of History* to stand alone – empirically. His understanding of world history was rendered intel-ligible and *demonstrable* by 'philosophy'. In this sense, 'philosophy of history' is not science of history, if 'science' means 'empirical science', nor is it merely a philosophical framework, a 'methodology' for his-torical inquiry. It *is* that, but it is *more* than that. Rather, for Hegel, philosophy of history is an *alternative* to history – not antagonistic to it, of course, but nonetheless, an autonomous inquiry.

It is thus that we must understand the text just quoted regarding the 'ideality' of 'the moments' of the State. This is the language of Hegelian *dialectics,* the realization of the Idea:

> Universal history . . . shows the development of the consciousness of Freedom on the part of Spirit. . . . This development implies a graduation – a series of increasingly adequate expressions or manifestations of Freedom, which result from its Idea. The logical, and – as still more prominent – the dialectical nature of the Idea in general, viz., that it is self-determined – that it assumes successive forms which it successively transcends; and by this very process of transcending its earlier stages, gains an affirmation, and in fact, a richer and more concrete shape; – the necessity of its nature, and the necessary series of pure abstract forms which the Idea success-ively assumes – is exhibited in the department of *Logic.* (Hegel, 1956, p. 63)

This is hardly the place to attempt an explication of Hegel's *Logic* or to develop an analysis of how the self-determining Dialectic of Idea operates. We should notice, however, that Hegel's Absolute Idealism is a *realism* in the sense that the empirical (the phenomenal) is concrete and is the manifestation of the Idea, the abstract, which is nonetheless *real*. It is just in this sense that Plato is a realist. As Taylor says, 'Hegel's idealism, far from being a denial of external material reality, is the strongest affirmation of it; it not only exists but necessarily exists' (Taylor, 1975, p. 109). Hegel is also a 'rationalist' in the clear sense that Plato is a rationalist. While Hegel does not decry 'appearance', he affirms that knowledge is not *of* or *restricted* to the empirical. There is, for him, a reality which transcends appearance, and of which appearance is a manifestation. But this 'reality' is Idea. As Taylor remarks, 'Absolute idealism means that nothing exists which is not a manifestation of the Idea, that is, of rational necessity' (p. 110).

This, of course, was exactly the focus of 'materialist' criticism of Hegel, which will be discussed in the next chapter. We can summarize Hegel's philosophy of history as 'idealist' in at least three important senses:

1   It has the Idea of Freedom as the *telos* of history.
2   Hegel's *empirical* concern is with the realm of thought, the ideas, beliefs, or more generally, the culture and the 'spirit' of a State. These are embodied in institutions, to be sure and thus we cannot overlook institutions. But we investigate them so as to discover the norms, values, goals, and beliefs that people live by, to grasp what motivates them *by virtue of* their institutions and their roles in them.
3   The 'mechanisms' of historical process are to be found by philosophy – in the Dialectic of the Idea.

These ideas have had a surprising vitality, as we shall see. Long after 'social science' had rejected the third, it remained commited to the second, and perhaps also to the first. What Iggers (1968) calls 'The German Conception of History' (the topic of chapter 7) owes its existence to the second. And, as I shall argue, Max Weber and, later, Talcott Parsons are unintelligible without due acknowledgment of the power of that tradition.

In the next chapter, we turn, however, to the symmetrical idea of a materialist theory of history.

6

Scientific Socialism:
Marxian Dialectics

Recovering the intervention of Marx and Engels into the problem of defining a human science involves all the problems of recovering the thought of any of the figures discussed so far; but it is complicated by three additional difficulties. First, Marxism is a living doctrine or, better, a whole family of living doctrines. Many people identify themselves as Marxist social scientists, but, although they put forward an enormous range of ideas about what it means to be a Marxist, each is ready to vindicate his or her particular view on the basis of Marxist texts. But, compounding the difficulty is the fact that different interpretations give rise to different notions about what might constitute a *Marxist politics*. Marxism has never been merely an issue for 'academic' debate; from at least the second International on (1889–1914), these differences have had genuinely monumental practical consequences.[1]

Second, what came to be the dominant conception of 'Marxism' towards the end of Engels's life, but probably not before the Second International, had as its texts very little of what today we think of as the corpus. Before the publication of the *Marx–Engels Gesamtausgabe* between 1927 and 1932, not only were most of Marx's so-called early writings unknown – the critique of Hegel's philosophy of the state, the 1844 'Paris manuscripts', including the famous fragments on alienated labor, and the notebooks of the same year, including the now often quoted Theses on Feuerbach – but *The German Ideology,* written jointly by Marx and Engels between November of 1845 and October of 1846 had been left, unfinished and unpublished, 'to the gnawing criticism of the mice'. Further, the important *Grundrisse,* a massive work of Marx dating from 1857–8 and containing some sketchy but remarkable

---

[1] The flavor of what is meant here is caught by Stephen Cohen, 1974.

intimations of his philosophy of science, was not published until 1939–41.

Third, we have the problem of the collaboration of two authors, each with a singularly powerful mind, each producing separate manuscripts alongside their collaborative efforts. Engels, born two years after Marx, in 1820, outlived Marx, who died in 1883, by 12 years. As we shall see, the last 25 years or so of Engels's life were important to the project of defining what has to be termed 'orthodox Marxism', the Marxism of the USSR.[2]

What follows does not pretend to be a comprehensive account. I have focused on one theme, the idea of a materialist history. This does not mean that I discount or undervalue the doctrine of alienation or the critically important *Capital* or even the lesser-known but important political and historical writings – for example, the *Eighteenth Brumaire* or the writings on the Paris Commune. But in his *Anti-Dühring* (1878), a book which was enormously influential in the development of what became 'orthodox Marxism', Engels argued that 'socialism became a science' by virtue of two discoveries of Marx: 'the materialist conception of history and the revelation of the secret of capitalist production by means of surplus value' (Engels, 1939, p. 33). This chapter, then, makes the effort critically to comprehend materialist history.

MATERIALIST HISTORY

At the conclusion of chapter 5, I summarized Hegel's philosophy of history as idealist in three senses, briefly:

1   It had the Idea of Freedom as the *telos* of history.
2   Hegel's empirical concern was culture.
3   The mechanism of historical process was the Dialectic of the Idea.

Symmetrically, then, but in reverse order, we can say that a theory of history is materialist if:

1   The mechanisms of historical process are concrete mechanisms. 'Concrete' is meant in contrast to the abstractions of the Idea, and 'mechanism' may be illustrated by, for example, 'natural selection' in biological evolution.
2   One must consider as empirically pertinent facts other than, or in

---

[2] There is no fully satisfactory way to classify variants of 'Marxist' thought. 'Soviet Marxism' identifies a clear orthodoxy, but so-called 'Western Marxism' is useful mainly as a counter-term. For an interesting discussion, see Perry Anderson, 1976 and 1980. For a different point of view, see Andrew Arato and Paul Breines, 1979; also Mark Poster, 1975. Nor should we forget Chinese and other variants!

addition to, facts about culture, ideas, religion, and so on. One must consider, for example, the mode of production, 'what is produced and how it is produced'.

3 Either there is no *telos,* or if there is, it concerns the lawfulness of change rooted in the mechanisms of change.

It is perfectly clear that the first item was the point of departure for Marx and Engels. Moreover, their criticism of Feuerbach, the most important of the 'Young Hegelians', was that he had not gone far enough in his critique of Hegel, that he and the Young Hegelians had 'never left the realm of philosophy':

> Since the Young Hegelians regard concepts, thoughts, ideas, and all products of consciousness, to which they give independent existence, as the real fetters of man – while the Old Hegelians pronounced them the true bonds of human society – it is obvious that the Young Hegelians have to fight only against the illusions of consciousness. (Easton and Guddat, 1967, p. 407)

The Young Hegelians had rightly criticized Hegel's abstract dialectic of the Idea, but as the title of the joint work *The German Ideology* is meant to convey, and as the Preface to part I makes clear, the Young Hegelians were still 'philosophers'; they still dealt 'in the realm of pure thought'; they were concerned only with ideology – the illusions of consciousness, and in particular, of course, the illusions of religion. But, 'None of these philosophers ever thought to look into the connection between German philosophy and German reality, between their criticism and their own material environment' (1967, p. 408). They had all accepted the premises of 'philosophy'. The Old Hegelians celebrated, as Hegel said, 'the Right and Order' which 'ideas' had sustained, whereas the Young Hegelians found them to be 'fetters'. To be sure, Feuerbach had succeeded in his effort to 'unmask human self-alienation . . . in its *holy form,* but if it were to be unmasked in its unholy form, it would be necessary to examine the 'real relations' of people, not merely people's ideas about themselves. For Marx and Engels, then, it is not just ideas which need to be changed but the 'material environment' as well. It is thus that 'the philosophers have only interpreted the world in various ways; the point is, to change it' (1967, Theses on Feuerbach, p. 402).

It is just here that Marx and Engels abandon philosophy for science: 'We know only one science, the science of history. . . . We will have to discuss the history of man, since almost all ideology ["philosophy"] amounts to either a distorted interpretation of this history or a complete abstraction from it' (1967, p. 408). There follows the famous text:

The premises from which we start are not arbitrary . . . they are the real individuals, their actions, and their material conditions of life, those which they find existing as well as those which they produce through their actions. (pp. 408f.)

It must be emphasized that the 'materialism' in 'historical materialism' need not have any more content than what has just been suggested; that if one wants to understand history, one must look at the conditions of life – how people work, with what, how they are related, and so forth. It is not possible on his view to understand history via the abstractions of Hegelian dialectics or, as important, by looking only at *Geist,* the ideas which are expressed by 'real individuals'. It is worth noting that the phrases, 'historical materialism' and 'materialist conception of history' are not found in Marx's writings at all. Engels first used the latter expression in 1859, in a review of Marx's *Contribution to the Critique of Political Economy,* and the second, now taken to define scientific socialism, was first used in English in 1892, again by Engels.

But it would be an enormous mistake to suppose that ideas are irrelevant to materialist history. The point is not that ideas are irrelevant, or, as we shall see, that they are somehow 'reducible' to material conditions, but, as the text just quoted says, that ideas have no independent existence. Thus, as Marx and Engels have it: 'Consciousness can never be anything else except conscious existence, and the existence of humans is their actual life-process.' Hence,

The ideas which these individuals form are ideas either about their relation to nature, their mutual relations, or about their own nature. It is evident that in all these cases these ideas are the conscious expression – real or illusory – of their actual relationships and activities, of their production and commerce, of their social and political behavior. The opposite assumption is possible, only if, in addition to the spirit of the actual and materially evolved individuals, a separate spirit is presupposed. (1967, p. 414)

It may be, of course, that it is hard to believe that an entire philosophical and historical tradition exists which *either* explicitly affirms the independence of ideas or, as in much social science, carries on *as if* they had an independent existence. But otherwise, it is hard to see why this misunderstanding is so rampant. The idea that our ideas about ourselves, our politics and commerce, can be 'real or illusory' – true or false – is absolutely central to Marxism – and, as I shall argue in chapter 13, the possibility of distinguishing between true and false ideas about ourselves presupposes the possibility of a realist conception of social science.

More needs to be said about the 'materialism' in 'historical material-ism', but first, we shall note that although *The German Ideology* contains the *germs* of a materialist theory of history, it hardly contains anything like a complete account. Indeed, this is nowhere to be found! The *locus classicus* of the theory is in the Preface to *The Critique of Political Economy,* the book which, as I have noted, prompted the Engels review in which the term 'materialist conception of history' was used for the first time in print. However familiar this text may be, it still seems best to quote it almost in full:

> In the social production of their existence, people [*Menschen*] inevitably enter into definite relations, which are independent of their will, namely relations of production appropriate to a given stage in the development of their material forms of production. The totality of these relations of production constitutes the econ-omic structure of society, the real foundation, on which arises the legal and political superstructure and to which corresponds definite forms of social consciousness. The mode of production of material life conditions the general process of social, political and intel-lectual life. It is not the consciousness of people that determines [*bestimmt*] their existence, but their social existence that deter-mines their consciousness. At a certain stage of development, the material productive forces of society come into conflict with exist-ing relations of production or – this merely expresses the same thing in legal terms – with the property relations within the framework of which they have operated hitherto. From forms of development of the productive forces these relations turn into fetters. Then begins an era of social revolution. The changes in the economic foundations lead sooner or later to the transformation of the whole immense superstructure. (Marx, 1970, pp. 20f.)

The German *bestimmt,* usually translated 'determines', already creates problems since English speakers, influenced by the notion that causality means 'whenever this, then that', tend to think of determination as a sufficient condition, not, as here, as a direction, influence, constraint, or 'conditioning'. Thus, as already emphasized, the idea that 'social exist-ence' – not merely existence – 'determines their consciousness' means, at the very minimum, that ideas do not have an independent existence, that, as in Comte (above), the *forms* of consciousness and the particular beliefs of a social group are the outcome of everything true of their *social* lives – a fairly innocuous claim and, of course, the basic premise of any sociology of knowledge. It cannot mean that we need to look at people's brains!

It is also clear that the famous architectural metaphor of 'foundations' and 'superstructure' implies, at a minimum, that not any superstructure can be built on any foundation, but rather that the foundation constrains or limits the possible superstructure. But it might mean, *in addition,* that the foundation *causes* the superstructure in the sense that it brings it about. Indeed, this is the way it has often been read. Several of Engels's formulations provide support for this reading, especially his acknowledgment that once there is a superstructure, it can affect the foundation. On this reading, then, there is the possibility of mutual causality. But once this idea is allowed, the *primacy* of the foundation is threatened. I do not intend to pursue this problem here;[3] my aim, for the present, is simply to note that the idea of 'historical materialism' is anything but clear.

Another critical question is the very distinction between 'foundation' – the 'economic structure' – and superstructure. An excellent case can be made, I believe, for the view that Marx saw this distinction as restricted in application to a capitalist society, in which, as we have already seen, we can distinguish between 'civil society' and the state, and in which we can think of the production relations as straightforwardly constituted by the juridical relations of private property. But, as Marx seems to have discerned, the distinction is enormously complicated in pre-capitalist societies, in which it is hard to know what is not *essential* to the constitution of the production relations. The institutions of religion, for example, seem inseparable very often. But if so, is this 'foundation' or 'superstructure'?[4]

[3] This, of course, is the problem which generated the influential intervention of Althusser and Balibar, 1970.

[4] There is a great deal to suggest that Marx and Engels conceived of the foundation/superstructure distinction undogmatically. In *The German Ideology* they write:

> The fact is, then, that definite individuals who are productively active in a specific way enter into these definite social and political relations. In each particular instance, empirical observation must show empirically, without any mystification or speculation, the connection of the social and political structures with production (p. 413).

In a letter to Conrad Schmidt (1890), Engels notes that the materialist conception of history has 'a lot of friends . . . to whom it serves as an excuse for not studying history', and he repeats the famous remark of Marx, in the 1870s, that he was not a Marxist. Engels writes:

> All history must be studied afresh, the conditions of existence of the different formations of society must be individually examined before the attempt is made to deduce from them the political, civil-legal, esthetic, philosophic, religious, etc., notions corresponding to them. . . . But instead of this only too many of the younger Germans simply make use of the phrase, historical materialism . . . in order to get their own relatively scanty historical knowledge . . . fitted together into a neat system as quickly as possible. (Correspondence, pp. 472f.)

See Harrington, 1972. The problem has enormous implications for the study of pre-capitalist societies. The debate is brilliantly joined as regards ancient Greece and Rome in the writings of M. I. Finley, 1973, and G. E. M. de Ste Croix, 1981. See also Ernesto Laclau, 1971.

Finally, this text would seem to support a technologically determinist reading of historical materialism. Changes in 'material productive forces' come into conflict with 'production relations', and this causes changes in the whole superstructure. Thus, the 'motor' of history is technology. The idea is not restricted to the Preface, just quoted; it is found in the *Manifesto,* in which Marx and Engels write: 'the bourgeois by the rapid improvement of all the instruments of production . . . draws all . . . nations into civilization'. This view has never been short of defenders, and it constitutes the center of what might be called 'Second International Marxism', the Marxism which entered the twentieth century; and today it has its articulate, sophisticated defenders.[5] On the other hand, Engels refers to 'driving forces' (see below) and implies that the emphasis on 'the economic' was in response to those who failed to appreciate its importance in history. Indeed, there are pages and pages where there is no one driving force, where historical change is regarded as the result of 'innumerable intersecting forces, an infinite series of parallelograms of forces which give rise to one resultant – the historical event' (Marx and Engels, 1942, letter to Bloch). On this latter reading, then, people enter into 'definite relations' and these 'structure' their lives; but it may be that the 'structures' are more complicated than the Preface implies, and that, as Herder suggested, the 'forces' at work in history are more various than the simple schema of the Preface implies.

THE 'MATERIALISM' OF 'HISTORICAL MATERIALISM'

The problems of comprehending the Marxian materialist theory of history have been exacerbated, however, by some other pieces of unfinished business. I have in mind here the relationship of historical materialism to Hegel's dialectics *and* to the materialist critics of Marx and Engels. We can make an obvious transition to these problems by looking at an important text from Engels's *Ludwig Feuerbach and the Outcome of Classical German Philosophy* (1888), the last of Engels's reflections on the issues of this chapter:

> [People] make their own history, whatever its outcome may be, in that each person follows his consciously desired end, and it is precisely the resultant of these many wills operating in different directions and of their manifold effects upon the outer world that constitutes history.

So far, of course this could have been written by Hegel. So, too, the next few lines:

[5] See G. A. Cohen, 1978, and the critical review by Andrew Levine and Eric Olin Wright, 1980.

Thus it is a question of what the many individuals desire. The will is determined by passion or deliberation. But the levers which immediately determine passion and deliberation are of many different kinds. Partly they may be external objects, partly ideal motives, ambition, 'enthusiasm for truth and justice', personal hatred or even purely individual whims of all kinds.

Engels surely has rejected, in the manner of Herder, a Kantian notion of free will. The will is 'determined' in Aristotelian fashion by 'passion or deliberation'. Persons are 'motivated' – set in motion – for all sorts of *reasons*. This surely does not (yet) sound as if people are robots. The text continues:

But, we have seen that the many individual wills active in history for the most part produce results other than those they intended – often quite the opposite; their motives therefore in relation to the total result are likewise only of secondary significance.

The text is important, but not because it gives evidence regarding the question of whether people are robots. Rather, since unintended consequences are the stuff of history, we cannot explain what happens in history by appeal to the *reasons* which explain the actions of individuals. It is essential to see that this view is shared by the *idealist* Hegel and the *materialist* Engels. We should also stress that for Engels, motives are of 'secondary importance'. He does not say that they are of no importance, nor does he say that results are never as intended. More than motives are necessary if we are to explain history. It is here that Engels and Hegel part company; thus Engels:

On the other hand, the further question arises: what are the historical causes which transform themselves into these motives in the brains of the actors?
    The old materialism never put this question to itself. . . . On the other hand, philosophy of history, particularly as represented by Hegel, recognizes that the ostensible and also the real operating motives of men who figure in history are by no means the ultimate causes of historical events; that behind these motives are other moving forces, which have to be discovered. But it does not seek these forces in history itself, it imports them from outside, from out of philosophical ideology, into history. (Engels, 1935, p. 59)

Engels's objection to Hegel is clear enough, for his alternative is not. Indeed, the very formulation of the question, 'what are the historical causes which transform themselves into these motives in the brains of the actors?' is wildly misleading, for it offers that the problem is one of discovering not '*other* moving forces' in history, but the causes of the motives in the brains of the actors. Now 'old materialism', which I turn to next, *did* put *this* question to itself, a question which, as the foregoing makes clear, is utterly *irrelevant* to the problem at hand, the problem of explaining the movement of history. If unintended consequences are the stuff of history, then appeal to peoples' *intentions* cannot for the most part explain it, regardless of whether we can explain their intentions. Indeed, the question which the 'old materialists' did *not* ask, but which Hegel did, was the question of whether there are causes which are not reducible to individual motives. Hegel found these in philosophy, in the dialectic of the Idea. The question for 'materialist history' is, Is there any other place to look? I want to show now that Marx and Engels held that 'philosophy' in any of its forms could not answer this question, but that 'science' could. We need to show first that they recognized that 'old materialism' could not answer the question because it *could not have a viable concept of the social.*

THE ABANDONMENT OF PHILOSOPHY

An enormous amount of confusion has been generated by a failure to be historical as regards the genesis of Marxism. There are two respects to this failure. The most obvious is the failure characteristic of propagandists on both sides of the cold war ideology to define Marxism as a general philosophy, as so-called dialectical materialism. Dialectical materialism is a general philosophy, with an ontology, an epistemology, a philosophy of science, and all the rest, but while its roots are surely in Engels, it is a phenomenon of the 1890s, properly associated with Georgii Plekhanov (d. 1918), who popularized the term. The latter was evidently coined by Joseph Dietzgen in the 1870s (Jordan, 1967). Nevertheless – and this is crucial – Marx and Engels, from perhaps 1845 to the late 1870s were explicitly anti-philosophy. Like the positivists of the period, they were interested in distinguishing 'philosophy' from 'science', although as I said before, and will say again, the very idea of 'science' was still highly contestable.

This brings us to the second failure. 'Science' by then had become a *good thing.* There thus was a tendency to identify all sorts of inquiries in pursuit of 'knowledge' as scientific, an easy move, if we keep in mind the original sense of 'scientia'. But there was an increasing consensus that metaphysics, the pillar of traditional philosophy, was not science – or at least that it was not *empirical* science. Even Hegel, who continued to use the word *Wissen* to identify his inquiries, accepted the (fairly recent) distinction between empirical science and philosophy. Of course, unlike the positivist philosophers, he defended philosophy as an autonomous inquiry in pursuit of knowledge. The question, then, was whether the 'materialists' were scientists or philosophers? Were they, like Hegel, *metaphysicians,* standing alongside idealists, or were they aligned with anti-metaphysical positivists?

As we have already seen (chapter 1), the eighteenth century had left a muddle. On the one hand, the 'corpuscular philosophy' ('scientific atomism') had stimulated a host of 'materialisms'. These included the philosophies of Lamettrie, Baron d'Holbach, Pierre Cabinis, and many others. At the same time, the anti-metaphysical tension in Locke's *Essay* regarding 'substance' (see above) had been resolved in British and French empiricism – sensationalism. 'Substance' had been thrown out, and the knowable had been identified with what could be experienced, a view shared by Kant. By the time one gets to Comte and his near contemporary Hegel, metaphysics has become non-empirical, in the *new* sense of 'empirical', *and* anti-naturalistic. It has become 'transcendental', or *a priorist,* as, for example, in Hegel. But because of this, and despite their disclaimers, even anti-metaphysical positivists seemed for all the world to be materialists. If they were not idealists, indeed, what could they be? These writers include, for example, the 'ideologues' of France, Destutt de Tracy, among others, who, as noted earlier, stand behind St Simon and Comte. Completing the picture were the *new* materialists, the Young Hegelians, Feuerbach and company. This, I believe, was substantially Marx and Engels's understanding of the philosophical situation around 1845 (cf. Bender, 1983).

But for them, the issue was further complicated. As early as 1839 (in his notes for his doctoral dissertation), Marx had argued that of the two 'directions in philosophy', 'positive' and 'critical', only the latter was liberating. In their view, 'the positive philosophy' was incapable of overcoming the irrationalities then current. It was 'capable of achieving merely demands and tendencies whose form contradicts its meaning' (Easton and Guddat, 1967, p. 63) – an apt characterization, I think, of Comtean philosophy.

This analysis was extended by Marx and Engels in their collaboration entitled *The Holy Family* (1845). Here they linked their critique to 'the two tendencies in French materialism', both of which aimed at a supercession of philosophy. One tendency had its origins in Locke. Evidently, Marx and Engels had in mind here Condillac and the Ideologues mentioned above. This tendency 'leads directly to socialism'. It does so because:

> If [we] form all [our] knowledge, perception, etc. from the world of sense experience in the world of sense, then it follows that the empirical world must be arranged so that [an individual] experiences and gets used to what is truly human in it, that [one]

experiences [oneself] as [human]. (Easton and Guddat, 1967, p. 394)

Fourier 'proceeds directly' from this tendency in 'French materialism', as, one might add, Owen in England proceeded directly from Locke.

The other tendency in French materialism stemmed from Descartes. Marx and Engels called this 'mechanical materialism'. It 'merges into what is properly French *natural science*' (p. 388). As Descartes 'completely separated his physics from his metaphysics', 'his followers were by profession anti-metaphysicians, viz., *physicists*' (p. 388).

Marx and Engels find both tendencies 'progressive', this last as regards the development of 'positive science', the first as regards the attack on the eighteenth-century status quo. But materialism is severely limited. It becomes 'one-sided'.

> Sensuous knowledge loses its bloom and becomes the abstract sensuousness of the geometer. . . . Materialism becomes *misanthropic*. In order to overcome the misanthropic, incorporeal spirit of its own ground, materialism must mortify its own flesh and turn ascetic. (p. 391)

This is a powerful characterization *and* critique. The *matter and motion materialism* of the 'physicists' strips 'sensuous knowledge' of its 'bloom': the 'secondary qualities' are removed from the world, and physics becomes geometry. But, in addition, it becomes misanthropic in another sense: it is unable to say anything about *humanity, society, and history*, which is exactly the strength of the idealist Hegel! Indeed, if we look at the prevailing possibilties *within* philosophy – 'positive philosophy', French materialism, and Hegel and the Young Hegelians – it is small wonder that Marx and Engels should dispair of 'philosophy'. By 1843, at least, Marx's critique of the Young Hegelians had become a general criticism of philosophy.

In the writings of 1843 and thereafter, Marx argued that the philosophy of Feuerbach, itself an effort to overcome critically idealist extravagances, was not critical of itself. It never questioned, he insisted, its own presuppositions. In a well-known text, he argued that the demands of the 'critical critics', can only be realized 'by the negation of philosophy as philosophy' (Easton and Guddat, 1967, p. 256). This 'negation of philosophy as philosophy' had, as we shall see, enormous consequences. It was easy to believe, for example, that Marx had repudiated all that he had derived from Hegel, and that the later 'scientific writings' had made an 'epistemological break' with the earlier 'philosophical' writings. The half-truth in this is that, thereafter, having 'settled accounts' with 'the German ideology', Marx no longer wrote 'philosophy' or concerned himself with the 'problems' thereof, in particular, with those of epistemology or ontology. From then on he would do 'science'.

But two problems went unnoticed, problems which by the 1870s had become very clear to Engels. First, they had not escaped *having* an epistemology or an ontology, and, second, there remained a host of unresolved questions regarding what *science was*. From the *Communist Manifesto* (1848) on, it was clear that the socialism of Marx and Engels was to be a scientific socialism, but if, as I have been arguing, the very idea of science was contestable, still more, the idea of a science which was linked to revolution, and if Marx and Engels were not to address these issues, then 'Marxism' would be – and is – subject to some profoundly *different* understandings. Historical materialism as *the* science of history was not self-explanatory. Of especial importance in this regard was the epistemology and ontology of such a science. If it was not an idealism *or* a materialism, then what was it? And indeed, what exactly was the epistemological content of the famous, but tantalizing, fragments of the Theses on Feuerbach? If it be granted that the 'chief defect of all previous materialism (including Feuerbach's) is that the object, actuality, sensuousness is conceived only in the form of the object or perception, but not as sensuous human activity, practice [*praxis*], not subjectively', what is the payoff for *science*? Finally, there are the recurring references to 'dialectics', with the equally adamant disclaimers of its Hegelian heritage. Again, what was the upshot for the 'one human science', historical materialism? As I said, by the 1870s, all these questions had become clear to Engels.

ENGELS'S BELATED EFFORT TO FILL THE GAPS

The motivation for Engels's belated discovery was that the attacks on Marx and Engels by socialists were becoming increasingly influential, especially in Germany (Stedman Jones, 1973). These socialists, Eugen Dühring among them, were *materialists,* committed to the idea that 'science' was the only way to truth and that the truths of science showed that nature, including people and society, could be fully comprehended only in terms of a materialist – reductionist – ontology and epistemology. Engels's *Anti-Dühring* or, to give it its full title, *Herr Eugen Dühring's Revolution in Science* (1877–8) was Engels's first effort to meet this challenge. A second book, written in the mid-1870s and published posthumously as *The Dialectics of Nature* (1927), was conceived originally as 'anti-Bücher'. Büchner was another important materialist of the day, whose *Force and Matter* (1855) should be mentioned; others were

Karl Vogt (a member, says Engels, of 'the unthinking mob') and Jacob Moleschott.

A third book of the period, Engels's *Ludwig Feuerbach and the Outcome of Classical German Philosophy* (1888) aimed to provide 'a connected account of our relation to the Hegelian philosophy, of our point of departure as well as of our separation from it' (1888, p. 16). By this time, it was clear to Engels that he needed to articulate how 'scientific socialism' differed from both 'old materialism' and Hegelianism, young and old.

After retiring from business in 1870, Engels reported that he 'went through as complete as possible a "moulting" . . . in mathematics and the natural science' (Engels, 1939, p. 15). His motivation was clear enough. If he was to demonstrate that scientific socialism was scientific, he had to know what, in fact, science was. The period, of course, was an amazingly productive one for science. Chemistry had emerged and was making remarkable advances; the cell had been discovered; the transformation of energy had become a key idea in physics, and evolutionary biology had captured the imagination of almost everybody. The question for Engels was, did the breakthrough which he and Marx had achieved in human science have the same status as these achievements in natural science; and if so, what were the methodological, epistemological, and ontological premises which made this so? Engels was clear that these were philosophical questions.

In his *Dialectics of Nature,* he wrote that 'natural scientists believe that they free themselves from philosophy by ignoring it or abusing it' (1940, p. 183). But they are mistaken since, 'without thought', they make no headway. They unreflectively take their categories 'from the common consciousness of so-called educated persons', but this is 'dominated by the relics of long obsolete philosophies'. Or, alternatively, they appropriate their ideas 'from the little bit of philosophy compulsorily listened to at the University', which, he hastens to add, is 'not only fragmentary, but also a medley of views of people belonging to the most varied and usually worst schools'. Or finally, their ideas come from 'uncritical and unsystematic reading of philosophical writings of all kinds' (1940, p. 183). Indeed, 'those who abuse philosophy most are slaves to precisely the most vulgarized relics of the worst philosophies' (1940, p. 184). Given what was then happening to 'Marxism' as a science, Engels had surely to regret his earlier disavowal of philosophy *qua* philosophy.

Engels was a better-than-average philosopher, and he had done his homework. In *Ludwig Feuerbach,* referring explicitly to Hegel's refutation of both Hume and Kant, he writes: 'the chemical substances produced in the bodies of plants and animals remained just . . . "things-in-themselves" until organic chemistry began to produce them one after another, whereupon the "thing-in-itself" [became] a thing for us' (Engels, 1935, p. 33).

On the other hand, Engels foundered badly on the ancient problem of the relation between concept and reality, between knowing and being. *The Dialectics of Nature* is filled with fragmentary, unclear attempts to clarify this problem, all couched in the language of Hegel. But perhaps the clearest statement of his position is to be found in a letter of 1895 to Conrad Schmidt:

> The identity of thought and being, to express myself in Hegelian fashion, everywhere coincides with your example of the circle and the polygon . . . the concept of a thing and its reality run side by side like two asymptotes always approaching each other yet never meeting. . . . But although a concept has the essential nature of a concept and cannot therefore *prima facie* directly coincide with reality, from which it must first be abstracted, it is still more than a fiction, unless you are going to declare all the results of thought fictions because reality has a long way to go round before it corresponds to them, and then only . . . with asymptotic approximation. (Marx and Engels, 1942, p. 527)

It is hard to see what is to be made of the idea that the concept cannot 'directly coincide with reality?' Does it then *in*directly coincide? But what could this mean? How is this 'correspondence' to be established, and how are we to know that 'concept' and 'reality' are asymptotically approaching? This is, we should emphasize, a crucial question for the *realist,* which Engels surely is. But while he fails to solve this problem – it was solved by his near contemporary Helmholtz, as I shall argue – he surely has a point that either all 'the results of thought' are 'fictions', or we must find some way to discriminate between those which are and those which are not. In the absence of a healthy concept of reality, there is simply *no* way to do this.

Engels was also clear that the materialism of Dühring, Büchner, and others, like 'classical French materialism' (before Hume), was restricted by the level of natural science in the eighteenth century, the billiard-ball geometrical mechanics of the new physics.

> [The] exclusive application of the standards of mechanics to the processes of chemical and organic nature – in which processes it is true, the laws of mechanics are also valid, but are pushed into the background by other and higher laws – constitutes a specific but at that time inevitable limitation of classical French materialism. (1935, p. 37)

This is as clear a statement as one could have of the notion of a *stratified* reality, comparable to that articulated by Comte. The laws of mechanics are valid and do not cease to be determining at the chemical and organic levels. But at each of these levels, there are new (emergent) laws to be taken into consideration.

Moreover, there was 'a second specific limitation of this materialism'. It lay 'in its inability to comprehend the universe as a process – as matter developing in an historical process' (1935, p. 37). Engels's language is inexact and is open to various interpretations, but it seems that he is putting forward the view that 'in historical process' there is genuine novelty. Like Spencer (see above), he speaks of 'a long sequence of development from the simple to the complex'. 'Process' as conceived by the old materialism did not allow for genuine novelty, since it served only 'to produce the same results over and over again' (1935, p. 37).

But these altogether sensible ideas were obscured by arguing that the limitations of the old materialism could be overcome by a *dialectical philosophy* which, unlike the Hegelian, would be truly scientific. As Bhaskar has noted, 'dialectics' is 'possibly the most contentious topic in Marxist thought, raising two main issues on which Marxist philosophical discussion has turned, viz., the nature of Marx's debt to Hegel and the sense in which Marxism is a science' (Bottomore, 1983, p. 122).

It is not my intention to try to settle these issues, although there is no avoiding taking a position, and a few points seem clear enough. First, from beginning to end, Marx was, as Bhaskar writes, 'critical of the Hegelian dialectic as such and yet believed himself to be working with a dialectic related to the Hegelian one' (1983, p. 123).[6] Second, Engels's writings of the 1870s and after provided a definite, if unclear, theory of dialectics in which it is conceived as 'the science of the general laws of motion and development of nature, human society and thought' (Engels, 1939, p. 155). According to Engels, these general laws can be 'reduced' to three: the law of the transformation of quantity into quality, and *vice versa*; the law of the interpenetration of opposites; [and] the law of the negation of the negation (Engels, 1940, p. 26). These are all in Hegel, of course, but Hegel's 'mistake lies in the fact that these laws are foisted on nature and history and laws of thought, and not deduced [inferred] from them' (1940, p. 26). Third, the evidence, though slight, would seem to show that Marx was in agreement with at least 'the general thrust of Engels's intervention' (Bhaskar, in Bottomore, 1983, p. 127). Of

---

[6] Bhaskar, 1979 and 1983, has provided what in my view is the most adequate account of dialectics in Marx and of its proper application. This is not, I should emphasize, historical materialism, but the brilliant 'triple critique' of *Capital*, vol. 1. See also Sayer, 1979, a systematic reconstruction of Marx's philosophy of science. It is, however, a reconstruction. The *Grundrisse* is extremely important for this project, a work not known until 1939–41.

course, this has been important in the twentieth century in rationalizing 'dialectical materialism' as the official philosophy of Marxism. But even so, as regards historical materialism, dialectics has a relatively clear and uncomplicated sense and application. Consider in this regard the familiar passage from *Capital*: quoted in the *Anti-Dühring*

> That which is now to be appropriated is no longer the laborer working for himself, but the capitalist expropriating many laborers. This expropriation is accomplished by the actions of the immanent laws of capitalist development. One capitalist kills many. Hand and hand with this centralization develops, on an ever increasing scale, the cooperative forms of labor process. . . . Along with the constantly diminishing number of magnates of capital . . . grows the mass of misery, oppression, slavery, degradation, exploitation; but with this too grows the revolt of the working class, a class always increasing in numbers, and disciplined, united, organized by the very mechanism of the process of capitalist productivity itself. The monopoly of capital becomes a fetter upon the mode of production. . . . Centralization of the means of production and socialization of labor at last reaches a point where they become incompatible with their capitalist integument. This integument is burst asunder. The knell of capitalist private property sounds. The expropriators are expropriated. (Engels, 1939, citing *Capital,* vol. I, ch. XXXII)

In response to Dühring's attack on 'dialectic', Engels asks, 'where are the dialectical frills and mazes and intellectual arabesque; where the mixed and misconceived ideas as a result of which everything is all one in the end; where the dialectical miracles for [Marx's] faithful followers; where the mysterious dialectical rubbish' (Engels, 1939, pp. 146f.). And surely Engels is not mistaken in this. At least here there is no 'dialectical rubbish' or 'dialectical miracles' in which the contradiction of 'thesis-antithesis' magically brings forth 'the synthesis'. Capitalist production gave rise – because of what it is – to conditions which threaten it, period.

Engels insists that in contrast to Hegel, Marx proceeded empirically, 'on the basis of historical and economic facts'. The 'contradictions' of capitalist society are specific and are inherent in concrete reality – not in the Idea. The processes which define its movement create problems that are soluble only by transforming the system of processes. This is 'the negation of the negation' in capitalist society.

This 'negation of the negation' is an 'extremely general . . . law of development', which 'holds good in the animal and plant kingdoms, in geology, in mathematics, in history and philosophy'. But, says Engels, it does not 'say anything concerning the particular processes of development' (Engels, 1939, p. 154), nor for the same reasons does it say anything about the particular mechanisms of these particular processes. Marx proceeded 'empirically'; so does the geologist, the biologist, and so on.

We should here be struck by the comparison with Spencer's super-generalizations, also universally pertinent. But if this allows Engels to respond to Dühring's charges that no 'miracles' are involved, that in each case the problem is to discover empirically the particular mechanisms which instantiate these 'laws', then the most obvious objection is the utter vacuousness of 'the laws of dialectics' – not their mystery. Unfortunately, Marxists have been quick to gloss over their ignorance of specific mechanisms and to cut off criticism of their confidence in the 'laws' of development by appeal to the 'dialectical character' of the 'totalities' in question. In this sense, Dühring's criticisms have real force. 'Dialectic' becomes a polemical counter to 'old materialism', and as Dühring charged, the talisman linking Marx's 'faithful followers'. How many Marxists have accused their comrades – and others – of a failure to be 'sufficiently dialectical'?

MATERIALIST DIALECTICS OF PROGRESS?

No doubt Hegel's philosophy of history had a *telos*. But does the materialist history of Marx and Engels? The text just quoted by Engels from *Capital* has the negation of the negation leading to proletarian revolution. But Engels insists that, 'in characterizing the process as the negation of the negation, Marx does not dream of attempting to prove . . . that the process was historically necessary'. The text is important:

> On the contrary, after he has proved from history that in fact the process has partially already occurred, and partially must occur in the future, he then characterizes it as a process which develops in accordance with a definite dialectical law. That is all. (Engels, 1939, p. 147)

Is Marx's method wholly retrodictive and empirical? Is Engels implying that capitalism need not have occurred, but given that it did, we can explain its emergence? If so, then perhaps nothing is inevitable in history; everything could have been other than it was. Similar consider-ations apply to the development of capitalism's future and to what follows it. Surely the developments explained by Marxism, monopoly and centralization of the means of production, increasing proletarianiz-ation, and so forth, have 'partially' occurred, but what does it mean to say that the process 'partially must occur in the future'?

One interpretation might be that in capitalist society something approximating centralization and so on will continue, and that some sort of revolutionary movements will attend this, the result being some kind of transformation of capitalist society. This is vague, of course, but it is not utterly void of content. A second interpretation is more interesting – as well as being fully consistent with Marx's *realist* understanding of classical political economy.[7] On this view, in capitalist society there are processes governed by law, real tendencies which exist by virtue of the social relations which define capitalism. But *how* those processes develop and, especially, *what* actually results is *in principle not predictable.* While there is necessity, with its 'iron laws', there is also in history radical contingency, a straightforward consequence of the fact that there are 'innumerable intersecting forces, an infinite series of parallelograms which give rise to one resultant – the historical event' (letter to Bloch). The analogy to natural science is exact: theory tells us that it is necessary that bodies in free fall fall at the rate of $\frac{1}{2}at^2$; but of course, bodies never fall at $\frac{1}{2}at^2$ because they are never in free fall. What they actually do is a result of necessity *and* the infinity of circumstances in which bodies fall – that is, what actually happens is contingent.

On this understanding, the process laws of capitalism are laws, just as there are process laws, presumably, of other 'systems'. But this is not sufficient for a theory of *historical change,* since, while we can explain what did happen (given an understanding of the pertinent laws and contingencies), we cannot say that it had to happen or what *will* happen. It could have been the case, for example, that under circumstances other than those which in fact existed in Western Europe between the eleventh and sixteenth centuries, something other than capitalism *would* have emerged, just as today it may be that under circumstances not now known (or knowable), the process laws of capitalism will *not* lead to proletarian revolution.

So conceived, there is an exact parallel to biological evolution, properly understood, an analogy discerned by a reviewer of Marx's *Capital,* when he said:

> The scientific value of such an inquiry lies in the disclosing of the special laws that regulate the origin of existence, development and death of a given social organism and its replacement by a higher one. (Quoted in *Capital,* preface to the 2nd edition, 1970b)

The reference to 'the replacement by a higher one' spoils this, as perhaps Marx sees. After telling us that the writer has but 'pictured' the 'dialectic method', Marx writes:

[7] See Derek Sayer, 1979, and Anwar Schaikh, 1981.

Of course the method of presentation must differ from that of inquiry. The latter has to appropriate the material in detail, to analyse its different forms of development, to trace its inner connections. Only after the work is done, can the actual movement be adequately described.

This is no minor point regarding the organization of Marx's book. The point rather is this: as with biological evolution, we can – if but incompletely – reconstruct what *did* happen. That is, once we have an understanding of the operative mechanisms, *and* once we have established the contingent circumstances on which these operated, we can then explain what in fact occurred. The method is wholly retrodictive and empirical. 'After the work is done', *then* 'the actual movement' can be 'adequately described'. In no way does this imply that there is some invariable sequence of stages through which either organisms – or social systems – must pass; the pattern, if there is such, can be explained, but it could not have been predicted. Indeed, Marx could not have made it any clearer when in 1877 he wrote as follows to the editor of the Russian *Otyecestvenniye Zapisky*:

> [My critic] feels himself obliged to metamorphose my historical sketch of the genesis of capitalism in Western Europe into a historico-philosophic theory of the *marche générale* imposed by fate upon every people, whatever the historic circumstances in which it finds itself, in order that it may ultimately arrive at the form of economy which will ensure, together with the greatest expansion of the productive powers of social labor the most complete development of man. But I beg his pardon.
> ... Events strikingly analogous but taking place in different historic surroundings led to totally different results. By studying each of these forms of evolution separately and then comparing them one can find the clue to this phenomenon, but one will never arrive there by the universal passport of a general historico-philosophical theory, the supreme virtue of which consists in being superhistorical. (Marx and Engels, 1942, pp. 353–5)

I have argued that the historical materialism of Marx and Engels did not inevitably involve a materialist alternative to Hegelian teleological history, and that there were, for them, no *historical* laws, dialectical or otherwise. But there is no getting around the *rhetoric* of so much of the corpus. In *The German Ideology, The Manifesto,* and even *Capital,* Marx and Engels, the proponents of eighteenth-century 'stage theories' and Comte, speak of 'progressive stages', from 'lower to higher', from 'tribal ownership' to 'ancient communal and state ownership' to feudalism and capitalism and thence to socialism. And it was clear to them that

'Socialism *will* come'. The revolution of the proletariat is 'inevitable', and on and on. These claims and forms of utterance suggest that Marx and Engels – like Comte, Hegel, Spencer, Darwin, and indeed all nineteenth-century thinkers – did not free themselves from the idea that human progress was inevitable. Convinced, as they plainly were, that capitalism had established conditions for overcoming scarcity, that there were inherent contradictions in it, and that socialist revolution was imminent, they can easily be read as holding an immanentist view of history, complete with an eschatology. Indeed, while, as I have argued, there was a clear analogy to biological evolution, *properly understood,* Engels's famous graveside speech must surely have fuelled a positivist understanding of the Marxist 'laws of development'.[8] By the end of the nineteenth century, especially with the work of Plekhanov, Marxism came to have many of the features of a Comtean positivism joined with a Spencerian monism. It can hardly be doubted that Engels's unclear, belated, and inadequate philosophy of science had much to do with this. The formal consequences of his appropriation of Hegelian dialectic issued in a monistic hypernaturalism, comparable in many ways to that 'old materialism' which Engels had set out to refute, and finally in the absolutistic, dogmatic closure of Marxism in Soviet Marxism, the outcome of which we have not even begun to get behind us.

Herder's ideas did not, and perhaps could not, sustain a viable conception of a historical human science. Neither did the Dialectic of the Idea of Hegel. It may be that at a different time and place, the ideas of Marx and Engels could have sustained such a conception. In the next chapter, I turn to a third concurrent stream in German thought, the German conception of history which derives from von Humboldt and Ranke, includes the 'Historical School of Political Economy', and extends ultimately to Max Weber.

---

[8] Engels said: 'Just as Darwin discovered the law of development of organic nature, so Marx discovered the law of development of human history' (quoted by Mandelbaum, 1971, p. 76). Mandelbaum, whose account has substantially influenced my own, argues that Marx 'did not formulate any ultimate laws concerning the sequence of phases through which societies must necessarily pass' (p. 73), but concludes that Engels did. I have argued that neither did, although the case is less clear as regards Engels. Mandelbaum cites two texts which he takes to be decisive in this regard; but a close reading shows that they are not. It is one thing to argue that history is intelligible and another to accept that it is so by virtue of the lawfulness of historical change.

7

From Ranke to Max Weber

In the previous two chapters, we have looked at German attempts to develop theories of history, theories in which history was conceived as the unifying discipline of the human sciences, if not the exclusive human science. In this chapter we shall continue our review by discussing Ranke, Dilthey, Schmoller, and Max Weber. These thinkers represent, alongside Hegel and the Marxists, the third branch of nineteenth-century German conceptions of social science.

This chapter has three goals: to characterize 'historicism' and its 'crisis', at the end of the century; to argue that Schmoller and the 'Historical School of Political Economy' offered a viable alternative to classical political economy and that Max Weber played a key role in burying this alternative; and finally, and not unrelated to the first two goals, to give an account of Weber's profoundly ambiguous role in the genesis of modern sociology. While Weber is always associated with 'the theory of action', I contend that this is an error, that in fact, Weber continued, even as he altered, the tradition of German historical social science. In particular, the notion of 'ideal-types' arrived at by engaging the German historical tradition from Ranke to Dilthey, was Weber's way of making history intelligible without importing into his inquiry the idealist metaphysics of that tradition.

THE HISTORICAL SCIENCE OF RANKE

We may begin with a historical howler: the idea that Leopold von Ranke (1795–1886) is 'the prototype of the nontheoretical' and 'politically neutral' historian – and as Herbert B. Adams, writing in 1884 in the brand new *Johns Hopkins University Studies in History and Political*

Science, said, 'the father of scientific history'. Ranke earned the title, according to Adams, because he was 'determined to hold strictly to the facts of history, to preach no sermon, to point to no moral, to adorn no tale, but to tell the simple historic truth' (quoted from Iggers, 1983, pp. 63f.). As has been repeated many times over, for Ranke, the sole task of the historian was to give an account of things as they really are – *wie es eigenlich gewesen.*

The famous phrase, it seems, was originally used by Wilhelm von Humboldt in his important programmatic essay 'On the Historian's Task' (1821). But neither von Humboldt, the originating force behind the new University of Berlin, or Ranke were 'the soulless positivists' that Adams and a train of others supposed they were. Adams, a force in the institutionalization of history in America, had ideas about the nature of a scientific history which were utterly alien to Ranke, who, for all the world, was as metaphysical as you can get and whose inquiries were as politically committed as can be.

When Ranke joined the faculty of the University of Berlin in 1824, Hegel held a chair in philosophy, Schleiermacher taught theology, and Frederich Carl von Savigny and Karl Friedrich Eichorn, founders of the 'Historical School of Jurisprudence', held forth in the Faculty of Law. The group which included Schleiermacher, Savigny, and Eichorn was aligned with the famous Göttingen philologists Friedrich August Wolf and August Bockh, who had pioneered rigorous philological criticism of classical sources. This larger group, which Ranke joined, stood in opposition to Hegel and his dedicated legions, including Heinrich Leo, who had attacked Ranke's first book in an unsympathetic review. Leo's critical remarks were not directed at Ranke's 'empiricism', however. On the contrary, as Iggers reports, 'Leo based his criticism on grounds that Ranke would have accepted. . . . Ranke's style was poor . . .; he had introduced sentimentality into his narration, and lacked critical judgment in the use of his sources' (Iggers, 1983, p. 67). This was no 'philosopher' challenging a 'historian' for lack of 'philosophy'. Indeed, the disagreement between the opponents was in no way a disagreement between empirically oriented scientific historians and idealist philosophers, for none of them decried philosophy, and they all shared a set of basic convictions which today we think of as metaphysically idealist. These included the view that 'history is a meaningful drama'; that 'nation, people, state' are identical and historically unique; that, as against empiricism, there is a deeper reality behind concrete historical phenomena, a reality which it is the task of the historian to discover; and, finally, as Ranke put it, that 'the historian is merely the organ of the general spirit which speaks through him and takes a real form' (quoted by Iggers, 1983, p. 77).

A brief sketch of some of Ranke's key methodological and philo-sophical assumptions may help give the foregoing some substance. First, there is a central distinction which has a long history, running straight through to Max Weber and central to his concerns. Ranke wrote: 'There are two ways of acquiring knowledge about human affairs – through the penetration of the particular and through abstraction. The one is the way of philosophy, the other that of history (Iggers, 1973, p. 30). Herder had, in effect, rejected 'the way of philosophy', by this time resuscitated by Hegel. Ranke takes his stand with the way of history, of course, but his neo-Platonism is crystal clear, nonetheless.

Historical understanding is of the concrete, but it is of the uniqueness of a 'nation'. 'Facts' are crucial in getting at this, but there is a 'meaningful unity' which is *not* empirically evident. *Wie es eigenlich gewesen* does *not* refer to a purely 'factual' representation of the past, but to the past in its *essence* – the older meaning of *eigenlich gewesen*. As Humboldt had already said:

> An event . . . is only partially visible in the world of the senses; the rest has to be added by intuition, inference, and guesswork. The manifestations of an event are scattered, disjoined, isolated; what it is that gives unity to this patchwork, puts the isolated fragments into its proper perspective, and gives shape to the whole, remains removed from direct observation.

Accordingly, the historian

> must separate the necessary from the accidental, uncover inner structure, and make visible the truly activating forces.

The 'study of Ideas', *Ideenlehre,* makes history and philosophy co-incident:

> If philosophy were what it ought to be, if history were perfectly clear and complete, then they would fully coincide with each other. Historical science would permeate its subject with the spirit of philosophy. (In Iggers, 1973, p. 44, *passim,* from 'On the Historian's Task')

Ranke and Hegel share in the criticism of 'those historians who view all history merely as an immense aggregation of facts', just as they share the idea that discerning the underlying reality of history and its meaning is the task of the historian. What then is the disagreement between them? Ranke is suspicious of Hegel's effort to impose *a priori* principles on history and distrusts the tendency of 'philosophy' to minimize 'the reality of fact'. Moreover, and perhaps more important, he departs from Hegel (and moves toward St Augustine) in holding that we cannot fully grasp the meaning of history – 'Only God knows world history' – and in holding, *contra* Hegel, that the 'cunning of Reason' is predicated on 'a supremely unworthy conception of God and of Humanity'.

Other notions of Ranke's sound distinctly Hegelian:

> No state ever existed without a spiritual basis and spiritual content. In power itself a spiritual essence manifests itself. An original genius, which has its own life, fulfills conditions more or less peculiar to itself. It is the task of history to observe this life. (In Iggers, 1973, p. 80)

Ranke's 'state' is no Herderian *Volk,* and it is hardly surprising that the *Machtstaat,* best represented, as Iggers says, by the Hohenzollern monarchy of Prussia, is a distinctive feature of nineteenth-century German historiography. Political history *was* history.

Finally, while Ranke and those who followed him were 'historicists', because they were *also* neo-Platonists, they were also historical optimists. The point is important and is sometimes missed. 'Historicism' is a very ambiguous term. Let us take it here to refer to the idea that all concrete existence is historical, that history is a flux, and that all human ideas and values have a historical character. It may be, accordingly, that they have *nothing but* a historical character, and that therefore there are no transcendent or eternal norms or standards. In this sense, of course, both Marx and Herder are historicists. By 'Platonism' I shall mean the idea that, independent of concrete existence, there are transcendent 'Ideas', – or at least, norms and values. This notion does join coherently with historicism. One need only argue that it is in history that 'real value' and 'divine Will' are 'expressed' or manifested. When historicism rejects Platonism, there is a 'crisis', or so it has seemed to many. Once Hegelian ontology is rejected, the grounds for historicist optimism evaporate. Historical relativism and the meaninglessness of history are the consequences.

Roughly this is what seems to have happened. From Ranke to Droysen, Treitschke, and Meinecke, historicism was optimistic. As Iggers notes, none of the German 'liberal historians, – not Droysen or Sybel or Treitschke – thought of themselves as Hegelian. All rejected Hegel's systematic philosophy and 'his schematization of history'. But they all 'accepted his concept of the ethical character of the state and the meaningful development of history' (Iggers, 1983, p. 95). That they could do so was precisely *because* of the shared and taken-for-granted Hegelian *ontology.* It was thus not surprising, as Iggers rightly notes, 'that the "moderately liberal" historians could make their peace with Bismarck as easily as they did' (p. 119). Confident in the 'mission' of the state, German historians could applaud the 'reality' which Bismarck brought to the German 'nation'. Moreover, as everyone knew, 'democracy' was a confusion: 'sovereignty of the people' indeed!

But in the last quarter of the century a host of writers rattled the foundations of German historical optimism. With the coming of World War I the game was over. Iggers points out that, until quite late, German historical thought remained 'surprisingly immune' to the widespread disquiet. In Germany, Schopenhauer and, still more, Nietzsche had attacked Hegelian history and Hegelian ontology. Jakob Burckhardt in Switzerland, 'isolated among German-language historians', was critical of the idea of 'a wise "economy" in world history' (p. 129). And, of course, the poets and novelists of the period – Baudelaire, Proust, Dostoevsky – were each diagnosing the profoundly irrational character of humankind, the tragedy of human history, and the futility of reconstructive dreams.[1]

DILTHEY AND THE DILEMMAS OF HISTORICISM

Many of the tensions of this shift from optimism to pessimism are reflected in the work of Wilhelm Dilthey (1831–1911). His writings made their greatest impact only after World War I, the war that killed German idealist philosophy *and* German historical science. Nevertheless, Dilthey's *Introduction to the Geisteswissenschaften* (1883) – the German is deliberately preserved – was, as Max Weber says, 'the first comprehensive outline of a logic of the *non*natural sciences' (Weber, 1975, p. 94). It provides an ideal basis for discussion of a set of problems seen by some of Germany's most prominent intellectuals writing in the last two decades of the nineteenth century.

In Dilthey's view, the sciences had emancipated themselves from metaphysics; yet the human sciences were still struggling to identify themselves. From the eighteenth century, the latter had been dominated by the paradigm of natural science, and while 'the historical school' had brought about 'the emancipation of historical consciousness and historical science', they continued to lack a 'philosophic basis' (*philosophische Grundlegung*). It is clear that Dilthey wanted to rule out metaphysics as a ground for human science, and, in particular, that he rejected both the metaphysics of Hegel and of 'materialism'. What, then, could serve? Dilthey found the answer in epistemology, in particular, in 'consciousness': 'All experience has its original connectedness (*Zusammenhang*) in the conditions of our consciousness in which it appears, in the totality of our nature' (quoted from Iggers, 1983, p. 133). This gives Dilthey a way to distinguish sharply between two *kinds* of

[1] See, in addition to Iggers, 1983, H. Stuart Hughes, 1958; Gerhard Masur, 1961; Arnold Brecht, 1959; Fritz Ringer, 1969.

knowledge or science, *Naturwissenschaften* and *Geisteswissenschaften*. They are radically different because they rest on radically different 'foundations'. Moreover, while there are various human sciences, all, because they are concerned with 'historical social realities', require a distinct mode of historical analysis.

It is absolutely crucial to see the sense in which Dilthey's view is anti-metaphysical. For him, as for the positivists and neo-Kantians, all reality 'behind' phenomena is inaccessible to cognition. This means that knowledge of nature is severely constrained: 'We do not know of this external world through inferences from effect to causes or some corresponding process' (Dilthey, 1976, p. 162). Thus, 'phenomena' can be ordered, but their causes cannot be known. The 'thing-in-itself', nature apart from our consciousness, is unknowable. But this is not true of *Geisteswissenschaften*, since the data of the human sciences are the data of consciousness, and these may be known *directly*. As Iggers says:

> Understanding (*Verstehen*) is possible in the *Geisteswissenschaften* because life 'objectifies' itself in such institutions as the family, civil society, state and law, art, religion and philosophy. As products of life and spirit, these institutions can be understood. (1983, p. 139)

In the *Geisteswissenschaften*, we are not dealing with 'representations' of an unknowable external reality, but with the objects of consciousness themselves. In effect, there is no subject/object duality in the *Geisteswissenschaften*: 'The facts of our consciousness are nothing else but that of which we become conscious. Our hopes and aspirations, our wishes and desires, this inner world as such is the thing itself (*diese innere Welt ist als solche die Sache selber*)' (quoted by Iggers, 1983, p. 136; cf. also Dilthey, 1976, pp. 191ff.).

This formulation of the 'solution' to the problem of the foundations of knowledge in the human sciences involves some difficulties – of which Dilthey was aware. While Dilthey employs plural pronouns – 'our consciousness', for example – he nevertheless refers to 'this inner world'. This seems inconsistent. Dilthey saw that his view was vulnerable to radical subjectivism even though historically concrete social institutions could not be the 'product' of an individual consciousness. On the other hand, he refused a Hegelian solution, insisting that Hegel was mistaken in supposing that philosophy could ground itself in a Universal Reason, a metaphysical solution which was itself grounded in a faith in Divine Providence. For Dilthey, such a faith was no longer tenable. Dilthey wanted to remain *within* historical experience (*Erlebnis*), not transcend it: 'Philosophy must seek the inner connectedness of its cognition not in the world but in humanity' (Iggers, 1983, p. 143; cf. Dilthey, 1976, pp. 135, 154). Dilthey saw, rightly, that 'the first condition for the possibility of a historical science lies in the fact that I myself am a historical being' (p. 143). But what was the second condition, and the third? What else needed to be presupposed? Dilthey stepped gingerly into no-man's land. As Iggers observes, in a speech given in 1903 on the occasion of Dilthey's seventieth birthday, there was a note of genuine dispair as regards the dilemma he had raised and had not solved:

> I undertook to investigate the nature and conditions of historical consciousness – a critique of historical reason. This task led me to the most general of problems; a seemingly insoluble contradiction arises if we pursue historical consciousness to its last consequences. The finitute of every historical phenomenon, whether it be a religion, an ideal, or a philosophic system, hence the relativity of every sort of human conception about the connectedness of things, is the last word of the historical world view. All flows in process; nothing remains stable. On the other hand, there arises a need of thought and the striving of philosophy for universally valid cognition. The historical way of looking at things (*die geschichtliche Weltanschauung*) has liberated the human spirit from the last chains which natural science and philosophy have not yet torn asunder. But where are the means for overcoming the anarchy of convictions which threaten to break in on us? (p. 144)

This is a rich text. Hegel's absolute idealism gave us a concrete reality which not only existed, but which existed necessarily – your consciousness or mine notwithstanding. Grasping it, in all its necessity, was knowledge. So philosophy and history were coincident. For Dilthey there is *only* concrete history in flux and no necessity in the 'connectedness'. Connectedness is merely *our* connectedness, a historicism *without* redeeming transcendence – that is, without philosophy. Indeed, there is not even 'nature', for to bring 'a historical way of looking at things' to natural science, to break the chains which fetter natural science, is to make nature but *our* nature.

There are then two questions. There is first the question of whether these conclusions are tolerable philosophically? It is plain that for Dilthey they are not. The 'striving of philosophy for universally valid cognition' – the quest for the point of Archimedes – remained unabated. Short of certain *foundations* for knowledge, there is *mere opinion,* the 'anarchy of convictions'. Cognitive and moral relativism, always the specter of 'philosophy', must somehow be 'overcome'.

The second question is this: If we grant that 'nature' must be *our* nature, how do we make sense of 'our'? That is, even if cognitive relativism is tolerable, solipsism is not. But if not, what are the philosophical alternatives? Indeed, will this not require a metaphysics? And if not Hegelian, then what? Though this question was rejected by the anti-metaphysical philosophies of the nineteenth century, this question has not yet gone away – with important consequences for our conception of science, natural and social.[2]

Before turning to the thought per se of Max Weber, it is essential to flesh out more fully the context of his thought. Ranke and Dilthey were surely crucial here, but there was something else which was just as crucial.

The famous *Methodenstreit* ('Battle of Methods') is conveniently dated from the 1883 publication of Carl Menger's *Untersuchungen über die Methode der Sozialwissenschaften und der Politischen Ökonomie insbesondere,* a tract which, as Schumpeter puts it, was a systematic effort 'to vindicate the rights of theoretical analysis and to put the Schmoller school in its place'. Schumpeter cannot resist adding, 'and a very secondary place it was!' (Schumpeter, 1954, p. 814). In some ways, indeed, the key question was: How secondary was this place at just this time?[3]

The 'Schmoller school' referred, of course, to the group led by Gustav Schmoller (1838–1917), the second generation of the 'Historical School of Economists', the first generation of which had included Bruno Hildebrand and, especially, Wilhelm Roscher and Karl Knies. These last two writers became the focus of Max Weber's extended methodological critique to be discussed *in extenso* momentarily. It is easy, of course, to assume that when there is a struggle over ideas, those that are victorious ultimately conquered because they were the true ideas. This is surely the case here. From the point of view of standard histories of economics, the 'historical school' was but a temporary aberration. But despite the relatively stable institutionalization of 'Manchester' political economy in England and France, German intellectuals, nurtured on the idea that *any* social science had to be historical, did offer a genuine alternative to 'classical' political economy. There is no small amount of paradox in the fact that Max Weber, often and rightly referred to as part of the third generation of German historical economists played a role in

---

[2] Dilthey has in fact replaced epistemology with sociology of knowledge! But once epistemology is displaced by sociology of knowledge, then one is committed to being a realist ontologically, a point to be developed in part III below.

[3] Schumpeter was a party to the *Methodenstreit,* entering it in 1910, after it had pretty much run its course. Schumpeter's massive *History of Economic Analysis,* could not, of course, have been done by the kind of pure theorist which Schumpeter so persistently applauds. Indeed, Schumpeter's most important work is all fully in the spirit, if not the letter, of the Historical Economists!

the rout which the 'theoretical' (now 'neo-classical') school achieved over Schmoller's group.

Classical political economy was in trouble not only in Germany, but also in France and England. There were all sorts of reasons for this, but, at bottom, it stemmed from the real troubles in which capitalism was immersed. And the economists seemed to have nothing useful to say! As many were then arguing, the problems of political economy were its 'deductivism', its 'psychologism', and its abstract detachment from concrete reality. In England, in 1876, a group of 'eminent natural scientists' had argued that the Statistics and Economics Section (Section F) of the prestigious British Association be disbanded because 'neither had any serious scientific standing' (Abrams, 1968, p. 78). J. K. Ingram, himself a political economist, condemned Nassau Senior's attempt 'to deduce all the phenomena of the industrial life of communities from four propositions,' propositions about 'human nature'. William Booth, founder of the Salvation Army, pointed to 'the a priori reasoning' of political economy and to its 'want of reality' (1968, p. 78).

There was also the nagging question of policy and its relation to 'science'. In Germany, Schmoller had instituted the *Verein für Sozialpolitik* in 1872, precisely as a mechanism for responding to policy questions. But close on the heels of the *Methodenstreit* was the *Werturteilstreit*: must not social science be value-free, if it was to be a science? In England the argument was already in full swing. In 1878 the President of Section F of the National Association for the Promotion of Social Science bluntly asserted that 'political economy at the present hour is undergoing a crisis,' and he went on to diagnose this in no uncertain terms:

> When the cholera or the yellow fever visits a country, there is a rush for help and advice to its physicians. . . . In the war of classes political economy is absent. . . . Discordant opinions, theory and counter-theory, unintelligible language which sounds as jargon, grand deductions of which he does not understand a word, and all this on matters which belong to his everyday life. (Abrams, 1968, p. 76)

Ingram took advantage of his rostrum to urge that the association turn Section F into a sociology section! Once done, social scientists could then be part of a more general science of social causality.

Indeed, it was by no means evident that 'political economy', understood as an abstract deductivist theoretical discipline could survive this onslaught – either in England or in Germany, where it was far less comfortably established. Its opponents, including by this time Durkheim in France, were gathering steam, and the stakes were high. At issue was the idea of political economy as an autonomous discipline.

Schmoller and his school pulled no punches in this regard. For him, *Gesellschaftswissenschaft* was a unitary historical science which, he said, 'should study the relations not only between man and material goods but also between man and his fellows'. For him, 'the economic order was to be regarded as only an aspect and integral part of the entire social life and as such was to be evaluated from an ethical point of view' (cited by Iggers, 1983, pp. 131f.).

Schmoller was no 'secondary' figure in German social science. A professor of *Staatswissenschaften* at Halle and then in 1882 at Berlin, he was not only a key organizer of the *Verein*, but editor of the influential *Jahrbuch für Gesetzgebung, Verwaltung und Volkswirtschaft*, the leading journal for scholarly work in social science in Germany. And he was a prodigious scholar. Sometimes alone and sometimes with his associates, he produced a shelf of volumes on every aspect of German society. Nevertheless, a loser in the *Methodenstreit*, he has largely been forgotten. Indeed, it is now hard even to characterize him in terms of our disciplinary division of labor. He cannot be called an 'economist', since today that means a theorist of the Ricardo, Mill, Menger, or Samuelson variety, nor a sociologist or a political scientist. But then what? It is generally agreed that he wrote good *history*, even if, as Schumpeter suggests, it was boring history. Schumpeter is plainly hostile, but he is honest. He suggests that Ibsen's characterization of Dr Tessman in *Hedda Gabler* fits Schmoller – the tedious scholar of tedious details. But he says also:

> . . . the sum of Schmoller's work meant a tremendous advance in accuracy of knowledge about the social process. It must suffice to list the main headings: Economic (especially fiscal) policy and administration, the class structure of society, medieval and later forms of industry, especially of craft guilds and merchant guilds; the growth, functions and structures of cities; of bank credit; and (one of the finest pieces of Schmoller's work) of government and private enterprise. (Schumpeter, 1954, p. 810)

Schmoller was neither a Comtean nor a Spencerian, and he would have rejected, accordingly, the label 'sociologist'. Indeed, he was too German to have any patience with the idea that there were historical laws, discoverable by the methods of the natural sciences. In this regard Schumpeter says: 'Comte's suggestion was the very incarnation of the "naturalist error" and Comtist historical laws were shams' (p. 812). On the other hand, what he did was science, and it had a method. But its key premise was rejection of 'the method of isolation', the premise which guided political economy. As Schumpeter writes, 'nothing in the social cosmos or chaos is really outside of Schmollerian economics' (p. 812).

THE METHODOLOGICAL CRITIQUE OF MAX WEBER

Max Weber (1864–1920) was trained in jurisprudence and history and knew in his father's household Dilthey, Mommsen, Sybel, and Treitschke. He held chairs in political economy at Freiburg and Heidelberg, was Visiting Professor in Vienna, where Böhm-Bawerk, the famous marginalist critic of Marxian political economy, held forth, and in 1919, succeeded Lujo Brentano in the Munich chair. He died the following year. Weber came to maturity in a beehive of intellectual activity, at a period in which German society was undergoing some dramatic crises of transformation, and the 'mandarins' of the German university system were being faced with dramatic problems and choices. We will return to this, but for now we will concentrate on a 1903–6 monograph entitled *Roscher und Knies und die logischen Probleme der historichen National-oeconomie*. Originally published in three parts in Schmoller's *Jahrbuch*, *Roscher und Knies* is a remarkable and ill-comprehended, tract. A polemically constructed dialectical interaction of a welter of figures, from Dilthey to Mach, from Ranke to Menger to Husserl to Wundt, Weber's own position emerges only confusedly. But a consistent picture does emerge – different in fundamental ways from that usually associated with Weber.

Weber begins his account with an explication of a distinction employed by Roscher, but dating at least from Ranke. Roscher holds, he says, that there are two sorts of scientific investigation: 'one he calls "philosophical": the analytical comprehension of reality', whose 'purpose is generalized abstraction and the elimination of "purely contingent facts"'; the other termed 'historical', which consists in 'the descriptive reproduction of reality in its full actuality' (Weber, 1975, p. 55).

For Ranke, 'philosophy' was 'abstract', but it was less 'analytical' than Hegelian; but Weber's characterization of history is pure Ranke: *wie es eigenlich gewesen*. Weber has shifted the distinction twice over, however, since he adds that the older distinction reminds us of 'the contemporary distinction between nomological sciences and sciences of concrete reality, a distinction which appears most unambiguously in the methodological contrast between the exact natural sciences . . . and [Rankean] political history' (1975, p. 55). *This* dichotomy was by then very familiar, being found not only in Dilthey, but in Rickert, Menger, and Simmel, and in Windelband, who gave us the terms, 'nomothetic' versus 'idiographic' in his 1894 inaugural address as rector at Strassburg.

This distinction, of course, is not Ranke's. It concerns a distinction between *kinds of sciences*. There was, however, no consensus on the *basis* of this distinction or on its implications. This must be emphasized.

Writers could agree that there was a difference between natural and social science and disagree sharply on the nature and basis of the difference, but especially whether the difference stemmed from epistemological, ontological, or methodological differences.[4] Much of *Roscher and Knies* is aimed specifically at straightening this out. From here on, we may concentrate only on Weber's view of the matter. The key text is as follows:

> The philosophical sciences [i.e., the nomological sciences] have the following aim: to order an extensively and intensively infinite multiplicity of phenomena by employing a system of concepts and laws. In the ideal case these concepts and laws are unconditionally and universally valid. The concrete 'contingent' properties of the 'things' and events perceptually give to us, the properties which make them objects of perception are progressively stripped away. (pp. 55f.)

'Pure mechanics', the *abstract* science par excellence best illustrates this. 'Empirical reality is invariably *perceptual* and accessible to our experience only in its concretely and individually qualitative pecularities,' but this means that in the nomological sciences 'results' become 'increasingly remote from the properties of empirical reality', and concepts 'increasingly universal in extension' and 'increasingly empty in content [intension]'. By virtue of this, their 'domain is that set of problems in which the essential (*wesentlich*) features of phenomena – the properties of phenomena which are worth knowing – are identical with their *generic features*' (*gattungsmässig*) (p. 56f.). One can do physics precisely because the physical properties of mass and motion are 'worth knowing' and, *qua body*, these are the generic features of *all* bodies. The power to abstract from concrete particulars or to conceive an abstract, but lawful, order in the qualitative multiplicity of perceptual experience is nomological science.

By contrast, the 'sciences of concrete reality' aim at knowledge of the particular, but 'because of the logical impossibility of an exhaustive reproduction of even a limited aspect of reality . . . this must mean the following: knowledge of those aspects of reality which we regard as *essential* because of their individual *peculiarities*' (p. 57). In abstract knowledge, 'essential' coincides with generic; in knowledge of the concrete, 'essential' is what is important to us. The idea is further glossed:

---

[4] The problem of 'naturalism' has been needlessly confused by failure to be clear on this. Weber departed sharply from Dilthey, as Antoni (1959) rightly argues. While Weber held that there were differences, these did not 'concern differences in the concept of causality, the significance of concept formation, or the kind of conceptual apparatus involved' (Weber, 1975, pp. 185f.).

The logical ideal of [the sciences of concrete reality] is to differentiate the essential properties of the concrete phenomena . . . from its 'accidental' or meaningless properties and thereby to establish intuitive [i.e. direct] knowledge of these essential features. These concepts are meant to approximate a representation of the concrete actuality of reality by selecting and limiting these properties which we regard as 'characteristic'. (p. 57)

In concept formation one needs to 'represent' the concrete whole 'meaningfully' – that is, to identify it in its particularity. The idea, a version of Ranke's *Ideenlehre,* is, of course, the basis of the famous doctrine of ideal types. These concepts are rich in *intension,* in contrast to the concepts of nomothetic science, and, similarly, they are severely limited in *extension* (p. 58).[5]

It may seem that this distinction neatly divides the human from the natural sciences, but it does not.

With the exception of pure mechanics, on the one hand, and certain of the historical disciplines, on the other, it is certain that none of the 'sciences' which in fact exist can develop their concepts exclusively from only one of these two metatheoretical points of view. (p. 58)

It is not clear which 'sciences' Weber has in mind here. But in any case, we must not jump to the conclusion that the difficulty in developing useful 'generic concepts' for those 'certain historical sciences' stems from differences in their *ontologies.* Weber denies this explicitly. After developing an extensive argument, he concludes:

The logical peculiarity of 'historical' knowledge in contrast to 'natural-scientific' knowledge . . . has nothing at all to do with the distinction between the 'psychical' and the 'physical', the 'personality' and 'action', on the one hand, and the dead 'natural object' and the 'mechanical process of nature', on the other. (pp. 184f.)

This is a direct rejection of the view put forward by Dilthey and others that a different methodology is required for *Geisteswissenschaften* and *Naturwissenschaften* because the two sorts of 'science' rest on different 'foundations'. Weber has specific arguments against this view, but even if this is not Weber's view, why can the historical sciences not be nomothetic? In fact, for Weber, there is little doubt that they can. But

---

[5] The distinction, brilliantly exploited by Weber, between intension (connotation) and extension (denotation) had been familiar in the literature since Mill's *Logic,* a book whose influence in Germany has been underestimated. The extension of a term includes all the things to which a term applies. The intension is the meaning of the term, where 'meaning' is here left unexplicated.

unfortunately, a nomothetic historical science would be of absolutely no interest to us! We can begin to get at the reasons for this by considering Weber's brilliant critique of the positivist ideal of explanation of concrete particulars by subsumption under law.

WEBER'S CRITIQUE OF POSITIVISM

Comte was perhaps the first to suggest that historical explanations proceeded by subsumption under law. Weber saw clearly that while this pattern might fit the 'abstract' sciences, it could not apply to 'the sciences of the concrete'.

Weber distinguished between 'laws of nature', 'empirical generalizations' and 'causal propositions'. For him, laws of nature are *necessary*; it is thus that they are invariant and unconditional. And it is thus also that subsumption under law constitutes *explanation*. Weber, no Humean, takes this idea most seriously. 'Empirical generalizations' are 'correlations' – what we might call 'contingent regularities'. But their 'causal interpretation' is problematic, and hence their explanatory import is problematic. Finally, 'causal propositions' may be singular statements, since they denominate 'circumstances and changes within concrete reality' as 'effected' and as 'effective' (p. 196).

Roscher, 'like so many modern "sociologists"' who invoke the 'organic theory of society', supposes that he can treat *Volk* the way a biologist treats 'elephant'. 'With progressive completeness of observation', he can establish 'correlations' comparing their development. These, then, will be elevated to the status of 'natural laws', true of all *Volk* (p. 63).

This sort of effort, however, 'cannot be conceived as the ultimate *goal* of any science, neither a "nomological" nor a "historical" science, neither a "natural science" nor a "sociocultural" science' (p. 63). Indeed, even if we grant that these disciplines 'could establish an enormous number of "empirical" historical generalizations, these generalizations would have no causal status' (p. 63f.). For Weber, the *scientific investigation begins only after* these correlations have been established. At the point, then, at which we have such generalizations, the investigator has to decide: 'What sort of knowledge is the aim of the investigation' (p. 64). Three possibilities emerge. The first is the ideal of a nomothetic science, 'a choice in favor of generic features as the theoretical goal and the deductive arrangement of these features under abstract, generally valid formulae' (p. 66). So contrued, concept formation 'would have the purpose of reducing, insofar as possible, all the cultural phenomena to purely quantitative categories of some sort' (p. 64).

What is involved is clearly the progressive elimination of the features specific to concrete phenomena in favor of concepts which are 'increasingly universal in extension' and 'empty of content'. Such an approach is logically possible. The resulting 'system' would 'constitute an abstract representation of the features common to all historical events' (p. 64). But obviously, just for that reason, it would be *pointless*. Whereas a physics whose laws are true of all masses is not futile, a social science whose laws are true of all societies would be. Weber is further clear that this virtually eliminates the possibility of quantification in social *science* (though not in social research).[6] 'Mass' and 'energy' are 'reducible' to purely quantitative formulae; the 'essential' properties of concrete phenomena are not. One is here reminded of C. W. Mills double-barrelled polemic against 'abstracted empiricism' and 'Grand Theory' (Mills, 1959).

A second alternative is *Hegelian*. It attempts 'to surmount the "hiatus irrationalis" between concept and reality by the use of "general" concepts – concepts which, as metaphysical realities, comprehend and imply individual things and events as their instances of realization' (p. 66). For Roscher, who got his Hegel via Ranke, 'comprehensiveness of extension and comprehensiveness of content' are synonymous; for unless they are, no deduction from abstract laws to the concrete is possible. A *Volksgeist,* for example, may be real. But it is the product of countless cultural and natural influences and need not be 'manifested' or 'expressed' in *any* of them (p. 61). So much for Rankean history.

There is then Weber's alternative: construction of the concrete concept – the ideal type – in terms of which we attempt to 'understand' (*Verständnis*) reality, 'to understand its development, which is concretely determined, and its necessarily concrete patterns' (p. 64). To see what this means, we need to say more about the particular features of explanation in the human sciences.

THE CONCRETE SCIENCES AND 'INCALCULABILITY'

Knies holds, as do many others, that it is human 'freedom of the will' which makes a nomothetic human science impossible. Weber denies

---

[6] Although effectively obliterated in the twentieth century, the distinction, to be discussed in chapter 14 below, is straightforward enough. Social research generates data, statistics, and 'facts', and organizes these using whatever tools are available. Social science aims at explanation, including explanation of the 'correlations' produced by 'social research'. Weber and Schmoller (and Durkheim, below) encouraged and did both, but they never confused them. Though it is either not noticed or ignored, Weber turned in over 1,000 pages of research findings which, as P. F. Lazarsfeld was pleased to note, 'in style and format would not be easily distinguishable from the pages of our contemporary sociology journals' (quoted from Lazarsfeld's preface to Anthony Oberschall, 1965, p. 23).

this, and his reasons are the key to understanding his thought. They lead us, if indirectly, to his account of the genuine differences between the human and the natural sciences.

Weber argues that as regards most features of *any* concrete event, whether a human action or the splintering of a falling cliff, there is an irradicable 'incalculability'. Consider a boulder falling and splintering. Assume 'ideal conditions of antecedent observation'. Using 'the established laws of mechanics', we could calculate 'the occurrence and perhaps general angle of the splintering; also the general direction of the one fissure or another' (p. 122). But we could not calculate the number or shape of the fragments, the patterns which they formed when they come to rest or 'a veritable infinity of similar aspects' (p. 122).

All these things are governed by the laws of mechanics, but it is impossible to calculate them because, as the boulder rolls and strikes objects in its path, its path and velocity change. Similarly, as it fissures, the parts themselves become part of the continuous causal process, some interacting with others and their respective masses being altered as a result, and so on. So the 'concrete determinants are lost without a trace', Weber insists. This is an incalculability in principle, because, although the laws of mechanics never cease to 'determine' what is happening, the outcome is the result of continuous causal transactions. We cannot, for example, know in advance of a fissure what effects that particular fissure will have. We might think we could explain the effects afterwards by reconstructing the causal sequence in detail, what Weber calls 'a causal regress'. But we cannot even do that, he insists. To be sure, no one would be *interested* in doing this, and this is 'typical' as regards natural scientific explanations of concrete events.[7]

For Weber, because a concrete is 'an intensively infinite multiplicity of properties', its explanation will always be incomplete because we can never reproduce in their complexity all the causes which produced it. And if so:

> A sufficient condition for explanation in such cases is the following: in general, we can provide a 'comprehensible' interpretation ['*begreiflich*' *interpretiert*] of the concrete, individual phenomena. That is to say: an interpretation which does not contradict our nomological knowledge. (p. 123)

---

[7] The point should not be missed. Natural scientists do not, for the most part, concern themselves with trying to provide actual explanations of concrete events. Once having arrived at a theoretically satisfying account of some domain, they assume that the laws of that domain hold in the natural world, and that events involving them are governed by them. Everything, for example, is subject to the laws of mechanics, but we do not seek, nor do we need, an explanation of the positions and velocities of *every* mass in the universe. Celestial mechanics is unique in this regard, both because information about positions and velocities of masses in the solar system is useful and, because the solar system is for all practical purposes *closed*, it is available.

This text is crucial. It is clear that the basic sense of '"comprehensible" interpretation' applies in *any* concrete science: 'Consider not only sciences like meterology, but also sciences like geography or biology. . . . In the overwhelmingly typical cases they are obliged to reply by providing forms of causal explanation which, in principle, are quite similar to the trivial case just considered' (p. 123). An 'interpretation' rejects the possibility of 'a genuine causal regress' and settles for less. The less which is settled for is a 'causal' explanation which does not contradict our nomological knowledge. It makes the outcome 'intelligible'.

VERSTEHENDE SOZIOLOGIE

It should be clear already that insofar as the historical sciences are exclusively concerned with the concrete, historical explanation can be nothing more than 'a "comprehensible" interpretation'. And it is also clear that this idea applies to any 'science of the concrete'. Nevertheless, there are special features of 'the social-cultural sciences'.

Weber writes: 'In the analysis of human conduct, our criteria for causal explanation [in the foregoing weak sense] can be satisfied in a fashion which is qualitatively quite different' (p. 125). 'As regards the interpretation of human conduct, we can, at least in principle, set ourselves the goal not only of representing it as "possible" – "comprehensible", in the sense of it being consistent with our nomological knowledge. We can attempt to "understand" it' (p. 135). While in any case of explanation of a concrete, we must be satisfied with causal incompleteness, there are, as regards conduct, unique *teleological* criteria for satisfaction of the weak version of causal explanation.

'Teleological' rationalization can be used as a constructive device for the development of conceptual schemes. These conceptual schemes are of extraordinary heuristic value for the causal analysis of historical relations. On the one hand, these constructive conceptual schemes (1) can have a purely concrete character; hypothesis for the interpretation of single, concrete complexes. . . . On the other hand . . . these conceptual schemes (2) can be ideal-typical constructions of a general character, like the 'laws' of abstract economics which theoretically deduce the consequences of certain economic situations by presupposing strictly rational action. (p. 189)[8]

[8] In *Economy and Society*, this distinction is substantially repeated, suggesting that Weber did not alter his views on this fundamental issue. In that context, a third use is mentioned, unimportant for present purposes: 'In cases of sociological mass phenomena', we may seek 'the average of, or approximation to, the actually intended meaning' (Weber, 1978, p. 9).

Both of these applications involve ideal-typical conceptual schemes. I want to put off discussion of the first – Weber's main interest as a social scientist – and look now at the second, Weber's extraordinary, but generally ignored, defense of 'pure economics'.[9]

It was charged that theoretical economics was deductivist, abstract, and psychologistic. On *the usual view,* it had the *pretense* of being a nomological science, a view shared by both defenders and critics. This was not Weber's view of the matter, however.

We must distinguish between explanation via production of a valid law – as in nomothetic science – and explanation via the production of a teleological schema of rational action. These are, he says, 'polar opposites'. If the 'laws' of economics were laws, they could be refuted by a single case. But 'the ideal-typical constructions of economics – if they are correctly understood – have no pretensions at all to *general* validity' (p. 190). On the other hand, if they are but 'empirically valid generalizations', they cannot explain, since their causal interpretation is problematic. One cannot explain why E occurred by means of a generalization to the effect that usually E follows C – unless one can show *also* that C is cause or part cause of E. *Weber saw this problem to be intractable.* In *Economy and Society,* he offered three reasons: people may be unaware of their 'true' motives; similar acts may be differently motivated, and people may be subject to 'opposed and conflicting motives' (pp. 9f.; see also Giddens, 1971, p. 149).

On the other hand, such a generalization could be used as evidence for the pertinence of a 'teleological rationalization'. And if so, the adequacy criterion for the weak form of causal explanation is satisfied. Insofar as there is empirical warrant for the postulation of the teleological rationalization, *it explains by showing that the act is in accordance with some norm or rule.* It makes sense of the act.

It is absolutely crucial to see that, for Weber (and rightly), it is not the probability statement which explains, since, lacking a subjectively adequate interpretation, 'it is still an incomprehensible statistical probability' (1978, p. 12). In other words, the mere fact that 'this' almost always, or even always, follows 'that' is no warrant for ascribing *causality,* and thus, appeal to a pattern, by itself, cannot explain. On the other hand, having only a subjectively adequate interpretation gives no warrant for ascribing causality since, obviously, we need evidence that the schema applies in the particular case at hand.

[9] Carlo Antoni and, more recently, Goran Therborn are almost alone in seeing the pertinence of Weber's relation to pure economics. Antoni writes that it was Weber's intention 'to restore dignity to the laws of the Classical School' (Antoni, 1959, p. 169). Therborn is correct that Weber's *verstehende* sociology 'must be seen and analysed' against Weber's background as a historian and an economist, and that this is 'scarcely, if at all realized' (Therborn, 1976, pp. 272f.).

The 'laws' of economics are paradigmatic 'teleological rationalizations', ideal-typical constructions which make sense of economic activity. The economist who understands what he is doing is not saying that his deduction explains, still less predicts, concrete acts, or that the real actors are 'rational'. He is saying that his schema makes acts intelligible because his theory is a subjectively and empirically adequate interpretation. 'We do not "infer" . . . "actual action", but rather "objectively" possible complexes' (1975, p. 190).

This is a radically different understanding of economic theory, to be sharply contrasted with the realist interpretations which had been part of the understanding of the entire classical tradition, including Marx. For that tradition, economic laws had been understood as causal laws of the economic system, real tendencies which became realized, *ceteris paribus*. The fact that the *ceteris paribus* clauses were never, or almost never, satisfied, of course, meant that outcomes would almost always diverge from the predictions of the theory. 'Market price', for example, was not expected to be coincident with the 'natural price', given what we would today call 'exogenous variables'. Weber has radically reinterpreted economic laws as *schemata of intelligibility*.

But Weber's account is not 'instrumentalist' as that term has generally come to be understood. It is not the case, for example, that we postulate a rational actor and that this is justified because we get good 'predictions' – that is, that the test of the adequacy of a theory is its capacity to predict with reasonable accuracy what actually happens.[10] This is quite the opposite of Weber's view. On his view, whatever happens, *after* it happens, is made intelligible by the theory. Weber denies predictability as the goal of concrete science because of causal complexity. He takes second best: the capacity to provide a '"comprehensible" interpretation'. Weber defends theoretical economics by restricting its claims.

In like fashion, he meets the objection that pure economics is reductively psychologistic, that, for example, the 'law of marginal utility' constitutes 'an attempt to provide a "psychological foundation" of "economic value" (Weber, 1975, p. 277), or more generally that an imputation of maximizing behavior is psychologistic. Weber insists that 'in this view, misunderstanding of these constructs reaches its peak'. Indeed, 'they do not contain a single grain of "psychology" in any sense of this word'. What is plainly ignored, he says, is that these are ideal-typical constructions which regard objective economic relations, not the 'mental instincts' of actors. These critics fail to distinguish 'between "the principle of profit" in objectified economic management and the mental instinct of self-interest and selfishness in the human subject' (p. 202). It

[10] The classic account is Milton Friedman, 1973.

is the former, not the latter, which is the object of the teleological rationalizations of pure economics. 'Economic "laws"', as 'schemata of rational action cannot be deduced from a psychological analysis of the individual, but rather from an idealtypical reproduction of the competitive price mechanism of the objective situation as stipulated by the theory.' (p. 202)

For Weber, theoretical economics is not methodologically individualist, since it describes the relations of objective situations, relations not reducible to psychological states of the actors.

Weber's view of these matters did not win out. Perhaps this was because it was not clearly understood; but, more likely, it was because by the time that he was putting his ideas forward, positivist philosophies of science had already conquered. Moreover, while Weber was on the opposite side from Schmoller in the *Methodenstreit*, Weber's unique defense of pure economics did not rule out the historical science which Schmoller – indeed, which he himself – practiced. I will argue that Weber was in agreement with the *aims* of Schmoller and the Historical School of Economics.

HISTORICAL SCIENCE

Despite Weber's clear insistence that rationality assumptions in economics were not psychologistic, it is usually held that Weber defended 'motive explanations', the imputation of reasons as explanations of behavior; that, as Dilthey and others had argued, this was the basis of Weber's 'anti-naturalism'; and that, accordingly, it was the task of the social sciences to frame abstract teleological principles which 'explain' behavior. But Weber's critique of positivism was a critique not of the pertinence of causality to human science, but, as I argued earlier, of the whole subsumption model of explanation as it applies to concrete events and particulars.

There is a section of *Roscher and Knies* in which Weber has great fun with 'the problem of historical laws'. He refers to a verse by the humorist Busch which goes as follows: 'Whoever is pleased whenever he is distressed makes himself, on the whole, unpopular'. Weber comments: 'Since [Busch] conceives the generic features of this phenomenon quite correctly, not as a necessary truth, but rather as a rule of "adequate causation", the verse is an altogether irreproachable formulation of a "law of history".' But of course, it is hardly surprising that it is, since all socialized adults in every human society are well supplied with a battery of such 'laws':

Our imagination has been schooled in the world of our own everyday experience. In consequence, when we are engaged in 'interpreting' human action, we often omit the explicit formulation of the content of our experience into 'generalizations'. This would be 'a waste of time'.

Is a 'scientific' social-cultural science a search for laws then?

Would it make scientific *sense* for [the interpretative disciplines] to formulate special generalizations and so-called 'laws' that are intended to achieve abstraction? . . . Can this project be expected to produce useful new insights germane to their concrete problems? *In general* it is not in the least self-evident that this *must* be the case. (p. 107)[11]

Of course, *if* the generalizations of common sense are 'historical laws', then historical explanation can be said to make use of historical laws. And *if* sociology has the task of explaining behavior as meaningful and this requires appeal to teleological rules, then the task of a sociology can be said to be to 'formulate . . . so-called "laws" that are intended to achieve abstraction'. But it is clear that Weber's *Roscher and Kneis* cannot be cited as an authority for this (pervasive, but odd) view. Moreover, if we look at the work actually done by Weber, we can see that he was interested neither in a general theory of action nor in explaining concrete behavior – for reasons which I hope are clear by now. Rather, he aimed at an understanding – the word is carefully chosen – of the 'characteristic meaning of single, concrete elements together with their concrete causes and effects' – for example, of the advent of capitalism in the West, the differences in the structuring of authority in Confucian China and modern Germany and the causes thereof, and so on.

Rejecting the 'nomothetic' route *and* the Hegelian (1975, p. 22), this was his third way, which involved critically, his ill-developed notion of ideal-types, considered *not* as 'teleological rationalizations', as in pure economics, but as constructions allowing characterization of an institution or even a civilization in its 'individuality' *without* introducing Hegelian metaphysics. Ideal-typical concepts are neither generic nor metaphysical. Rather, they are conceptual constructs formed by abstraction and combination, by putting together, as Giddens says, 'an indefinite number of elements which, although found in reality, are rarely, or never discovered in this specific form' (Giddens, 1971, p. 141).

---

[11] Compare here Nietzsche (1957): In the natural sciences, 'the generalizations are the most important things', because 'they contain the laws'. But the historian's generalizations are useless, because 'the residue of truth, after the obscure and insoluble part is removed, is nothing but the commonest knowledge. The smallest range of experience will teach it' (p. 39).

Ideal types are not, accordingly, *descriptions*; nor are they *hypotheses* in the sense that they name possible existents which, *were* they to exist, would provide explanations.[12] Yet they aid in both description and explanation, because they enable us 'to become aware of the character-istic meaning of single, concrete cultural elements together with their concrete causes and effects'; because, as before, these thus become 'intelligible' (*verständlich*) (Weber, 1975, p. 65).

Weber contributed to subsequent confusions over these issues for one very large reason: he failed to work out his final views on the relation of the 'historical sciences' to the 'sociocultural sciences'. In *Roscher and Knies,* he seems content to employ one or the other of these terms, as one or the other was employed by whomever he is criticizing. But neither had any sort of settled meaning, and Weber could not, of course anticipate what the 'disciplines' would be like after his death. Nor could he know that his own work, itself no model of clarity, would figure so largely in these debates. But the uncritical use of the two terms by commentators who fail to notice that there is even a problem cannot be so excused.

In *Economy and Society* we have the much quoted 'definition' of sociology:

> Sociology (in the sense in which this highly ambiguous term is used) is a science concerning itself with the interpretative under-standing of social action and thereby with a causal explanation of its course and consequences. (1978, p. 4)

Later he writes:

> We have taken it for granted that sociology seeks to formulate type concepts and generalized uniformities of empirical process. This distinguishes it from history, which is oriented to the causal analysis and explanation of individual actions, structures, and personalities possessing cultural significance. (p. 19)

Finally, speaking about the now famous 'types of action orientation', he writes:

> Sociological investigation is concerned with these typical modes of action. Thereby it differs from history, the subject of which is rather the causal explanation of important individual events. (p. 29)

---

[12] Marx's key concepts are not ideal types: they are 'theoretical' in contrast to 'empiri-cal'; they *do* describe by referring to *reals*. They are thus like the concept of an ideal gas: a gas operating in theoretical closure. The fact that gases, like everything else, never operate in conditions of theoretical closure, does not make the concept of an ideal gas an ideal type in Weber's sense. An ideal gas is a hypothesis in the sense that, by postulating its existence, we can explain the behavior of gases which are *not* in conditions of closure. See chapter 13.

This is almost all we have specifically on the question of the relation of history to sociology as Weber conceived it. And no doubt, there is enough here to argue that Weber arrived at a unique conception of 'sociology' defined in terms of *Verstehen* (and thus in marked contrast to the conceptions of Comte and Spencer). The idea, then, that a sociology so construed 'seeks to formulate type concepts and generalized uniformities of empirical process' leads to the view that *Economy and Society* represents Weber's 'discovery' of a general theory of 'social and economic organization'. From here, of course, it is but a short step to Talcott Parsons's *The Structure of Social Action*.

On the other hand, if we take *Roscher and Knies* as only a little removed from the later *Economy and Society,* then 'sociology' is *propaedeutic* to history. On this view, *Economy and Society* is an exercise in concept formation, the working out of ideal-typical categories to be applied in historical research.[13] In a letter to von Below of June 1914, Weber wrote:

> We are absolutely in accord that history should establish what is specific to, say, the medieval city; but this is possible only if we first find what is missing in other cities. . . . And so it is with everything else. It is the subsequent tasks of history to find a causal explanation for these specific truths. . . . Sociology, as I understand it, can perform this very modest preparatory work. (Cited from Weber, 1978, p. lviii)

Nothing seems clearer than that Weber sought causal explanations of concrete wholes, and that, therefore, he was, on his own view, a *historian*. Which is to say that, for Weber, the real social-scientific problem is the explanation of what, to us, are the 'significant' events and differences which constitute human societies. So understood, there was but some 'very modest preparatory work' for 'sociology'. There is thus a double irony. Defender of 'pure economics' but no economist himself, Weber is credited as being a founder of modern sociology as an autonomous discipline, despite the fact that, in the last analysis, he remained firmly committed to the German idea that the human science par excellence is history.

[13] Therborn (1976) argues that 'sociology, in the sense Weber used it about his own work, was in fact not a new science of society but a type of social study which applied the epistemological principles of economics and history formulated by Weber in 1903–6' (p. 297). Following Winckelmann, the German editor of Weber's work, Therborn argues that 'Weber's magnum opus, *Economy and Society,* is to be construed . . . not as a "theory of social and economic organization" – as an English selection [by Talcott Parsons!] once presented it – but as a typology and a *Kasuistik*' (p. 287). See also C. A. Bryant, 1985, pp. 96ff. Bryant's account of Weber is extremely useful. Therborn also points out that it is an error to hold that Weber worked out his views in criticism of historical materialism (p. 276). See also Giddens, 1971, esp. pp. 192ff.

Weber has been called 'the bourgeois Marx'. This is, I believe, a very useful appellation – and for more than one reason. But perhaps it is Karl Löwith who identified the fundamental reason:

Neither the sociology of Marx, nor that of Weber, was confined by the boundaries of specialization. Yet it would be wholly mistaken to construe the fundamental universality of their sociological problematics as a mere 'sociologism' extending the limits of sociology as a specialized discipline. In reality, their approach expressed the transformation of Hegel's philosophy of objective spirit into an analysis of human society. (Löwith, 1982, p. 24)

8

Economy and Society:
The Sociology of
Pareto and Durkheim

In Germany, Schmoller lost the *Methodenstreit* and the *Werturteilstreit*. As to this latter 'battle', Max Weber's famous editorial of 1904 – what some commentators have called 'an outright attack' on Schmoller (Dahrendorf, 1961, p.2), had made his position clear: 'Normative propositions' and 'existential propositions' are 'logically distinct'. There is no deducing 'ought' from 'is' (Weber, 1949, p.51). While there is nothing original in this – it is in Hume and is repeated, for example, by the eminent Henry Sidgwick in his heated battle with the policy-oriented political economists of England – 'value neutrality' quickly became the watchword of the 'scientist' in his role *as* scientist. And a decade before the outbreak of the *Methodenstreit*, a group of economists, Menger in Austria, Schmoller's antagonist in the *Methodenstreit*, Leon Walras (1834–1910) in France, and W. S. Jevons (1835–82) in England, invented what we now call 'neo-classicism' – general equilibrium analysis based on the discovery that marginal principles can be extended to include production and distribution. That this involved an enormous simplification of the problem which had haunted political economy since at least Quesnay is hardly arguable. And no doubt it generated gigantic new spaces for novel mathematical techniques. Although the new ideas did not conquer the field all at once – there were holdouts in America well past the turn of the century – the new ideas certainly gave 'economists' added incentive to defend their preserve. I say 'economists' here, since it was also during this period that 'political' was dropped from 'political economy'. It does not appear, for example, in Alfred Marshall's *Principles of Economics* (1890), the work which gave neo-classicism its definitive form. There are two writers, important for later developments, who have not yet been brought into our account, writers who in crucial ways were on opposite sides in these two 'battles', even though both had fallen 'under the spell of Auguste Comte's writings' and otherwise had much in common. Both were contemporaries of Weber: Emile Durkheim (1858–1917), philosopher turned sociologist, and Vilfredo Pareto (1848–1923), economist turned sociologist. Both accepted a positivist version of lawfulness and of scientific explanation, which might have been predicted of Comteans, even those of an original sort. Both were anti-historical and were, for different reasons, genuine founders of quantitative sociology. Both thought of society as a 'system', though they differed critically over the elements constituting the system. And in a sense, both were imperializing sociologists: Pareto, by incorporating 'pure economics' into sociology, and Durkheim, more radically, by rejecting it altogether.

I begin with 'economics' and with the economist turned sociologist, Pareto. As Schumpeter has said, once the sociology, philosophy, and methodology in which it 'floats' is filtered out, Pareto's *Cours d'économie politique* (1896–7) 'is simply a brilliant Walrasian treatise' (Schumpeter, 1954, p. 860). It is that, but since the sociology, philosophy, and methodology are not flotsam and jetsam, I want to examine the connections of these. This provides the opportunity, then, to give a general sketch of the basic ideas of neo-classical economics in the form in which they existed at the turn of the century. My main aim in this brief account is to show that Schumpeter was correct in arguing that, for all the technical improvements in analysis that marginalism brought about, it represented no paradigm shift from classicism (see 1954, p. 892). If so, then Pareto's further generalization making 'sociology' the inclusive science, subsuming economics as a part, rested on foundations entirely familiar to Ricardo or Say. This makes the contrast to Durkheim in the second part of the chapter even more vivid.

THE NEO-CLASSICAL 'REVOLUTION'

The classicists had sharply distinguished exchange from use value. In a barter economy, the former was simply a ratio, the power of purchasing objects by comparison to other objects, whereas the latter was the direct usefulness or 'utility' of an object. It was assumed that the introduction of money made no difference since, as Mill argued, money was merely 'a store of value'. It was plain that things had to have some utility if there was to be any exchange, but it was a complete mystery how the two concepts of value were otherwise related. The famous 'paradox of value', that some objects having enormous use value, had no exchange value, and that others which had little use value had high exchange value, was a stumbling block for theory. The labor theory of absolute value, in Ricardo and Marx, was, of course, a response to this puzzle.

If, instead of use value, we introduce the idea of marginal utility, considered roughly as the idea that individuals have different categories of wants, or 'tastes' to use Pareto's term, which can be arranged in a definite order of subjective importance, we can then say that there is a definite sequence for additional increments of these goods as we go on consuming them.

There are three features worth noting: that the preference scheme is individual, that it is ordinal, and that, within a specified time frame, consumption of more of a product leads to smaller and smaller increments of utility, and, at satiation, to zero utility. Ordinality refers to the idea that while there is a definite order, 'utilities' are not measurable (cardinality). This seems to have been an enormous problem for the founders. It was overcome in a clear way by Pareto, who argued that measurability was an unnecessary assumption as long as we are interested only in a maximizing problem. One can observe preference behaviors, and no one doubted that people can consistently compare the satisfactions expected from different bundles of goods without actually measuring them – for example, whether one will get two times or three times more utility from item A than item B. The last idea of the three, the so-called law of diminishing marginal utility, is an intuitively plausible idea and is essential in the solution of the maximizing problem, since it generates a maximizing rule.[1]

All this is beautifully expressed by an 'indifference curve' introduced by Edgeworth but put to work by Pareto in a novel way. In the simplest case, we can represent an infinite series of combinations of two objects to which an economic individual is indifferent (see figure 8.1).

In figure 8.1, point *m* represents the choice of one unit of bread and one unit of wine, whereas *m'* represents an equally desirable combination, more wine and less bread, and so on along the whole line *ns*. Similarly, the curve *n's'* represents an infinite series of choices preferred over *any* of the choices on curve *ns*. As a rational maximizer, of course, our actor would prefer to be on curve *n's'* rather than *ns* even if he is 'indifferent' as regards his position on each of the individual curves. The bases for indifference and exchange are the personal and interpersonal comparisons of marginal utilities: movement from one point on a given person's indifference curve indicates a gain in utility from one product that is matched by a loss of utility from the other product.

[1] Worth mentioning is the fact that it was Samuelson who showed that the so-called consistency postulate was all that was needed for the maximizing problem, creating then a *pure* theory of choice. See Samuelson, 1938.

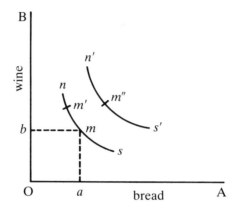

Figure 8.1   Indifference curve

The upshot is this: in effect, we are now in a position to explain exchange value in terms of use value. Thus we can imagine two barterers in open negotiation as represented in figure 8.2.

The coordinate axes for the first individual are OA and OB, for the second, wα and wß; *t*, *t'*, *t''* ... and *s*, *s'*, *s''* ... represent their respective indifference curves. An 'equilibrium' is indicated by *c*, which determines the exchange ratio of A to B.[2] As with the classical analysis, however, nothing changes with the introduction of *n* parties or *m* commodities or with the introduction of money; indeed, 'measurability' comes to utility if there is a correspondence between products with utility and a conventionally accepted standard commodity, a 'numeraire', in terms of which all exchange relations can be expressed. If the product represented on the B axis (figure 8.2) is money, taken as numeraire, the exchange ratio is a *price*.[3] But the idea is further generalizable so that we have the basis for a *logic of choice* – applicable not merely to consumer goods, but to any context of 'rational' choice, including therefore the whole area of *production*. Iron or fertilizer, water or labor power thus have 'use value' in this new sense, since they acquire indices of economic significance based on the same principles of rational choice as operate on the consumption side. Thus the allocation of factors of production, the 'supply side', falls under the same principles as 'the demand side'. Finally, by virtue of the foregoing, the distribution of

---

[2] This is *an* equilibrium, not *the* equilibrium, unless further constrained by a budget curve or price ratio. And even then it may not be unique.

[3] Compare Marx's analysis of the fetishism of commodities in *Capital*, vol. 1.

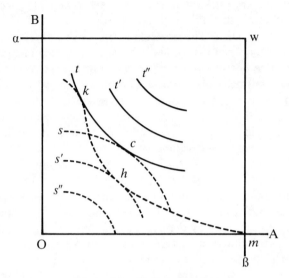

Figure 8.2   Exchange ratios

both costs and incomes falls under the same principles. As Schumpeter notes, 'the whole organon of pure economics thus finds itself unified in the light of a single principle – in a sense in which it had never been before' (1954, p. 913).

We should pause to notice here that, since on the consumption side, the economic significance of goods was to be derived from an aggregate of the indifference curves of actors for given products, there was a problem from the beginning regarding the analysis of the relative contribution of the factors of production. Plainly, all the factors are requisite insofar as withdrawing any one of them – labor, tools, natural resources, and so on – will result in no product. Menger seems to have been the first to solve the problem. He acknowledged that one could not in principle separate the factors, since the cooperation required for production was conjoint, radically unlike the 'cooperation' between parties in a barter relation. He argued, however, that it was not necessary to separate these factors – for example, the relative contribution of the worker versus the relative contribution of the machine she or he runs – since, for analysis, it is sufficient to determine their *marginal* contributions. The idea is attractive enough, even if it does involve some very strong assumptions.

As Schumpeter writes, these marginal contributions 'can simply be found by withdrawing successively small quantities of each requisite of production, keeping the others constant each time, and ascertain the loss of satisfaction that this will cause consumers of the product or products' (1954, p. 914). The problem is simply that there is no way to determine the marginal contribution of, say, a worker independent of the market price of the product he or she is producing, and this means that unless these prices are social optima, there is no way to equate the value of the worker's contribution to the wage rate. It is exactly the situation as regards the price of the commodity represented on axis A in figure 8.2. Marshall argued, correctly, that marginal utility can be known *because* people are willing to pay different prices for different consumption bundles. But that their personal buying decisions are related to the numeraire – that is, to a budget constraint – does not imply, contrary to general equilibrium theory, that these prices are social optima. Of course – and this is crucial – the whole problem is conveniently swept away by the simple expedient of arguing that, with perfect competition and in perfect equilibrium, we can solve the set of equations which show that the money wage rate equals the physical marginal increment due to the last 'increment' of labor, multiplied by the equilibrium price of the product. That is, *if* we assume economic rationality on the part of all the actors, full information, independence of decisions, large numbers of actors, substitutability over the possible range of imputs, and much else besides, then the theory is coherent;[4] *and if nothing else were happening in society,* it would be explanatory.

For Durkheim, this was, it seems, too much to ask. Accordingly, he rejected the program *in toto*. By contrast, since, on his view, something else is always happening in society, Pareto was led to argue that pure economics was no more than a subsystem which somehow had to be integrated into a general sociological theory. But this takes us to the last point we need to make as regards the neo-classical 'revolution'.

The theory, of course, is indispensably mathematical, requiring the

___

[4] Almost all 'popular' accounts of the market rationality of capitalism cheerfully confuse what Menger rightly distinguished. People *do* 'cooperate' in a barter relation, but this must be sharply distinguished from the cooperation of two men digging a ditch or a bricklayer with his hod-carrier. And these two cases are different in important ways. It is easy to see how one might determine the relative contributions of two diggers to their product, the hole, and then value their contribution proportionately, the man who is twice as productive, say, is entitled to twice the proceeds. But how does one do this with the bricklayer and the hod-carrier? The resultant brick wall is more valuable than it would have been had the bricklayer or the hod-carrier worked alone. But what is their relative contribution? There is no *physical* way to distinguish their marginal products. The theory tells us that this does not matter, since the price of the jointly constructed wall is determined through comparison to two singly constructed walls. Accordingly, the value of the relative contributions to the more valuable wall becomes determinable. One begins to see the importance of the assumptions, violated at every turn, especially in the field of production.

development of various markets, described by means of a series of equations embodying their conditions and relations. It goes without saying that the phenomenal twentieth-century development of these ideas, like the twentieth-century developments in modern logic with which they converge, require on the part of their practitioners considerable mathematical skill, imagination, and investment. But for all that, it cannot be denied, I think, that Walras, Menger, Marshall, Pareto, and others

> added nothing to the ideas of the preceding period concerning what it is that happens in the economic process and how, in a general way, this process works out; or to put the same thing differently, they saw the subject matter of economic analysis, the sum total of things that are to be explained, much as Smith or Mill had seen them, and all these efforts aimed at explaining them more satisfactorily. (Schumpter, 1954, p. 892)

Of course, they added enormous detail to the older account as they cleaned up and corrected the cruder efforts of the classicists to give an account of how an exchange system works; and in doing so, they further mystified what was already of enormous ideological use. They still assumed, that is, that the constituents of the economic system were individuals, functionally characterized as 'firms' or 'households'; they still assumed that it made no difference in the exchange system that only some people owned and controlled the productive resources. They still assumed that the whole analysis could be founded on the 'rational' behavior of economic individuals, so that, for example, demand schedules for products were aggregations of individual indifference curves. They still assumed 'perfect competition', although equilibrium analysis highlighted the interdependence of 'variables' in the simultaneous equations. Finally, they assumed, after Mill had settled 'the unsettled questions', that political economy was 'an abstract science', not a Baconian science, and thus that its conclusions, 'like those of geometry, are only true, as the common phrase is, in the abstract' (Mill, 1874; above, chapter 3) *except that by this time,* there was neither a realist underpinning to its claims nor, as in Mill, an acknowledgment of its limits as an explanatory or predictive science, a fact appreciated by Pareto, but not, it seems, by many others. Indeed, by this time, not only was political economy under attack, but it was under attack by a competing imperialist discipline: sociology. It is here, then, that we can see the respective postures of Pareto and Durkheim.

PARETO'S SOCIOLOGY

One cannot help but be impressed by the erudition of Pareto, who was as familiar with ancient Greece and Rome as he was with the sophisticated mathematics which propelled equilibrium analysis. Moreover, he was especially alive to the philosophical, and especially the methodological, controversies of his time. The first volume of his *Trattato di sociologia generale* – hereafter referred to by its English title, *Mind and Society* – has four chapters devoted to his philosophy of science and two chapters concerned with clarifying 'non-logical conduct' – pertinent to 'economics' only as regards 'tastes' and thence, 'since tastes are taken as data of fact', wholly to be ignored. As givens, they are not explained, but they can function as 'premises' in explanation. The situation, crucially, was otherwise with 'sociology', understood to be 'the synthesis of [law, political economy, political history, the history of religions, etc.] (Pareto, 1935, vol. I. para. 1). Indeed, the characteristic feature of Pareto's *sociology* – in contrast to his economics – is the overwhelming importance of the *non-rational*.

We can begin with his philosophy of science, what he calls 'the logico-experimental standpoint'. Since it contains no novelties, it can quickly be characterized. Pareto writes:

Metaphysicists generally give the name of 'science' to knowledge of the 'essences' of things, to knowledge of 'principles'. If we accept that definition for the moment, it would follow that this work would be in no way scientific. Not only do we refrain from dealing with essences and principles: we do not even know the meaning of these terms. (para. 19)

The theme, familiar since Comte, has Hegel as Pareto's supreme culprit. It is repeated often and sometimes in alternative formulations. A favorite example of 'metaphysics' in economics concerns the 'problem of value': 'Metaphysically, people have used an entity called value taken as a constant cause of variations in price' (para. 104). Or, symmetrically, 'to say that "force" is the "cause" of motion is to think one is saying something and to say nothing – to define an unknown by an unknown' (para. 496).

For Pareto, 'scientific laws are . . . nothing more than experimental uniformities' (para. 99). 'Laws imply no necessity' (para. 69). 'Scientific law must . . . be taken as prefaced by the restriction: *within the limits of time and space known to us*' (para. 97). 'Modern scientists study the movements of the stars directly, and go no farther than required for establishing uniformities of such movements.' One may ask, 'What is gravitation?', but 'celestial mechanics can dispense with a solution to it. So long as its equations hold, it matters little how they are obtained' (para. 92). As Pareto had noted in his earlier (1906) *Manual*, 'it can be said that establishing a theory is something like passing a curve through a number of fixed points. An infinite number of curves can satisfy this condition' (Pareto, 1971, pp. 31f.).

Finally, 'explanation consists solely in putting the fact that is to be "explained" in relation with other facts' (para. 533). 'The positions of heavenly bodies are calculable via the equations of dynamics.' This, and nothing more, he insists, is scientific explanation (para. 534).

It is not difficult to see how this thoroughly positivist view of scientific law and scientific explanation could rationalize mathematical economics. Even so, a fairly evident problem, among the many which might be mentioned, is the confirmability of the 'equations' of general equilibrium theory – in contrast to the confirmability of the equations of dynamics in application to 'heavenly bodies'. This, as we saw, forced Weber to a novel understanding of the role of the equations of 'pure economics'. By contrast, it led Pareto to see economics as a subsystem of sociology. The problem, as he saw it, was the economic outcomes were affected by non-economic 'variables', and especially variables rooted in human irrationality.

Volume II of *Mind and Society* is devoted entirely to the 'Analysis of Sentiment', Pareto's general name for the various manifestations of non-rational behavior. It involves his theory of 'residues', 'residues' because they are 'constant' – what is left over when the countless variations have been removed. A residue, in this sense, is the root or basis of a non-logical action or reasoning, a kind of primitive psychological tendency. Residues get rationalized. That is, people seek to explain and justify them. Pareto calls these rationalizations 'derivations'. The result is a 'derivative', or a non-logico-experimental theory. That is, non-rational behavior can be explained by showing that it results from a false 'theory' held by the actor. It is Pareto's aim, then, to disentangle such theories. Unsurprisingly, they characteristically 'transcend experience'. This is, evidently, an effort in the sociology of belief, or, more accurately, the psychology of belief.

It will not pay to assess the viability – indeed, intelligibility! – of his complicated taxonomy of 'residues', or the parallel taxonomy of 'derivations', the task of volume III. One senses elements of Bacon's 'Idols of the Mind' and, indeed, anticipations of Lévi-Strauss! Some of the categories seem rooted in biology – for example, 'the sex residue' (paras. 1324–96) – whereas others are not – for example, 'asceticism' (paras. 1163–1206). All his categories are richly illustrated. Pareto was acquainted with an enormous store of fact and fancy.

Three points do warrant comment however. First, as I noted above, properly speaking, Pareto's theory is a psychology, rather than a sociology, of belief. We will pursue this point later, noting here merely the reason for this. Pareto's methodological individualism does not allow a place for the *sui generis* social, what Durkheim called 'social facts'. Second, Pareto's effort is in no way *historical*. He is interested in the constants which determine 'social equilibrium'. 'The sentiments or instincts that correspond to residues, along with those corresponding to appetite, interests, etc. are the main factors in determining the social equilibrium' (para. 875). Historical examples are illustrative and comparative, serving to get at the basic and universal 'determinants' of social equilibrium. Finally, Pareto is quite clear that, as regards theories of all kinds – including therefore 'logico-experimental theories – one can do a psychology of belief – 'seek the manner of their genesis . . . and the reasons for their acceptance'. But such an inquiry cannot replace 'the objective standpoint': 'Whether a theorem of Euclid is true or false, and how and why he came to discover it, are two separate questions' (para. 855). For Pareto, in marked constrast, for example, to Dilthey, the psychology of belief has *no epistemological* consequences.

Social equilibrium

Volume IV pulls together Pareto's program for sociology: the application of general equilibrium theory to society taken as a social system. The opening paragraph asserts:

> The form of a society is determined by all the elements acting upon it and it, in turn, reacts upon them. We may therefore say that a reciprocal determination arises. Among such elements the following groups may be distinguished: 1. soil, climate, flora, fauna, geological, mineralogical, and other like conditions; 2. elements external to a given society at a given time, such as the influences of other societies upon it – external, therefore, in space; and the effects of the previous situation within it – external, therefore, in time; then 3: internal elements, chief among which, race, residues (or better, the sentiments manifested by them), proclivities, interests, aptitudes for thought and observation, state of knowledge and so on. Derivations also are to be counted among these latter. (para. 2060)

This *sounds* like Montesquieu or Herder or perhaps even Hegel or Marx. But *the similarity is wholly superficial*.

First, the 'internal elements', which for Pareto are dominant, have their bases in 'residues', which are 'constants'. This means that 'the molecules of the social system' are 'individuals, who are possessed of certain sentiments, manifested by residues' (para. 2080). The geographical elements are 'undoubtedly very important', but no direct examination of them is attempted. Instead, 'they are accounted for indirectly by taking as data of fact the residues, proclivities and interests of human beings who are subject to them' (para. 2064). 'Race', we should note, is put right alongside 'residues' as a determinant.

Two sets of 'external elements' are distinguished. The invasion of society A by society B is an element that is 'external' (in space), one that has effects on B in a clear enough way. Yet is is hard to see how Pareto is conceiving of the effects of the past, revealingly titled 'external' (but in time!). This is a serious problem for any methodological individualist and most clearly reveals Pareto's distance from Montesquieu, Herder, Hegel, Marx, or Durkheim. For them, as for Pareto, we might say that society is a system of elements. But whereas, for Pareto, the elements are exclusively individuals; for the others, there are *also* relatively enduring relations, structures, *Geist, mentalités*, social facts, and so on.[5]

A further big difference needs to be noticed. For Pareto the 'social equilibrium' constituted by the inter-relations of individuals is dynamic, moving through successive states in a lawful way. But although he heaps scorn on the idea of 'progress', he remains a Comtean in a crucial sense. Given the determinateness of each state and its successive transformations, there is, for him, a 'normal' trajectory for each particular 'form of society'. Pareto's version of a system does not exploit the *organic* analogy of system maintenance or 'growth', even if his language is misleading in this regard. The key idea for him is that the system is *fully deterministic* in the same sense that the solar system is fully deterministic. *It is a closed system of law-governed relations.* Pareto has a picture of a gigantic set of equations of many, many variables and unknowns, such that their simultaneous solution would exhaustively determine the successive states of the system.

> In order thoroughly to grasp the form of a society in its every detail it would be necessary first to know what all the very numerous elements are, and then to know how they function – and that in quantitative terms. . . . The number of equations would have to be equal to the number of unknowns and would determine them exhaustively. (para. 2062)

For Pareto the *big* problem arising from this picture was not one of principle, but the technical problem of making the calculations, 'the

---

[5] None of these writers, I believe, gave a satisfactory account of this important difference but that problem, to be addressed in chapter 13, need not be pursued immediately.

practical difficulty of solving the equations' (para. 2062, note 1). The economic system was but 'a small fraction of the social system as a whole'. Even then, 'in the case of 100 individuals and 700 goods there would be 70,699 conditions. . . . We would have to solve a system of 70,699 equations' (1971, para. 217).[6] He takes it for granted that quantified indices of the countless variables might be achieved (*Mind and Society*, para. 144), and he seems not in the least bit put off by the prospect of establishing the system of equations which would generate determinate 'states'. Of course, he made *zero* contribution to realizing either goal. Still, Pareto is rightly thought of as one of the founders of a quantitative sociology – and an optimist *in extremus*. He acknowledges that he would be content with even 'imperfect knowledge of the equations' (para. 2062, note 1). Pure economics had shown the way. The imperfect knowledge gleaned there, he insists, has proved to be 'of great help' in the solution of particular problems.

I need not try here to assess this last claim. On the other hand, lest the point be missed, the problem is *not* whether, as Pareto has it, the successive states of the social system are fully and lawfully determined, nor that these states are the causal outcomes of a host of 'elements' acting and in turn being acted on. Both these ideas, I believe, are eminently valuable, although they demand a great deal more analysis than Pareto or anyone before him provided. The problem as regards Pareto's vision of sociology is rooted in his philosophy of science and ultimately in his ontology: Are these 'laws' mathematical functions of variables? In Weber's terms, can social science be an abstract science? Indeed, can any sense be given to the idea that *the social system* or, for that matter, *the system of the world*, is a *closed* system. Only if these are like the solar system, considered abstractly, can the laws of society or of nature be mathematical functions of variables.

Elites and masses

Up to this point, I have avoided the substantive themes in Pareto's sociology. It will hardly do to ignore these, however, especially his theory of elites, which has had an enormous influence on the social sciences. As Bottomore (1964) has argued, Pareto defined 'elites' in two ways, as 'the people who have the highest indices in their branch of activity' (Pareto, 1935, para. 2031) and as 'a governing elite', as distinct from a 'non-governing elite' (para. 2032) which, together, are distinct

---

[6] An econometric model produced by Data Resources has 898 variables and 800 equations. A Burroughs 7800 computer, which fills an entire room, does the computations. See *The New York Times*, National Economic Survey, 8 January 1978, p. 11. Computational capacity has increased enormously since then, and in principle there is no limit.

from a 'lower stratum, the non-elite' (para. 2034). The first idea is innocuous politically and sociologically since it could affirmed by an equalitarian as well as an elitist. There could be 'elites' in this sense in a fully egalitarian society! No egalitarian, as far I know, has argued for a condition in which there is no excellence. The second idea is a horse of a different color. It is one of a family of theories each of which was directed at Marxism, at socialism – indeed at democracy in the traditional sense of direct participation of the people in political affairs. Here we should include Pareto's near contemporaries Gaetano Mosca (*Elementi di Scienza Politica* of 1896) and Robert Michels (*Zur Soziologie des Parteiwesens in der modernen Demokratie* of 1911).

These theories held that in every society, no matter how constituted, a minority would control politics. The choice of words here is important. 'Domination', 'Rule', 'Governance', 'Leadership' have very different connotations – indeed, they reflect very different conditions in the constitution of society, from say, the tyranny of masters over slaves to the relationship between an oligarchy and the *demos* in the ancient *polis* to the legitimated authority of the modern nation state to the influence of a Pericles among citizens, who, through voting, make the decision which affects them all. Elite theory aims quite deliberately to minimize, if not dissolve these differences. Indeed, the idea precisely is to leave the impression that the relations between ruler and ruled, governors and governed, elite and masses, leaders and followers are effectively the *same* relation.

This is clear enough in Pareto, whose argument takes a distinctly Machiavellian turn. Pareto's focus is the double-barrelled problem of how elites 'circulate' and how they maintain their ability to command. His key 'analytic' device is 'residues', the psychological characteristics of elites and masses, how they change and how they figure in 'social equilibrium'. Here Pareto's selective historical examples succeed in mystifying the very different historical circumstances of power and authority.

There are two types of 'governments', those 'relying chiefly on physical force and on religious or other sentiments' and those 'relying chiefly on intelligence and cunning' (Pareto, 1935, paras. 2274, 2274). They result from differences in the 'residues' of elites and masses. For example, governments of the second type 'have governing classes in which Class I residues ["the instinct for combinations" (para. 889)] predominate, as compared with Class II residues ["group persistences" (para. 991)]' (para. 2276). Further subdivisions allow for a host of generalizations – for example, circulation of elites is generally very rapid in governments of subtype IIb, a type which fits Athens, Rome at various times moments under the republic, many medieval republics, and 'the very important type of government flourishing in our day –

government by 'speculators' (para. 2275). These governments are expensive, but they 'produce actively'. And, of course, sufficient juggling of 'residues' yields a variety of other such generalizations – along with the pretense, at least, of real scientific explanation.

Elite theory is surely motivated by a Comtean fear of the lower classes. Indeed, Comte would have approved of the sentiment expressed by Pareto in this text (which is but one example among many):

> Those who demanded equality of citizens before the law certainly did not foresee the privileges which the masses now enjoy. . . . Those who demanded freedom to strike did not imagine that this freedom, for the strikers, would consist of beating workers who wanted to continue to work and setting fire to factories with impunity. Those who demanded equality of taxes to aid the poor did not imagine that there would a progressive tax at the expense of the rich. . . .
>
> The great error of the present time is believing that men can be governed by pure reason without making use of force. . . . The most peaceful people are forced, by the governments which have left only that way open to them, to band together and to resort to threats and violence to defend their interests. . . .
>
> A consequence of the heterogeneity of society is that rules of conduct, beliefs, morals, should be, in part at least, different for the different parts of society in order to obtain maximum utility for the society.

Indeed,

> the equality of citizens before the law is a dogma for many people, and in this sense it escapes experimental criticism. If we want to discuss this in a scientific manner, we will see immediately that it is not at all evident *a priori* that such equality is advantageous to society; moreover, given the heterogeneity of society itself, the contrary appears more probable. (Pareto, 1971, paras 106–10)

Mosca summarizes the Comtean point succinctly: 'In the world in which we are living socialism will be arrested only if a realistic political science succeeds in demolishing the metaphysical and optimistic methods that prevail at present in social studies' (quoted by Bottomore, 1964, p. 12).

DURKHEIM'S SOCIOLOGY

The ideas of Pareto and Mosca were directed against socialism, but they could be liberalized to make them precursors of the theory of democratic elites – or they can be read as precursors of fascism. Michels, the protégé of Weber whose career was blocked in Germany because he was a Social Democrat, ended his career in Italy, a personal friend of Mussolini and a professor at the militantly fascist University of Perugia.[7]

Emile Durkheim was, as Lukes says, 'a socialist of sorts' but at the same time, like Pareto, a moralistic conservative. Yet his conservatism was sociologically motivated – a fact of some importance. Durkheim has been ably discussed elsewhere. In what follows I will highlight two topics: his concept of 'social facts' and his concept of sociological explanation.

Durkheim visited Germany in 1885-6. As Lukes demonstrates, he was in total agreement with Schmoller's critique of political economy, that it was abstract, deductivist, unreal, and psychologistic.[8] But, given that these were his criticisms, he clearly could not go the way of Pareto. Rather than generalize pure economics, he had to start from a different place. He agreed with Comte that the laws of society were no different from those governing the rest of nature, and he agreed with him, ultimately, that psychology had nothing to offer to sociology. Psychology and political economy assume that 'the individual . . . is the sole tangible reality that the observer can attain', and thus 'the only problem that science can pose is that of discovering how the individual must behave in the principal circumstances of economic life, given his nature' (quoted by Lukes, p. 80, from *Cours de science sociale* of 1888). But 'the psychological factor is too general to predetermine the course of social phenomena. Since it does not call for one social form rather than another, it cannot explain any of them' (Durkheim, 1938, p. 108).

Rather, there are irreducible 'social facts' – that is, 'ways of acting or thinking with the peculiar characteristic of exercising a coercive influence on individual consciousness. (Durkheim, 1938, p. liii). 'Social facts do not differ from psychological facts in quality only; they have a

---

[7] Democratic elite theory, defined broadly, comprises Walter Lippman, *The Phantom Public* (1925) and *Essays in the Public Philosophy* (1955), Ortega y Gasset, *The Revolt of the Masses* (1930), Karl Mannheim, *Ideology and Utopia* (1936), and James Burnham, *The Machiavellians: Defenders of Freedom* (1943). Schumpeter's *Capitalism, Socialism and Democracy* (1943), and especially his argument that democracy is rightly characterized as a system in which there is competition for the vote, has been enormously influential. See also H. D. Lasswell *et al.*, *The Comparative Study of Elites* (1952). R. A. Dahl's now classic *Preface to Democratic Theory* (1956), whose concern was to define 'democracy' in conditions of the 'real world', stands as both the beginning and the end of tradition of democratic elite theory. See, for example, C. W. Mills, *The Power Elite* (1958); C. A. McCoy and John Playford, eds., *Apolitical Politics: A Critique of Behavioralism* (1967).

[8] '[Economists] study the facts that they deal with as if these formed an independent whole which was self-sufficient and could be explained in isolation. Now in reality economic functions are social functions, integrated with other collective functions; and they become inexplicable when they are violently separated from the latter. Workers' wages do not depend simply on the relation between supply and demand, but on certain moral conceptions. . . . Examples of this could be multiplied' (quoted by Therborn, 1976, pp. 253f.; see also Lukes's brief summary of 'La Science positive de la morale de Allemagne', in Lukes, 1972, pp. 86–95.

different substratum; they evolve in a different milieu; and they depend on different conditions' (1938, p. xlix).

In a period of ferocious anti-metaphysical empiricist individualism, Durkheim struggled to articulate an anti-individualist and naturalistic conception of 'society'. 'Social facts' were still 'facts', even if they were of a different kind. But in seeking to articulate this difference, he promoted some confusions which are still with us. He says,

> What is so readily judged inadmissible in the matter of social facts is freely admitted in the other realms of nature. Wherever certain elements combine and thereby produce, by the fact of their combination, new phenomena, it is plain that these new phenomena reside not in the original elements but in the totality formed by their union. The living cell contains nothing but mineral particles, as society contains nothing but individuals. Yet it is patently impossible for the phenomena characteristic of life to reside in the atoms of hydrogen, oxygen, carbon and nitrogen. (Durkheim, 1938, p. xlviii)

A functioning system may have properties not predicable of any of the elements of the system. Is society a system in the required sense? If so, what are these properties, and what are its 'parts': individuals, structures, or what? But in any case, the issue is not whether society has properties that are different from the properties of the individuals who comprise it, but whether individuals in association have *individual* properties not predicable of them were they *not* to exist in association; or whether, more generally, it is their specific forms of association that gives them the properties they have. If they did not exist in association, they would not even have *human* properties, just as was argued by Rousseau, Herder and Comte. It was in this radical sense that psychology, for Comte, was a non-existent discipline. If we understand methodological individualism as the docrine that social facts can be explained solely in terms of facts about individuals, then, when we consider properties uniquely characteristic of persons – that is, features or capacities not predicable of inorganic or subhuman entities – the problem is not how to give a strictly individualist explanation of human behavior, but *how to even talk about such action in the absence of irreducible social predicates!* This is what Durkheim has his hands on with his doctrine of the 'collective consciousness'.

It may be, *as well,* that 'society is not a mere sum of individuals' and that 'the system formed by their association represents a specific reality which has its own characteristics' (1938, p. 103). The idea that society is a system in the sense that molecules, cells, or organisms are systems is, as I argue later, probably disastrous. But this is utterly *irrelevant* to the problem at hand. One can deny that society is a system in this sense and still insist on the irreducibility of 'social facts'.

There was a second confusion passed on by Durkheim. He picks up his account of the 'externality' of social facts by noting that 'this does not mean that they are not also mental after a fashion, since they consist of ways of thinking and behaving' (1938, xlix). One can hear Mill or Pareto say, 'How can they be mental "after a fashion"?' Either they are, or they are not. If they are, then they are psychological facts. Indeed, the thesis that an idea can be mental – in somebody's mind – and yet social remains the least understood thesis in the literature of social science and, as we shall see, a fundamental stumbling block for an empirical psychology. Durkheim was bound to confuse his readers when he asserted that

> the states of the collective consciousness [*la conscience collective*] are different in nature from the states of the individual conscious-ness; they are 'representations' of another type. The mentality of groups is not the same as that of individuals; it has its own laws. (1938, xlix; see also Lukes, esp. pp. 230–6)

Durkheim has here multiplied the requisite entities, with consequences that become increasingly clear in his later thought. Chief among these was his shift from an emphasis on the material conditions of activity as *causes* of 'representations' to the idea that these were but *preconditions* of representations, ultimately *irrelevant* for sociology.[9] As Lukes re-marks, 'Durkheim had by the time of his latest writings come very close to maintaining that symbolic thought is a condition of and explains society' (Lukes, 1972, p. 235). This road, which connects to Neoplatonism and leads directly to twentieth-century structuralism, is the direct result of Durkheim's unsatisfactory formulation of the problem of social facts, a problem concerning the relation between persons and society, between agency and structure. Durkheim sees that 'mentalités', like language itself, are irreducibly social. It's not, however, that 'society' has proper-ties not predicable of individuals but that, apart from society, individuals have different – non-human – properties. Society is *constitutive* of personhood, but exists only as *incarnate* in the 'minds', acts, and products of persons.

[9] Therborn (1976) notes rightly that the difference between Marx and Durkheim does not primarily concern their conceptions of man; it is rather than for Durkheim, 'the social "infrastructure" is a social substratum in the same sense that human physiology is an organic substratum of psychology' (p. 256), an analogy endorsed by Durkheim in his *Sociology and Philosophy*. This idea is disastrous for both sociology and psychology. Just as physiology becomes *causally* irrelevant to psychology, so 'social morphology' becomes causally irrelevant to sociology: a double dualism: individual 'representations' and indi-vidual bodies; collective representations and material activity.

Similarly, 'consciousness' is *only* the conscious*nesses* of *individuals* –
even if 'mentalités', like languages, are *sui generis* real and *incarnate*
only in individual consciousnesses. The collective consciousness has no
'states' if by this we mean 'states of a substratum different from states of
persons'. But because *mentalités* are incarnate in persons does not make
them psychological facts. Durkheim's naturalistic critique of methodological individualism was incomplete.[10] What he needed and sorely
lacked is something akin to Giddens's idea of the duality of structure
(Giddens, 1979; Bhaskar, 1979): that social structures (including language,
'mentalités', relations constitutive of institutions) are the medium and
product of the acts of conscious agents, social constructions which,
because they always pre-date individuals, play a causal role in their
epigenesis. Durkheim diagnosed the limits of the empiricistic individualisms, but he gave an erroneous account of 'social facts'. Not only
was there an unresolved tension in his thought regarding the radical
difference between a 'materialist' and an 'idealist' philosophy of society
(see chapters 5 and 6) but, he needlessly imported into his account the
disastrous idea of 'social organism'. It was in terms of both these notions
that he was so valuable to later 'structural functionalism'.

Functionalism in Durkheim

'Functionalism' is a term with many meanings. Durkheim was a critic of
that version of functionalism which he attributes to Comte and Spencer.
He writes:

> Most sociologists think that they have accounted for phenomena
> once they have shown how they are useful, what role they play,
> reasoning as if facts existed only from the point of view of this role
> with no other determining cause than the sentiment, clear or
> confused, of the services they are called to render. (1938, p. 89)

We must be careful here. Durkheim opposes the idea that individuals or
groups voluntarily bring into existence what they clearly or unclearly
recognize as needed. The idea is familiar enough in the liberal tradition
of social thought, of course (see chapter 2). Its flaw is its voluntarism, its
failure to acknowledge that 'social facts' are mainly the unintended
consequences of intentional acts.

But one can 'objectify' functions and argue merely that, in fact, some
element serves a 'need', whether or not it was intended to do so. The
'need' may be some postulated or supposed human need, from the need
for food to the need for love. One might then affirm that the family, for

[10] See chapter 13 for an analysis of the critical differences between this and an
alternative realist formulation.

example, satisfies these needs, but without affirming that it was any-body's intention to create families. Although Durkheim has been read as holding some such view, it runs counter to his persistent criticism of the idea that social facts can be deduced from 'human nature', another thesis he attributes to Comte and Spencer. For Durkheim, it is wrong to argue that social forms can be explained as the means, intended *or* unintended, artificial or natural, in terms of which the needs of human nature are satisfied (1938, p. 98).

Finally, one might hold that society is a 'system' which, *as* a system, has needs. There are then two questions which might be asked:

> When . . . the explanation of a social phenomenon is undertaken, we must seek separately the efficient cause which produces it and the function it fulfills. . . . We must determine whether there is a correspondence between the fact under consideration and the general needs of the social organism . . . without occupying our-selves with whether it is intentional or not. (p. 95)

Durkheim held that a social fact was not explained by showing that it was 'useful', since this did not explain 'how it originates or why it is what it is' (p. 90). And he acknowledged that a social fact can exist 'without being at all useful'. But consider his 'first rule' for sociological method: 'A social fact is normal, in relation to a given social type at a given phase of its development, when it is present in the average society of that species at the corresponding phase of its evolution' (p. 64). That is, Durkheim is committed to the idea that society is an organic unity which, like an organism, is capable of living, dying, changing, and evolving. Indeed, its 'evolution' is unilinear, as in Comte.

Two assumptions are involved here: the idea that society is a totality, and the Comtean notion that societies, like organisms, have a lawful 'development'. Molecules, cells, and organisms are obvious totalities, being compounds of elements whose causal 'co-operation' gives them the properties they have. But it is not so clear how one theorizes that society is a totality in this sense. There is first of all the problem of boundedness. One can theorize and experimentally isolate boundaries of molecules. Organisms are patently no problem. Indeed, the temp-tation here has been to deny ecological facts in coming to an under-standing of organisms. Second, as regards societies, there is the problem of defining what counts as 'system-maintenance'. The idea can be given a plausible sense in molecules, cells, and organisms. Moreover, in a living system, we can theorize and produce evidence for a concept of what is 'normal' and of 'normal development', and we can speak unproblematically about its death. Is this sensible as regards societies? Third, we have been able to theorize *mechanisms* of system-maintainance in living things – for example, homeostasis – and in artifacts – for example, thermostatic control systems; but, as above, there is an overwhelming temptation for the social theorist to move from metaphor to confusion; to suppose, for example, that society is a teleological system in the sense that there *must* be some sort of negative feedback bringing about 'adjustment' of the system.

Durkheim was uncritical in all these matters. He held that as regards 'the social organism', there are 'normal' and 'abnormal' states and developments. Indeed, this was his way to solve the philosophical problem of 'fact' and 'value'. As is well known, Durkheim diagnosed 'anomie', inequality, and inadequate organization as the fundamental ills of industrial capitalism. But for him, these were 'abnormal', but temporary, aberrations (see Lukes, 1972, pp. 172–8). On his view, St Simon was essentially correct in arguing that 'industry had been, up to the present, placed under subordination of powers which rose above it', that 'these powers retrogressed irretrievably', and that 'this situation is unhealthy and the cause of the crisis which we suffer' (Durkheim, 1958, p. 202). But on his view, St Simon was wrong in supposing that once 'the old powers' had disappeared, all would be well. Comte was more nearly right in seeing that, given the ills, the problem now was moral and pedagogical, and that a new positive force was demanded: to develop a new moral order consistent with industrial society. Ideas had now to catch up with the new realities.

It is easy to produce texts which suggest strongly that Durkheim's ideological 'solution', like Comte's, was reactionary. For example, in *Socialism and St Simon*, he wrote:

> What is needed if social order is to reign is that the mass of men be content with their lot, is not that they have more or less but that they be convinced they have no right to more. And for this, it is absolutely necessary that there be an authority whose superiority they acknowledge and which tells them what is right. (1958, p. 200)

On the other hand, in contrast to many today who are in sympathy with Durkheim's sociologically motivated conservativism, Durkheim acknowledged the 'injustices of contracts', where 'one social class is obliged, in order to live, to offer its services at any price, while the other can do without them' (quoted from Lukes, 1972, p. 175). He insisted that planning was essential to combat the anarchy of production, and that workers and employers would need cooperative institutions if the pathologies of capitalism were to be overcome. But, of course, Durkheim, unlike his erstwhile followers, was a penetrating critic of the scientific pretensions of 'pure economics'.

The task of sociology

In this last section, I want to argue that there was a wide gap between Durkheim's official doctrine and his sociological practice, a gap which can be explained and which explains a great deal of contemporary sociology. Some earlier themes can be joined and some additional focal points addressed.

Chapter IV of *The Rules* begins with an account of the polarity between 'historians' and 'philosophers', a polarity familiar since Ranke (see chapter 7). 'For the historian, societies represent just so many heterogeneous individualities.... For the philosopher ... all these individual groupings, called tribes, city-states, and nations, are only contingent and provisional aggregations with no exclusive or separate reality' (1938, p. 76). The sociologist can go between the two: 'Between the confused multitude of historical societies and the single, but ideal, concept of humanity, there are intermediaries, namely social species' (p. 77). Because societies are social organisms, there can be social species, and because there are social species, 'variations are not of such a nature that they deny all scientific treatment' (p. 77). It is clear that Durkheim is responding to the problem which Weber's notion of ideal types was meant to solve, but that for him, a 'scientific treatment' *is* a treatment which demands *generalization*. We need to discover propositions of the form 'All *F*'s are *G*'s', or at least of the form 'Most *F*'s are *G*'s'. The contrast to Weber is remarkable. From Weber's point of view, Durkheim is another Roscher, a generalizing 'sociologist', trapped by a wholly spurious biological metaphor (see chapter 7).[11] Indeed, it is quite amazing how so many have missed this and thus have happily joined Weber and Durkheim. This stems from an inadequate understanding of the methodological issues at stake.

The most useful way to proceed is to take seriously Durkheim's two claims that all sociology asks is that 'the principle of causality be applied to social phenomena' (1938, p. 141), and that 'comparative sociology is not a particular branch of sociology; it is sociology itself' (p. 139). What is at stake, then, can be couched in terms of the questions: What is the principle of causality? and What is the comparative method? On both

---

[11] Therborn calls our attention to a text in *The Division of Labor* (1947) directed against Savigny: 'One finds classified there, not social species, but historical phases, which is quite different'. France, he notes, has passed through 'very different forms of civilization', but 'it is impossible to admit that the same collective individuality can change its species three or four times. A species must define itself by more constant characteristics.... It is even very probable that the same industrial, scientific and artistic civilization can be found in societies whose hereditary constitution is very different' (p. 174f.). Therborn observes rightly that Durkheim 'sees national societies as resembling biological organisms' (Therborn, 1976, p. 250).

topics, Durkheim consciously proceeds from Mill. He adopts 'the method of concomitant variations or correlation' as *the* method of sociology, and he rejects Mill's analysis of causality.

Durkheim saw that Mill's analysis of causality was confused, but, unfortunately, his version was no improvement. It will be recalled that Mill held to a Humean constant conjunction conception of the causal relation, denying all necessity between 'cause' and 'effect'. He also asserted the famous doctrine of the 'plurality of causes': 'It is not true . . . that one effect must be connected with only one cause, or assemblage of conditions. . . . One fact may be the consequent in several invariable sequences' (Mill, 1930, III, ch. 10, para. 1). Durkheim attacks 'this supposed axiom' and its presupposition head-on:

> [It] . . . is, in fact, a negation of the principle of causality. To be sure, if one believes with Mill that cause and effect are absolutely unrelated, there is nothing contradictory in admitting that an effect may sometimes follow one cause and sometimes another. If the relation which unites C to A is purely chronological, it does not exclude another relation of the same kind which would unite, for example, C to B.
>
> If, on the contrary, the causal bond is logical, it could not be indeterminate. If it consists in a relation resulting from the nature of things, a given effect can maintain this relationship with only one cause, for it can express only one single nature. (1938, p. 127)

Durkheim wants to restore 'determinacy' to the causal relation, and he was correct in this. Calling the relation 'logical', however, did not help, especially given that it was just at this time, with the giant advances in modern logic (see chapter 9), that 'logical' had come to mean 'conceptual'. There is a flavor of the older realist conception in his formulation, and this smacked then, as now, of 'metaphysics'. It was not pursued by Durkheim. What he did, instead, was to argue that there was a class of causes for each class of effects, that, as he said, 'if suicide depends upon more than one cause, it is because, in reality, there are several kinds of suicides. The same is true of crime' (1938, p. 129). The problem of science was to establish such causal laws. The experimental methods were the means.

There is a sense in which this analysis is both better and worse than Mill's. It is better insofar as Durkheim sees that science is impossible with the Humean notion of causality. It is worse insofar as Mill allowed himself what he called 'the admixture of effects', 'a concurrence of two or more causes, not separately producing each its own effect, but interfering with or modifying the effect of one another' (Mill, 1930, III, ch. 10, para. 4). This problem and the problem of the plurality of causes shows that Mill was sensitive to the problem of causality in the real world where, as Weber, Engels – and the common person – sees, everything that happens is a complex causal product, an admixture of effects of many causes, and where, in common parlance, a person may die, for example, from a variety of 'causes'. The plurality of causes and the problem of the admixture of effects raises complete havoc with the experimental methods, a fact fully emphasized, of course, by Mill.

Durkheim was not *entirely* insensitive to the real difficulties of isolating causes in *his* sense. Mill's famous methods of agreement and difference were not available for sociology since 'they suppose that the causes compared either agree or differ by one single point' (Durkheim, 1938, p. 129) and this is impossible to come by. After eliminating the method of residues as 'of no particular use in the study of social phenomena', he affirms the viability of the method of concomitant variation or correlation: 'The mere parallelism of the series of values presented by the two phenomena, provided it has been established in a sufficient number and variety of cases, is proof that a relationship exists between them.' Indeed, this is 'direct proof' that 'they are united by an internal bond' (p. 130).

But there are dangers: 'The concomitance may not be due to the fact one phenomena is the cause of the other but to the fact that they are both the effects of the same cause, or, again, that there exists between them a third phenomenon . . . which is the effect of the first and the cause of the second. The results to which this method leads need, therefore, to be interpreted' (p. 131). This problem is revolvable, however, by means of the logic of the crucial experiment, by finding a 'control' case.

In *Suicide*, for example, by including French Jews in his scheme, he could show that commercial activity, urbanization, and education were but 'measures' of 'individualism', not independent causes of suicide (Stinchcombe, 1968, p. 27). He was thus able to conclude that 'excessive individuation' was the cause of 'egoistic suicide'.

Now in fact this program is so much nonsense, and it is surprising that readers have been so tolerant. No science could proceed on the assumptions of the official doctrine. But then, Durkheim's concrete work doesn't either. The official doctrine has it that the aim of science is to secure knowledge of causal laws construed as empirical invariances and that the method of correlation is the means to this end. Ideally, we should be able to find the cause, either 'a single antecedent' or 'a single set of antecedents' for every effect.

As is well known, Durkheim distinguished between egoistic suicide and altruistic suicide. This was a consequence of his notion, contra Mill, that 'a given effect' can maintain a 'determinate' (logical? necessary?)

relationship 'with only one cause'. Since 'excessive individuation' or, remarkably, 'insufficient individuation' in the case of 'altruistic suicide' are 'causes', 'suicide' had to be of two sorts. But more fundamental is the assumption that we are to think of the causal relation as some sort of connection between 'variables', 'dependent' and 'independent'. It is this understanding, of course, which is at work in the usual (multivariate) understanding of Mill's 'experimental' methods, where 'hypotheses' pick out candidates for 'dependent variables', properly defined (Lazarsfeld and Rosenberg, 1955).

Suicide, of course, is an 'effect', but this must mean that suicides have causes. Indeed, it seems obvious that, as Giddens says, 'it is a social fact in itself, the outcome of a complex set of events involving numerous social actors: relatives, friends, doctors, police, coroners, etc. These phenomena cannot be studied by means of suicide statistics, because they are involved in the very creation of such statistics' (Giddens, 1978, pp. 116f.). The official doctrine has the cart before the horse. If we could understand the complex causal factors at work in individual 'suicides', not only the factors which lead people to take their own lives, but the way these acts are identified and so on, we could explain the *suicide statistics,* an accomplishment which would also enable us to explain the different *rates.* If the variable 'suicide' is strongly correlated with the variable 'excessive individuation', then that is because there is something about the causes of individual 'suicides' which is represented by the concept 'excessive individuation'. What is needed – but what is forbidden for the method – is an analysis of these causal mechanisms as they operate in explaining suicides. As I will argue in chapter 13, the point is perfectly general and can easily be missed. Quantitative research involving multivariate analyses and so on confuses *explacandum* for *explacans.* It offers patterns as explanations, a task for which they are unsuited, whereas it is the patterns which need explaining.

Durkheim's work is a perfect example, as well, of the way that this is mystified. His book *Suicide* does contain some genuine explanations. The ideas of 'anomie', 'social integration', and 'urbanization', are concepts characterizing social relations, 'social facts' as 'ways of acting and thinking with the peculiar characteristic of exercising a coercive influence on individual consciousness' (1938, p. liii). It is just because they are this that they can figure in the *causal* explanation of individual suicides (and thus also in explaining differential rates of suicide). One might say here that Durkheim's concept of social facts, often read as social structures, gives rise to a *realist* understanding of his social science, in which the critical concepts are promissory notes on the causal mechanisms operating in society. Saying that anomie is a condition of society is, in this sense, like saying that a compound is water-soluble.

This is what does the explaining, even if it is the empiricist notion of 'correlations' which pretends to do so.

Moreover, it is this realist reading of Durkheim which leads to the comparison with Weber, since he also can be read as holding the view that social structures structure action. We can round this out by comparing Durkheim with Weber on how this functions in their very different conceptions of comparative method.

Weber's point of departure was this:

> The type of social science in which we are interested is a *science of reality* [*Wirklichkeitwissenschaft*]. Our aim is the understanding of the characteristic uniqueness of the reality in which we move. We wish to understand on the one hand the relationships and the cultural significance of individual events in their contemporary manifestations, and on the other the causes of their being historically *so* and not *otherwise*. (Weber, 1949, p. 72)

Time- and space-bound historical configurations must be characterized ideal-typically and explained causally. Both tasks require a comparative method. Ideal-typical characterization involves the study of concrete *ways of thought and action* with an eye toward identifying the specific *uniqueness* of the configuration, a task realized only by means of comparative study. For example, one might say, with Pareto, that in every society there is 'political command'; but the specific relations and ideology can be grasped only by seeing how the extensive land empire of Rome's slave economy made for a politics different from that of Athens's territorially inelastic thassalocracy, that both of these were radically different from the politics of the non-expansionistic medieval republics, which were different again from those of modern capitalist nation-states, each of which again are different in important ways. The causal question, not completely satisfiable, could be put into a manageable frame by the same device. For example, if 'ascetic Protestantism' and 'the spirit of capitalism' were causal consequences of the transition to 'capitalism' – all ideal-typical concepts in a Weberian frame – then they should be absent in pre-capitalist societies. Comparative method could serve to test whether this was true or false.

Durkheim's *official* doctrine was, as I noted, a multivariate strategy in which "variables' were shown to be directly 'connected'. But the real interest lies in his efforts to eliminate *structural conditions* as either unnecessary or insufficient causes of *individual* suicides. Including French Jews in the suicide study showed that people whose lives are structured by commercial activity, urban life, and high levels of education are not, *for these reasons*, more likely candidates for suicide. It is this, of course, which has led so many writers to notice similarities between Weber and Durkheim in the use of comparative methodology. The similarity, let it be emphasized, is between Weber and *some* of Durkheim's practice – not between Weber and Durkheim's official doctrine. There is another difference of no small importance.

Durkheim, but *not* Weber, wanted to compare 'species' of 'social organisms'. The metaphor of 'species' finally did Durkheim in, but one might be generous here and note that by 'species' one might mean merely 'type' or 'set' defined in this way or that. Thus, one might learn something from the comparison of 'social revolutions'. One might, for example, get a clearer idea of the structural conditions causally relevant to the French, Chinese, and Russian revolutions (Skocpol, 1979). Indeed, as in the Weberian frame, such analysis is unavoidable, even if, failing to acknowledge that it is unavoidable or what it is really for, it may be done badly.

But if one supposes that a species of social organism is a totality in the sense that an organism is, then it is easy to suppose *also* that it has a 'normal' development and finally, that there is in history a unilinear evolution. I earlier indicated how the distinction between 'normal' and 'pathological' infected Durkheim's social science, and I conclude by noting that, despite his protestations to the contrary, *The Division of Labor in Society, Primitive Classification* (with Marcel Mauss), and *The Elementary Forms of Religious Life* are each marked profoundly by the characteristic nineteenth-century assumptions of unilinear evolution. These are especially apparent in his comparative work, in which commitment to the generalizing idea of a social species led him to abandon history for spurious cross-sectional analyses, comprehended as causal developments over time, a trap fallen into by modern writers who should know better. One example from Durkheim will illustrate the point. In *The Elementary Forms,* as Kapsis points out, Durkheim compares Australian and American Indian tribes 'as if they were sampled from a single society at different points in time' on the grounds that they are members of 'the same social species' and thus can be taken to represent 'two successive movements of a single evolution' (Kapsis, 1977, p. 354). By parity of reasoning, why not consider three members of the same 'social species' at different times, so as to discover why in each of them there was, for example, a social revolution? One might then arrive at the 'scientific' and 'explanatory' generalizations 'When there are conditions, $n_1, n_2, \ldots n_x$, a social revolution is highly probable', or 'If there is to be a social revolution, then conditions, $n_1, n_2, \ldots n_x$, are necessary'. But this is not to mediate between the claims of historians and the claims of sociologists. It is rather, as I have been arguing, to abandon history, to adopt a notion of scientific explanation which is fully positivist, and ultimately, to hold with Pareto that the world system is closed.[12]

The next chapter begins at the beginning, as it were, and makes the effort to sketch, against the background of what has already been said, the career of psychology as an empirical science.

[12] Just as there was a gap between Durkheim's official doctrine and his practice, some modern inquirers generate useful results despite their explicit methodologies. See my 1981 review of Skocpol's *States and Social Revolutions*.

9

The Genesis of Psychology

It has been a premise of this book that neither 'science' nor, *a fortiori*, the branches of the social sciences are 'natural kinds'. As 'disciplines', they have been constituted by human practices, and their constitution therefore has a history and might have been other than what it in fact has been. This idea is especially critical with respect to 'psychology', because in psychology, more than in any other contemporary branch of science, it is only too easy to read this history backwards, to take some idea of 'psychology' as it is presently constituted and then to find in the past a continuous line of development of that idea, supposing this to have been the 'natural' development in which the discipline was progressively liberated from its pre-scientific past.

Psychology, of course, was for a long time intimately related to philosophy; indeed, although the two were separated by Kant, it was not perhaps until the end of the nineteenth century that the divorce became final. But, contrary to the standard view, it is a main contention of this chapter that we shall not get a handle on the history of 'scientific psychology' unless we see clearly what this divorce ruled out. Once 'epistemology' had been discovered and had become the foundational inquiry, the possibility of a non-reductionist physiological psychology was out of the question. Writing before Hume and Kant, Hartley (1749) proceeded 'naively', attempting to solve the problem which Locke had put aside, that of how 'vibrations' in the central nervous system give rise to 'ideas'. For Hartley, this question, as Rorty puts it, was like the question 'How are telephones possible?' That is, it was a scientifically tractable question. But Hume thought otherwise, and after Kant, as Burnyeat (1984) has argued, our innocence was lost. And, as everyone knows, innocence once lost can never be regained. An empirical science needed 'foundations' in experience, and if so, there was no way to close the gap between the phenomena of consciousness and what is not in consciousness. It seemed to most that there were but three choices: to go with Kant and reject the possibility of a scientific psychology; to go the route suggested by Hume and developed by Mill and the 'associationists'; or, to remain committed to the idea of a secure empiricist foundation and go with Mach for what, I shall argue, is a physiological psychology without physical *causes*. Moreover, as this suggests, there has been a systematic failure to discriminate between the salient issues and different positions, largely because, since Kant, writers have agreed with Kant in making epistemology independent of and prior to 'science', and in supposing that everyone is either an 'empiricist' or a Kantian. As regards the history of psychology, this has fuelled two additional confusions: that wrought by putting Mill, Spencer, Helmholtz, and Mach together as 'empiricists' and that wrought by supposing that if 'mind' is to be active and unitive, as it is in Kant, only idealism is possible.

There were good historical reasons for the bifurcation of what we now call 'epistemology' and what we now call 'psychology'. Some of these were broached in chapter 1. It may be well here to summarize the conclusions of that chapter which are of importance for what follows.

First the savaging of naive realism drove a wedge between 'inner' and 'outer', creating the modern problem of knowledge. How can our ideas correspond to what is not in the mind? Second, Hume 'solved' the mind/body problem (as formulated by Descartes) by thoroughly 'operationalizing' science. His 'scepticism' was a gentleman's scepticism, a scepticism not over whether there was an 'external world' (or 'other minds'), but about any 'theory' which went beyond experience. Third, Kant sought to refute scepticism once and for all, but the net result was that scepticism was 'moved upstairs to the transcendental level' (Burnyeat, 1984, p. 250). The plain man says 'The stove is warm', and that is fine as long as one remains uncritically within the empirical realist (naive realist) world of the plain man. But the philosopher knows better: there is no way to close the gap between 'things in themselves' and the contents of consciousness. This is a complicated story, and it will be well to pick up the threads of the argument before Hume and Kant, with Hartley (1705–57), physician, philosopher, and Christian.

THE HUMAN UNDERSTANDING

Hartley picked up where he believed Locke and Newton had left off. In his *Observations on Man* (1749), he provided a complete system, beginning with an account of how our 'ideas' are generated and going on in part II (of his 1,000-page treatise) to considerations of 'the Duty and

Expectations of Mankind', including a discussion of 'the Being and Attributes of God', and the 'Terms of Salvation'.

Hartley is remembered as the 'founder of British associationism', as precursor of a tradition which runs from him to James and John Stuart Mill to Alexander Bain, founder of the British journal *Mind,* and thence to Titchener, who brought 'empiricistic' British 'psychology' to America. But this will not do. Hartley's 'psychology' was a thoroughgoing physiological psychology which offered a causal account of sensation in terms of Newton's theory of vibrations. Contrary to what Boring (1929) says, Hartley was no 'psycho-physical parallelist'. In noting that 'the Doctrine of *Vibrations* may appear at first Sight to have no Connexion with that of *Association*' (Hartley, 1966, p. 6), he seems sensitive to what we think of as the mind/body problem. But he insists, nonetheless, that 'if these Doctrines be found in fact to contain the Laws of the Bodily and Mental Powers respectively, they must be related to each other, since the Body and Mind are'. And, critically, *this relation is causal*: 'One may expect, that Vibrations should infer Associations as their Effect, and Association point to Vibrations as its Cause' (p. 6).

What follows, then, is an attempt to show how Newton's 'aether' hypothesis can be brought to bear on the issues raised by Locke. Sensation causes vibration which sets in motion the infinitesimal particles of 'the medullary Substance', which finally arrive at the appropriate locations in the brain. At this point, then, 'it seems reasonable to expect that, if a single Sensation may leave a perceptible Effect, Trace, or Vestige, for a short time, a sufficient Repetition of a Sensation may leave a perceptible Effect of the same kind, but of a more permanant Nature, i.e., an Idea' (p. 57). It is appropriate to call this an 'associationist' account if we keep clearly in mind that, in Hartley's view, his real innovation was in joining Newton to Locke to show how 'vibrations' leave a 'Vestige' which becomes the *material* for compounding the complicated 'Ideas' which are characteristic of human understanding.

It took no time at all for some distinguished writers to entirely excise the 'vibrations' part of the story. Joseph Priestley (1733–1804) produced a 'condensed version' of Hartley's work in 1775, a version fully consistent with the new *empiricistic* conception of 'scientific philosophy'. He stripped it of what related 'to the doctrine of vibrations, and the anatomical disquisitions', on the grounds that these were 'difficult and intricate', and he eliminated the 'whole system of moral and religious knowledge'. 'However excellent', they were, he said, 'in a great measure, foreign to it' (cited from Huguelet's very useful introduction to Hartley's *Observations,* 1966, p. xii). James Mill picked up where Priestley had left off. Familiar not only with Hartley's work but also with what had transpired in between – including therefore Hume's analysis of experience and causality – Mill launched the understanding of 'associationism' which became characteristic of British 'empirical psychology'.

Priestley was not alone in ridding Hartley of his 'materialism'. Coleridge, as 'a compleat Necessitarian', liked Hartley's work so much that he had named his first son David Hartley Coleridge. But, as Huguelet points out, sometime in 1797 or 1798, Coleridge 'became disenchanted with Hartley's mechanical psychology and passive necessitarianism'. Now under the influence of Kant and German thought, he rejected Newton 'in favor of a creative mind working upon an ideal reality'. His second son, born in 1798, was named 'Berkeley', after the bishop of Cloyne. Coleridge's turn to German metaphysics had effects on British letters, but not on British 'science'. In the nineteenth century, British 'scientific philosophy' was strongly anti-metaphysical and anti-sociological. These two features put it in sharp opposition to German 'scientific thought', a fact of some importance for this chapter. But it would be an error to suppose that because British thought was anti-metaphysical and anti-sociological, there was already a consensus regarding the nature of 'psychology'. At this point we can distinguish two competing notions: the associationist psychology of the two Mills, and another, the line which followed Hartley. We will look first at the pertinent pages of J. S. Mill's influential *Logic* of 1843.

BRITISH ASSOCIATIONIST 'PSYCHOLOGY'

It will be recalled that while working on the *Logic,* Mill was reading Comte. It will also be remembered that in Comte's hierarchy of the sciences, there was no place for 'psychology', a word that was only then coming into use. Comte held that 'psychology' had to be metaphysical; that mind, ego, and the like were but *useless* abstractions, remnants of our previous metaphysical stage. His associate Laurent, writing in 1826, had put the matter succinctly in arguing that whereas physiology 'stops where the phenomena are wanting, psychology abandons observation to mount by the inductive path to causality, to substance' (Boas, 1924, p. 282). It is clear that, by this time, almost everyone could agree on the metaphysical character of causality and substance, 'empiricists' and Kantians. It is clear, too, that this would argue decisively against Hartley's program, a fact clearly seen by Mill.

As I emphasized before, the basis of Comte's hierarchy of the sciences was his conviction that nature was stratified, that everything was governed by the laws of physics, that some things were subject, in addition, to the laws of physiology, and that others – humans – were subject to the laws of sociology. Accordingly, Comte did not argue that psychology had been *replaced* by physiology. The place of physiology in the hierarchy of sciences was right below that of sociology, the science of humans as social beings. Animals, like humans, perceive, feel, and are purposeful, and inquiry into their perceiving and so on was the proper domain of physiology, a biological science. But physiology was not a human science, because it did not treat what was *distinctive* of humans. This meant that, since humans were everywhere social and were so *by virtue of* social phenomena, one could explain human nature by understanding society, but not the other way around.

Mill agreed with Comte that if psychology were to be a science, it would have to rid itself of metaphysics. But he saw Comte as having gone too far in eliminating the possibility of psychology. Mill's concern was to give some non-metaphysical and non-socially produced content to the human part of 'human nature'.

He did this by arguing that 'the laws of the mind . . . comprise the universal abstract portion of the philosophy of human nature' (Mill, 1930, VI, ch. 5). Of course, one must distinguish 'mind' from its 'sensible manifestations'. As Laurent had noted, inquiry into the former was metaphysics. But Mill could accept part of Comte's view, since 'states of mind are immediately caused either by other states of mind or by a state of the body' (ch. 4). The former fall under *the laws of mind*; but, since 'sensation' always has 'for its proximate cause some affection of the portion of our frame called the nervous system', the latter are properly matters of physiology. Mill agreed also with Comte that the 'science of the formation of character' – 'ethology' – was *not* psychology, since this surely involved considerations of the distinctly social and historical. Mill thus eliminated from psychology everything but the 'laws of the succession of states of mind' – British associationism, as that has come to be understood. Mill got what he wanted: a universal non-physiological psychology and a social human nature, a combination, I take it, that today would be widely accepted. Mill's program was coherent, nevertheless, since he did not see psychology as pretending to explain 'behavior'. Physiology, a biological science, could explain 'sensation'; whereas ethology, a social science, could shed some light on socially produced human character. Given this and the biography of a person, one might begin to explain individual behavior. The idea that psychology could be the *science* of behavior would have amused Mill.

SPENCER'S AESTHO-PHYSIOLOGY

The other line of thought is a neglected chapter in the history of British psychology (see Danziger, 1982). I refer here to a continuation of what Hartley began, the mid-nineteenth-century physiological psychology of W. B. Carpenter, Professor of Physiology at the Royal Institute and

Thomas Laycock, Professor of Medicine at Edinburgh and, more important, Herbert Spencer, whose radically rewritten *Principles of Psychology* (1st edn, 1855; 2nd edn, 1870, 72) needs to be discussed. I cannot here go into any detail regarding thought of Carpenter or Laycock; all three attempted to explain 'psychological' phenomena in terms of physiological processes, but Spencer clearly recognized what had become the epistemological problems standing in the way of a scientific psychology. Spencer has been ill understood, despite the ground-breaking account given by Mandelbaum in 1971. It is my suspicion that orthodoxy in the histories of psychology and epistemology is so deeply entrenched that it is easy to exclude Carpenter and Laycock in histories of psychology on the grounds that they were 'primarily' physiologists. Moreover, it is even easier to miss the meaning and the significance of Spencer's notion of 'transfigured realism'.

Spencer argued that physiology must exclude *all* reference to consciousness: 'Physiology is an objective science; and is limited to such data as can be reached by observations made on sensible objects'. 'It cannot ... properly appropriate subjective data; or data wholly inaccessible to external observations' (Spencer, 1902, p. 48). On the other hand, inquiry could not be restricted to the laws of the successive states of the mind, since one could never show how these were connected with changes in the environment. It wasn't that associationist principles were irrelevant; there were 'connexions between the internal phenomena', and clearly these needed to be understood. What was required, however, was another kind of inquiry, called by Spencer 'aestho-physiology', which would discover the connections between the data of consciousness and objective phenomena *within* the organism. Eventually, then, these had to be connected with what was going on in the environment *outside* the organism. This, then, would comprise psychology, a science which *depends* on both physiology *and* aestho-physiology:

> ... that which distinguishes Psychology from the sciences on which it rests, is, that each of its propositions takes account both of the connected internal phenomena and of the connected external phenomena to which they refer. ... [A psychological proposition] is the connection between these two connections. ... The distinction may be best explained in symbols. Suppose that A and B are two related manifestations in the environment – say, the colour and taste of a fruit; then so long as we contemplate their relation by itself, or as associated with other external phenomena, we are occupied with a portion of physical science. Now suppose that *a* and *b* are the sensations produced in the organism by this peculiar light which the fruit reflects and by the chemical reaction of its

juice on the palate; then, so long as we study the action of the light on the retina and optic nerves, and consider how the juice sets up in other centres a nervous change known as sweetness, we are occupied with facts belong to the sciences of Physiology and Aestho-physiology. But we pass into the domain of Psychology the moment we inquire how there comes to exist within the organism a relation between *a* and *b* that in some way or other corresponds to the relation between A and B. Psychology is exclusively concerned with this connection between (A B) and (*a b*) – has to investigate its nature, its origin, its meaning. (Spencer, 1902, I, pp. 132f.)

Having lost his epistemological innocence, Spencer was profoundly sensitive to what were by then obvious objections to his program. He observed that 'each individual is absolutely incapable of knowing any feelings but his own'; that, accordingly, it is only through one's 'reasonings' that one can infer that with the actions of other bodies 'there go internal states of consciousness like those accompanying [the] external actions of one's own body'; that even if this is true – as he does not seriously doubt – it is still not demonstrable experientially that 'what he knows under its subjective aspect as feeling, is, under its objective aspect nervous action'; and, finally, having 'learnt at second hand, through the remotely-inferential interpretation of verbal signs', that others, 'like himself', have a nervous system, he further infers that he has a nervous system like those others and thus reasons that his own sensations are due to 'disturbances which the outer world sets up at the periphery'. This only begins to suggest 'the remotely-inferential character of the belief that feeling and nervous action are correlated' (pp. 98ff.). But however indirect and 'remotely inferential', 'the evidence of this connection is so large in amount, presents such a congruity under so great a variety of circumstances, and is so continually confirmed by the correct anticipations to which it leads, that we can entertain nothing more than a theoretical doubt of its truth' (p. 100).

The upshot is a 'transfigured realism', which 'simply asserts objective existence as separate from and independent of subjective existence' (Spencer, 1902, II, p. 494). Transfigured realism is not 'the Realism of common life – the realism of the child or the rustic', since, critically, no relation in consciousness can 'resemble, or be in any way akin, to its source beyond consciousness' (*ibid*; see also 'The Relativity of Relations between Feelings', I, sec. IV). While 'internal feeling' – the phenomenon of consciousness – 'habitually depends upon an external agent, yet there is no likeness between them in either kind or degree' (I, p. 194). Put simply, I may have the perception of a red tomato, and this is confirmed intersubjectively. But there is absolutely no reason to believe that in the external, 'objective' world, there are red tomatoes. There are causes of 'the molecular motions' of our nervous system, but of course, this is an inference. It is, in fact, what we earlier termed 'transdiction', except that it is now turned on the very question of a scientific psychology.

Nevertheless Spencer is still fully in the grip of Hume and Kant, and thus he is easily read as holding to some sort of psycho-physical parallelism. As Mandelbaum notes, for Spencer, 'science would be transcended and metaphysics would set in if one tried to form any conception of how motions in the nerves "produce" sensations, or how complex associations of these ideas can lead to those efferent nerve impulses which eventuate in action. To attempt to go behind the verifiable correlations between these utterly different types of concept would be to introduce notions which it is not in any way possible to verify within experience' (Mandelbaum, 1971, p. 304). Spencer was still the positivist in holding that *causality was empirical invariance*. But if so, all one can do is to 'correlate' introspectively identifiable 'feelings' and brain processes; and in turn correlate these with 'related manifestations in the environment'. It is, as we shall, but a very short step from here to Mach's thoroughgoing phenomenalism.

Spencer was never part of the scientific establishment of his native country, and British psycho-physiology was largely forgotten, in part because of powerful developments in nineteenth-century Germany, where, it should be emphasized, physiology had broken away from anatomy and had established itself firmly in the new university system (see chapter 10). Oxford and Cambridge, with roots in the Middle Ages, were still tied to the old order. As a consequence, neither science nor medicine had a place there. Indeed, the fact that in Great Britain 'psychology' was dominated by philosophers owes much to this circumstance. With only a few notable exceptions, such as Sir Charles Bell and François Magendie, nineteenth-century developments in physiology, psycho-physiology, and psycho-physics were of German provenance: the work of Johannes Müller, E. H. Weber, J. E. Purkinje, A. W. Volkmann, and, in the next generation, K. von Vierodt, F. C. Donders, H. Aubert, Gustav Fechner, Helmholtz, and finally Wundt (Turner, 1982). All these men were fully committed to the development of experimental techniques, but all were, at the same time, unabashedly 'philosophical', a consequence of the form of institutionalization of nineteenth-century German universities. For the purposes of this sketch, three figures are central: Helmholtz, Wundt, and Mach.

HELMHOLTZ'S ALTERNATIVE

Hermann von Helmholtz (1821–94) 'was a very great scientist, one of the greatest of the nineteenth century'. So writes Boring at the beginning of his chapter examining Helmholtz's contribution to 'experimental psychology' (1929). An army surgeon in Berlin, Helmholtz read his famous paper on the conservation of energy before the *Physicalische Gesellschaft* in 1847, became professor of physiology and general pathology at Königsberg in 1849, invented the ophthalmoscope in 1851, and published the first volume of his *Handbuch der physiologischen Optic* in 1856 and his *Tonempfindungen* in 1863. He was called to a chair of physics in Berlin in 1871 and continued to publish and lecture on physics, philosophy, and psycho-physiology until his death in 1894. All this is well known. What is less well known is that he considered psychology to be, in effect, a general epistemology – with striking parallels to Spencer.

Briefly, Helmholtz held that what we can know is circumscribed by the nature of our sense organs and central nervous system. But this was not empiricism as Mill understood it, nor was it Kantianism with a transcendental ego. Rather, it was a kind of physiological Kantianism, in which the structures of experience are a function of our sense organs, the 'unconscious inferences' (*unbewussten Schluss*) of the central nervous system, and input from the 'external world'. On his view, 'experience' is a 'sign', not an 'image' or 'reflection', of the external world. Just as language is a system of signs, so are sensory perceptions, except that, because humans have a definite sensory system, perceptions as signs are not arbitrary. In Kantian fashion, Helmholtz distinguished sensations and perceptions, the latter being 'interpretations' which depend on unconscious inferences. And, as in Spencer, this depends on preservation of a subject/object distinction. But the 'object' is not the experienced object, a 'red tomato', say. 'Red tomato' is an interpretation. And crucially, as Locke – but not Hume and not Spencer – had held, causality was the generative power of an object, neither the phenomenally manifest relations of events nor invariances which are, as Mach argues, 'mathematical functions'. That is, both the 'objects' at the object end and the mediated objects of the ordered phenomenal field are known only by virtue of the causal powers of 'things' in the world. Both are known only inferentially, the former as the theoretical entities of physical theory – for example, unobservable atoms – and the latter as outcomes of the unconscious inferences of the central nervous system. This was Spencer's transfigured realism coupled with a realist understanding of causality.

This must not be missed. Just as the Cartesian destruction of naive realism had made a theoretical physics possible, so it seems to have made a theoretical psychology impossible. There seemed to be no way to close the gap between 'objects' in the world and the contents of consciousness. Indeed, if causes are constant conjunctions established *in* experience, 'psychology' must be either metaphysical or associationist.[1] Helmholtz took the bull by the horns, by, in effect, accepting the Spencerian argument in favor of what Spencer had called 'transfigured realism' and by insisting that there was nothing metaphysical about *causes as in principle unwitnessable productive powers.* 'The word *Ursache* (which I use here precisely and literally) means *that existent something (Bestehende) which lies hidden behind the changes we perceive.* It is the hidden but continuously existent basis of phenomena' (Helmholtz, 1971, p. 521).

The fundamental problem of 'psychology', then, was not to explain, as per the metaphysicians, the nature of mind or, as per Mill and the associationists, the laws of the mind independently of physiology, but rather to see how 'information' flowing to the 'mind' could issue in meaningful experience. This implied a research program focused on the scientific problem of how mechanisms possessed by sentient organisms could be lawfully related to mechanisms in the physical world.

While I have no doubt that this was Helmholtz's program, he never called it a program for psychology. At this time, psychology had neither a fixed subject-matter nor an institutional location. Helmholtz rarely used the term 'psychology', and when he did, he seems usually to have meant what we call 'philosophy'. He saw himself as having contributed to 'sensory physiology' and to 'philosophy' in the non-technical sense that regarded the study of knowledge. While he would have admitted that epistemology had a normative or regulative dimension, it was not philosophy, if by that one means, as we do today, that science was independent of it.

The nativism/empiricism debate

There were some genuine difficulties in Helmholtz's ideas, of course; yet, his program was buried not because of the emergence of a superior

[1] Although it cannot be pursued in detail here, I believe that William James's remarkable *Principles of Psychology* (1890) made an attempt at resolving this dilemma. It was an ultimately unsuccessful attempt precisely because James, like Spencer, was caught in an empiricist notion of causality. In his *Principles,* James took what he called 'a strictly positivist point of view', defined psychology as 'the Science of the Mental life, both of its phenomena and their conditions' – physiologically and in the 'outer world', but balked because 'the relation of knowing is the most mysterious thing in the world'. Indeed, 'if we ask how one thing [a person] can know another [the physical world] we are led into the heart of *Erkenntnisstheorie* and metaphysics' (1950, I, p. 210).

alternative but for philosophical and institutional reasons. One substantive issue worth looking at is the famous 'nativism/empiricism' debate.

This argument was not, as Boring would have it, between Kant and
Fichte on the one hand and the British psychology of the two Mills on
the other, because the parties to the debate sided with neither (Pastore,
1974). We need one of Helmholtz's terms of art: 'local signs', understood as spatially different retinal locations of the same sensation – for
example, a particular shade of red. According to Helmholtz:

> The difference between the two opposing views is as follows: The
> empirical theory [Helmholtz's] regards the local signs . . . as signs
> whose signification must be learned, and is actually learned, in
> order to arrive at knowledge of the external world. It is not
> necessary to suppose any kind of correspondence between these
> local signs and the actual differences of spatial location they
> signify. The nativist theory, on the other hand, supposes that the
> local signs are direct perceptions of actual differences in space,
> both in their nature and in their magnitude. (Helmholtz, 1971,
> p. 197)

On the nativist view, no learning is necessary for our spatial intuitions,
since there is an immediate 'correspondence' between the retinal 'sign'
and the objects of a structured world. On Helmholtz's view, 'none of
our sensations give us anything more than signs for external objects . . .
and we learn how to interpret these signs only through experience and
practice. For example, the perception of differences in spatial location
can be attained only through movement; in the field of vision it depends
upon the movement of the eye' (1971, p. 196). The nativist 'assumes that
the laws of mental operations are in pre-existing harmony with those of
the outer world', making veridical perception an unexplained miracle.
But there need be no miracle. There is an exact parallel in language
learning. If we assume a child with fully intact perceptual and cognitive
abilities, the child can learn to 'correlate' wholly arbitrary signs with
what is signified. Simlarly, before this occurs, we learn to 'interpret' our
perceptual signs as correlated to the external world, all quite 'naturally'.
On the other hand, while the 'interpretative' machinery, which is
substantially pre-conscious, admits of a great deal of slippage – indeed,
its very imperfections count against 'the idea of a pre-established
harmony between the inner and the outer world' (1971, p. 240) – our
sensory system, like the systems of other percipient organisms, – is
effective, and we do learn to use it. Helmholtz's view is fully Darwinian:
evolution gave organisms cognitive mechanisms which allow their successful engagement with nature; and, depending on the species, there
will be a greater or lesser degree of 'learning' in coming to cope with the

environment. Since organisms must move in their environment if they are to learn, Helmholtz had the concept of an active organism. His use of 'experience' was the trial-and-error engagement of the active organism using its sensory machinery to acquire 'knowledge' of the external world.

Unconscious inferences

Helmholtz was fully aware that referring to unconscious mechanisms as 'inferences' was bound to arouse opposition, since the term, then as now, suggested a 'logical conclusion'. Inference was taken to be a capacity only of 'the highest operations of mind' (1971, p. 217). Yet, he insisted, 'there appears to me in reality only a superficial difference between the inferences of logicians and those inductive inferences whose results we recognize in the conceptions we gain of the outer world through our sensations' (p. 217). There was one difference, and it was not superficial in one sense, that 'the former . . . are capable of expression in words, while the latter are not' (p. 217). Yet this difference was not sufficient to justify the depreciation of *Kennen* as against *Wissen*. The Kantian restriction of judgment to inferences expressible in words and his failure to carry out the analysis of intuition into 'the elementary processes of thought' were obstacles to acquiring an understanding of how we come to know. 'These judgments or inferences will, of course, remain unknown and inaccessible to philosophers [psychologists!] as long as they inquire only into knowledge expressed in language' (1971, p. 391).[2]

While the story is far too complex to try to tell here, we can at least take note that it is also during this period that 'logic' began to separate itself from 'psychology'. With the important technical advances of Boole (1854), Jevons (1869, 1881), Peirce (1870, 1885), and Frege (1879, 1884) came the possibility of realizing the idea of a formal logic that would fully ground science. But 'the new logic' was not about 'reality' as Aristotle had believed; nor was it about the psychology of reasoning – that is, it was no 'psychologism'. If logic was to be the science of sciences, it could not depend on the new upstart science of 'psychology'. As is well known, Gottlob Frege was critical in this regard, convincing not only Bertrand Russell and the positivists, but Edmund Husserl as

[2] This 'philosopher's' prejudice remains with us, for example, in the widely shared assumption of 'cognitive psychology' that where there is cognition there is linguistic representation, or that 'information-processing' must be 'described in terms of the semantic and syntactic relations among content-specifying sentences'. See chapter 14. Similarly, 'inference' in 'unconscious inference' requires neither a capacity to project hypotheses, nor the availability of predicates to serve as 'evidences'.

well. Indeed, after 1900, 'psychologism' became a bad joke, not to be taken seriously by anyone.[3]

The logician's anti-psychologistic prejudices were only part of the problem that Helmholtz had to face with his idea of 'unconscious inferences'. Just as serious were positivist objections to the postulating of mechanisms which were purported to 'lie behind' phenomena and which, even worse, were supposed to have causal powers. Further, Helmholtz lacked an articulated theory of mind. While he clearly did not follow Mill, he also rejected the Kant/Fichte notion of mind as transcendental ego. Helmholtz saw the latter as leading to an idealism, which, although not ultimately refutable, was nonetheless implausible on the evidence (1971, pp. 385ff.). By the middle of the century, both 'mind' and 'matter' had rigidified as Cartesian substances, and for Helmholtz and the positivists they were merely metaphysical notions, not scientifically respectable. On the other hand, Helmholtz seems to have seen the mind/body problem as a pseudo-problem, although not for the reasons offered by Mach. That there was an independently existing external world was the only plausible scientific hypothesis; and of course we are conscious beings. The scientific problem, however, was how to understand this causally – a task which did not need a transcendental ego or *either* of the Cartesian substances – even if it required that the furniture of the world include structures and mechanisms of more than one kind, structures which are nomically related and can be theorized.

There was another problem. Turner has suggested that, while Helmholtz's program was plausible, 'obviously the new psychology could not accept such a limited program' (Turner, 1982, p. 172). Yet, then as now, those who wanted psychology to be a *science of mind* could not proceed empirically – for what turned out to be two very powerful reasons. First, as only Spencer and Helmholtz seem to have noticed, such a program *presupposes* some answers which could be provided only by a limited program of the Helmholtzian sort. A learning theory, for

---

[3] For a discussion of the technical advances leading to *Principia Mathematica*, see W. and M. Kneale, 1962. For an excellent account of the background of 'psychologism' in Germany, of Husserl's shift from psychologism to transcendental phenomenology and of the differences and similarities between Frege and Husserl, see Marvin Farber, 1943. It can hardly be doubted that for Frege, Husserl, and Russell, anti-psychologism was motivated by the wish to defeat relativism, or that Platonism was ever far away. Of course, more recent empiricist philosophy of logic has depended on the myth of analyticity. On the other hand, if logic and mathematics are but bodies of skills, beliefs and thought processes into which psychologically competent individuals are socialized, then any thoroughly naturalistic and empirical inquiry of knowledge is 'psychologistic'. J. S. Mill fired the first psychologistic shot, and a second salvo came from Helmholtz, a fact of some importance for the interpretation of his thought. See his two essays, both titled 'The origin and meaning of geometric axioms', 1870, 1878. Other versions of late nineteenth-century 'psychologisms' are found in the writings of Theodore Lipps, J. E. Erdmann (who was evidently the first to use the term), Lange, Sigwart, Heyman, and, of course, Wundt.

example, which assumes that the learner already has meaningful perceptions simply assumes away the fundamental problem of learning. In
taking the contents of consciousness not as what needed to be explained,
but as unexplainable explainers, defenders of the science of mind did
just this. That this approach, rooted in introspection, dead-ended was
hardly surprising. Nor is it surprising that psychology was then redefined
as the science of behavior. Having assumed that humans have meaningful experiences, it was then easy to assume this away as irrelevant.
People could be treated as mindless, and learning could be defined as
change in behavior! Second, there was the problem that mind is social,
a fact fully appreciated by Helmholtz and Wundt.

THE ROLE OF WUNDT

The revisionist understanding of the 'founder' of modern experimental
psychology has picked up momentum (Danziger, 1979a, 1980a, b;
Leary, 1979; Reiber, 1980; Woodward and Ash, 1982). I will concentrate on Wundt's role as regards the disciplinary definition of experimental psychology.

Wundt was not the first to use the phrase 'physiological psychology'.
Moreover, he seems to have benefited from his reading of Bain's *Senses
and the Intellect* (1855). Bain, who is wrongly regarded as a kindred
spirit of Hartley, *was* a psycho-physical parallelist. It was thus that he
could establish the quaint precedent of beginning with a chapter on the
nervous system and then promptly forget about it when it came to *real*
psychological questions. Wundt thought otherwise – at least, he *initially*
thought otherwise. His *Grundzüge der physiologischen Psychologie* (1st
edn, 1873) was a huge success. As any number of writers have said, it
was the first of Wundt's two great achievements which launched psychology as an autonomous science. The other, of course, was the
founding of his laboratory in Leipzig in 1879.

No doubt the world was ready, prepared by the remarkable advances
in physiology, neurology, and psycho-physics. Wundt seems to have put
it all together: brain localization, sensory physiology, psycho-physics,
will, memory, and cognition. In America, William James acclaimed the
Grundzüge with enthusiasm. So too did Sully in England. Both saw 'the
new psychology' to be a physiological psychology. F. A. Lange, author of
the famous *History of Materialism,* pounced on the following text in the
Grundzüge:

> It is clear that the forebrain in which the most significant functions
> of the cerebral cortex are concentrated, transforms sensory stimuli
> into extraordinarily complex movements of many forms. . . .

Everything which we call Will and Intelligence resolves itself, as soon as it is traced back to its elementary physiological phenomena, into nothing but such transformations. (Wundt, 1873; quoted by Diamond, 1980, p. 62)

Wundt's book was seen to represent a project wholly in keeping with the ideas which Helmholtz and the psycho-physicists had been putting forward, and the term 'physiological psychology' was meant to capture this. Yet, as Diamond points out, it was just this view of the matter which Wundt later characterized as a 'widespread misunderstanding' about the nature of the new discipline (1980, p. 62).

What happened is clear enough. 'Physiological psychology' was 'experimental psychology', a term which Wundt had already used in his *Beiträge* of 1862. An inquiry which was 'experimental' was surely 'scientific'. But was there any necessity that 'experimental' be *physiological*? It was just this link which Wundt broke.

Diamond has provided the valuable service of translating and collating the changes in the opening pages of the five editions of Wundt's *Grundzüge,* between its first publication in 1873 and the last edition of 1908–11. The upshot of these changes was a clear shift in the relation of physiology to psychology, from a physiological psychology to the definition of experimental psychology as an autonomous discipline entirely independent of physiology. It will suffice here to quote one of the later texts:

Of the two tasks that are . . . implied by the name of physiological psychology – one methodological, relating to the use of experiment, the other amplificatory, relating to the corporeal basis of mental life – it is the former that is more essential to psychology itself, while the latter has value chiefly with respect to the philosophic question about the unity of life processes. (Quoted by Diamond, 1980, p. 169)

The latter is a 'philosophic' question – that is, a *non-scientific* question. Even so, there is the studied ambiguity of 'more essential' and 'chiefly', leaving some measure of unclarity as regards the precise scientific relevance of physiology for psychology. This is characteristic of everything that Wundt wrote on the subject thereafter, even if today it is agreed that Wundt thoroughly divorced psychology from physiology (Boring, 1929; Leary, 1979; Reiber, 1980). Wundt was crystal clear on the positive subject-matter and tasks of 'experimental psychology': 'The immediate contents of experience which constitute the subject matter of psychology are under all circumstances processes of a complex character.' Accordingly:

... scientific investigation has three probems to be solved. . . . The *first* is the *analysis* of composite processes; the *second* is the *demonstration of the combinations* into which the elements discovered in the analysis enter; the *third* is the *investigation of the laws* that are operative in the formation of such combinations. (Wundt, 1897, p. 25)

Conspicuously absent is the relation of 'the immediate contents of experience' to anything except *other* contents of experience. It was just this definition of psychology's problems, along with Wundt's assertion that 'introspection' – *innere Wahrnehmung*, not *Selbstbeobachtung* – was the 'foundation of psychology' (Danziger, 1980a), that Wundt came to be seen as the introspectionist *par excellence* and a German associationist who, having left physiology to the physiologists, was now moving in the direction of the truth of British empirical psychology.

But there were two aspects of Wundt's notion of 'experimental psychology' which were decidedly *un*-British: his view that mind was active and unitive, and his view that it was social. The first had been a key characteristic of German 'psychological' thought from Leibniz on. In his *New Essays on the Human Understanding,* Leibniz had attacked Locke on just this point and it was a dominant theme in Kant's 'antipsychological' epistemology (Leary, 1982).

Wundt appropriated the key idea of 'apperception', arguing that its central mechanism, 'psychic causality', was a form of causality which differed sharply from physical causality. In contrast to physical causality, psychic causality was *directly known*. Physical causality, according to Wundt, was an indispensable 'supplementary concept' of natural science, as was the idea of matter itself. Neither were needed for 'psychology'. Moreover, as Danziger points out, apperception played a key role in Wundt's system, expressing his dynamic standpoint, 'the attitude which caused him to characterize his own system as "voluntaristic"' (Danziger, 1979a, p. 216). Rejecting the British view (including that of Spencer) that the mind was a passive receptacle for impressions, Wundt held that the power of 'selective attention' and 'discriminative judgment' was central.

The idea that mind was social was a legacy of the neo-Kantian tradition of German Idealism, in which the 'subjective mind' was transcended in favor of an 'Absolute Mind'. The crucial empirical implication of this, as we saw in chapter 5, was the idea that the contents of subjective consciousness have an objective, social, historical source. Wundt's largely ignored multi-volumed *Völkerpsychologie* (1900–20) represents the culmination of this tradition in German thought – like the idea of an active and unitive mind, the idea of an objective, social mind arrived in Britain late, toward the end of the century.

Wundt seems to have agreed with Helmholtz that psychology was restricted to a limited program, since the functioning of 'the higher mental faculties' takes one inevitably into the realm of the irreducibly social. It ws just this, incidentally, which so much impressed Durkheim (Lukes, 1972). Accordingly, Wundt distinguished two kinds of psychology: 'experimental' and *Völkerpsychologie* – 'ethnic' or 'social' psychology. There are, he wrote, 'certain facts at the disposal of psychology, which, although they are not real objects, still have the character of relative permanence, and independence of the observer' (Wundt, 1897, p. 22) – Durkheimian criteria of 'objectivity' and 'externality'. These facts are 'unapproachable by means of experiment in the common acceptance of the term'; they are 'mental products that have developed in the course of history, such as language, mythological ideas, and customs' (1897, p. 23). They can be studied only as *Geisteswissenschaften*.

When it came to formulating the limit of his program, Wundt was no clearer than Helmholtz. Leary has suggested that Wundt confined his program to examination of the 'basic processes involved in the lower mental activities such as sensing, perceiving, feeling and willing' (Leary, 1979, p. 234). Was 'cognition' to be excluded entirely? Since 'unconscious inferencing' is involved even in perception, according to Helmholtz, is this a 'cognitive process?' The problem continued to haunt us.

Nevertheless, empirical psychology, replete with laboratories and experiments, had finally come into its own. Wundt had fought two battles to make psychology an autonomous science, one against the philosophers, the other against the physiologists. There is a sense in which he won them both, even if, ultimately, he lost the war over the subject-matter of 'the new psychology', first to Mach and a vibrant new version of positivist philosophy of science and then to the Americans and behaviorism.

THE VICTORY OF POSITIVISM

In the nineteenth century, physical science surely came of age; and as I will argue in the next chapter, the 'industrialization' of science made it, for the first time in human history, a fundamental force in the everyday lives of ordinary people. It was not just that new discoveries were being made, in chemistry, electricity, and medicine, but that by finding a place in the university, modern science forged institutional links with business, industry, and the state and began to compete with the 'liberal arts', especially 'philosophy', as 'the true educator' of society's elites. This shift, critical for the argument of this book, had another upshot, also critical for the present argument, namely the emergence of a large group of reflective, vocal, and authoritative 'philosophers' of the now mature natural sciences. This group of natural scientists *turned* philosophers included G. R. Kirchoff, Wilhelm Ostwald, Ernst Mach, Ludwig Boltzmann, Karl Pearson, Henri Poincaré, Pierre Duhem, William Thomson (Lord Kelvin), Helmholtz, and his pupil Heinrich Hertz, to name only the most notable. There was one idea which they all shared: that science was totally separate from metaphysics. But there was disagreement over what this meant concretely. In this section, we will examine the disagreements. After these debates, by perhaps World War I, 'philosophy of science' was uniformly positivist. It is not hyperbolic to say that the consequences of this were simply enormous.

Piérre Duhem's *La Théorie Physique: Son Object, Sa Structure* was one of the later writings of the group just named. The first edition, which appeared in 1906, brought together articles which had appeared in 1904 and 1905 in the *Revue de Philosophie*; but the first chapter is an excellent introduction to the debates among physicists during the previous 25 years or so.

Duhem perspicuously discerned two answers to the fundamental question regarding the aim of physical theory. The first is this: 'A physical theory . . . has for its object the explanation of a group of laws experimentally established' (Duhem, 1954, p. 7). According to the second: 'A physical theory . . . is an abstract system whose aim is to *summarize* and *classify logically* a group of experimental laws without claiming to explain these laws'. But the seemingly innocent idea of 'explanation' is a problem. Duhem offers this: 'To explain (explicate, *explicare*) is to strip reality of the appearances covering it like a veil, in order to see the bare reality itself' (1954, p. 7). But this makes science subordinate to metaphysics. To illustrate this, Duhem offers four 'explanations' of the phenomena of magnetism. For Aristotelians, the alteration of form imposed on matter is the underlying reality producing the phenomena. For the 'Newtonian philosopher faithful to . . . Father Boscovich', matter is resolved into point-masses, between any two of which the inverse square law applies, and so on. Atomists insist that this won't do, however, since, in their view, matter is composed of small, hard, rigid bodies. But Cartesians say that matter is 'essentially identical with extension in length, breadth, and depth, as the language of geometry goes'. In their efforts to explain the phenomenon of magnetism, each of the schools accuses the other of introducing 'occult causes', but, of course, this criticism can be applied to each of the 'scolding schools' in turn. Since all agree on the phenomena can we, then, 'assign an aim to physical theory that would render it autonomous', that is, independent of metaphysics? Following Ostwald and Mach, Duhem asserts: 'A physical theory is not an explanation. It is a system of mathematical propositions, deduced from a small number of mathematical principles, which aim to represent as simply, as completely, and as exactly as possible a set of experimental laws' (p. 19). By 'represent' Duhem does not mean that the system of propositions *describes* a structure which is causally responsible for the phenomena and which, were it to exist, would explain them – for example, the fact that iron filings polarize in a magnetic field. Indeed, this idea of explanation is metaphysical, for the simple reason that causes which 'lie behind phenomena' are unknowable, being in principle unobservable. For an empiricist such as Mach, a 'representation' is merely a set of concepts which, by organizing experience, provide an 'economical' schema for experience. Mathematical functions are thus 'abridged descriptions' of what occurs in experience. 'Knowing the value of the acceleration of gravity, and Galileo's laws of descent, we possess simple and compendious directions for reproducing in thought all possible motions of a falling body. A formula of this kind $[d = \frac{1}{2}at^2]$ is a complete substitute for a full table' (Mach, 1945, p. 193). This 'compendious representation of the actual, necessarily involves as a consequence the elimination of all superfluous assumptions which cannot be controlled by experience, and above all, of all assumptions that are metaphysical in Kant's sense' (Mach, 1959, p. xl). When Mach says, then, that physics is not explanatory, but descriptive, 'descriptive' refers to what is *in* experience, 'arranged in an economical order' (Mach, 1945, p. 197).

The neo-Kantian alternative is in agreement that metaphysics must be eliminated, but it views 'representation' differently. For Hertz and Boltzmann, for example, *Darstellungen* ('representations') are consciously constructed schemes, *Bilder* (pictures or 'models') which *define reality*. As Janik and Toulmin have pointed out, Hertz was deeply bothered by the question of what sorts of things Maxwell's equations asserted about the deep nature of electromagnetism, but then it occurred to him that 'Maxwell was saying nothing at all about the physical nature of these phenomena' (Janik and Toulmin, 1973, p. 142). Hertz said: 'To [the] question, 'What is Maxwell's theory?' I cannot give any clearer or briefer answer than the following: Maxwell's theory is the system of Maxwell's equations' (quoted by Duhem, 1954, p. 80). Let it be emphasized that on both these readings, a third, realistic possibility is excluded, namely, that the equations are only *part* of the theory, and that another part is an iconic model meant to 'represent' a hypothetical mechanism whose real existence would explain the observed phenomena. The Kantian alternative must not be confused with this idea. The former makes no existential claims. Theories are 'representations', not descriptions – even hypothetical descriptions. And this means, as Hertz acknowledged, that the question of the truth of the theory was never a question of whether theory gave correct or nearly correct descriptions of 'reality'. Thus it was easy for both empiricists and neo-Kantians to appeal to the principle of consistency and the 'economy of thought' as *exclusive* criteria of theory. And it was easy for both to take on instrumentalist aspects, so that theory would serve to 'anticipate experience', an idea which could also be appropriated as a criterion for theory acceptance: whether it allowed 'good predictions'.

There were writers who surely sounded like realist holdouts. Duhem points to the 'English' physicists Thomson and Maxwell. Thomson insisted: 'I never satisfy myself until I can make a mechanical model of a thing. If I can make a mechanical model, I understand it' (quoted by Duhem, 1954, p. 71). For Duhem this is characteristically 'English'. 'The Englishman', he writes, 'finds the use of the model so necessary to the study of physics that to his mind the sight of the model ends up being confounded with the very understanding of the theory' (1954, p. 71). Indeed, Maxwell's *Treatise on Electricity and Magnetism* and Thomson's *Lectures on Molecular Dynamics* were 'in vain attired in a mathematical form', being but successions of models, 'each representing a group of laws without concern for the other models representing other laws' (p. 86). Duhem admits that this was not metaphysics, since 'the English physicist does not . . . ask any metaphysician to furnish the elements with which he can design his mechanisms'; he does not ask or claim to know 'what the irreducible properties of ultimate elements of matter are', nor does 'he aim to deduce his model from a philosophical system' (p. 74). But for Duhem (following Poincaré), these models 'are paintings, and the artist, in composing them, has selected with complete freedom the objects he would represent and the order in which he would group them. . . . The logician would be out of place in being shocked by this: a gallery of paintings is not a chain of syllogisms' (p. 86). This loss of logical rigor is more than annoying to Duhem. All these paintings, however lovely, are unnecessary – as efforts at explanation or even as 'fruitful for discoveries' (p. 94). Indeed, doesn't the model-builder himself warn us that the models he proposes are not explanations? Thomson is quoted: 'Although the molecular constitution of solids supposed in these remarks and mechanically illustrated in our model, *is not to be accepted as true in nature*, still the construction of a mechanical model of this kind is undoubtedly very instructive' (quoted from Thomson, *Lectures on Molecular Dynamics*, p. 131, by Duhem, 1954, p. 75). If they are *not* to be accepted as 'true in nature', how can they be explanatory? They are 'fictions', and fictions are dispensable. Perhaps these models are useful for instruction – although it is doubtful that Duhem would have assented even to that. Indeed, even Helmholtz seems to have capitulated. In his Preface to Hertz's *Die Principien der Mechanik* (1894), he contrasts Maxwell's use of iconic models with Hertz's notion of 'a very general representation of facts and their laws by the system of differential equations of physics'. While he could not rise any objection in principle 'against a method pursued by such great physicists', he remarks: 'I must confess that I remain attached to this latter mode of representation' (quoted from Duhem, 1954, p. 100). Of course, neither this text from Helmholtz nor the one cited above from Thomson are decisive as regards the issues at stake. As for Helmholtz, he wrote too much against this interpretation of science for us to assent to Duhem's efforts to include him in the positivist camp (Mandelbaum, 1971, ch. 14).

NEUTRAL MONISM, PHENOMENALISM, AND 'PURE EXPERIENCE'

At the turn of the century, philosophy of natural science and scientific psychology shared a commitment to 'experience'. Mach, as already mentioned, was critical in this, but there is a close relationship between his view and what seem to us now to be the origins of rather different, competing views. In this regard, William James and Edmund Husserl immediately come to mind but the work of Richard Avenarius is our best introduction in this regard.

In his *Kritik der reinen Erfahrung* (1888–90), Avenarius pursued the Kantian project of avoiding the Scylla of materialism and the Charybdis of idealism by arguing that philosophy must restrict itself to a description of the world as it is presented to us in ordinary experience: 'The important thing for experience is how it is characterized, not what exists without it' (quoted by Janik and Toulmin, 1973, p. 135). As Janik and Toulmin rightly observe, Avenarius effectively 'bracketed' ontological questions, much in the spirit, if not the letter, of Husserl's later 'descriptive psychology'. Moreover, influenced by the 'act psychology' of Brentano, Avenarius, like Husserl, recognizes no consciousness which is not consciousness *of* some object. Consciousness is irreducibly intentional. But here the similarity ends, for Husserl went on, in the spirit of Kant, to argue against 'psychologism', and ultimately, for a 'transcendental phenomenology' which could provide the 'presuppositionless' ground for natural science.

Avenarius, along with Mach, went in a different direction from both Helmholtz and Husserl, a direction pursued also by James. For them, 'pure experience' was the meeting place of *realism* and *solipsism*. There was no 'mind/body problem'; nor was there an 'other minds' problem.

There were just relations in experience.[4] And since there were just different relations, we could reject the dichotomy between physical research and psychological research. Writing in his enormously influential *Analysis of Sensations* (1883).[5] Mach could conclude:

The great gulf between physical research and psychological research persists only when we acquiesce in our habitual stereotyped conceptions. A color is a physical object as soon as we consider its dependence, for instance on a luminous source, upon other colors, upon temperatures, upon spaces, and so forth. When we consider, however its dependence upon the retina . . . it is a psychological object, a sensation. (1959, p. 17)

Then, contra Kant *and* the realism of Helmholtz:

For us . . . the world does not consist of mysterious entities which by their interaction with another, equally mysterious entity the ego, produce sensations, which alone are accessible. For us, colors, sounds, spaces, times, . . . are provisionally the ultimate elements, whose connexion it is our business to investigate. (1959, pp. 29f.)

We can see how positivist philosophy of science enters. The task of science is the 'compendious' or 'economical' arrangement of these 'connexions'. As this involves 'the elimination of all superfluous assumptions which cannot be controlled by experience, and above, all, assumptions which are metaphysical in Kant's sense', 'a whole series of troublesome pseudo-problems at once disappears' (p. 210). The 'dualist' question 'How is it possible to explain feeling by the motion of the brain?' can never be answered, for 'the problem is not a

---

[4] See especially William James, 'Does "consciousness" exist?' (1904; in McDermott, 1967). James approved of Mach's views on these critical matters. James offered a 'radical empiricism', and Mach is often termed a 'phenomenalist'. But James was willing to offer that 'there was only one primal stuff or material of the world, a stuff of which everything is composed, and if we call that stuff "pure experience", then knowing can easily be explained as a particular sort of relation towards one another into which portions of pure experience may enter' (p. 170). As James's shift regarding the intelligibility of the knowing relation suggests (see note 1), radical empiricism represents, I believe, a decided shift from the tentative indirect realism and naturalistic epistemology of *Principles*. (See Gerald Myers, 1986.) R. S. Cohen, 1970, provides an excellent review of Mach's ambivalences.

[5] Janik and Toulmin note that 'seldom has a scientist exerted such an influence upon his culture as has Ernst Mach' (1973, p. 133). His psychology influenced the aesthetics of *Jung Wien*. Hoftmannsthal was in his debt. *The Man Without Qualities*, by his pupil, Robert Musil, describes a Machist world; Kelsen's positivist theory of law shows his influence. Neurath founded the Ernst Mach *Verein*, a forerunner of the Vienna Circle, acknowledging the enormous debt of twentieth-century logical empiricism to Mach. Einstein began as a Machist and James referred to Mach as a 'pure intellectual genius'. Finally, his views became so popular among Marxists that Lenin felt compelled to respond with his polemical *Materialism and Empirio-Criticism* (1908). This remarkable book defended realism, but offered a horrendous 'reflection' epistemology as a counter to Machism.

problem' (p. 208). The world consists of 'elements' (sensations) that are connected in different ways. If we 'neglect our own body' and consider only those elements which make up 'foreign bodies', we are physicists. If we consider these in relation to our own bodies, we are in the domain of 'physiological psychology' (p. 210). This was a devastatingly simple solution, a solution which could incorporate the 'psycho-physics' of Fechner and Helmholtz *and* the new physiology. Indeed, in Mach's hands the new science of psychology was strictly parallel to the new physics. As a fully empirical physics did without atoms, matter and occult material causes, what was needed was an empirical physiological psychology without minds and 'psychic causality'. Just as physics experimentally relates 'color' to its 'luminous source', to 'temperature' and so on, so physiological psychology relates 'color' to occurrences on the retina. Indeed, apart from some important technical differences in formulation, Mach's program for psychology was substantially Carnap's. For both, there is no epistemic difference between the statements 'This wooden support is firm' and 'Mr A is excited' (Carnap, 1932–3). The statements of physics, like those of psychology, depend only on inductive generalization from 'perception-sentences', and neither require that we postulate some 'occult power' or 'entity' which 'stands behind' our perceptions but itself 'remains unknowable'. Moreover, it is hardly surprising that this program coincides so exactly with American behaviorism. Though Watson shifts his attention to 'behavior' and appropriates the language of 'stimulus' and 'response', as in Mach and Carnap, methodological 'objectivism' means exorcizing the metaphysical and, exactly as was supposed to be the case in physics or chemistry, restricting psychological statements to objects and events accessible to independent observers. On this view, if 'Mr A is excited' is a typical psychological sentence, then psychology might try to show that this can be lawfully correlated with observable physical events. But these might be of various sorts, from happenings in the brain to measurable changes in blood pressure to more overt 'behaviors'. It has often been noted that Watson was indiscriminate in this regard. But so was Mach and Carnap. One of Skinner's 'contributions', of course, was his outright rejection of physiology. But what we need to notice here is that, judged epistemically, it does not matter whether the terms in psychological laws are physical, physiological, or molar-situational. As Mach said, with the conception of mathematical function, we can display simple *or* complicated relations 'according to what is required by the facts under consideration'.

In the decades following the turn of the century, but decisively with World War I, psychology and the social sciences became self-consciously 'empirical sciences'. But first we must see how the materials discussed up to now were put to work in this development.

Part II
The Modern Social Sciences

10

Capitalism, Science, and the University

In part I of this book, I attempted to sketch the development of the key ideas in the genesis of our thinking about a human science. These are the materials out of which the modern social sciences were constituted. By 'the modern social sciences' I mean the familiar disciplinary divisions of the social sciences as they are now institutionalized in the modern university. It is an important fact that this institutionalization was given its present form in the American university system, beginning with the creation of the first university in the United States, Johns Hopkins in 1876. Harvard and Yale were but 'colleges', offering only undergraduate degrees. This process was substantially completed by the end of World War I, by which time the 'disciplines' had pretty much defined their boundaries, their tasks, and their methods. While dissidents have continued to attack these and there have been changes, the latter have been surprisingly superficial, a result of the fundamental commitments which form the subject-matter of the present chapter.

In the next chapter, we will look in more detail at the key figures in the struggles of the various disciplines to achieve autonomy. As I shall suggest, the Americanization of social science will spread to Berlin, Oxford, and the Sorbonne only much later and not without opposition. At Oxford, for example, 'experimental psychology' didn't get a building until 1947. But then, Oxford and Cambridge, notoriously backward in 'science' from at least the seventeenth century on, didn't feel the need to build a physics laboratory until 1871. Men like Cavendish and Joule could afford private laboratories, and Count Rumford, founder in 1799 of the Royal Society, could assure Davy and Faraday the freedom to pursue their inquiries.

In this chapter, I identify three developments which, taken together, help us to understand why the specific constitution of the social sciences was what it was. The first is the uneven development of industrial capitalism, first in Great Britain and then, at about the same time, in the last half of the nineteenth century, in Germany and the United States. Coupled with some other factors in the national histories of these modernizing nations, this unevenness had two critical consequences: first, there were differences in how and when 'the social question' emerged, and second, there were differences in the way the state responded. The second development, not unrelated to the first but not reducible to it either, is the development of higher education. Oxford, Cambridge, and the Sorbonne had medieval roots; the *École Polytechnique*, founded in 1795; the University of Berlin, founded in 1810; and the Johns Hopkins University, established in 1876, were the creations of modernizers. I shall argue that this bears fundamentally on the specific relationships of the university to the state and to industry and thus on the nature of the state's response to both the social problem and industrial capitalism. Finally, as part of these processes, there was the development of the natural sciences themselves, in particular, their industrialization, first in Germany in the second half of the nineteenth century and then in the United States.

INDUSTRIAL CAPITALISM, THE STATE, AND THE SOCIAL PROBLEM

There is some truth in the idea that Great Britain experienced 'evolution' rather than 'revolution'. The English civil wars were surely bloody enough, and the road of 'primitive accumulation' – transformation to the social relations of capitalism – was certainly violent enough. Nevertheless, it is not unreasonable to say that, between 1688 and 1725, Britain had achieved a capitalist society and a stable regime of King-in-Parliament, a *proto* modern state, if not a modern state in the strictest sense (Plumb, 1967). And with this, industrial capitalism literally exploded. One statistic gives the picture. In 1760, 2.5 million pounds of raw cotton sustained an industry mostly dispersed around the countryside, and all the work was done by hand. By 1798, 22 million pounds of cotton were imported; by 1850, the figure was 366 million pounds, and the factory system dominated the production of textiles (Landes, 1969, pp. 41f.).

During the English civil wars, Oxford and Cambridge had tried to remain aloof from the strife but, as 'producers of parsons', it was inevitable that they would come under attack. The 'radicals' – that is, those who rejected any sort of state church – failed just as completely as did the political radicals. As Hill notes, 'the *ancien régime* came back to

Oxford and Cambridge, if to nowhere else in the kingdom'. One consequence of this was that 'modern science had to develop, slowly, elsewhere: in the Royal Society of London, in the dissenting academies' (Hill, 1972, p. 132). Indeed, albeit with some notable exceptions – for example, Sir Isaac Newton, Professor of Mathematics at Cambridge – what we think of as British 'science' went on almost completely outside the university, from its most illustrious beginnings in the seventeenth century until very late in the nineteenth.

That the *whole* story of the Industrial Revolution in Britain can be told without essential reference to any innovation in the understanding of nature – despite widespread misunderstanding on this critical point – is important, and it is a topic to which I will return. At this point, however, we should take note of some other well-known aspects of this great revolution. First, it fundamentally altered the world; second, it was not 'from above'; and third, it created 'the social problem'. A contemporary observer noted:

As a stranger passes through the masses of human beings which have accumulated round the mills and print works . . . he cannot contemplate these 'crowded hives' without feelings of anxiety and apprehension almost amounting to dismay. . . . There are mighty energies slumbering in these masses. . . . The manufacturing population is not new in its formation alone: it is new in its habits of thought and action, which have been formed by the circumstances of its condition, with little instruction, and less guidance, from external sources. (Quoted by E. P. Thompson, 1963, pp. 190f., from a contemporaneous account)

Thompson remarks that it was 'as if the English nation entered a crucible in the 1790s and emerged after the wars in a different form. Between 1811 and 1813, the Luddite crisis; in 1817 the Pentridge uprising; in 1819, Peterloo; throughout the next decade the proliferation of trade union activity, Owenite propaganda, Radical Journalism, the Ten Hours Movement, the revolutionary crisis of 1831–2; and beyond that, the multitude of movements which make up Chartism' (1963, p. 191).

There was no revolution, of course. The 'Great Reform Bill' extended the franchise to holders of property worth £10; and the 1834 Poor Law Act and the Ten Hours Bill were passed. We need to be reminded, perhaps, that a survey undertaken in 1831 and communicated to Lord John Russell, 'stated *unanimously,* that the £10 qualification did not admit to the exercise of the elective franchise a single person who might not safely and wisely be enfranchised: that they were surprised to find how comparatively few would be allowed to vote' (quoted by Thompson, 1963, p. 818). Indeed, that same official inquiry noted that 'of the working classes not more than one in fifty would be enfranchised by the Bill'. Adult male suffrage went to perhaps 15 per cent with the passage of the Reform Bill. The Poor Law Act was more effective. As Hobsbawm writes:

> There have been few more inhuman statutes than the Poor Law Act of 1834, which made all relief 'less eligible' than the lowest wage outside, confined it in the jail-like work-house, forceably separating husbands, wives and children in order to punish the poor for their destitution, and discourage them from the dangerous temptation of further paupers. (Hobsbawm, 1968, p. 89)

As noted, for these Acts of Parliament, 'statistics' were needed. 'Political arithmetik' already had a good start in Great Britain, as of course, did political economy. Phillip Abrams reports that Nassau Senior, the first incumbent of a chair of political economy at Oxford (1825), began a routine inquiry into the proposed Poor Law Bill and transformed it 'into one of the most sweeping and meticulous fact-finding investigations ever conducted in the area of social economics' (Abrams, 1968, p. 10). English 'social research' had definitely been born.

In the case of England, the need for 'social research' would generate its own institutions, institutions which were quite independent of the well-established universities. In 1833, 13 'gentlemen', who by their own testimony 'felt a strong desire to assist in promoting the progress of social improvement', formed the Manchester Statistical Society (Abrams, 1968, ch. 4). This was followed in short order by the formation of the Statistical Society of London. Its founding members included Thomas Malthus; John McCullough, first incumbent of the chair of political economy at London's University College; Richard Jones; and an eminent group of MPs, notables, and professionals. As Abrams notes, 'in its early years the Council of the Society often looked like a subcommittee of a Whig cabinet'.

The Society divided itself into four sections: 'economic statistics', 'political statistics', 'medical statistics' ('vital' statistics we would now say) and 'moral and intellectual statistics'. This last, fascinating category succinctly reflects the methodological assumptions of mid-nineteenth-century 'social science', 'psychologism', and 'moralism'. The category concerned itself with 'the condition of the people' and included statistics on poverty, crime, and illiteracy. For the men of the Statistical Society, 'the condition of the people' was of great importance, for one did not need to have socialist learnings to see that trouble was on the horizon, and that reform was sorely needed. What was needed first, however, was 'facts'.

As *Meliora: A Quarterly Review of Social Science* put it, 'statistics . . . are the bone and sinews, the nerves and muscles of legislation; reforms are impossible without their aid'. But, as Abrams points out, 'the moral imperative to social action and the morally based understanding of society are still plainer': 'In every view of the subject it concerns the statesman, the patriot and the Christian, to promote a healthier and purer morals among the people, and medically to deal with the diseases which endanger our social welfare (quoted in Abrams, 1968, p. 39). The 'diseases' these reformers had in mind were not solely organic. Indeed, they included ignorance, 'spiritual destitution', 'impurity', pauperism, crime, and intemperance, this last being a fundamental concern: 'The singling out of drink as the critical social problem, often as the cause of all the others, was very representative of the new social science.' The most affluent, hard-working, and Christian nation in the world was also 'confessedly the most drunken'. The social problem *was* a moral problem and was, accordingly, a problem of how to restore the morals of individuals.

It is difficult to overestimate the importance of this perception of 'the social problem', but not difficult to explain it. Not only did it serve the interests of both government and industry, but methodological individualism was deeply rooted in British thought, a coincidence of epistemological and political individualism. Nor should we be deceived by the fact that, as Abrams observes, the ameliorists did not utterly lack a sense of social structure. Indeed, it is quite impossible not to import into one's analysis some sense of this, a point noted in my earlier account of Hobbes and Adam Smith. And that is as true of current 'analyses' of social problems as it was of those of the ameliorists. Just as patterns could be recognized in the statistics which were assiduously gathered – between for example, public drunkenness and ordinary crime, or prostitution and opportunities for reliable income – so today, it is hard to ignore similar patterns. Yet how easy it was (and is) to blame individuals and ignor causes. Thus, the high crime rate was explained in terms of 'the ignorance and weakness of moral principle to be found among the working classes', and a remedy was to pay workers at a time when it would be difficult for them to spend their money on drink (Abrams, 1968, pp. 40f.).

What Abrams calls the ameliorist movement in Britain produced, in 1857, the National Association for the Promotion of Social Science. In 1880, when the movement peaked, its council included 31 peers, 48

MPs, 19 Doctors of Law, 14 Fellows of the Royal Society, and 'numerous' baronets, knights, ministers of the Church of England, professors and Fellows of the London Statistical Society. But at this point, the 'consensus' seems to have fractured. The cause, as now seems clear, was the discrediting of the 'science' of political economy, caused by its incapacity to respond to capitalist crisis. Not only was political economy incapable of explaining the deepening cycles of depression, but the well-intentioned fact-gatherers were providing no useful solutions to the mounting social problems. Indeed the economic crisis which began in 1873 seems to have squashed the potential for a more authoritative 'social science' in Great Britain.

It is well to observe here, as Hobsbawm remarks, that 'the British middle-class citizen who surveyed the scene in the early 1870s might well have thought that all was for the best in the best of all possible worlds' (Hobsbawm, 1968, p. 126). After all, it seemed that Britain's workers had been tamed to capitalism – the 1848 revolutions which nearly ripped Europe apart had made barely a tear in the social fabric of Britain; the incredible expansion of the 'second phase' of the Industrial Revolution, led by the railroads, had raised the standard of living, and the franchise had been regularly extended since the breakthrough of 1832. What is now known to economic historians as the Great Depression was a surely a large setback for Britain, but, as every well-born Englishman knew, Britain would survive. At the same time,

> The 'Great Depression' cannot be explained in purely British terms, for it was a world-wide phenomenon, though its effects varied from one country to another and in several – notably the USA, Germany and some new arrivals on the industrial scene as the Scandinavian countries – it was on balance a period of extraordinary advance rather than stagnation. (Hobsbawm, 1968, p. 126)

This needs to be emphasized. 'The last capitalist revolution' had been fought in the American Civil War (Moore, 1966, ch. 3), and the Bismarckian forced march into nationhood had unleashed forces fettered by the older arrangements. Within 35 years, the United States and Germany would be first-rate world powers. But there was a price to be paid. In Germany 'the social problem' would bring Germany precariously close to socialism (Schorske, 1955), and in the United States the social problem would have to be faced for the very first time – even if it was not then squarely faced. Between Germany, the United States and England, there was a usually overlooked but critical difference. It was the role of higher education.

HIGHER EDUCATION IN GERMANY

The French Revolution and the era of Napoleon brought an enormous increase in the centralization of political authority and in the participation of the middle classes in politics, changes that had been made in England a full century earlier. This new development put new demands on government. On the continent generally, education became 'the "monopoly" of the state' and 'a means by which . . . groups which had been oppressed and in opposition to the traditional ruling group could become integrated in the existing order' (Gilbert, 1965, p. 320 *passim*). We can get the necessary flavor of this, perhaps, by looking briefly at higher education in Germany.

The Prussian General Code of 1794 established 'a basic legal framework which was to remain in force until the advent of National Socialism' (Ringer, 1969, p. 23). Crucial for our purposes was the establishment of schools and universities as state institutions. After 1810, Prussian censorship provoked the ideal of academic freedom and, with Wilhelm von Humboldt in charge of the newly created Section for Culture and Education of the Prussian Ministry of the Interior, the University of Berlin was founded. Not a creature of the past, like the University of Halle, the premier institution for the education of Prussian bureaucrats, still less like Oxford or the Sorbonne with their medieval roots, Berlin was constituted with the *philosophische Fakultät* pre-eminent. 'Each field taught within the framework of the philosophical faculty . . . gave particular knowledge as well as a general philosophical education' (Gilbert, 1965, p. 325). The ideals of *Lernfreiheit* and *Lehrfreiheit* – freedom for both learner and teacher – were seen as requisite to the 'disinterested' pursuit of truth. It was not that the university would not train civil servants and teachers but that these would be 'enlightened'. Their education would not be restricted to the obsolete pseudo-knowledge of the older institutions. The ideology and constitution of the University of Berlin had enormous influence; not only did it establish a pattern for the education of German academics which gave them a different orientation, both intellectually and politically, from their counterparts elsewhere, but it also provided the basis for a kind of institutionalization of 'disciplines' which became a model for subsequent universities.

The idea paid off. The German university system of professional chairs, seminars, and institutes provided cadres for the modernized state and promoted specialized research in all the advancing sciences. By the mid-nineteenth century, German 'science', especially chemistry, mathematics, physiology, and physics, had achieved distinction. In the German system, each seminar and institute ideally had its own quarters, research facilities, library, and staff. The existence of a seminar or institute depended on the eminence of a professor, often an internationally known figure in his field.

There was a tremendous proliferation of seminars and institutes in Germany in the last third of the nineteenth century, as a result of *direct state action.* German unification had come late, and Bismarck was active in building the requisites of a modern state. He was also active in utilizing Germany's resources to promote industrialization. The university was part of this. McClelland reports that between 1873 and 1914, 173 *new* institutes were formed (McClelland, 1980, pp. 279f.). Most of these were in the natural sciences including medical specialties. Some were in 'old' disciplines such as hygiene, neurology and sexual disorders – indeed, in just those specialites which allowed for the medicalization of the exploding social problems of industrializing Germany. Exactly as in to Britain, though some 30 years later, 'social research' began in earnest in Germany; and Germany's version of the British National Association for the Promotion of Social Science, the *Verein für Sozialpolitik,* was established, with the aim of encouraging the sharing of technical and scholarly knowledge and providing a vehicle for direct influence on social policy. But there was another, critical change to which the Germans made a singularly important contribution. Following Ravetz (1971), it can be called 'the industrializing of science'.

THE INDUSTRIALIZING OF SCIENCE

While no one today would deny that 'sociology of science' has something useful to say about 'the social influences' on scientific practice, the way science develops, and the applications of scientific knowledge, it is all too readily assumed that science is that activity which is defined by something called 'the scientific method' and that, critical to 'scientific method', is 'prediction and control', the ultimate certification of the validity of scientific theory. On this view, although the sciences differ in their subject-matter, they share in a method. The method critically involves the testing of hypothesis, and this is the test of prediction: 'If we do such-and-such, then so-and-so will happen.' One goal of science is explanation, of course, but since a scientific explanation has the same logic as a prediction, we can say that the capacities to predict or, by virtue of this, to generate effective technologies, are the most adequate marks of a science.

This image of science is of very recent vintage, dating from around the turn of the century. Positivist philosophy provided the explicit rationale for it, but critical institutional changes made this rationale convincing. We can say that this image characterizes 'technocratic science' or, better, 'industrialized science'. Legitimated, then, by a positivist philosophy of science, industrialized science is a symbiosis of science, business, industry, and the state. In this century, it has become an absolutely essential part of the basic mode of production in a modern economy.

SCIENCE AND TECHNOLOGY

There are two main causes of the characteristic misconceptions about the relationship of science and technology. The first is the historical coincidence of the rise of modern science and the Industrial Revolution. The second is an anachronistic reading of the history of science, according to which modern science was not merely coincident with the Industrial Revolution, but was essential to its occurrence.

It is easy to show, however that the story of what we call the Industrial Revolution of the eighteenth and most of the nineteenth centuries can be told without essential reference to advances in our understanding of nature. As Landes has argued, the series of inventions which began in cotton manufacture (and generated the factory system), 'can be subsumed under three principles: the substitution of machines . . . for human skill and effort, the substitution of inanimate for animate sources of power, in particular the introduction of engines for converting heat to work; [and] the use of new and far more abundant raw materials' (Landes, 1969, p. 41). *None* of these depended in any way on innovations resulting from the scientific revolution which began with Copernicus and culminated in the seventeenth century in the work of Galileo, Newton, Harvey, Boyle, Descartes, among others. I want to revert to an alternative 'Baconian' tradition of natural science momentarily, but, though we may include this in as part of 'the revolution of modern science', it is quite clear that it played but a negligible role in advancing our understanding of the physical world. Some 'experiments' by Baconians did play a role, but as Kuhn (1977) has noted, these all had their roots in the older tradition. The men we think of as the key figures in the revolution of modern science, the men named above, revolutionized what must be called the 'classical physical sciences' – astronomy, physics, and geometrical optics – sciences which were 'mathematical sciences', both in antiquity and later. As Kuhn has summarized the situation: 'In fact, . . . despite the hortatory claims of Bacon and his successors for three centuries, technology flourished without significant substantive imputs from science until about one hundred years ago' (p. 142).[1]

---

[1] Of course, if one begins with a Baconian and positivist conception of science, then one ends up writing a different kind of history. T. S. Ashton's *The Industrial Revolution* is typical of such an approach: 'The stream of English scientific thought, issuing from the teachings of Francis Bacon, and enlarged by the genius of Boyle and Newton, was one of the main tributaries of the industrial revolution' (p. 12f.).

Moreover, as Kuhn notes (in agreement with Koyré and Butterfield), 'the scientific revolution' was a revolution in the mathematical (classical) sciences and is 'more accurately ascribed to new ways of looking at old phenomena than to a series of unanticipated experimental discoveries' (Kuhn, 1977, p. 46). It is important to see the force of this, since it is widely held image that the fundamental feature of the scientific revolution was the application of 'experiment', the Baconian trumpeting of 'scientific method' as 'twisting the lion's tale'.

In the older tradition, 'experiments' were substantially 'thought experiments'. This view endured – indeed, it still endures. Galileo surely did experiments, but, as Kuhn writes, 'he is even more noteworthy as the man who brought the medieval thought-experimental tradition to its highest form' (1977, p. 42). Descartes and Newton (like any decent theorists in our own time!) persistently employed the 'thought-experiment'. Of course, there were committed (hands-on) experimenters, and there were critical differences in the aim and nature of their experiments by comparison with those of the older tradition.

The fundamental interest of these Baconian experimenters was in seeing how nature would behave under 'unnatural', contrived, previously unobserved circumstances, by 'twisting the lion's tale'. Their experiments might or might not be guided by 'the corpuscular philosophy'. For the corpuscular theorists – Gilbert, Hooke, Boyle – the gap between 'theory' – now usually dubbed 'their metaphysics' – and possible outcomes was so vague that one could hardly call any of their experiments 'tests', a fact of some importance as regards the later antimetaphysical attack so neatly summarized by Duhem (above, chapter 9).[2] The Baconians scorned 'thought experiments' and were fanatical as regards accuracy of reporting; moreover, critically, they went to the workshops of craftsmen and alchemists for any sort of apparatus or device which might increase their capacity to manipulate nature to see what it would do. It was in this context that the first link was made between the new 'scientists' and the older technologies. Indeed, while Baconianism contributed little to the development of the classical sciences, it gave rise to a large number of scientific fields, often with their roots in prior crafts. Important here are the study of heat and of chemical phenomena. Indeed, the main techniques, reagents, and instruments of what we call chemistry go back to long before the scientific revolution.

[2] The idea that one experiments when one 'tries it to see what happens' is Baconian and is far removed from the sort of experiment required to test a theory or hypothesis. A real test requires having a carefully articulated theory which has some definite testable implication and then establishing conditions of experimental closure so that the expected consequence is *allowed* to manifest itself. Closure, of course, is but an ideal, and in practice it is extremely difficult to even approximate it. See Bhaskar, 1976. The idea that scientific theory is validated by 'the millions of experiments going on in real world', such as getting rock-and-roll from one's FM receiver, is a misconception. The latter might work even if the 'theory' was far wide of the mark. See Bunge, 1967.

There were some advances in the eighteenth century as regards heat and chemical phenomena, but they remained undeveloped and un-systematized. Results were qualitative and vague, restricted in large part to the repeated demonstration of previously unknown effects, 'natural magic' contrived in the 'laboratory'. Again, in no sense could it be said that this growth contributed either to the Industrial Revolution or to a more adequate understanding of nature.

A key event in this regard was the establishment of the *École polytechnique* during the 1790s. Determined to surpass English achieve-ments, the revolutionary government of France invented a new sort of educational institution which combined study of classical subjects in the sciences with inquiry into the *ars méchaniques,* including the new Baconian sciences of heat, magnetism, and chemistry. Lavoisier had published his fundamental *Traité* in the year of the Revolution (and by virtue of his status and politics had been guillotined). Under the mathematizing influence of Laplace, the men of the *École* – Fourier, Carnot, Poisson, Ampère, Fresnel, and others – literally transformed these sciences thereby breaking down the wall that had separated the classical, mathematical, physical sciences, from the Baconian sciences. This development was accelerated in Germany, where it was possible to institutionalize these topics in institutes of the University. In addition, the Germans in the 1850s pioneered the *Realschule,* a secondary school which, in contrast to the traditional *Gymnasium* with its emphasis on antiquity, was specifically organized to educate students in those new 'knowledges' pertinent to modernizing society.

As a result of these developments, the first *technologies* to be genuinely influenced by increased scientific knowledge began to appear. Organic chemistry was the 'science', and the chemical industries were the ben-efactors, first with aniline dyes (1856), then with cellulose derivatives: lacquers; photographic plates; celluloid, the first modern plastic (1868), artificial fibers (1889), synthetic resins (1909), chemical fertilizers, and, of course, poison gas, the invention of which allows us to call World War I 'the chemists' war'. Not only was much of the theoretical and experimental work at the basis of the organic chemical industry German, but, as Landes notes, the production of alizarin, by Perkin in England and Graebe and Lieberman in Germany in 1869, was 'the last of the great British discoveries and the first of a long series of major dis-coveries by German laboratories; it marked a shift in the locus of innovation. It also symbolized the arrival of an era of purposive research' (Landes, 1969, p. 274). Finally, and not unrelated, German industry was quick to cash in on the new opprtunities. By the 1880s, Badische Anilin, Hochst, AGFA, and others had about one half of the world market. By the turn of the century, it was around 90 per cent.

Electricity was a scientific curiosity at the start of the nineteenth century. Over the next eighty years or so, we can identify a series of largely unconnected innovations, practical and theoretical: Volta's chemical battery (1800), Oersted's demonstration of electromagnetism (1820), Ohm's Law (1827), the experiments of Arago, Faraday, and others on electromagnetic induction, the invention of a self-executed electromagnetic generator (1867–7), Gramme's ring dynamo (1870), culminating in the first public power station in Europe in 1881 (Goldalming in Britain by Siemens Brothers). In 1879, the incandescent lamp was marketed, and Siemens demonstrated the first electric railway at the Berlin Industrial Exposition. Electrochemistry and electro-metallurgy became viable industries (aluminium manufacture and caustic soda process, 1886; Siemen's electric furnace, 1878).

For the first time, then, the general public could experience directly the results of science, the scientific capacity to produce 'natural magic', astonishing effects utterly independent of any intervention of the super-natural, devices, machines, and technologies which harness nature, put it to work – all for the sake of an easier and better life. These changes could not but impel new confusion over 'science', which had been 'liberated' from 'philosophy' for only a mere 150 years or so.

Initially the product of leisured elites, scattered across Europe and with only meager institutional resources, 'scientists' had found a place in the universities, especially in Germany. These 'academic scientists' were, as already noted, reflective and increasingly authoritative, as a result of the plain evidence of their achievements. But they reflected not only on the epistemology of science, its rejection of metaphysics and its separation from religion, but on the role of science in the world. In an 1862 address, Helmholtz offered a concept which combined the older idea that 'science' was the disinterested pursuit of truth with the new idea that science was a productive force: 'Whoever, in the pursuit of science, seeks after immediate practical utility, may generally rest assured that he will seek in vain. All that science can achieve is perfect knowledge and a perfect understanding of the action of natural and moral forces' (Helmholtz, 1971, p. 140). At the same time, 'all nations are interested in the progress of knowledge for the simple reason of self-preservation'. Accordingly,

> men of science form, as it were, an organized army labouring on behalf of the whole nation, and generally under its direction and at its expense, to augment the stock of such knowledge as may serve to promote industrial enterprise, to adorn life, to improve political and social relations, and to further the moral development of individual citizens. (1971, p. 40)

Helmholtz's words were well chosen, not merely the metaphor of 'an organized army', but that this army was under the direction of the nation and its concern was *such* knowledge as may first of all 'promote industrial enterprise'.

Thenceforth, there would be 'pure' science and 'applied' science: 'whatever contributes to the knowledge of the forces of nature and the powers of the human mind is worthwhile and may, in its own proper time, bear practical fruit, very often where we least expect it' (p. 40). Helmholtz was correct in judging that the early discoveries of modern science were only then beginning to 'bear practical fruit', and that such fruit was very often 'where we least expect it'. What his own argument suggested, however, but what he seems not to have seen, is that interests in the 'practical fruit' would soon *define and propel* research, which up to that point had been pursued for the sake of disinterested knowledge. Indeed, the effort to distinguish between 'pure' and 'applied' science and to separate both from 'technology' was itself a product of this transformation.

The problem is multifaceted. On the one hand, once the tail began to wag the dog as industrialization proceeded, the distinctions, offered specifically in response to threats against the independence of scientific work, became increasingly problematic. Thus, is research defined and funded by the United States Defense Department 'pure'? (Ravetz, 1971, ch. 2). On the other hand, as Landes has reminded us, there is a large gap between the discoveries of theoretical science and their application to technology, a gap that is mediated by applied scientists who offer generalizations derived from theory, by engineers who take these, along with a host of other considerations – economic, legal, and social – and seek the solution to some particular technological problem, such as the building of a bridge or a Star Wars defense system (Landes, 1969, esp. pp. 323ff.; Bunge, 1967). Third, it is easy to mistake the source of an advance in technology, whether from new knowledge of laws of nature or successful engineering. During the Industrial Revolution, for example, the 'heavy chemical industry' was vital, since the mass production of inorganic agents – alkalis and acids – was essential to large-scale textile manufacture. But such production was not made possible by breakthroughs in our understanding of chemical phenomena. On the contrary, they were largely the result of techniques developed by craftsmen engaged in technical problem-solving. Moreover, as Landes writes, 'the more successful enterprises were characterized not so much by innovations in chemical process as by the effective organization of the factors of production within the prevailing scientific and technological framework (Landes, 1969, p. 113). Finally, scientifically *in*adequate theories are very often technologically adequate. Ptolemaic astronomy, for example, *remains* the cosmology for sublunar celestial navigation.

The industrialization of science was combined with a positivist theory of science (see chapter 9 above) – a combination which guaranteed that, thenceforth, the pursuit of truth *would be identical with* an instrumentalist, technocratic conception of science. A theory was true *if and only if* it had a practical application. If the true is that 'which works', then Bacon's aphorism that 'human knowledge and human power meet in one' takes on a new meaning – *not* the capacity to penetrate to the hidden truth characteristic of Greek science, *not* the Stoical capacity to safeguard oneself from that which is not under one's control and to learn to live in harmony with nature, *not* the Christian or Islamic or, more generally, the religious capacity to appreciate the magnificence of Nature. Power is now domination: the capacity to control and manipulate.

It is no wonder that Bacon is of such interest to critics of 'modern science'. In seeing positivist/industrialized science as science *tout court*, we look for its first voice, find Bacon, make him into a positivist, elevate him to an overblown prominence, and explain 'science' as *inherently* aimed at domination – what the *friends* of science call 'prediction and control'.[3] To be sure, the Baconian idea of science is a vital part of our shared understanding of 'science'. Indeed, it is no exaggeration to say that *because* it is a fundamental feature of Americanized social science and thus constitutes the main vehicle for introducing people to 'science' and to 'scientific method', it *dominates our thinking about science*.

The emphasis on experiment as the key feature of science is Baconian – even if the experiment may be but vaguely related to some theoretical idea, and even where, as in social science, the 'experiment' is merely 'a good prediction'.[4] The amassing of data which are then analysed for patterns is Baconian. The emphasis on 'remaining close to the facts' – especially in the early stages of a science is Baconian. Finally, it is surely true, as I noted above, that the Baconian sciences grew out of concerns and techniques which were the property of craftsmen and alchemists,

[3] As the previous note suggests, we need 'good predictions' to validate theory; but these predictions are the predictions of a good experiment; or where this is quite impossible, we can use a real world (open system) opportunity to test an implication of theory. Eddington's famous photographs from Africa of the image of a star just outside the sun's disk supported Einstein's special theory of relativity. Einstein's own thought experiments had by this time convinced him of the correctness of the theory, so that when Eddington asked, 'What if there had been no confirmation?', Einstein is reported to have answered, 'Then I would have been sorry for the dear Lord – the theory is correct.' See Holton, 1968.

[4] Among the sophisticated, there are two kinds of social-scientific analogs to the Baconian 'experiment'. The first consist of quantitative techniques – multiple regression, factor, and path analysis, and so on – in which the 'test' is whether, 'given sets of data', some other 'equation' will give us 'as good a prediction'. See chapter 13. The other kind involve 'comparative studies', as per Durkheim. Among the less sophisticated [sic], all one need do is to compare, for example, the Soviet Union and the United States, this being a good 'test' of capitalism versus socialism.

and that Bacon, *by virtue of* his blindness to the scientific work of his own physician, Harvey, and that of the 'mathematicians' Gilbert, Copernicus, Galileo, and Kepler, was single-mindedly committed to the idea that knowledge was specifically for practical use, for 'the relief of man's estate'.

Baconian ideas did not reflect 'classical' science, but they have come home to roost, even if, for reasons which he could not have imagined, 'science' has had more success in constructing instruments of annihilation than in 'relieving man's estate'. Indeed, it is not unreasonable to say that today 'science' *is* 'industrialized science' *is* 'technocratic science', and that in critical ways, this is a fundamental problem of our time.[5]

THE AMERICAN UNIVERSITY AND THE GENESIS OF THE SOCIAL SCIENCES

We can now try to fit the last piece into the puzzle. Everyone knows that following the Civil War, the United States went through a period of phenomenal economic development, and that this was attended by urbanization, a new wave of immigration, and the emergence of 'the social problem'. Yet, as in the case of German industrialization, the role of the university is not usually emphasized.

Before Johns Hopkins became a university in 1876, there were no universities in America. There were, of course, 'colleges', institutions in which the undergraduate curriculum – there was no graduate curriculum – was uniform, prescribed, and traditional. It consisted largely of Greek and Latin, mathematics, rhetoric, the rudiments of physics and chemistry under the rubric 'natural philosophy', and some biology, botany, and geology. The curriculum culminated in moral philosophy, often taught by the president of the college or one of its most distinguished faculty. This might include anything from Aristotle to Montesquieu to the Scottish philosophers to the political economy of Mill.

Americans, no doubt, were sensitive about their backwardness. One measure of this was the desirability of study abroad, especially in Germany. Herbst reports that between 1820 and 1920 almost nine thousand Americans entered German universities. Before 1870, most of them sought professional training in medicine and the natural sciences. But by 1878, students of *Geisteswissenschaften* and the liberal arts outnumbered those in law and theology (Herbst, 1965, p. 8). As noted, German science was internationally regarded, and the system of *Lernfreiheit* was doubly attractive to students coming from the restric-

[5] Nothing has replaced Ravetz, 1971, as an introduction to this problem. Ravetz is not optimistic.

tive atmosphere of American colleges, an atmosphere geared to and fully apt for training preachers. Moreover, middle-class Americans were aware of the parallel, rapid emergence of the United States and Germany as world powers. Scholars returning from Germany, sensitive to the changes going on in both German society and German universities, were eager to transform American colleges in the direction of German *Wissenschaften* with their professional and research oriented outlook. In perhaps characteristic American fashion, it was not long before they outdid their exemplars.

The result was the coincident and mutually reinforcing development in America of the seminar which, as Herbst reports, was 'deliberately modelled after the laboratory approach of the natural sciences', of departments of specialized instruction and research, and, finally, of Ph.D. programs. While it seems that the seminar came to America a bit earlier than either departments or graduate programs, these last have no history before the 1870s. Both represented America's successful effort to professionalize its educational system. Some dates and examples will serve to illustrate what was happening.

Although the exact date and place is still contested, America got its first psychological laboratory sometime in the 1870s. By 1882, there were 18 psychological laboratories in the United States, and by 1904, there were 48! By 1917, the British publication *Who's Who in Science* could report that America had more psychologists than the combined numbers in England, France, *and* Germany (Camfield, 1973).

The first graduate program in the social sciences was Columbia's School of Political Science, founded in 1880 by German-trained John W. Burgess, a notorious racist judged even by the standards of his own time. The Columbia School, the model for those which followed very soon after, included courses in history, economics, geography, and politics. Sociology was not added until 1891 (Somit and Tanenhaus, 1967). The world's first sociology department, established at the University of Chicago by German-educated historian Albion Small, had as its staff: Charles Henderson, a Baptist minister and the university chaplain; Frederick Starr, who had been employed by the American Museum of Natural History; and Marion Talbot, the assistant dean of women (Kuklick, 1980).

Then came the professional associations and journals: the American Historical Association (1884) and its *Papers* (1886); the American Economic Association (1892) and its *Publications* (1886); the American Psychological Association (1892); the American Academy of Political and Social Science (1889); the American Political Science Association (1903) with its *Proceedings; The American Journal of Sociology* (1895); and the American Sociological Society (1903). *Political Science Quarterly* had been established by the Columbia School in 1886, and Harvard had started the *Quarterly Journal of Economics* that same year.

The structural changes in the American university and the acceleration of professionalism have no real parallel anywhere, not even in Germany. So, too, the phenomenal growth of the university. McClelland (1980) reports that in 1870 the student population in Germany stood at 14,000. By 1900 it was 34,000, and by 1914 it had reached 61,000. In the United States there were 154,300 undergraduate students and 2,400 graduate students in 1890; by 1900, the numbers were 231,000 and 5,000; by 1920, an astounding 582,000 and 15,600; and by 1930, 1,053,500 and 47,300! Most of these were being absorbed by the mushrooming new 'departments' in the branches of the 'social sciences'. One can get some idea of this by noting that in the first year of its existence (1904) the American Political Science Association had only 214 members, whereas six years later the figure had jumped to 1,350.

The conditions for a technocratic kind of social science were almost perfect. Nowhere in the world was the opportunity and the need as great as in the United States at this time. The same crisis which had jolted Great Britain and undermined political economy there had just the reverse effect in America, promoting fantastic new growth possibilities for a professionalized, practical social science and for a revitalized raw-boned competitive capitalism – the classic image of *laissez-faire* political economy (Hofstadter, 1955, ch. 4). The Germans had indeed shown the way, not just in professionalizing the academy, but more recently, in industrializing science. Finally, and in part as a result of this, the very idea of 'science' had been transformed, from the practically irrelevant *theoria* of the past to a *practically* productive and predictive *instrument* whose ultimate vindication was its capacity to generate technologies 'for the relief of man's estate'.

In marked contrast to the nations of Europe, the United States did not have a feudal past; so it did not have any of the legacies of that past, neither *ancien régime* nor a university system which had been the instrument of an *ancien régime*. To be sure, as the ruling classes of Europe underwent *embourgeoisement* or were replaced, the university adapted to the new conditions. But its class base remained, well past the period which, for our purposes, is critical. In Europe, the professoriate was, as one writer says, 'a Mandarin class', a closed corporation legitimated by tradition and class position whose authority and power was firmly established (Ringer, 1969).

This is crucial in explaining European *resistance* to the new social sciences. Already privileged and influential in the highest circles of government and finance and, in Germany and France, key figures in the state monopoly on education, the professoriate had no wish to alter its ways. Add to this the generational conflict, enormously exacerbated by the system of chairs and, in Germany, of institutes funded solely on the basis of the organizing professor, and it is hardly surprising that in Europe, critics of the intellectual *status quo* could not, even in the prevailing conditions of disarray, breach the intellectual establishment. Two consequences followed. On the one hand, the most firmly established social science, political economy was able to sustain itself in the university, prompting in the cities of Europe a proliferation of socialist centers of teaching and learning. On the other hand, the elite of the universities could continue, at least until the catastrophe of World War I, to conceive of themselves as the guardians of both national culture and of those ideas and values requisite to reproducing the patrician class of which they were key members.

But the United States was 'bourgeois' from the beginning. As Bledstein puts it: 'Americans lacked tradition as a source of authority, but they did not lack "science"' (Bledstein, 1976). When faced with the gigantic new problems of urbanization, immigration, race, poverty, and class war – even socialist and anarchist ideas – Americans, proceeding from where they were, would generate solutions which would take as given both middle-class dominance of society and the middle-class ideology of 'freedom'. Shored up by some carefully directed violence, racist and ethnic politics could easily be joined to the politics of economic growth, and in turn, both could be joined to technocratic solutions. The university could play a key role in all of this.

While the topic is enormously complicated and this is not the place to attempt anything more than a sketch, it is critical to emphasize that the middle-class ideology of America was deeply rooted (Hartz, 1955), that until after the Civil War black slaves constituted a substantial portion of America's 'working class' (Genovese, 1965), that between the end of the Civil War and World War I the world's largest immigration to a single nation took place, an immigration that would generate a highly fragmented non-native American working class (Steinberg, 1981), and, finally, that the net effect of the Great Depression which in the capitalist world ran from 1873 to 1896 would be, for the United States, an extraordinary advance rather than a reversal or stagnation (Hobsbawm, 1968). The United States was not entirely 'exceptionalist', if by that one means that it never faced class war – the first 'Red Scare' of the late 1870s and 1880s (Avrich, 1984) and the second, in the immediate post–World War I period – were more than sufficient to call for full-scale, if selective, repression (Zinn, 1980). But the United States was different enough not to call for a Bismarckian anti-socialist law (1878) (Barraclough, 1962) and different enough for Americans to *share a belief* that there was nothing wrong with their country's basic institutions and that, accordingly, 'problems' could be dealt with in a piecemeal, ameliorative fashion. But of course, this was exactly the ideology of a technocratic social science.

In the view of the new professionals, the problem was not class war, but 'ignorance'. William Watts Folwell on the occasion of his inaugural address at the University of Minnesota, one of the big land-grant universities of America's heartland, put the matter clearly. After identifying what he took to be the main areas of difficulty, 'the migration of races' and 'the sudden growth of cities', he noted: 'We are building our great national fabric according to rule of thumb'. Americans were 'merely empirics', 'journeymen', when it came to dealing with the gigantic problems of a rapidly growing nation. What was needed, he insisted, was to construct a solid basis of science, 'not only under the technical arts and learned professions but under commerce, government, and social relations' (quoted by Bledstein, 1976, p. 284).

This idea could not have been alien to his audience or to the new professionals returning from German universities. Were social inquiry and criticism to continue to be the province of 'metaphysical philosophers', the likes of Henry George, or of dilettantish political reformers such as Jane Addams or W. E. B. DuBois, or of irresponsible journalists like Jacob Riis or Lincoln Steffens? Why should social problems be less subject to *scientific* solutions than any other problems? But if social scientists were to be *professionals* with legitimate claims to authority and autonomy, they must mark out their own scientific territory and establish their own system of credentialling. It was clear to them what this meant: they must constitute *disciplines,* deliberately and systematically, in exactly the manner in which everyone said natural science was constituted, the manner in which any true science must be constituted.

While this did not occur overnight, it did occur in a remarkably short time, in just two generations. The Americanization of the social sciences, their constitution as modern social sciences, was not a deliberate plot to depoliticize the new problems, to reduce them to strictly 'scientific terms' so that they could be put under the tutelege of 'experts', thereby disenfranchising those who had fought so hard to win the franchise, although this was, it is fair to say, a consequence of this process. Many of the founders of American social science, as we shall see, were true 'progressives', men who were deeply concerned and politically committed to the improvement of conditions of life and the elimination of misery. But the issue here is their *beliefs about science,* about what it could do, given the chance. And the chance once given, was taken. Indeed, given the circumstances, what else would we expect?

In the next chapter, this will be fleshed out discipline by discipline. It is easy to show, I believe, that the social sciences were Americanized in the two generations between 1880 and World War I, that the latter buried irremediably any possible alternative, and that by the 1930s American scientism and scientific socialism were the legitimating scientific ideologies of a badly polarized world.[6]

---

[6] On the macroscopic level, there is much sense in the idea that there are two dominating conceptions of social science in the world, 'bourgeois' and 'scientific socialist'. The roots of the former are, as this history has argued, coterminous with the beginnings of modern society in the West. The latter stems from the Second International, with roots in Engels (chapter 5), but was not realized until the era of Stalin. It is, of course, a profoundly sad fact that these have so much in common! But, since 'science' is now industrialized everywhere, this is hardly surprising. Of course, there have always been 'dissident' voices – on both sides.

11

The Americanization of
Social Science

America's first professional social scientists were Americans educated in Germany, and the founding of institutionalized social science in America was in its first stage fully under the dominance of scholars who had been trained in Germany and had returned to the blossoming American university scene. The list of names is a stunning catalogue:

William G. Sumner: Marburg and Göttingen, Yale.

Herbert B. Adams: Heidelberg, Johns Hopkins.

John W. Burgess: Leipzig and Berlin, Columbia.

Richard T. Ely: Halle, Heidelberg, Geneva and Berlin, Johns Hopkins and Wisconsin.

John Bates Clark: Heidelberg and Zurich, Columbia.

Henry W. Farnam: Strassburg, Yale.

Frank J. Goodenow: Paris and Berlin, Columbia.

Arthur T. Hadley: Berlin, Yale.

George E. Howard and Leland Stanford: Munich and Paris, Nebraska.

Edmund J. James and Simon N. Patten: Halle, Pennsylvania.

E. R. A. Seligman: Berlin, Heidelberg, Geneva, Columbia.

Albion Small: Berlin and Leipzig, Chicago.

Frank Taussig: Berlin, Harvard.

William James and Frank Tillinghast: Berlin, Harvard.

Edward Wheeler Scripture: Leipzig, Berlin and Zurich, Yale.

E. B. Delabarre: Freiburg, Brown and Harvard.

James Mark Baldwin: Berlin and Leipzig, Princeton.

W. L. Bryan: Würzburg, Clark.

James McKeen Cattell: Göttingen and Leipzig, Princeton and Columbia.

G. Stanley Hall: Bonn and Berlin, Johns Hopkins.

Franz Boas: Heidelberg, Bonn and Kiel, Clark and Columbia.

This generation had the task of trying to transplant German ideas about social science and German ideas about the role of the social scientist in modern politics to the alien soil of North America. As Albion Small recalled, these ideas 'were not taken over bodily', not 'reproduced here inscribed upon tables of stone, visible, intelligible, categorical'. Continuing with a rich religious metaphor, so character-istically American, Small noted that the German tradition 'was brought as ambition to count in the work of bringing forth things new and old from the scripture of human experience, of using them so as to help American society become wise unto salvation' (Small, 1924, p. 326). But aside from being infused with German social science and Puritan redemption, the scholars of this generation were republicans and re-formers – middle-class and middle-of-the-road. For the most part, they did not shed the American sense of 'freedom', and they valued co-operative self-help and 'social ethics', not socialism – not even the limp socialism of the *Kathedersozialismus* of the *Verein* group. They were German, however, in thinking of *Geisteswissenschaft* as a kind of historically oriented unified social science with overlapping, non-discrete, connected concerns. And they still believed that policy judgments could be just as 'scientific' as any other judgments.

Some of these ideas created serious problems for the founders. The United States was not Germany, and in more ways than one. It had a British heritage, not only of constitutionalism, but also of individualism, and both had profound effects on early American thinking about human affairs. It was no mean feat to reconstitute and mesh this with the Hegelianized approach of the German tradition. Indeed, although there is a sense in which Albion Small and John Dewey actually succeeded in this, they were not the people who ultimately defined American social science.[1]

In addition, structural conditions constrained the possibilities for social science in the United States in ways different than in Germany: there the professoriate was established; in America it had yet to achieve

---

[1] A gap in the present account is the absence of discussion of the roles of James and Dewey in the struggle to generate American social science. Both were critical influences initially, and though each had very different programs for psychology and social science, ultimately their impact in this regard was probably slight. Indeed, their work in psychology stands radically opposed to what became the dominant view. Nevertheless, it is not uncommon to suppose that they contributed to the development of technocratic science in America. In my view, this reading requires both bad history and a misunderstanding of 'pragmatism'. Pragmatism came quickly to be misunderstood as a version of technocratic philosophy, in part because technocratic philosophies came to dominate American culture and also because pragmatism, like positivism, had an impatience with traditional 'meta-physical' philosophy. In this regard, see Dewey's brilliant 1908 review of James's *Prag-matism* (1916). Although the issues are far too complicated to settle here, it is clear that the primary thrust of pragmatism, was, like Marx's, to make social *praxis* a fundamental category (Bernstein, 1971). We are fortunate to have recent and highly original books on James by Gerald Myers (1986), and on Dewey, by Ralph W. Sleeper (1986).

authority. And it had to do so in the face of opposition from local elites – clergymen, lawyers, and merchants – who were themselves being challenged by the new big-monied men: the Vanderbilts, Harrimans, Goulds, Rockefellers, Carnegies, and Morgans – men who were coming to be increasingly courted by the boards of trustees of the exploding new universities. The University of Chicago, for example, was the lucky recipient of Rockefeller money. Thorstein Veblen, today identified as 'an iconoclast', exactly because, like Dewey and Small, he had ended up falling out of the mainstream, put it this way: 'The rule of the clergy belongs virtually to the prehistory of the American universities. . . . The substitution is a substitution of businessmen and politicians; which amounts to saying that it is a substitution of businessmen' (Veblen, 1951, p. 46). The development of corporate society with the setting up of trusts and the growth of labor unions, both of which accelerated between 1893 and 1904, called for an American version of a corporate response from the university. Finally, at just the time when the German-trained Americans needed the most clarity, their German teachers found themselves at the intellectual barricades: by the end of the century, the *Verein* group had substantially lost both the *Methodenstreit* and the *Wurturteilstreit,* and Droysen and the establishment historians were being hard-pressed to enter the modern era. Even more critically, it was now easy to think of 'science' in technocratic terms.

Veblen saw clearly what was happening. 'Academic social scientists' succumbed to the temptations and pressures of this new order of things. Given the 'exigencies of competitive academic enterprise in America', with 'businessmen' as executives of the new universities, there was little choice but to reward those who enhanced the position of the university in the larger community. One consequence was distraction from the goals of science: 'It is not simply that the vulgar, commonplace convictions of the populace . . . receive considerable attention in this field of moral and social sciences', but that 'a jealous eye must be had to the views and prepossessions prevalent among those well-to-do classes from whom the institution hopes to draw contributions to its endowment' (1957, p. 134). The upshot is the substitution of 'homolectical exposition' for science. Veblen had an old-fashioned view of science. For him, it was 'inquiry into the nature and causes, the working and the outcome, of [the] institutional apparatus' (p. 132). But even if this sort of inquiry 'should bear no colour of iconoclasm', its outcome 'will disturb the habitual convictions and preconceptions on which they rest'. Instead, the 'putative leaders of science' 'enlarge on the commonplace', put aside questions of causes in favor of questions of use, 'on what ought to be done to improve conditions and to conserve those usages and conventions that have by habit become embedded in the received scheme of use and wont, and so have been found to be good and right'. The result is 'a "science" of complaisant interpretations, apologies, and projected remedies' (p. 136). The problem was not so much that social scientists were reformers, but rather that they weren't scientists.

This first generation struggled with some real dilemmas: how to be German professors in a rapidly changing America, and how to be 'scientific' (and thus 'objective') and at the same time have a political impact. Then, there was the problem of social science versus social scien*ces*. Could social scientists in America have authority without having some specialized 'discipline'? Was 'a science without an identifiable central problem . . . a science at all' (Becker, 1971, p. 82). The first generation did not succeed in resolving these dilemmas. The second generation, students of that German-trained first generation, decided to be American professors in America. They marked out their territories, defined social science in positivist and ahistorical terms, and adopted an unabashed technocratic stance. This is the difference between the younger Albion Small and the older Albion Small, betwen Boas and Lowie, between Burgess and Merriam, between Ely and Irving Fisher, between William James and J. B. Watson.

After the catastrophe of World War I, it seemed clear to everyone that they had made the right choice. Thenceforth, Americans would set the style in 'social science'. In Europe, the Bolshevik Revolution, the rise of fascism, and the Second World War persistently aborted, but never annihilated, alternative discourses, especially those nurtured on or in response to the possibility of a Marxist social science. But it was not until the present period, beginning perhaps in the sixties during the Vietnam war, that American social science, like the United States itself, lost that hegemony which it began to acquire in the inter-war period.[2] But we need to see in a clearer way how social science came to be Americanized.

POLITICAL SCIENCE

We will begin with what is the oldest of the 'disciplines', albeit the one which in one sense at least, was the least successful in making itself into

---

[2] If it is true, as is argued here, that the process of Americanization was complete by the 1930s, it would take another book to discuss the problems and developments in Europe in the inter-war period and after. National socialism and fascism had a devastating and complicated impact, of course, but the destruction of social democracy and Stalinization was also critical.

While it is not my intention in this book to attempt to trace the developments in America since the 1930s, it is my view that although there were variations in the pattern – for example, in psychology where early behaviorism gave way to 'the Age of Theory' which gave way to Skinner, and so on – the basic assumptions remained unchallenged. An excellent and brief review can be found in Handy and Kurtz (1964) and Handy and Harwood (1973). Moreover, there were always dissidents, and often they were well-known figures.

an autonomous social science. 'Political science' dates from Aristotle's *Politics*, and between then and now, one can track an immense variety of lineages, strands, and developments of which two were discussed earlier. One is, the idea that politics can be derived from 'human nature', a development which became, in the eighteenth century 'the science of government'. These ideas, of course, would have puzzled Aristotle. The 'science' of government was most at home in Great Britain, but it also had plenty of advocates in the French Enlightenment. This conception of political science, it should be noted, allowed for a particularly clearcut division between political science and political economy, especially when, with the marginalist 'revolution', political economy became 'economics'. The other tradition was German and included the complex of inquiries perhaps best captured by the term *Geisteswissenschaft*. There were at least two strands to this. One emphasized comparative and systematic study of the state and its role in the histories of human civilization; we think here, of course, of Savigny, Ranke, and Droysen, the teacher of Burgess and of both C.K. and H.B. Adams. The other strand was also closely aligned with history; but in the view of Roscher, Knies, Schmoller, and the Historical School of Economists, *Sozialwissenschaften* and *Sozialpolitik* absorbed economics.

Were it not for the fact that, almost without exception, the founders of political science in America had been trained in Germany, mostly in the 1870s, the obvious solution to the institutional problem of political science would have been to define it as the science of government.[3] But as with 'political economy', as we shall see, it will take a generation to get *back* to this tradition, to de-Teutonize political science and political economy in America.

The first question which Burgess at Columbia, Herbert Baxter Adams at Hopkins, and Charles Kendall at Cornell had to face was that of the subject-matter of political science and the sense in which it is a science. The immediate practical issue was its relation to the discipline of history. Americans accepted the view of Droysen. As Adams put it: 'History is Past Politics and Politics present History' (Somit and Tanenhaus, 1967, p. 25). This phrase was inscribed in his seminar room at Johns Hopkins and was the *leitmotif* of the influential Johns Hopkins's *Studies in Historical and Political Science*. Burgess agreed, arguing that 'Political Science must be studied historically and history must be studied politically in order to [obtain] a correct comprehension of either. Separate them, and the one becomes a cripple, if not a corpse,

---

[3] It is of some interest to notice that Harvard, one of the best established of America's 'colleges', and the bulwark of the eastern (and Anglo-Saxon) establishment, was least interested in 'political science'. It had (and has) a department of government. The first prominent political scientist to gain a Harvard Ph.D. was William Bennett Munroe, in 1900.

the other a will-o'-the-wisp' (quoted from Herbst, 1965, from the 1896 Annual Report of the American Historical Association).

Since, for Burgess and Adams, political science contained an element of 'philosophical speculation', when it was 'true and correct', it was 'the forerunner of history'. Political science, accordingly, had a claim superior to that of history. History established 'facts' but lacked 'political reason' (Somit and Tanenhaus, 1967, p. 26). The members of the American Historical Association were 'astonished and dismayed' at this assessment. Could 'political scientists' and 'historians' live together in peace? But even among political scientists, there was disagreement. W. W. Willoughby argued that political science was related most closely to sociology; and Munroe Smith saw it as overlapping with law and economics. W. G. Sumner, political scientist cum sociologist cum political economist, who held the chair of political and social sciences at Yale College was, despite his German training, an American Spencerian and like Willoughby and Smith, he saw the social sciences as separated from history, but otherwise as non-discrete.

But, like the Germans, the whole of the first generation was clear about political science being policy-oriented. Of some 135 articles in the first 5 volumes of *Political Science Quarterly,* at least 83 deal directly with 'contemporaneous events' (Somit and Tanenhaus, 1967, p. 44). Indeed, beginning in the 1880s, but especially from the 1890s on, social scientists had special reasons to be interested in the problems which politicians had to address:

> The development of regulative and humane legislation required the skills of lawyers and economists, sociologists and political scientists. . . . Controversy over such issues created a new market for the books and magazine articles of experts and engendered a new respect for their specialized knowledge. Reform brought with it the brain trust. (Hofstadter, 1955, p. 155)

But just as with the British Poor Law Act, 'reform' was not necessarily 'humane'. One topic with enormous currency was immigration. The eminent Professor Burgess, who had much to say on this topic, gives us a solid glimpse into those 'prepossessions' which Veblen saw as being enlarged upon by 'our leading scientists'.

In Burgess's opinion, Teutonic political genius 'stamps the Teutonic nations as the political nations *par excellence,* and authorizes them, in the economy of the world, to assume the leadership in the establishment and administration of states'. The use of force was justified because 'there is no right to the status of barbarism'. It followed that immigration to the United States must be severely limited: 'We must preserve our Aryan nationality in the state, and admit only such non-Aryan race-elements as shall have become Aryanized in spirit and in genius by contact with it'. This excluded Slavs, Czechs, Hungarians, and South Italians. What of the undesirables already in the United States? For Burgess, a step in the right direction would be for 'every Irishman to kill a Negro and be hanged for it' (quoted from Herbst, 1965, pp. 121f., from Burgess, *Political Science and Comparative Constitutional Law* (1890), 'The Ideal of the American Commonwealth', *PSQ* (1895) and 'Some Impressions of the United States', *Fortnightly Review* (1882).

The questions of the subject-matter and scienticity of political science continued to be clouded when the first decades of the twentieth century arrived. Somit and Tanenhaus (1967) observe that in the period from 1903 to 1921, there was very little discussion or systematic analysis of the proper division between political science and the other sciences and that what there was tended to be brief and 'from the pens of European scholars'. They would seem to be correct, however, in judging that it was not that the issues had been resolved. Rather, as the early departments at Columbia and Johns Hopkins gained prestige and new departments came into existence, at first combined with other 'social sciences' and then give autonomy, as 'political scientists' acquired 'visibility' as 'experts' – Woodrow Wilson, it is worth remembering, first became prominent for his work in public administration – and as political scientists acquired an organization, which, in the words of Willoughby, 'would do for political science what the American Economic and American Historical Association were doing for economics and history' – in short, as political scientists acquired some professional and institutional standing – the problem became less acute. In this, of course, political scientists were involved in a tacit conspiracy with members of the other 'branches' of the social sciences. Each branch was engaged in the same struggle at the same time. Whatever unclarity remained, it was tolerable as long as no one 'discipline' was in a pre-eminent position.

But perhaps the key fact in the Americanization of political science was the change in the nature of graduate education. In 1904 almost half those holding positions in the American Political Science Association had been German-trained; this proportion fell to a third in 1914, and of the 18 members added to the Executive Council, only three had studied on the Continent. An American Ph.D. in a 'discipline' made its holder a 'professional' in that discipline – even if he may have been hard-pressed to define the discipline's special subject-matter.

Ironically, it was not a professional political scientist, nor even a member of the American Political Science Association who offered the most penetrating contemporary account of political science as a science. Yet this account, found in Arthur Bentley's remarkable *Process of Government* (1908), was utterly ignored by the profession until perhaps the 1930s. Bentley's book was unfriendly to the social science of the day, dismissing key ideas of Small, Lester Ward, Dicey, and others as 'verbiage'. For him, political science was literally dead, and, critically, it was evading its central problem: 'the activities which are politics'. But Bentley was an outsider, and it would take some time for the insiders to catch up. In the ensuing years, a recurring theme, especially in the adresses of Association presidents, was the question of the scientific status of political science. Henry Jones Ford and Jesse Macy variously exhorted the membership to be less 'descriptive and historical' and to develop principles 'universal in application' (Somit and Tanenhaus, 1967, pp. 77f.). It was World War I, however, which finally crushed German-inspired historical political science in America.

Charles Merriam's clarion call of 1921, 'The Present State of the Study of Politics', came in the wake of that demise. His essay set a tidal wave in motion, leading to the establishment of an Association Committee on Political Research, to three national conferences on the science of politics, and in 1925; as Somit and Tanenhaus remark, 'to the creation of the Social Science Research Council' – financed, it is worth mentioning, by Rockefeller money.

Merriam's essay is a naked positivism – sometimes reading as if whole sentences had been lifted from Comte. For example, he writes that with a scientific politics it would be possible to have 'a more intelligent control of the process of government' and thereby facilitate 'the conscious control of human evolution toward which intelligence moves in every domain of human life' (Somit and Tanenhaus, 1967, p. 11). At other times, he sounded more like Karl Pearson, with his emphasis on 'hypotheses', 'precise evidence', 'relations of variables', and so on. Finally, Merriam strongly endorsed the appropriation by political science of the methods and results of psychologists and statisticians. With reference to the historical, legal, and comparative approaches to politics – that is, to the German approach – Merriam insisted, 'I am not suggesting that we ask our older friends to go', but it was nevertheless clear that if they were to stay, they would be welcome only insofar as they adopted the rigorous canons of scientific research of a 'new science of politics'.

Merriam was not completely successful, of course. Had he been, we would not have the recurring efforts to appropriate the methods and assumptions of more successfully realized social sciences: the 'behavioralism' of Lasswell or Truman, the survey-research approach of Berelson and Key, the functionalism of Easton of Almond, the 'operationalism' of Dahl and Oppenheim, the game-theoretic approach of Luce and Rogow, the decisionist approach of Simon or Tullock. Of course, European streams of thought continued to infect American political science – aided and abetted by Hitler. Indeed, the list of names of German political scientists who came to the United States is quite remarkable: Leo Strauss, Eric Voegelin, Theodore Adorno, Max Horkheimer, Karl Wittogel, Herbert Marcuse, Franz L. Neumann, Carl J. Friedrich, Hans Morgenthau, Otto Kirchheimer, Karl Deutsch, and, somewhat later, Hannah Arendt. Between these writers and their students, and the dissidents in the American tradition, American political science has continued to have a slightly fragmented character and to be persistently 'unscientific' at its edges.

ECONOMICS

Economics was not Americanized. Even more than political science, it needed to be de-Germanized so that it could return to that mainstream of thought whose roots were in Quesnay and Smith.

It seems that the first chair in political economy, then a branch of moral philosophy, was at King's College, now Columbia, sometime after 1786. Up to the 1880s, the pattern of political economy in America was more characteristic of France than of England. America's leading figures – Francis Wayland, Amasa Walker, and Henry C. Carey – were strongly under the sway of the optimistic views of J. B. Say and Frederic Bastiat. 'Free-traders', these men exhilarated in the 'laws of the market' and saw the United States as the veritable paradigm of the competitive market economy ensconced in classical theory. Adopting Say's Law that production begat consumption, Carey maintained that the economy could only expand, and there would be increasing munificence – growth at its very best. Sumner saw a flaw in Carey's optimistic scenario, judging

that when population was scarce relative to the land available for appropriation, the standard of living would be high and equality would prevail; but that when crowds of land-hungry workers had to compete for increasingly scarce means of life, that idyllic condition would give way to one of fierce competition, misery, and class antagonism. There was nothing to be done about this, Sumner insisted. Anticipating the lifeboat ethics of our own day, he argued that helping the poor would only make things worse in the long run (Sumner, 1883).

As the 1870s began, John Bates Clark, Seligman, Ely, and Taussig, among others, were pursuing their education in Germany; and Menger, Jevons, and others were in the process of inventing marginalism. Clark was an early exponent of the new theory and, if Schumpeter is correct, may claim to have been an independent discoverer. But the others came back convinced that the Historical School's critique of 'Smithianism' as deductivist, abstract, and unhelpful was correct. These writers, impelled by the Great Crash of 1873, rejected *laissez-faire* and looked to the *Verein für Sozialpolitik* as a model for the social reform of society.

In 1884, E. J. James and Simon N. Patten decided that a society patterned on the *Verein* would

> combat the widespread view that our economic problems would solve themselves, and that our laws and institutions which at present favor individual instead of collective action can promote the best utilization of our material resources and secure to each individual the highest development of all his faculties. (Quoted from Dorfman, 1949, vol. 3, p. 205)

These were heady ideas, far too radical for economists facing the constraints pinpointed by Veblen (see above). But the efforts of James and Patten to organize economists did not pass without effect. Richard T. Ely, 'that excellent German professor in an American skin' (Schumpeter, 1954, p. 873), succeeded in bringing together 'liberal' economists who, 'in pursuit of free inquiry', as Clark put it, organized 'a Political Economy Club on a rather progressive basis' (1954, p. 206). This would eventually become the American Economic Association; but there were some conflicts of doctrine that would first have to be resolved.

The initial 'Statement of Principles' had been blunt. It had asserted that 'the conflict of labor and capital has brought into prominence a vast number of problems, whose solution requires the united efforts, each in its own sphere, of the church, of the state, and of science' (quoted from Wesley C. Mitchell, 1969, p. 233). The statement noted that 'while we appreciate the work of former economists, we look not so much to speculation as to the historical and statistical study of actual conditions of economic life' (1969, p. 233). What was needed was social research and historical understanding – not the pure theory of the classicists.

In order to secure enough members to get the organization going, Ely and his group found it necessary to add the following qualification to the statement of principles: 'This statement was proposed and accepted as a general indication of the view and purposes of those who founded the American Economic Association, but it is not to be regarded as binding upon individual members' (1969, p. 235). But within three years (1887), the constitution was disembowelled, only the first 'objective' was left in tact: 'the encouragement of economic research'. Seligman subsequently insisted that the changes were not made 'in deference to a coterie'. We can believe this and still believe that the group who led the movement were asking their colleagues to bite off more than they could chew.

It is noteworthy that the most distinguished spokesmen for 'the old school', the tradition of Ricardo, Say and Mill, was a distinguished mathematician and astronomer Simon Newcomb. In an unsigned review of his colleague Ely's *The Labor Movement,* Newcomb described the book as 'the ravings of an anarchist and the dreams of a socialist' and concluded that 'Dr. Ely seems . . . to be seriously out of place in a university chair' (quoted from Dorfman, 1949, p. 163, from *The Nation,* 1886). Nicholas Murray Butler, then merely a tutor on Burgess's Faculty of Political Science at Columbia, suggested in a similarly unfriendly review that the book favored 'a socialist programme' and pointed out that Ely was 'careless' in not seeing that the problem was 'intemperance, [the] imperfect ethical development of man, . . . unchastity, ignorance of the simplest law of political economy, and in fact the wickedness of human nature' (1949 p. 163). This was, of course, the familiar moralistic assessment of the British ameliorists. The charges of 'socialist' were new – the beginnings of by now familiar American red-baiting. Ely himself had two years previously denounced 'rebels against society' who stood for 'common property; socialist production and distribution; the grossest materialism, . . . free love . . . and . . . anarchy' (quoted by Herbst, 1965, p. 189, from *Christian Union* (April 1884). Ely called himself a 'progressive conservative'.

It has rightly been said that American social science of the 'progressive period' was an important aspect of the whole atmosphere of reform (Hofstadter, 1955), but, as noted earlier, one must be wary of what was meant by 'reform' concretely. In addition, one should also notice that once the un-radical 'radical' critics of American society – Ely, Small, Veblen, and Beard – had been painted as 'mad anarchists' or 'dreamy socialists', middle-class men with middle-class ideas could define a neat middle-of-the-road 'reformist' program. Compared to Europe, the United States lacked a large, radical labor movement, and in consequence the *characteristic* role of the social scientist would be to act as the voice of middle-class yearning for reform.

By 1890, most of the leading members of the 'old school' had become members of the American Economic Association – with the notable exception of Sumner, who by this time was more usually identified with the new science of sociology. American economics could say that it had cleansed itself of its German – and 'socialistic' – tendencies and was now back on that good and true path so well marked by Anglo-Saxons.

One could argue, of course, that the rout was not complete, that out of the original movement came the American 'institutionalists' – the 'maverick' Veblen, his student Wesley C. Mitchell, and John R. Commons. That their work left an indelible mark on our thinking – sometimes unacknowledged – suggests the challenge of their approach. That few – albeit a notable few – have followed in their footsteps suggests that, of the social sciences, economics, with a good head start, was most successful in institutionalizing itself as a 'science'.[4]

SOCIOLOGY

With regard to sociology and anthropology, we can, following Becker (1971), concentrate on just two men, Albion Small and Franz Boas. As Becker shows, Small achieved scientific standing for sociology, but at the price of abandoning his earlier views of its nature and role. In effect, therefore, we have two Smalls, the German Albion Small and the American Albion Small. In the case of anthropology, the shift was from Boas's conception of an ethically significant science of man to a conception of it, by his student Robert H. Lowie, as a specialized value-neutral discipline: the ethnographer as neither antiquarian nor romantic purveyor of 'an exotic milieu' (Lowie, 1937).

It is not insignificant that Small saw Lester Ward as having 'improvised an entirely mistaken interpretation of cause and effect when he led Americans to believe that they owe sociology to Comte'. It was Small's contention that 'the efficient cross-fertilization came from the German tradition' (Small, 1924, p. 315). Small does not deny, of course, that Ward, whose work 'occupies in general sociology very much the place of the Tower among the institutions of London' (p. 341) 'avowedly represented the Comtean succession, while William G. Sumner and Franklin H. Giddings developed . . . the initiatives of Herbert Spencer' (p. 329). But Small is not wrong when he reminds us that, by 1890, 'the academic atmosphere of the United States was thick with germs of ideas which came from or through [the] German tradition' (p. 328).

After offering, in 1904, the first textbook of sociology (with George E. Vincent), Small wrote *Adam Smith and Modern Sociology: A Study in the Methodology of the Social Sciences* (1907), *The Cameralists: The Pioneers of German Social Polity* (1909), *The Meaning of the Social Sciences* (1910), and *The Origins of Sociology* (1924). In all these, his concerns and commitments are wholly those of the German Historical School. In the 1907 book, he wrote that 'modern sociology is virtually an attempt to take up the larger program of social analysis and interpre-

---

[4] Phillip Klein (1983) provides a brief, but excellent, appreciation of Wesley Mitchell, a student of both Veblen and Dewey at Chicago. It is well to notice that Myrdal, Galbraith, Leontief, Kuznets, and E. S. Mason, for example, stand in the lineage of Veblen and Mitchell. Leontief created a stir in 1975 when he resigned from the renowned Harvard economics faculty, calling for its 'temporary disenfranchisement' and the hiring of an additional faculty with a 'wider range of interests'. Harvard had replaced Kuznets, Mason and the Marxist Samuel Bowles with a group of 'high-powered theoretical and mathematically astute economists' (*New York Times*, 5 February, p. 1).

tation which was implicit in Adam Smith's moral philosophy, but which was suppressed for a century by prevailing interest in the technique of the production of wealth' (quoted by Becker, 1971, p. 12). In Small's view, 'Smithianism' would have puzzled Adam Smith; there was even in Smith a project for a human science which was buried by the praxiology which we now call 'economics'. In his *Origins of Sociology*, Small picked up this theme, but he omitted Smith, tracing sociology from the Cameralists to Savigny to Ranke to Schmoller. The book contains an extensive account of the 'Menger–Schmoller debate' and of the later 'Schmoller–Treitschke controversy' in which Treitschke railed against the German *Sozialdemokratie,* from which, in Treitschke's view, 'no really fruitful new idea has sprung' (Becker, 1971, p. 260).

Small was profoundly alive to 'the social question' and, like his *Verein* teachers and Ward, he wished 'to base reform on sound knowledge of the social process'. Since the social process was the outcome of many concurrently operating causes, nothing was irrelevant to the task. But if so, didn't that make sociology an out-and-out imperialistic discipline? While the older disciplines – history, economics and political science – were struggling to identify a subject-matter, here was sociology being the bully. 'Who would transact with such a monster? Who would welcome its meetings? Who would be comfortable with its aims and findings, if these aims and findings were in explicit defiance of what one was doing oneself?' (Becker, 1971, p. 18).

Small was out front in acknowledging the problem. In the last chapter of the *Origins of Sociology* (1924), Small criticises himself. In his 1890 syllabus (which later became his textbook), he had written that 'sociology is the science which has for its subject-matter the phenomena of human society, viz., the varieties of groups in which individuals are associated, with the organization, relations, functions and tendencies of thee various associations', *or,* 'in other words, Sociology is the science which combines and correlates all the special sciences' (pp. 344f., emphasis omitted). He comments: 'It would require a high voltage of imagination to invent a more cheerful *non sequitur* unafraid' (pp. 344f.). Indeed, this is no 'in other words'. The two definitions are inconsistent. The first makes sociology the exclusive human science; the second assigns it no subject-matter at all!

Small finally decided against the German Historical School and Ward, explaining away imperialistic enthusiasm as the 'sin' of 'amateurish ambition'. His generation was convinced that current methods were inadequate, and that 'methods must be devised for learning more about human affairs' (p. 346). He concluded apologetically that this really was all that 'the early innovators' were committed to. He was now (1924) prepared to settle for a definition of sociology which would effectively make it a *method* and a *technique without a subject-matter*: 'A sociologist, properly speaking, is a man whose professional procedure consists in discovery or analysis of categories of human group composition or reaction and behavior, or in use of such categories as means of interpreting or controlling group situations' (p. 348). The old idea that establishing the *causes* of social problems was *the* goal, and that this demanded a unified social science was gone. As Veblen observed, it was unsettling to the *status quo*. Sociology, too, would clean up its act.

Becker suggests that Small was all but 'fated' to become a methodologist rather than a human scientist: 'He seems to have been caught up ideologically in following out what he had to do – as editor of the *Journal,* as chairman of the leading sociology department, as propagandist for the new discipline, as public relations man, as theoretical and practical technician' (Becker, 1971, pp. 24f.). Of course, even if Small had not been caught up ideologically, he could not have stemmed the tide. The new generation, trained in statistical methods, with mutually reinforcing motivations to win promotions and to produce the 'facts' needed by presidents, mayors, and corporations, would not be likely to opt to antagonize their colleagues in the quiet conspiracy in which there was plenty for everyone.[5] The complete denouement, kept at bay during Small's lifetime, was given 'a fitting voice' just three years after his death. William F. Ogburn, in his presidential address to the American Sociological Society concluded:

Sociology as a science is not interested in making the world a better place in which to live, in encouraging beliefs, or in spreading information, in dispensing news, in setting forth impressions of life, in leading multitudes, or in guiding the ship of state. Science is interested directly in one thing only, to wit, discovery of new knowledge. (Quoted from Becker, p. 28)

Impelled by 'successes' in behaviorist psychology, by the vigorous operationism of Percy Bridgman's *The Logic of Modern Physics* (1927), and by the methodological rigor of Vienna positivism, which had been

[5] By 1915, Small sensed that the social sciences had become 'a pack of mongrels', each fighting for their scrap:
In the universities, the decisive question has usually been, not what aspects of reality most urgently demand investigation, but with what sort of material one could most certainly establish oneself as a teacher. . . . Not a division of social science in the United States has fully defended itself against the lure of profits from textbooks . . . the more obvious deferring of the question, What most needs to be investigated? to the question, What sort of mental pabulum will the market digest? (Quoted by Becker, 1971, p. 23, from 'Fifty Years of Sociology in the US (1865–1915)')
Small had no idea, of course, that his early effort at textbook writing would set such a precedent!

exported to the United States, it was not long before Stuart Dodd, G. A. Lundberg, F. S. Chapin, and others were spelling out the meaning of a 'professional procedure' for sociological research. The protests of R. S. Lynd (1939) and later of C. W. Mills (1959), would make them no friends in the now solidly established 'profession' of academic sociology.

ANTHROPOLOGY

Franz Boas, says Becker, 'practically single-handedly fashioned a successful academic discipline of anthropology in America'. Boas faced problems comparable to Small's. This is not surprising. In the first place, the histories of anthropology and sociology were not, until then, very different, if indeed they were different at all. The same big names recur: Rousseau, Buffon, Comte, Spencer, Tylor, and Frazer. We can think of others, of course, which appear in one, but not in the other – for example, Paul Broca, who founded the Society of Anthropology in Paris in 1859. The possibility of a different history was due, in part, to the possibility of what we now call 'physical anthropology', in contrast to 'social anthropology'. From early in the nineteenth century, the study of humanity had involved the direct study of human pre-history, through the study of bones, skulls, relics, and artifacts. Anthropology thus had museum links; but it also had links to 'psychology'. Indeed, Boas's first academic appointment was in G. Stanley Hall's psychology department at the new founded Clark University which Hall headed; and his second appointment, as lecturer and then professor of physical anthropology at Columbia, came about through the instrumentality of the psychologist J. McKeen Cattell (Herskovits, 1953, pp. 13f.). The more usual arrangement, of course, had anthropology originally in the same department as sociology.

If anthropology was 'the science of humanity', a description which seems to date from approximately 1795 (Becker, 1971, p. 77), then, like sociology, it too was an imperialistic discipline. Of course, for most of the century, there were no professional anthropologists or sociologists; students of people and society were all lawyers, classicists, physicians, philosophers, or just plain 'learned'. The problem would nonetheless have to be faced in the American university.

Franz Boas was German-born and -educated – as a physicist and a geographer – but his trip to Baffin Land in 1883–4 turned his attention to ethnology. He tells us that, early on, he aligned himself 'with those who are motivated by the affective appeal of a phenomenon that impresses me as a unit, although its elements may be irreducible to a common cause'. In a spirit common to Max Weber as to many of his time and place, 'the problem that attracted me was the intelligent understanding of a complex phenomenon. When from geography my attention was directed to ethnology, the same interest prevailed' (Herskovits, 1953, p. 10). Herskovits writes that no one label applied to Boas because every label did. He was historicist, diffusionist, evolutionist, functionalist, and psychologist (p. 68). But by 1904, he was apologizing for his holism and pluralism:

> Conscious of the invigorating influence of our point of view and of the grandeur of a single all-compassing science of man, enthusiastic anthropologists may proclaim the mastery of anthropology over older sciences that have achieved where we are still struggling with methods, that have built up noble structures where chaos reigns with us, the trend of development points in another direction, in the continuance of each science by itself, assisted where may be by anthropological methods. (Quoted by Becker, 1971, pp. 96f.)

Like Small, Boas proceeded from a youthful *Schwärmerei* of an 'all-compassing science', that would be methodologically open to the idea that anthropology was but a handmaiden to the autonomous method-secure sciences 'that have built up noble structures': *that* was some shift.

In addition to the problem of having to settle for a more modest role for anthropology in order to secure its scienticity, Boas had another problem in unilinear evolutionism. Indeed, the two problems were not unrelated.

Science, presumably, is the search for laws. In the nineteenth-century French and British traditions, human science was the search for laws of progress. But if unilinear evolution were the case, then history, anthropology, and sociology would be the same discipline. Boas saw no merit in unilinear evolution, and still a German at heart, he believed that history could be scientific *without* laws. He also insisted, in good German fashion, that each culture had to be understood in terms of its own historical process. But this didn't help, since if anthropology were to be conceived an *idiographic* science, it would still not be distinguishable from history! Was Maitland correct in saying that 'anthropology must choose between becoming history or nothing'? (quoted in Becker, 1971, p. 89).

One way out was to argue that anthropology *as a science* had no historical dimension and that it was concerned only with *social process itself*. The upshot was the American brand of anthropology: Culture and Personality, psychological anthropology – 'a logical, even apodictic outcome of Boas's own vision' (Becker, 1971, p. 87). The main goal was not to reconstruct the past, but to determine 'the processes by which certain stages developed'. In this way, the union of individual psychology and culture could be elucidated. Neither Comte, who would have found this combination unintelligible, nor Spencer had anything useful to say on this score. Anthropology could start afresh. Indeed, as is now plain, the impetus would come from Galton and, after the turn of the century, from the psychology of Freud.

Culture and Personality was a form of functionalism, and in England, Bronislaw Malinowski and A. R. Radcliffe-Brown were articulating their own versions of it; but there was a critical difference between the American view and both the British and the French versions which had been inspired by Durkheim and developed by Henri Hubert, Marcel Mauss, and Lucien Lévy-Bruhl. Boas agreed with all these writers that good ethnography demanded 'the close observation and description of the daily life of a primitive people' (Herskovits, 1953, p. 67), and as far as 'functionalism' was concerned, he had himself been an early critic of the curatorial practice of the synoptic museum, 'because if a specimen is isolated, "we cannot understand its meaning"' (Lowie, 1937, p. 142). The big difference, especially between the Durkheimians and the Americans was the pertinence of psychology. For the Durkheimians, including here Radcliffe-Brown, anthropology was substantially independent of individual psychology: the individual as individual was irrelevant. Not so for the Americans, who had been very much influenced by the 'psychology of individual differences'. Indeed, as Lowie was to insist, 'original nature' may differ racially as well as individually and, 'as *verae causae,* these must enter into our accounts of cultural differences and of cultural change' (Lowie, 1937, p. 266). For Lowie:

A general human explanation breaks down when diversity, not likeness, is to be explained. Here psychology might still conceivably render service by tracing group differentiate to original nature, but to nature racially circumscribed. Actually, to be sure, any differences in endowment that may exist are not congruous with cultural differences. This, however, is far from maintaining that the races are alike. To quote Thomas's reasonable conclusion: 'It is to be emphasized that there are no proofs that the mind is of precisely the same quality in all races and populations. It is not improbable that there is a somewhat different distribution of special abilities, such as mathematics, music, etc.'. (Lowie, 1937, p. 285)

Lowie also quarrelled with the Durkheimian idea 'that one explains customs and beliefs by showing "how each one of them is an example of some general law of human society"' (1937, p. 233). But this did not mean that for him anthropology was an idiographic science. The problem was not the appropriation of the subsumption model of explanation from the French and British traditions, but the nineteenth-century view of 'general law'. For Lowie, 'correlations' are 'the closest approximation ethnology is likely to achieve to the ideals of natural science . . . yet [the] scientific respectability of the anthropologist remains unimpaired so long as he co-ordinates with a maximum of attainable efficiency, the particular phenomena he studies' (p. 288). And in another place, keenly aware of the work of Mach and Pearson, he noted that 'generalizations do not have to be universal in order to be useful'. 'The progress of ethnography lies in the ever-increasing better-founded determination of functional relationships between descriptively isolable elements' (quoted by Becker, 1971, p. 103).

Becker's conclusion is apt:

> On the face of it, Lowie has here kept the broader historical-evolutionary interest; but this is only an appearance. Since the whole story will never be known, the purpose of anthropology is to keep filling in. Generalizations do not have to be universal; they merely have to be useful – useful to the purpose of the discipline. The purpose of anthropology has become solely self-furthering. (p. 103)

HISTORY

The idea of history has recurred in all the preceding discussions. And of course, we must remind ourselves that the Americanization of the social sciences involved both their separation from one another and from history. Higham notes rightly that 'the real problem in early twentieth century America was not one of emancipating history from science, but rather the reverse: preventing science from repudiating history' (Higham *et al.*, 1965, pp. 108f.). As social scientists deserted history, 'historians', defensively, confronted the question of a scientific history. But 'historians' must be put in quotes, for, prior to the last quarter of the nineteenth century, the professional historian was an oddity.

In America, during the seventeenth century, it was Puritan clergymen who wrote history; in the eighteenth and nineteenth centuries, it was patricians – for example, Thomas Hutchinson, Francis Parkman, Henry Adams, and Theodore Roosevelt. As late as 1884, there were only 20 full-time teachers of history in the 400 or so institutions of higher learning in America. A decade later, there were 100, and by 1909, remarkably, the American Historical Association could claim 2,700 members! (Higham *et al.*, 1965, pp. 4, 10).

Herbert B. Adams, head of the Graduate Program in Historical Studies at Johns Hopkins, was trained in Germany, and one might have expected that he would articulate a Rankean conception of history. It is true that he insisted that Ranke was 'the father of scientific history', but his conception of Rankean history was a distortion, as noted in chapter 7 above. *Wie es eigentlich gewesen* did not spring from positivism. But by the time that most of the Americans arrived in Germany, Ranke had retired and the positivist burst had exploded in German natural science. Finally, while one can easily overwork the idea that 'practical-minded' Americans eschewed 'speculation', there was a long-standing British anti-metaphysicalism in America's essentially anti-intellectualist history.

America's historians did have a philosophy of history, of course; along with everyone else, they accepted completely the idea that progress was inevitable. Still, American historians were contemptuous of 'philosophy of history' and were utterly distrustful of the idea that history was an 'art' and that historians were 'literary artists'. Finally, 'whereas literary amateurs dealt extensively in personalities, the professionals prided themselves on tracing the evolution of institutions' (Higham, 1965, p. 97). Their history thus had greater affinity with that of the Englishman Buckle than with that of the German Droysen, even if there was in Schmoller and his group, a German version of this. From the point of view of the 'amateurs', the American assiduousness for 'facts' and deprecation of literary genius were the most appalling features of the new professionals. Theodore Roosevelt, one of the more famous of the amateurs, was led to explode:

> After a while, it dawned on me that the conscientious, industrious, painstaking little pedants, who would be useful in a rather small way if they had understood their own limitations, had become because of their conceit distinctly noxious. They solemnly believed that if there were enough of them, and that if they only collected enough facts of all kinds and sorts, there would cease to be any need thereafter for great writers, great thinkers'. (Quoted by Higham *et al.*, 1965, pp. 8f.)

The scientific history of the first generation lacked the powerful – and spurious – generalizations about the past which the older and bolder historians had sought; but far worse, it lacked useful generalizations about the *present*. And this was exactly the wrong time to be accused of irrelevancy:

> The social scientists, ironically enough, were plunging into a piecemeal empiricism of their own at the very time they were criticizing historians for neglecting general theories. But the social scientist's empiricism – their surveys of urban slums, their bureaus of municipal research, their statistics on commodities, transpor-

tation and prices – was excitingly contemporary. *Their* facts concerned the practical problems that most of the American people
after 1900 wanted solved. (1965, p. 110)

It was against the background of these changes that James Harvey
Robinson published his famous manifesto of historical reform, *The New
History* (1912). The 'new' history was surely aimed at the 'old' history of
the founders, but 'the sharpness of the attack obscured its somewhat
superficial character' (Higham *et al.*, 1965, p. 104). The dissenters
appropriated most of the basic assumptions of the founders and added
some new ones. Critical among the innovations was the 'presentism' of
the new history. 'History would thereby become, as never before,
pragmatically useful' (1965, p. 111). The idea was at least implicit in the
writings of policy-oriented German theorists, and, as noted earlier,
Albion Small and John Dewey were developing a 'functional ethics'
from the same materials. The second move seemed original by illicit
comparison. It insisted on breaking the concentration of German historiography on politics and political elites, 'the narration of meaningless
names or potentates and battles'. The new history would be institutional
and far more inclusive. It would look to 'social forces' (a favorite phrase
of Frederick Jackson Turner). Without being committed to 'the
Feuerbach–Marx determinism', it would recognize that civilization 'has
a fundamental economic basis'. As Robinson was aware, in this, the
new history looked more like the history of Schmoller and the Marxian
variants (Robinson, 1912, pp. 8, 50).

It is some paradox that, while the Americanized social sciences were
institutionalizing a self-conscious methodological individualism, the historians were going in the opposite direction. As I argued in chapter 8,
there is an *inherent* connection between methodological individualism
and a non- or anti-historical approach, since without even the idea of
relatively enduring *sui generis* social structures, it is hard to see what
social process could be about. This methodological rift between history
and the social sciences, a rift which manifests itself as a key characteristic of contemporary mainstream social science, was masked by inherited confusion over the issues. Indeed, it still is!

Moreover, at this time, a third feature of the new history contributed
to the obscuring of this fundamental separation. The new historians
would ally themselves with the social sciences; taking a cue from old-
style sociology and anthropology, the new history would be the synthesis of the social sciences. The older idea that there were laws of
history, was revived, but they were construed as laws of society, a
radical difference. The idea, then, was that the special social sciences
would generate these laws, and that the historian would then incorporate them into an integrated historical view.

Looked at from one point of view, this was eminently plausible. But, in fact, the social sciences seemed to be incapable of generating the requisite 'laws', and historians continued to speak uncritically of 'historical laws'. Worse, they seemed, at least, to leave no room in history for agency. There were only 'social forces'. For many, the new history of Robinson, Turner, and Beard was uncomfortably 'deterministic'.

In the 1920s, Harry Elmer Barnes, a student of Robinson's, became the herald of the promised marriage between history and the social sciences. His *The New History and the Social Studies* (1925), *History and Social Intelligence* (1926), and other writings are full of promise, but, of course, the marriage was never consummated. Carl Becker, in a review of Barnes's 1925 book, perhaps expressed the historians' view of the matter when he said that 'knowing the newer sciences of geography, anthropology, psychology, sociology, politics, economics and ethics, or some part of them, may indeed be useful. But the systematic mastery of so many disciplines is not for all.' He concluded that in order to write a good book, 'the historian will chiefly need . . . intelligence, experience of men and things, insight into human conduct, literary ability, and last but not least knowledge (the more the better, whether of the newer or the older sciences of mankind), knowledge of the subject-matter first of all, then of anything in heaven or earth that may have bearing on it' (quoted by Saveth, 1964, pp. 8f.). Social scientists would be content, as C. W. Mills has so neatly put it, with that 'dull pudding called sketching in the historical background' (Mills, 1959, p. 154). As part of the 'the democratic theory of knowledge', in which all facts are equally important, American inquiry into the human condition has been supremely tolerant, pervaded by a spirit of live and let live.

One final consequence must be noted. By the 1930s the presentism and activism of the new historians had been thoroughly de-fanged. Relativism, implicit in the new history from the beginning, but brought clearly to the surface by Becker, now unhinged the ideal of objectivity. With this, the old idea of a 'science of history' appeared as 'mere bunk' (Clarence Alford, quoted by Higham *et al.*, 1965, p. 123). Beard, who had always believed that 'science, facts, and the scientific method' could provide 'inescapable and irrefutable policies', no longer thought so. In a rousing address entitled 'Written History as an Act of Faith', Beard made a plea for the emancipation of history *from* science, with a view to restoring morals and politics to historical writing. The rift between history and social science was now complete. The stage was all set for the enthusiastic reception of Talcott Parsons's remarkable *The Structure of Social Action* (1937), an ahistorical, 'objective', idealist, functionalist, voluntarist, and empiricist picture of the interconnectedness of society (see Gouldner, 1970).

PSYCHOLOGY

If consensus around a 'paradigm' is a test of a 'mature science', then economics is the most successful of the social sciences; psychology cannot hold a candle to it in this regard. But if sheer numbers of professional practitioners is the test of the successful institutionalization of a 'science', then psychology is the winner hands down. Moreover, psychology is the exemplar of the Americanization of social science. It had an advantage in this regard from the beginning. One astute writer has noted that as regards the lifework of the founders of American psychology – James, G. S. Hall, J. M. Baldwin, J. McKeen Cattell – 'their youthful travels in Germany appear to have been almost totally irrelevant' (Danziger, 1979b, p. 33). There were good reasons for this. First, there was no consensus in German psychology about its tasks; and, in particular, the relation of physiology to psychology was profoundly muddled. Even if we include Wundt's work as the most powerful influence on German psychology, it will be remembered that he had a pluralist vision of psychology and considered his own version of 'experimental psychology' to be but a small part of it. Second, for institutional reasons, German psychologists never tried to separate psychological concerns from philosophy. Because philosophers had institutional authority, psychology was defended in terms of its relations to philosophy – the senior 'discipline' (Danziger, 1979b, pp. 34f.; Leary, 1979). This was not possible in America. Third, all the leading figures – Helmholtz, Wundt, Brentano, Stumpf, Ebbinghaus, and Mach – were interested exclusively in the generalized normal human adult mind – not in 'the psychology of individual differences', a feature of that segment of British psychology which was inspired by Darwin, especially, of course, through the work of his half-cousin Sir Frances Galton (1822–1911). In this, psychologists in America would be spiritual cousins. Finally, none of the Germans had offered a clear way to make psychology a socially useful discipline. But this was a prerequisite for the *de nova* institutionalization of psychology in America. Redefining psychology as 'the science of behavior' would eventually do the trick.

Writing in 1929, Boring summarized the situation beautifully:

> By 1900 the characteristics of American psychology were well defined. It inherited its physical body from German experimentalism, but it got its mind from Darwin. American psychology was to deal with mind in use. . . . Thorndike brought the animals into the formal laboratory, . . . then went over the study of school-children and the mental tests increased. Hall helped here too with his

pioneering in educational psychology. . . . Then Watson touched a match to the mass, there was an explosion and behaviorism was left. (Boring, 1929, p. 494)

In 1869, Galton had published *Hereditary Genius,* followed by *English Men of Science* (1874) and *Natural Inheritance* (1889). Incorporating and extending the statistical ideas of Quêtelet, Galton was the first to apply the normal law of error to the measurement of mental ability. He developed the 'index of correlation', 'r', which was brought to its present
form by Karl Pearson, Galton's successor at the Francis Galton Laboratory for National Eugenics and the British trumpet for the philosophy of Ernst Mach. But, as Boring notes, 'the movement in psychological testing is essentially American' (1929, p. 546). Hall and Cattel had prepared the ground; and Boas, along with Jastrow, Bolton, Thorndike, Woodworth, Helen Thompson, and others, devised tests. Lewis M. Terman complained in his 1906 doctoral dissertation that 'one of the most serious problems confronting psychology is that of connecting itself with life'. Eighteen years later, as the force behind the army testing program and as the newly elected President of the American Psychological Association, Terman could declare with enthusiasm and no small measure of truth:

It is the method of tests that has brought psychology down from the clouds and made it useful to men; that has transformed the 'science of trivialities' into the 'science of human engineering'. The psychologist of the pre-test era was, to the average layman, just a harmless crank, but now that psychology has tested and classified nearly two million soldiers, has been appealed to in the grading of several million school children; is used everywhere in our institutions for the feeble-minded, delinquent, criminal and insane; has become the beacon light of the eugenics movement; is appealed to by congressmen in the reshaping of national policy on immigration; is furnishing high-powered explosives for the social reformers of one wing, while serving at the same time as target drawing the hottest fire from the other wing – no psychologist of today can complain that his science is not taken seriously enough. (Quoted by Samelson, 1979, pp. 106f.)

'The psychology of individual differences' and the whole technology of testing provided a *raison d'être* for psychological science but, as Samelson notes, this was 'only a part of the effort to rationalize and bureaucratize the world' (1979, p. 155). Indeed, the whole idea of a psychology of the 'mind in use' was part of this. Thus, while E. L. Thorndike did bring animals 'into the laboratory', his animal psychology was not inspired by a Helmholtzian interest in discovering the mechanisms of 'unconscious inferencing'. Quite the contrary, like his work in educational psychology, it was inspired by an interest in prediction and control. For Thorndike, as Boring put it, 'animals show in their learning no evidence of inferential reasoning or what we should nowadays call "insight", but learn simply by the chance formations or associations in their random experience' (Boring, 1929, p. 555). From the point of view of prediction and control, the 'law of effect' was quite sufficient. With the coming of behaviorism, *The Journal of Animal Behavior* was merged with *Psychobiology* to form, in 1921, *The Journal of Comparative Psychology*. Thenceforth, differences between research on animals and research on people could be effectively ignored. It wasn't, however, just a matter of humans becoming mindless; intelligent animals lost their intelligence as well.

As everyone knows, Watson's 1913 programmatic statement was aimed against 'introspective psychology' and was justified as an effort to advance a truly scientific psychology. Watson was abetted in this by Cattell, Baldwin, and Walter McDougall, who in 1908 had written the first textbook to *define* psychology as 'the science of behavior'. Like all other American psychologists, these men were interested in the 'mind in use', which is to say, in behavior. And Watson was aided by the complete victory on the Continent and in Great Britain of Mach's version of positivist philosophy of science – including, if less obviously so, his version of 'physiological-psychology'. There were, of course, other and perhaps even more direct influences on Watson, but that is hardly the point. Watson had the good fortune of 'touching a match to the mass'. None of what he said was new, including the idea that scientific psychology's 'theoretical goal is the prediction and control of behavior' (Watson, 1963, p. 158).

Watson, like Terman, seems to have understood what was going on around him. In that same programmatic paper, he observed that it gave him 'hope' that his position was 'defensible' since

> Those branches of psychology which have already partially withdrawn from the parent, experimental psychology, and which are consequently less dependent upon introspection are today in the most flourishing condition. Experimental pedagogy, the psychology of drugs, the psychology of advertising, legal psychology, the psychology of tests, and psychopathology are all vigorous growths. (1963, p. 158)

It should be emphasized here that it mattered far less that behaviorism sought to expunge introspection than that it codified the idea that 'experimental psychology' should model itself on 'applied psychology' and that the theoretical [sic] goal of scientific psychology was 'the prediction and control of behavior'. There is in this, a final, wonderful, historical coincidence. The term 'social science' had long carried an unfortunate association with 'socialism', a fact of some significance in the anti-Communist America of the 1950s. Bernard Berelson, Ralph Tyler, and others, urged by the Ford and Russell Sage foundations, saw fit to replace the potentially embarrassing label 'social science' by 'behavioral science', making standard what was already explicit in some quarters and implicit in all others. Without any remorse or conceptual embarrassment then, the human sciences would now unite in seeing themselves as jointly concerned with 'behavior' and with individuals who could be both mindless and asocial, the 'happy robots' of 'The Great American Celebration'.

Part III
Realist Philosophy of Social Science

12

The Critique of Empiricism

In part III we turn specifically to philosophy, and in this chapter to the philosophy of natural science. I will sketch and critique the dominant empiricist conception of science – the 'standard view' – and try to provide a realist alternative. In the two chapters that follow, this will be brought to bear in a sketch of a realist philosophy of social science, including, in chapter 14, a philosophy of psychology.

I argued in part II that the turn of the century saw the institutionalization of the human sciences in their modern form, and that, for all practical purposes, the process was complete by the decade following World War I. The first decades of this century also saw the full realization of the philosophy of science as a fundamental concern of professional philosophers. Bertrand Russell and his Cambridge colleague G. E. Moore, whose initial goal was 'a cleansing of Victorian philosophical stables, to be followed by the reconstruction of philosophy in new and unambiguous terms' (Toulmin, 1969, p. 28), ushered in 'the Age of Analysis'. Russell's insistence that logic was 'the essence of philosophy' was propelled by Wittgenstein, who, after crediting Frege and Russell, announced that, 'on all essential points', he had found the 'final solution' to the problems he had addressed (Wittgenstein, 1921, p. 5). The 'new logic' provided the tools for a systematic re-articulation of the critical work of the philosopher/physicists. A self-conscious 'philosophy of science' was the result. But if this were not enough, the first decades of the century saw, as well, a revolution in physics, with relativity and quantum mechanics.

This revolution and the philosophy of science movement – twentieth-century logical empiricism – were not sufficient causes of the form and materials of twentieth-century mainstream social science. By the first decade of the century, the powerful anti-metaphysical bias of late nineteenth-century empiricist philosophy had already taken hold, along with the idea that scientific laws were 'functional' and preferably quantitative, and that explanation was derivation. The shift to a technocratic conception of the goal of science had already had an impact, so 'prediction and control' were by now primary. Moreover, the redefinition of philosophy as logical analysis was reinforcing the idea of value-neutrality for both science and philosophy. Vienna positivism was not a wholly novel phenomenon; it was, rather, a far more precise program for some older ideas. Because World War I had settled the argument between the 'scientists' and the 'metaphysicians', in favor of the former, Vienna positivism was well received in Europe and was easily transplanted to the fertile soil of American social science. Because it could provide a full-fledged technical apparatus for a rigorous re-articulation of the basic assumptions of the newly emerged disciplines of the empirical social sciences, social scientists were eager to put it to work.

This body of thought, though persistently under attack and revision, has been the conventional wisdom for about 50 years now. Indeed, the root ideas are so taken for granted, so much the basis for education in the social sciences, so much a feature of the conventional discourse of the social sciences, including that of its critics, that it is well-nigh impossible to grasp the full implications of these beliefs.

Moreover, it is next to impossible to accept the idea that there may be a large gap between the practices of the natural theoretical sciences and the philosophy of science which is offered as a 'rational reconstruction' of these, that there may be very little resemblance between the work-site practices of these sciences and our widely shared understanding of 'science'.[1] Einstein, often ahead of most people, began his 1933 Herbert Spencer Lecture at Oxford with a significant prescription: 'If you want to find out anything from the theoretical physicists about the methods they use, I advise you to stick closely to one principle: Don't listen to their words, fix your attention on their deeds' (quoted by Holton, 1968, p. 178). But if the practices of physical scientists bear little resemblance to the dominant philosophy of science, it is no exaggeration to say that,

[1] The label 'theoretical physical science' is critical and I have in mind here work-sites such as the Cold Spring Harbor Laboratory and Princeton's Institute for Advanced Studies. The problem is that 'science' is not one thing, not even at a sufficient level of abstraction. Think only of the differences between the goals and work-site practices of 'computer scientists'; population geneticists at Cambridge University; biologists in comparative taxonomy at Queens College; a hemotologist working on folic acid deficiency; chemists at Stanford working on neuroleptics and chemists at Max Factor; the educational psychology of a Skinnerian attached to San Quentin prison and at the New School for Social Research; inquiry into the economy in progress at Rand Corporation, the Bureau of Labor, the London School of Economics; cancer research at Cold Spring Harbor and at the Texas Medical Center; astrophysics at Rome Air Development and at Princeton.

in consequence of their relatively late beginnings as 'sciences', *the practices of mainstream social science have long since been constituted by it.*

Yet, in the last several decades, every key tenet in this 'standard view' has been either abandoned, liberalized to the point of triviality, or thoroughly undermined. It may be well to list these events here:

1 The abandonment of the phenomenalist program as regards macro-objects and the theoretical entities of physical science (Carnap, 1928, 1936–7; Quine, 1951; Carnap, 1956; Hempel, 1958).

2 The abandonment of the verifiability theory of meaning (Ayer, 1936; 2nd edn, 1946; Hempel, 1950; Quine, 1951).

3 The dissolution of the idea that scientific theories are axiomatic systems formulable in the extensional logic of *Principia Mathematica,* including the idea that the non-logical terms divide into two disjoint 'vocabularies', 'observational' and 'theoretical' (Rudner, 1966; Suppe, 1974).

4 The acknowledgment of the pertinence of a realist interpretation of theory (Hempel, 1958; Nagel, 1961), under criticism from Sellars (1949; 1956, 1958, 1961), Smart (1956), Feyerabend (1958), and Shapere (1960, 1966).

5 The dissolution of the analytic/synthetic distinction (Quine, 1951; Putnam, 1962).

6 The abandonment of the program to generate an inductive logic suitable for science (Hempel, 1943, 1945; Carnap, 1945; Popper, 1935; Goodman, 1946, 1954).

7 The dissolution of the idea that verification/confirmation/falsification is rule-determined and grounded in theory-neutral 'basic sentences' (Carnap, 1936–7; Popper, 1935, 1963; Kuhn, 1962; Toulmin, 1972; Feyerabend, 1962; Lakatos and Musgrave, 1970).

8 The liberalization of the 'covering law', 'deductive-nomological' conception of explanation (Hempel and Oppenheim, 1948; Hempel, 1965) and the articulation of alternatives by Scriven (1962), Harré (1970), Bhaskar (1975), and Aronson (1984).

9 The bankruptcy of 'reductionism', and the liberalization of the unity of science program (Carnap, 1938; Nagel, 1961; Feyerabend, 1962; Schaffner, 1967), with an alternative conception of 'stratification' by Polanyi (1968), Weiss (1971, Bhaskar (1975), and Wimsatt (1976).

10 The incapacity to provide an adequate analysis of 'laws of nature' (Chisholm, 1946; Goodman, 1954; with alternatives by Bohm, 1957; Bunge, 1959; Harré, 1970; Dretske, 1977).

11 The critique of Humean causality (Bunge, 1959; Harré and Madden, 1975; Bhaskar, 1975).

It seems that no one believes any longer in the standard view in its entirety; yet, because it is easy to pick and choose among its elements, it continues to be taken for granted as the basis of all popular and mainstream social scientific discourse. Although a number of recent writers – Harré (1970) and Bhaskar (1975) – have pointed out that its various elements stand much like a house of cards, this has barely seeped into the literature. In what follows, I will pursue this idea, to show that there is a pair of cards in the house which supports the whole edifice and that, if the pair if withdrawn, it is easy to see both why the remaining elements are as they are and why they could not be sustained.

The key cards are the 'metaphysical' problem of the 'external world' and the problem of causality. The key theme is the empiricist idea that a scientific explanation must eschew appeal to what is in principle beyond experience. To anticipate, then, once causality is rendered as per Hume *or* per Kant, 'transdiction' (chapter 1) is no longer allowed; this requires restriction of science to 'the empirical world' (empirical realism or phenomenalism), a phenomenalist or instrumentalist treatment of theory and a logicist explanation of theory acceptability; it demands that 'laws of nature' be universals of the form (x) $(Fx \supset Gx)$ (creating the problem of contrafactuals, the paradoxes of confirmation, and leaving the problem of induction unsolved), and that explanation be derivation, which in turn entails the symmetry of explanation and prediction and permits an extensionalist account of the unity of science. The motivation for this is the demarcation of science from metaphysics; the tool is extensionalist logic (Brown, 1977).

THE REJECTION OF REALISM

In the 1893 edition of his *Allgemeine Chemie,* Ostwald dropped hypothetical entities altogether. Mach demonstrated that Newton's definition of mass co-ordinated with no observables whatever, that absolute space was 'a conceptual monstrosity', and that there was little hope of reconciling the ideas of the ether, matter, and electricity in terms of the mechanical properties of atoms. Maxwell's equations could be interpreted, as by Hertz, as 'representations' which say nothing at all about the physical nature of the phenomena 'represented'. The whole drift of physics was in the direction of a phenomenologically based science of correlated observables.

As Holton has shown, all this was liberating to the young Einstein. His first paper on relativity in 1905 shows the influence of Mach on two counts: first, in its recognition of the need to carry out an epistemological analysis on the meaning of space and time, and second in its supposition that reality is 'what is given by sensations, the "events", rather than putting reality on a plane beyond or behind sense experience' (Holton, 1970, p. 170). But, as Holton notes, the paper manifests an opposing belief, 'that "reality" in the end is not going to be left identical with "events"' (p. 171).[2] At about the same time, Max Planck, a key innovator in what later became quantum mechanics, was railing against Mach's positivism. His 1896 paper 'Against the New Energetics' was a first blow. This was followed by the now famous attack in 1909, in which he insisted that a basic aim of science is 'the finding of a fixed world picture independent of the variation of time and people', or in other words, 'the complete liberation of the physical picture from the individuality of the separate intellects' (quoted by Holton, 1970, pp. 172f.). And by 1918, Einstein had diverged decisively from his earlier Machism and was very close to Planck's stubborn realism.

Schlick had taken Mach's chair at Vienna, but from 1910 to 1925, he held to a critical realism (Feigl, 1969). By 1930, however, he had withdrawn to what he took to be a metaphysically neutral position. By then the Vienna Circle had become a powerful intellectual force. Einstein, now in full agreement with Planck, whose realism was uncompromising even in the face of the difficulties of the quantum theory,[3] wrote a letter to Schlick in which he said:

> In general your presentation fails to correspond to my conceptual style insofar as I find your whole orientation so to speak too positivistic. . . . I tell you straight out: Physics is the attempt at the conceptual construction of a model of the *real world* and its lawful structure. . . . In short, I suffer under the unsharp separation of Reality of Experience and Reality of Being. . . .
>
> You will be astonished about the 'metaphysicist' Einstein. But every four- and two-legged animal is de facto in this sense a metaphysicist. (Quoted by Holton, 1970, p. 188)

Einstein is here rejecting the 'epistemological turn' which makes the realms of being and 'experience' coterminous. We cannot get 'out of' or 'behind' experience, so, if science is the effort to *know* what is beyond or behind experience, it must be, in Kant's sense, 'metaphysical'. The

[2] In an excellent book, Michael Friedman (1983) has shown both how positivism was involved in Einstein's work on relativity and that relativity requires a realism. See also Arthur Fine, 1984.

[3] Quantum mechanics continues to raise some profoundly complicated problems, of course. J. C. Polkinghorne (1984) has given what seems to me to be the most recent and useful account. He remarks, 'I have never known anyone working in fundamental science whose work was not motivated by desire to understand the way the world is' (p. 79), and he concludes that whatever else may be said about the problems raised by quantum mechanics, the solution is not to be found in abandoning realism. I am indebted to Robert Weingard for the foregoing reference and for his help on the pertinent issues, which will not be pursued here.

last sentence of the quotation above could have been written by Helmholtz. Even if a sentient being cannot get beyond *its* experience, it is not a solipsist![4]

Writing the next year (1931), Planck was even clearer:

> The essential point of the positivist theory is that there is no other source of knowledge except the straight and short way of perception through the senses. . . . Now the two sentences: (1) *there is a real outer world which exists independently of our act of knowing* and (2) *the real outer world is not directly knowable* form together the cardinal hinge on which the whole structure of physical science turns. And yet there is a certain degree of contradiction between these two sentences. . . . Therefore, we see the task of science arising before us, an incessant struggle toward a goal which will never be reached, because by its very nature it is unreachable. It is of a metaphysical character, and, as such, is always and again beyond our achievement. (Quoted by Holton, 1970, p. 189)

In his 1932 rejoinder to Planck's essay, Schlick jumped on the allusion to Kant and metaphysics: 'Nature, and everything of which the physicist can and must speak belongs, according to Kant, to empirical reality, and what that means is . . . explained by him in just the way it must be by us. . . . Hence the physicist cannot appeal to Kantian philosophy; its arguments lead only to the empirical world which we all acknowledge, not to a transcendent world' (Schlick, 1959, p. 101).

Schlick is clear about the meaning of the term 'transcendent world'. It 'stands behind' the empirical world, where 'behind' means that 'it cannot be known in the same sense as can the empirical world, that it lies beyond a boundary which separates the accessible from the inaccessible'. 'Cannot be known in the same sense', of course, means ultimately that it can not be known at all, since propositions about it either meet the test of verifiability or they do not. If they do not, they cannot be (scientifically) known; if they do, then positivism and realism 'are not in opposition', since 'propositions concerning bodies [material bodies or the hypothetical entities of physics] are transformable into equivalent propositions concerning the occurrence of sensations in accordance with laws' (1959, p. 107). 'The empiricist does not say to the metaphysician "what you say is false", but, "what you say asserts nothing at all!"'

Neither Einstein nor Planck were satisfied with this response, but it

---

[4] In a brilliant, brief piece written for the Schilpp volume on Russell (1951), Einstein repeated these themes and noted that from Hume's critique, 'one is easily led to believe that all those concepts and propositions which cannot be deduced from the sensory raw-material, on account of their "metaphysical" character, are to be removed from thinking.' But 'this claim – if only carried through consistently – excludes thinking of any kind as "metaphysical"' (pp. 288f.).

must be admitted that neither of them seemed able then to do more than insist that there was a huge difference between their realism and Schlick's 'empirical realism'. However, they had accepted the *terms* of the empiricists (including Kant). They knew that to do science, they had to go beyond experience. They thus admitted to being metaphysical – unavoidably so. But they were told that if they were doing science, they couldn't be metaphysical; so, when they *thought* they were going beyond experience, they really were not. Einstein and Planck did reject *bad* metaphysics, 'empty talk', but how could they respond to the positivist for whom *all* metaphysics was nonsense?

'THE EXISTENCE OF THE EXTERNAL WORLD'

Common sense surely presupposes the existence of objects which exist independent of experience, and it is realist in believing that the nature of such objects can be known. But 'naive', or 'direct', realism is almost certainly false. Naive realism holds that the actual properties of physical objects are those which we ascribe to them on the basis of sense perception, that, for example, lemons are yellow and sour. It is easy enough to provide convincing arguments for the falsity of direct realism (arguments as old as Protagoras), and I shall not labor the point here. But the odd thing is that, with very few exceptions – for example, Spencer and Helmholtz – these arguments have led to various forms of positivism. That is, instead of moving in what would seem to be the natural direction, toward a view in which independent objects stand in a causal relation to perceivers, almost the whole of the scientific and philosophical tradition since Hume has taken the tack that what lies beyond possible experience is a matter for metaphysics, not science. The reason for this, almost always missed, turns on the question of *causality*. The most expeditious way of demonstrating this is by reference to a rather long quotation from Bertrand Russell's very influential 1914 essay 'The relation of sense-data to physics'.

> Physics is said to be an experimental science, based on observation and experiment. . . .
> What can be learned by observation and experiment? Nothing, as far as physics is concerned, except immediate data of sense; certain patches of colour, sounds, tastes, etc. . . .
> The supposed contents of the physical world are prima facie very different than these; molecules have no colour, atoms make no noise, electrons have no taste, and corpuscles do not even smell.
> If such objects can be verified, it must be solely through their

relation to sense-data; they must have some kind of correlation with sense-data, and must be verifiable through their correlation *alone*.

But how is the correlation itself ascertained? A correlation can only be ascertained empirically by the correlated objects being constantly found together. But in our case, only one term of the correlation, namely the sensible term is ever found; the other term seems essentially incapable of being found. Therefore, it would seem, the correlation with objects by sense, by which physics was to be verified, is itself utterly and forever unverifiable. (Russell, 1957, p. 140)

There are now four ways to go: critical realism, a 'metaphysically neutral' phenomenalism[5] (or empirical realism), skepticism, or some version of Kantianism. In the essay quoted above, Russell has opted for the metaphysically neutral route, the way of Mach, of Carnap and Schlick (after 1925), and indeed, following their abandonment of phenomenalism, of Popper, Hempel, and Nagel as well.

Following on his rule that, 'whenever possible, logical constructions are to be substituted for inferred entities', Russell argued that 'we may succeed in actually defining the objects of physics as a function of sense-data'. With the new techniques of modern logic available, this phenomenalist research program must have seemed quite possible. Indeed, there was no doubt in Russell's mind that it was: 'Just insofar as physics leads to expectations this *must* be possible, since we can *expect* what can be experienced.' In effect, skepticism was just too intolerable. The phenomenalist program, of course, was most meticulously attempted by Carnap (1928) and popularized by Ayer (1936), even though by that time Carnap had already abandoned explicit definition for 'reduction sentences' (Carnap, 1936–7). He was now content to accept that science could be safely grounded in the *empirical realist* – naive realist – terms of ordinary experience. Indeed, by 1950, the 'myth of the given' was shattered; the principle of verifiability had been compromised to triviality; 'correspondence' rules had replaced 'reduction sentences'; and the

---

[5] The formulation of the phenomenalist position is critical. At a minimum, it involves two theses, that there are 'sense data' and that we never perceive material objects. Moore and some American realists held to both, but defended realism understood simply as the idea that material objects exist even when they are not perceived. They never determined satisfactorily to themselves or to their (objective) idealist critics the *relation* between sense data and material objects. Madden and Hare (1976) make a convincing case that William James tried a third route, by attempting 'to introduce objective reference into a private data scheme' (p. 114). Phenomenalists also tended to hold that the distinction between the mental and the physical was to be drawn within the range of sense experience. Mach is the paradigm, but James seems also to have made this move. A fourth thesis, true of Mill, Russell, Carnap, and Ayer held that material objects are, as in Mill, 'permanent possibilities of sensation', or in twentieth-century formulations, constructions out of sense data: phenomenalist 'reduction'.

whole program had become so thoroughly liberalized that the original goal, the grounding of science in the security of 'the empirical', had effectively been forgotten. Naive realism was not only the starting-point for science, which it always is; it was also the starting-point for a scientific epistemology. 'Theoretical terms' were not like the 'meta-physical' utterances of Heidegger, since theories, taken as wholes, were 'interpreted' formal systems, 'anchored' in the 'soil of experience' (see Suppe, 1977, pp. 50ff.).

What were Russell's reasons for rejecting critical realism? If the 'empiricist' route failed, we could avoid skepticism only if we knew 'some principle *a priori,* without the need of empirical verification, e.g., [that] our sense-data have causes other than themselves, and that something can be known about these causes from their effects'. Russell, never a dogmatist, was willing to countenance this move – if necessary – but he made it plain that if this step is taken 'physics ceases to be empirical'.

Why is this? It is clearly impossible that we could have *empirical* knowledge of the *causes* of our 'sense-data' (experience) since, on Russell's Humean reading of causality, to ascertain a causal relation, one must ascertain *empirically* a constant conjunction between the 'cause' and its 'effect'. Of course, it was precisely because Kant saw that such limits made science *impossible* that he took the transcendental route and was led to argue that causality was a category of mind – one not found in experience at all. But in *either* case, what we have called 'transdiction' (see chapter 1) is illicit. The possibility of transdiction is the critical difference between empiricists, here including Kant, and a critical realist. The issue is not whether theories are 'free inventions of the mind', for the critical realist can agree that, as social products, theories are 'inventions'. Rather, it is whether we can say that we have knowledge of causes in nature which are in principle not to be experienced nor to be defined in terms of experience.

We can see how this relates to the positivist treatment of the hypothetical entities of the sciences. Assuming that they are somehow given 'empirical meaning', is there a further claim that they exist? If so, it could then be said that they could have causal properties which would go toward explaining what happens in the world – including, then, *our* empirical world. If the answer is 'yes', then, both Hume and Kant are wrong about causality. In other words, critical realism presupposes scientific realism in the sense that theoretical terms may have a non-observable reference. By virtue, then, of the causal properties of the theoretical 'thing', the theory is capable of explaining. We need to spend a moment on the empiricist treatment of theory so as to see how theoretical terms became a source of empiricist bafflement.

PHENOMENALISM, INSTRUMENTALISM, AND SCIENTIFIC REALISM

The replacement of 'inferred entities' by 'logical constructions', of course, was the program of the phenomenalist reduction, but it haunted empiricists even after that program had been abandoned (Smart, 1956). The abandonment of phenomenalism as regards macro-objects and the acceptance of what Carnap called the 'thing-language' (Carnap, 1936–7) resulted, as noted, in 'empirical realism'. In effect, naive realism was the epistemological point of departure for science. The only problem, then, was to anchor, *logically,* theoretical terms to the empirical world, to provide some *rule of inference* which would allow us to apply terms meaningfully.

By the time of his 1958 'Theoretician's Dilemma', Hempel was experiencing considerable discomfort with these ideas. In a revealing sentence, he asked: 'Why should science resort to the assumption of hypothetical entities when it is interested in establishing predictive and explanatory connections among observables' (Hempel, 1965, p. 179). It is very easy to accept uncritically Hempel's formulation of the goal of science, to accept that explanation is derivation, and hence that it is symmetrical to prediction. And if so, it is easy to see why the 'perplexing problem' arises, for, as the psychologists Hull and Skinner[6] had argued,

> Unless there is a weak spot in our causal chain so that the second link is not lawfully determined by the first, or the third by the second, then the first and third links must be lawfully related. If we must always go back beyond the second link ['the intervening variable'] for prediction and control, we may avoid many tiresome and exhausting digressions by examining the third link as a function of the first. (Quoted by Hempel, p. 186, from Skinner, 1953)

'Lawfully determined' here means 'uniformly associated' or 'invariant', and Skinner's paradigm is a version of Carnap's 'reduction sentence'. If so, the 'second link' does not function in 'prediction and control' – explanation! – so it is unnecessary. This gives rise to the 'theoretician's dilemma'. If the theoretical terms 'serve their purpose' and 'establish definite connections among observable phenomena', they can be dispensed with (as per above). But if they do not 'serve their purpose', they

---

[6] It is fascinating to note that after the positivists had convinced the psychologists that science was what the positivists said it was, positivists tended to use examples and arguments from psychologists to make their points. This was not merely easier and safer: if the arguments of chapters 1, 9 and 14 are sound, it was inevitable, precisely because empiricist epistemology depended upon a psychology constrained by its presuppositions. For a suggestive early treatment, see Koch, 1964.

are surely unnecessary, since lacking 'definite connections' to 'observable phenomena', they are meaningless.

Hempel saw that the 'dilemma' does not go away with the weakened notion of theory as an 'interpretative system', or with a consistent instrumentalist conception of theory according to which the sentences are not 'significant statements', either true or false, but are 'convenient symbolic devices in the transition from one set of experiential statements to another'.[7] Indeed, Hempel rightly concludes that the dilemma rests on a false premise, in that theoretical terms play a different role than that assumed by the 'dilemma'.

At this point, Hempel is only inches away from abandoning the empiricist understanding of theory. But he is still not there. He admits that 'to assert that the terms of a given theory have a factual reference, that the entities they purport to refer to actually exist, is tantamount to asserting that what the theory says is true' (Hempel, 1965, p. 219); moreover, it is the case that 'in publications dealing with problems of theoretical physics, or biology or psychology . . . sentences containing theoretical terms are normally treated on a par with those which serve to describe empirical data' (p. 221). That is, scientists are realists, not instrumentalists. To think of theory in other than realist terms 'would be a hindrance rather than a help'.

But, not noticed by Hempel, is the fact that if the theory is true, then because these entities exist, they can have causal properties. But in that case, since they could *in principle* be non-observables – for example photons – the empiricist (Humean) notion of causality would have to be abandoned; moreover, the whole covering law model of explanation would be thrown in doubt. Indeed, while Hempel now sees that 'the theoretician's dilemma . . . took it to be the sole purpose of a theory to establish deductive connections among observable sentences' (p. 222) and that *this is a mistake,* he does not see that, unless one drops Humean causality and the covering law model of explanation there is no way for a theory to achieve 'systematic economy and heuristic fertility' or to provide for the possibility of 'inductive explanatory and predictive use' (p. 222).

[7] In the locus classicus of 'the standard view', Ernest Nagel sought to dissolve the realism/instrumentalism debate. He concluded that 'the opposition between these two views is a conflict over preferred modes of speech' (Nagel, 1961, p. 152). The difference between the two is clear enough: for example, either the theory that a gas is a system of rapidly moving molecules is a *description of reality,* or it is not. If *not,* then the theory might be 'a rule which prescribes a way of symbolically representing for certain purposes, such matters as the *observable* pressure and temperature of a gas' (p. 129, my emphasis). But, of course, to say that a gas is a description of reality is *not* to say, as Nagel seems oddly to assume, that it is a description of something that can be observed. The idea that a theory was an interpreted axiom system along with the deductive-nomological notion of explanation went a very long way, of course, to obscure this difference.

That an iconic model was essential to theory-construction (even with quantum theory), was urged by Campbell (1920/1957), Hanson (1958), Nagel (1961), and Hesse (1962, 1966), but it was not perhaps until Harré's 'Copernican revolution' in the philosophy of science (1970) that the incompatibility of this idea with 'deductivism' was demonstrated. What results is an inversion of the deductivist notion of theory: the core of a theory is not the never fully formalizable aspects of it, aspects which can conveniently be constrained for experimental and practical purposes,[8] but the iconic model which is offered as representing a real causal mechanism. On this view, theory depends on non-propositional ideas, on non-deductive relationships and intentional meaning relations, and on metaphor and analogy which only socialization into a science can provide.

CAUSALITY AND EXPLANATION

It may be that the most direct way to see how these ideas come together is to take a rather simple illustration and pursue it. The example given below aims to show how theory, causation, and explanation are systematically misconstrued by the standard view, and what a viable realist alternative looks like.

Assume a broken water pipe at Cove Road, Oyster Bay, in the early morning of 17 January 1986, when the temperature fell to −4°C. This situation seems just right for the familiar deductive-nomological account of scientific explanation (Hempel, 1965). We have candidates for law-like statements and satisfaction of the instantial conditions; hence we deduce the event to be explained.

But problems arise over what in the 'sketch' is left out – left out are the *et ceteras* and *ceteris paribus* clauses. Both need to be filled in if the law-like statements are to be true and non-trivial and if the deduction is to succeed. So we must ask, what else has to happen when air temperatures fall if water is to freeze? What conditions can't be present?

---

[8] An excellent example is provided by Weininger (1984) in discussing the relation between quantum mechanics, which lacks an adequate iconic model, and molecular chemistry, which has one. Quantum-mechanical calculations yield results which fully conform with experimental findings, but usually unnoticed is the fact that 'most calculations employ the fixed, or "clamped", nucleus approximation, which considerably simplifies the task of doing the calculation. In the fixed nucleus approximation the nuclei are treated as classical particles and confined in their "equilibrium" positions' (p. 939). Indeed, Woolley has contended that this is more than a matter of convenience, but is motivated at least in part by the 'felt need' to make contact with the classical idea of molecular structure. That is, 'by adopting the fixed nucleus approximation quantum chemists guarantee that they will achieve results that are interpretable in term of one or more molecular structures' (quoted by Weininger, p. 940). I use this example below in discussing the unity of science program.

Suppose, for example, that the pipes in question are in a crawlspace which is not heated but are adjacent to a heated room and that the door between is open. Is sufficient heat available to prevent freezing? Suppose that on the previous three days the temperature was below 0°C and the same door was closed, but the pipes did not break. Perhaps this was because although the water froze, the pipes, being made of copper, expanded sufficiently. But perhaps they were at their limit on the night of the 17th. But how do we build 'sufficiently' into our laws? Indeed, there is a suspicion that triviality is the price of deducibility.

But the idea of deducibility itself raises some questions. We might go the way of Dretske (1977) and argue that if the laws in question are of the form $(x)(Fx \supset Gx)$, then the inference, 'this is an F' (this Fs), hence, 'this must be a G' (This Gs), is formally valid, but irrelevant. 'The fact that *every* F is G fails to explain why *any* F is G.' 'Entails' is exactly the wrong relation for explanation. F-ness is *nomically* linked to G-ness.[9] The 'must' is in the wrong place, since it is between premise and conclusion and not between the properties or between the event and the conjunction of causes which produced it. Or we might say (following Scriven, 1962) that, while the deductive pattern at least maintains the hold on the individual case, anything less than that – the so-called 'inductive-statistical' pattern – sharply reveals the non-explanatory character of the covering law model. Knowing that 67 per cent of Fs are Gs fails to explain why some particular F is G; perhaps 67 per cent of people exposed to Herpes I contract it, but that hardly explains why Sam contracts it, however much contact with the virus is necessary for contracting it. The 'must' of explanation needs to be maintained, but it is not a logical 'must' at all.

As Dretske writes, the standard construal that a law of nature is a universal truth plus X, where X discriminates between any true statement of the form $(x)(Fx \supset Gx)$ and a law, depends on some deeply held empiricist prejudices, but in particular on the atomist idea that everything in the universe is but contingently related (Chisholm, 1946). A nomic connection must be 'matter of fact', but for the empiricist it cannot, therefore, be necessary. But if so, X cannot be filled in. Accordingly, 'to say that a law is a universal truth having explanatory power is like saying that a chair is breadth of air used to seat people. You cannot make a silk purse out of a sow's ear, not even a very good sow's ear; and you cannot *make* a generalization, not even a purely universal generalization explain its instances' (Dretske, 1977, p. 262).

How does this work in the example? Evidently, to explain the broken

---

[9] Compare here the Goodman paradox: 'All emeralds are green' and 'all emeralds are grue' differ because the former expresses a generalization rooted in complicated nomic connections.

pipes, we need to know something about the ordinary things involved, about water, copper piping, the movement of air, and about what tends to happen when other things happen. We have to know what things can and cannot do. Water tends to freeze when its temperature is reduced to freezing-point; it doesn't turn purple or explode. This is sufficiently law-like, of course, but its analysis is not of the form $(x)Fx \supset Gx$. Rather, we need something more like: 'When C, A tends to Phi in virtue of its structure S.' This is *not* a more complete version of the $(x)(Fx \supset Gx)$ formulation. Phi-ing is a causal power, a dispositional property of A which need not be *witnessable*. We do not need to observe phi-ing to be able to say that As do tend to Phi – *if* we can say (even with Hempel) that our theory about A is true.

Moreover, that A has the power of phi-ing means that it has that power even when it is not 'triggered' by C (the realist interpretation of dispositions) and, even more than that, that when it is triggered by C, it may phi but have *various effects, some of which may be manifest, others not. That is, that phi is a tendency means not* that when C, A *usually* does such and such (though that may also be true). It means that unless something prevents it, under conditions C, A *does* Phi. Because A will not generally be in a condition of closure – that is, it will be part of a nexus of other causes, in conjunction (or mediation) with these – it can be a party to all sorts of 'effects' or outcomes.[10]

On the Humean account, all we can look for are relations between manifest events or occurrent properties. Of course, there can be no *nomic* relation between these. On the one hand, since events (and empirical properties) are best construed as complex causal outcomes, laws will not be about classes of events (or properties) but about the 'structures' and the dispositional properties to which they give rise. In the formula above, S is the structure which constitutes (or is partly constitutive of) A. S is a theorized molecule, a magnetic field, a space–time cone. It is a contingent fact that water is H_2O and that it freezes, but if our theory is true, it *must*. Dispositional properties, phi-ing, and so on, are necessary because A is S and Ss phi.

There is no Platonism. First, knowledge of such properties is *a posteriori*. Second, there is no requirement that these properties or the 'things' which incarnate them are either universal or eternal. Versus a Platonism, the properties do not exist independently, nor are they 'essences' in the sense that the property 'determines' the 'nature' of the 'thing'. Quite the opposite, it is the theorized mechanism which gives rise to the property and explains it. Nor is this an 'essentialism' in the sense that it is possible to give an 'ultimate' explanation. Finally, all that

---

[10] See the account of tendency in chapter 3, of Engels in chapter 6, of Weber in chapter 7, and of 'the plurality of causes' in chapter 8.

is required metaphysically is the assumption that there are 'things' which exist independently of us and that these can be theorized. As Barnes has argued, an 'essentialist strategy' is characteristic of scientific work. 'Given the range of possibilities both for imposing pattern and adapting pattern, simultaneously if need be, which the form of the language of essences makes available, this is not to be wondered at' (1982, p. 82).[11]

Experience gives us the pre-theoretical 'things' and events of sedimented experience. In everyday life, we experience patterns – not invariances. Water freezes and pipes break at low temperatures. What we call 'water', of course, is not just H_2O – the purest of it contains other things. So it is a compound in this obvious sense. But at another level, a molecule of H_2O is itself a complex of hydrogen and oxygen atoms, which at still another level, are each complexes of protons, electrons, neutrons, and so on. These novel things – molecules, fields, space–time cones – are the product of theoretical work, but although, if our theories are true, they are real, they exist in the world in complex relations. Ordinary water almost always freezes when its temperature is lowered to 0°C, because ordinary water is mostly H_2O, H_2O – theoretical water – has the causal property of freezing at 0°C, and in the environment in which the temperature of (ordinary) water is usually lowered to 0°C, there are generally few factors present that would interfere with the exercise of this causal property.

The discovery of these things involves what has been called 'transdiction' (and 'retrodiction'). To put it crudely, we believe that these things exist and have the powers we say they have because, if they do, we can make sense of the world we experience. We arrive at critical realism when the idea is turned on experience itself. Consider the statement 'Sulphur is yellow.' This is often supposed, in naively realist terms, to be an inductive generalization about sulphur or, worse, a law of nature. But it is a poor candidate for either. It presupposes, of course, a transaction with a percipient, and thus it is as much a generalization about human percipients with a particular (and psychologically theorizable) perceptual system as it is a generalization about sulphur. Whether yellow is manifest – whether we *see* yellow, in other words – depends at the very least on the surface structure of sulphur which, science tells us, reflects light of wavelength 5745 Angstrom units, on the causal properties of light, and on the little understood perceptual mechanisms of human perception. That is, there are nomic relations here, but they are not as the empiricist has them. And of course, we

[11] Barnes suggests that an essentialist mode of cognition (as opposed to some particular theory of essences, for example, a current science) may be the 'general mode of cognition of any human community, deriving from innate structures involved in the epigenesis of linguistic and inferential skills' (1982, p. 82). The idea is found in James's *Principles of Psychology*, chs 21 and 28.

might be presented with sulphur and *not* see yellow for a host of reasons – all of which might be explicable in terms of the nomic relations existing between percipient beings and the 'external world'.[12]

More generally, the apparent invariants of everyday experience are poor candidates for the 'laws' of the Deductive–Nomological model of explanation, even with a host of *ceteris paribus* clauses thrown in. Of course there are patterns: water freezes, sugar dissolves, sulphur is yellow; but we must not be tempted into the subsumption model by these. As these examples suggest, our everyday causal knowledge, unaffected by empiricist mythology, is less a knowledge based on past regularities between 'events' and more a primitive knowledge of causes understood as the particular tendencies of the particular things of everyday experience.

We need knowledge of these causes if we are to succeed in explaining events, but we need, as well, *historical* knowledge. We need to know that a sequence of events and changes occurred such that, in regard to the structured properties of the relevant 'things', there was a conjunction or configuration causing the pipes to burst when they did. We have to know the temperatures of the previous nights, the position of the door in the crawlspace, the fact that the copper had expanded to its limits, and so on. That is, there is an enormous difference between explanation in the concrete world (see Engels and Weber, above) and explanation under conditions of experimental closure, when complicating causal factors are either controlled or constant.[13]

Recognition of the indispensability of history in explanation shows why there is a radical asymmetry between explanation and prediction. To predict on the 16th that the pipes *would* break on the 17th, we need the appropriate causal knowledge, but we also need grounded knowledge that the temperature will fall again, that the pipes are at their limits, that the door will again be open, and so on. But obviously, no matter how well grounded this knowledge, an indefinite and infinite

---

[12] As Turvey, Shaw, Reed and Mace (1981) have shown, misperception is regularly misconstrued in establishment thinking about perception. A straight stick immersed in water appears bent. 'The situation of straight-stick-immersed-in-water must structure the light in a way that is physically sincere. The differential in refractive indices between the media of air and water cannot be compromised [as laws of nature]. Therefore, there is no intelligible sense in which it can be claimed that the stick ought to appear straight if perception were free of error and if perception were direct' (p. 274), a point advanced, as the authors note, by the realist philosopher F. J. E. Woodbridge in 1913.

[13] Bhaskar (1975) has provided the rationale for experiment in science. To say that a theory gives good predictions means that one can devise an experiment or find a real-world situation in which phenomena which are both theoretically necessary consequences of the structure and are not manifest (because of causal complexity, the system being open) are demonstrated. Not having available a way of distinguishing between the empirical, the actual, and the real, empiricists must collapse prediction in the real world into prediction under closure.

number of things could happen, any one of which would falsify the prediction. Moreover, at least some of these things are in principle unpredictable. This is because, *necessarily,* the future is never exactly like the past. Thus, everything that happens alters the configuration of relevant structures, and thus, while not everything is connected to everything else, if you hang a light bulb in *your* basement, it has no causal effect on *my* pipes, but if *I* hang a light bulb in my basement, it surely does. The point deserves emphasis. Even if the world were 'Aristotelian' and all 'structures' were eternal and unchanging in themselves (which is not the case), their relations would always be different. This is precisely the insight of 'process' philosophies and of Peircean 'tychism'.

On the empiricist view, the world is a determined concatenation of contingent events; on the present view, it is a contingent concatenation of ensembles of complexly related stratified structures. On the empiricist view, science requires system closure – ultimately (as in Pascal and Pareto) closure of the world system. On the present view, it requires only that there is a causally efficacious real world in which 'structures' have sufficient endurance in time for us to be able to theorize about them.

THE PROGRAM OF THE UNITY OF SCIENCE VERSUS STRATIFICATION

The abstractive interrogation of nature which has produced scientific theory has proceeded unevenly, and this has important implications. One consequence is that, while the scienc*es* tell us what the world contains – atoms and molecules, cells and mammals, fields and forces – their theories do not tell us how these various 'things' relate in what is presumably a single reality (Hull, 1974). Indeed, in marked contrast to the program of the unity of science, it is by no means clear *how,* or even *that,* these can be conjoined to reflect the various 'unities' of either naive experience or the theoretical sciences. As Hull has noted, 'considerable contingency exists between the phenomena at various levels as they are now analysed – and in some cases the analyses are even incompatible' (1974, p. 134). Three implications follow. First, although theoretical manageability requires that we think in terms of isolability and system closure as regards the domain under study, it is almost certain that an enormous number of extra-systemic causal transactions are continually taking place, transactions which are frighteningly complex (Weiss, 1971; Grobstein, 1976). Second, whereas each of the theories may give an account of processes essential to its level of concern – the subatomic, molecular, cellular, and so on – each individual theory has an impoverished view of more inclusive levels (Wimsatt, 1976). This is true, we should hasten to add, not merely of complex unities such as organisms, but of the molecule itself. For example as R. G. Woolley (1978) has argued, features that are assumed to be intrinsic to the molecule simply disappear when the usual simplifying approximations in quantum calculations are dropped. Thus, 'among the properties "created" by the many-body system, are the *size* and *shape* of an individual atom or molecule' (quoted from Weininger, 1984). Indeed, it seems that 'molecular structure results from an *interaction* between a molecule and its environment in a way for which *ab initio* theory cannot yet account' (p. 939).

The upshot of this example (and others from biology could be produced) is that the whole Chinese box picture of the program of the unity of science is optimistic to the point of being ludicrous. We must here be brief.

The sense of 'reduction' which has the greatest plausibility is that of reduction of theory. In order to carry this out, one must achieve at least a partial translation between the key terms in two theories – for example, the identification of 'temperature' with 'mean kinetic energy of molecules', or in the very problematic case of the reduction of Mendelian genetics from molecular genetics, the identification of 'gene' with some specifiable segment of DNA and RNA, and of predicate terms like 'dominance' with molecular mechanisms (structures) of such and such a sort. Translatability between theories is, of course, an essential formal condition of reduction, but there are other conditions, formal and substantive, which must be met but which need not be mentioned here. What does need to be noticed is the following.

First, reduction of theory requires two well-established theories which could stand in the requisite relationship. There are few such candidates in the physical sciences and none in the social sciences. Second, this sort of reduction, if successful, is not committed to the idea that *events* identified in the language of the reduced theory can be explained solely in terms of the reducing theory. It holds only that the principles of the reduced theory are themselves to be 'explained' in the sense of being derivable from the reducing theory – that is, that there is a systematic (logical) relation between these. For example, from molecular genetics one can deduce the principles (laws) of Mendelian genetics. But if nature is stratified, then events described in the language of the reduced theory (for example, the birth of an albino mouse) will need for their explanation principles (laws) from a variety of levels. Third, and related to the foregoing, a successful reduction does not make the properties denoted by the terms of the reduced theory any less real. Gases continue to have temperatures, even if temperature is the causal outcome of the statistical regularities of the aggregated behavior of their constituent molecules. Finally, the very idea of theory-reduction may be methodologically useless, counter-productive even. Like *most* of the philosophy of science stemming from the heyday of twentieth-century philosophy of science, the idea represents a *logical reconstruction of a finished science*, not a guide to discovery. As Hull writes regarding the relationship between Mendelian genetics and molecular genetics, 'at the very least the formal relations between these two theories are so complex and the reconstructions necessary for any detailed derivations so massive that the efforts to reduce Mendelian genetics to molecular genetics seems hardly worth the effort' (Hull, 1974, p. 44). He concludes that 'no one is currently engaged in producing such derivation, and there seems no good reason to do so'. But, 'according to the logical empiricist analysis of reduction, this is precisely what they should be doing' (1974, p. 44).

TRUTH AND THE ACCEPTANCE OF SCIENTIFIC THEORY

The whole of the preceding has assumed that some good sense could be given to the idea that there are true theories of science. It is time to turn to this difficult problem. Regarding this topic, the recent trajectory has been astounding. It has gone from confident verificationism to a more modest confirmationism to Popperian falsificationism to Kuhn's ambiguous attack on the 'rationality' of science to Feyerabend's all-fours epistemological anarchism; from the idea that there had to be an algorithm to might makes right to anything goes (Lakatos and Musgrave, 1970).

Confirmationism was weak verificationism (Carnap, 1936–7). Scientific propositions need not be shown to be true; they need only be shown to be probable. The underlying assumption of the confirmationist was the possibility of an inductive logic, construed on the basis of the extensionalist model of Russell and Whitehead's *Principia Mathematica*. By the 1940s at least, Carnap and Hempel had recognized that this was part of the nexus of problems set off by Hume, and that such a logic was absolutely central to the promised 'rational reconstruction' of science. After all, rational belief was not a matter of 'animal faith'. Inference was *logical*; that is, there must be 'purely formal criteria of confirmation . . . similar to that in which deductive logic provides purely formal criteria for the validity of deductive inference' (Hempel, 1965, p. 10).[14]

Neither Russell nor Popper were so sanguine. Russell continued to

---

[14] For some of the relevant debate, see Manicas, 1971. I will show in the next chapter how critical logicist assumptions have been made in the development of recent psychology.

have doubts about the viability of empiricism on exactly this score, moving from a Platonism (1903) to a 'solipsism of the moment' (1927) to his final view, that 'causality and induction, in their traditional [i.e., Humean] forms, cannot be quite true'. Moreover, he concluded that it was 'by no means clear what could be substituted for them' (Russell, 1948, p. 180). Popper, of course, shared in the interest in distinguishing science from metaphysics, and likewise insisted that the objectivity of science depended on there being 'an empirical basis'. But it was clear to him that the confirmation route was a dead-end. Popper, like Russell, recognized the full force of Hume's critique of causality and the problem of induction which it had raised. He saw that, given Humean constraints on inductive inference, a scientific theory could have *no* logical warrant. This, too, is sometimes missed. It was not that it lacked the warrant of a *demonstration,* but that, on Humean premises, one could not even warrant *probabilities* (Popper, 1934, 1963). Falsification, however, was *deductive (modus tolens).* Thus, scientists imaginatively 'conjecture' hypotheses. What makes a hypothesis scientific is the fact that one can put its elaborated consequences to the test. Those which are *not* 'falsifiable' (for example, the theories of Marx and Freud!) are not scientific. Those that can be tested and survive attempts at refutation are, thereby, 'corroborated'.

Unfortunately, this is not much help either. Not only are there a host of problems associated with Popper's empiricist commitment to 'basic sentences' and with the Duhem/Quine contention that hypotheses can never be tested in any thing like the requisite isolation; but, more critically, 'Popper's method is self-defeating because if you adopt the aim of science as he describes it, his method seems pointless. . . . In practice, Popper's method would amount to a skepticism that would trivialize science as we know it' (Lieberson, 1983, p. 44). The point is that scientific practice has stronger commitments.

As I have insisted, scientists assume that transdiction and retrodiction – inference to the best explanation – are perfectly licit modes of reasoning (Hanson, 1958). One may indeed speculate as to why anyone would have thought otherwise? As Einstein noted, they were made to seem otherwise only by a 'fateful "fear of metaphysics" . . . which has come to be a malady of empiricistic philosophizing' (in Schlipp, 1951, p. 289).

Secondly, but worthy of emphasis, the twentieth-century version of science, logical empiricism, was profoundly impelled by the innovations and promise of modern logic. 'Logicians' since Aristotle have tried to guarantee the rationality of science by showing that its conclusions answer to the canons of logic. Aristotelian canons have themselves, of course, had an enormously influential history. When these were undermined in the eighteenth century and the 'problem of induction' emerged, 'science' was in trouble. But the new logic of Russell and Whitehead's *Principia* seemed to totally redefine the possibilities of showing that the sciences answered to these canons. Indeed, the extensionalist spell of *Principia* combined so neatly with the older empiricism that it seemed to be a marriage made in heaven.

But of course, even if scientists accept that 'transdiction' and 'retrodiction' are licit forms of reasoning, and even if it be admitted that Hempel's theoretician's dilemma was falsely posed, we still have the problem of discriminating between explanatory theories.

It would be wonderful to be able to say that we now know exactly how to do this. But, unfortunately, we do not. Indeed, once one gives up the idea of a theory-neutral 'data base', a 'foundation' in experience for science; once one abandons the program of replacing 'inferred entities' with 'logical constructions'; and once one yields, with Kuhn, to the idea that there are no *rules* for the acceptability of theory, no algorithms, and that no logic, deductive or inductive will suffice, then one must assent to a thoroughly contextual and historical conception of knowledge. On this view, knowledge is a *social product,* and the standards of inquiry are generated in the course of inquiry. This is a relativism. But it is not an irrationalism, because it presupposes a realism (Manicas and Rosenberg, 1985).

NATURALIZED EPISTEMOLOGY

There are two major constraints on socially produced knowledge. The first is an independently existing world; the second involves the socially (and thus historically) constituted practices (languages, techniques, and so on) themselves. The independently existing world is never known as it is – in itself – since it can be known only as mediated by those selfsame socially constituted forms. But to have communication and to avoid solipsism, it is not necessary that there be 'shared experience', a universal logic, or 'a commonly shared core of beliefs' whose meaning is fixed by 'shared standards of truth and of inference' (Lukes, 1982; Davidson, 1974). All that we need is a non-experienceable world which is part-cause of our experience. On the other hand, because that world is not experienced, though its mediated effects are, there is no way of escaping relativism – relativism, but not epistemological nihilism. Indeed, once it is admitted that 'there are no extra-natural and extra-social grounds of rationality and truth in the *a priori,* the analytic, the necessary, and *a fortiori* that no transcendental argument or rational intuition can claim to have access to such grounds' (Hesse, 1980, p. 37), we are left with an epistemological naturalism in which 'knowledge, mind and meaning are part of the same world that they have to do with, and . . . they are to be studied in the same empirical spirit that animates natural science' (Quine, 1968, p. 185).[15]

This is not the place to develop these critical ideas which we owe to Herder in the eighteenth century, to Marx, Helmholtz, and Spencer in the nineteenth, to Dewey and Wittgenstein and, more recently, Kuhn, Toulmin, Hesse, and especially Barry Barnes and David Bloor.[16]

The main idea is plausible enough. Indeed, were it not for particular turns taken in the history of the Western scientific and philosophic tradition, the particular form of separation of science and philosophy (see chapter 1), the conceptualization of 'sociology' and 'psychology', and the 'philosophy of science' of the late nineteenth century and recent past, the main idea would hardly need arguing. It holds, briefly, that humans and human cultures relate symmetrically to a natural world, which they shape and which shapes them. Being capable of making apt responses to the causal imputs from this world, humans learn, and collectively they develop social patterns which, in turn, become causal factors in their reproduction. In the chapters which follow, more will be said about what this means for psychology and the social sciences.

It holds as well that 'knowledge' is conventional in the sense that it is an *artifact,* a social construction, and that there is no good reason to believe that such constructions *must* converge. We may assume – on the evidence – that as members of a species with similar evolutionary pasts, we have similar infra-psychological powers, perceptual and cognitive, and thus that there may be elements of our experience – the stubbornness of sensation, for example – which are more or less 'universal'. Indeed, this contingent possibility, which would have to be accepted as a consequence of inquiry, has often been taken as a philosophical necessity – in the form of a Kantian transcendental ego or in the form of 'sense data' or 'basic sentences'. But even if it were established that there are elements of our experience which are universal, since human epigenesis is social, a naturalized epistemology must reject an epistemological individualism and hold that, as Bloor puts it, 'society gets into knowledge right at the ground floor, in the most elementary steps of language learning, and in the most elementary

---

[15] Quine's naturalism is not 'half-hearted', but it remains epistemologically individualist in the sense that, for him, a naturalized epistemology is a physiological psychology, having no need of a sociology of knowledge.

[16] Manicas and Rosenberg (1985) clarify and defend the 'strong programme in the sociology of knowledge' which has been developed in many books and articles by Barry Barnes and David Bloor. Much of the relevant bibliography is contained therein. The relation to Wittgenstein is brilliantly developed by Bloor (1983); that to Kuhn in Barnes (1982).

links that are forged between concepts and the world' (Bloor, 1982, p. 305). Again, this has critical implications as regards psychology and the social sciences, to be pursued in the next chapter.

On the present view of knowledge, to say that a belief or theory is true is to say that it asserts or captures or portrays the way the world is, that the belief corresponds to reality, that the theory is about reality as it truly is. But if that is what 'is true' *means,* it is not the case that the *test* of truth is correspondence with reality. There is no way to compare the belief or theory to theory-neutral reality. There is no way to escape present experience, experience which is the net result of causal inputs from nature *and* the social world. This was, if you will remember, the nub of the 'metaphysical' problem as discerned by Einstein and Planck. It is the reason why the problem of 'science' – of *knowledge* – cannot finally be solved.

On this view, the idea of 'truth' is *not* dispensable (as pragmatic philosophers usually argue), since once we take a fully social view of knowledge, we see that talk about truth performs a social role – in argument, criticism, persuasion, and, more generally, in the fixing of belief. If our beliefs were solely determined by stimulation from the external world (epistemological individualism), the idea of 'truth' would be dispensable, for it could not then perform this role. As David Bloor has argued, because our knowledge is socially produced, there is 'a continuing problem of maintenance'. 'Nature has power over us, but only [people] have authority' (Bloor, 1976, p. 36).

In the spirit of Peirce and Dewey, then, we can see that there are different types of *cultural practices* which have been employed as mechanisms for the fixing of belief, and in this spirit we can suggest a more useful way to respond to the Popperian problem of demarcation and the empiricist problem of the acceptability of theory.

The practice of classical science generated two ideas which as ideals have been critical to the institutionalization of theoretical science in the West: the idea that no belief ought to be closed to scrutiny (Peirce) or to criticism (Popper), and the idea that there are particular criteria, pertinent to the judgment by peers, of scientific truth (Dewey, 1938; Toulmin, 1961, 1972; Kuhn, 1962, 1977).

The first involves all the conditions associated with the familiar idea of free inquiry, an idea *never* fully realized, and with the industrialization of science, increasingly compromised. I do not refer only to 'Lysenkoism' here, but to the enormous constraints generated by the fact that research is now capital-intensive; that the researcher is not an independent agent; that, because research can be 'classified' or be the 'property' of the institution funding it, results can easily be suppressed, falsified, or amended; that institutional control of publication can prevent criticism;

and that, because the number of journals is so large that no one keeps up, and because of competitive pressure, 'shoddy science' has become characteristic (Ravetz, 1971). I noted earlier that the industrialization of science may be the most critical political problem of our day. The possibility that the ideal of free inquiry is so far from being realized that 'science' has no future is real enough. In any case, we ought not to minimize the problem. The idea that 'truth' will be victorious is empty, since, if one takes seriously the idea that knowledge is a social product, then truth is merely the product of specific truth-producing social practices.[17] It is not, in other words, as if there were some Platonic propositions out there to be discovered; there is only the natural world which causally impinges on us and which we comprehend (and experience) via socially created forms. The term 'shoddy science' does not refer to science deflected from truth, but to scientific practice which does not answer to the social conditions of free inquiry. A great deal more might be said here, but the general picture is clear enough.

The second idea has been the focus of epistemologists of science though, excepting Kuhn and Toulmin, they have usually missed the main point. Kuhn has suggested that there are five characteristics of a 'good' scientific theory:

1   It should be accurate; which means that, within its domain, experiment should be in agreement with theory.
2   It should be consistent, both internally and with existing theory.
3   It should be of broad scope, explaining more than it set out to explain.
4   It should be simple.
5   It should be fruitful; that is, it should disclose new phenomena or order previously unnoticed relationships among phenomena already known. (1977, p. 322)

But, as Kuhn goes on to say, the criteria are imprecise, and 'when deployed together, they repeatedly prove to conflict with one another' (p. 322). Moreover, and in part because of the foregoing, these criteria 'are not by themselves sufficient to determine the decisions of individual scientists', whose collective judgment is what determines when a theory is accepted into the body of knowledge. Since 'every individual choice between competing theories depends upon a mixture of objective and subjective factors, or of shared and individual criteria' (p. 235), the actual situation is not as it has been described by the standard view, a fact not denied by Kuhn's critics. But the actual situation is *epistemologically* relevant, since on the view of knowledge urged in the fore-

[17] 'Progressive realism', understood as the idea that scientific knowledge is moving toward a fully accurate description of the real mechanisms of the world, cannot be sustained except perhaps as a normative ideal.

going, 'scientific knowledge' is none other than what is actually produced. On the other hand, we can make perfectly good sense of a distinction (never precise or absolute) between science and non-science. Very roughly, theoretical, fundamental, explanatory, classical science is just that set of practices in which the social conditions of free inquiry are realized and whose practitioners are socialized and guided by the five criteria for theory choice outlined above. Moreover, the same argument shows that scientific belief is not either the product of 'mob rule' *or* of rationality as defined by the standard view. There is a third choice. Because there is a independently existing world which impinges on us, science is possible. When, then, the social conditions for science are more or less satisfied, we have the (idealized) analogy of a jury trial in which all the relevant evidence is produced, in which the jurors then negotiate from their respective postures, and from which a collective judgment eventually emerges. Neither 'mob rule' nor the rationality of epistemological individualism.

Of course, we cannot be sanguine here. As noted earlier, the social conditions for scientific knowledge have never been fully realized, and it may well be the case that the *ideal* of scientific practice sketched above is by now beyond recovery. Indeed, if it is true that mainstream social science began with a set of constituting beliefs in a social condition antithetic to the realization of social scientific knowledge; that, for the most part, it is dominated by the attributes of industrialized science; and that 'classic science' is an increasingly marginalized aspect of actual research in physical science, we can hardly be optimistic about the future.

13

A Realist Social Science

Chapter 10 suggested that the differences among theoretical science, applied science, and technology were rapidly being eroded. There is now a growing critical literature which shows that our customary understanding of the distinctions between these is not as straightforward as one might have supposed (Ben-David, 1971; Kuhn, 1977; Mayr, 1982; de Solla Price, 1982). Nevertheless, it is crucial that the distinctions be acknowledged. My aim in this chapter is to defend social science as a theoretical science which, like physical science analogs, seeks to understand the world. This task must be distinguished from other familiar tasks of existing social-scientific practice, especially 'social research', the effort to develop data about society, and 'applied social science', whose ostensible task is to use knowledge to solve some of life's social and individual problems. I will have something more to say about applied social science in the next chapter. But in the interest of precluding needless confusion and misunderstanding, it may be well to add a few words on the idea of social research.

As noted in part I, social research emerged with the modernizing processes of the modern state. There can be little doubt that today, governing depends heavily on information provided by social researchers – from demographic data to data about unemployment, the balance of trade, the inflation rate, crime, health, and welfare. Some of this information is reliable, some not. This is not the place, however, to attempt to discuss the problems, which range from familiar statistical problems to more serious conceptual issues, like those associated with data on unemployment or 'crime', for example (Reiman, 1984). Nothing in what follows argues against the desirability of good information and, hence, the need for good social research. Rather, what is contended is that social science ought not to be conceived *exclusively* as social research.

No one, I think, would maintain that social science is identical with *statistical* inquiry, but it is a widely shared opinion that the methodology of social research generates an explanatory capacity and that, accordingly, 'social research', broadly construed, is identifiable with social science. This view is not restricted to so-called 'quantitative' researchers; the confusion has infected *all* mainstream social science. In the last part of this chapter, I will try to make clear how this is the case.

The main goal of the chapter is to sketch a realist conception of social science as an alternative to the mainstream view. I noted in the Introduction that the most important way in which the present study is incomplete lies in the absence of an account of the arguments regarding the nature and tasks of the social sciences since the 1930s, and especially since World War II. This last period has been an especially fertile one. But, while much work remains to be done, there are now a number of very good discussions of various aspects of it.[1] Before starting on my sketch, which draws heavily on this work, it may be useful to characterize, if briefly, a portion of the discussion, recognizing that the characterization may ultimately turn out to be a caricature.

THE RECENT DEBATE

The recent debate in the philosophy of the social sciences has turned on two related polarities, that between a 'subjectivist' and an 'objectivist' pole, and that concerning the relationship of agency to structure. The first has been haunted by the specter of philosophical idealism, the second by that of a world without agents. While there are some very critical differences among them, it is not impossible to include in the subjectivist approach all of the following: phenomenology (Schutz, 1962), versions of ethnomethodology (Garfinkel, 1967), the post-Wittgensteinian views of Winch (1958), and versions of hermeneutics and critical theory (Gadamer, 1960; Habermas, 1968; Ricoeur, 1970; Taylor, 1971).

The point of departure of these views is criticism of the objectivism of 'positivist' social science. Again, with differences, this criticism concerns the failure of mainstream theory even to acknowledge that the social world is constituted by agents and thus becomes intelligible only insofar as one can discover the meanings or intentions of those agents. The radical objectivist treats meaningful action as 'behavior', but even those who do not – for example, Merton – because they remain wedded to the

---

[1] Included here are books by Jay (1973), Poster (1975), Pettit (1975), Bernstein (1976), Anderson (1976, 1980, 1983), Giddens (1976, 1979), Buck-Morss (1977), Bhaskar (1979), Kurzweil (1980), McCarthy (1981), James (1984), and Skinner (1985).

hypothetical-deductive model of explanation, take social reality for granted and thus treat it the way they treat the natural world. The objectivists thus misconstrue 'explanation' and never address the question of how social reality is constituted and maintained (Natanson, 1963). Worse, the 'objectivity' of social science as the dispassionate and detached view of the social world is but the standpoint of the person as alienated. Society and culture, as in Talcott Parsons, become autonomous *things* which constitute persons instead of being constituted by them (Gouldner, 1970).

According to the view presented here, these criticisms are wholly on the mark, but in saying that the specter of philosophical idealism haunts these views, I mean that, as regards the social world, these views tend to undermine an appearance/reality distinction; in Marxist terms, these views rule out the possibility of 'false consciousness'. Put simply, while it is true that the social world is constituted by agents and has meaning by virtue of this and that, accordingly, we must appeal to the cognitive resources of agents if we are to offer adequate descriptions of the social world, it may be the case that the understandings that agents have of their social world is incorrect (Gellner, 1970; MacIntyre, 1970). Social science needs to do more than give a description of the social world as seen by its members (ethnography); it needs also to ask whether members have an adequate understanding of their world and, if not, to explain, why not. 'Critical theory', with its antecedents in the Marxism of the Frankfurt school, acknowledges this, of course. Yet recent critical theory, since Habermas (1968), has taken an idealist turn (McCarthy, 1981, pp. 96ff.; Keat, 1981). The problem is to accept the 'hermeneutic circle' and, at the same time, to sustain the possibility of critique: to acknowledge that there is no neutral or transcendental standpoint, but to hold also that *explanatory* social theory, insofar as it exposes domination concealed *as* domination, is inherently emancipating (Bhaskar, 1979, 1982). This suggests, as I will argue, the need for a realist conception of social science.

The second polarity, between agency and structure, overlaps with the first, but it is most familiarly associated with French 'structuralism'. Sartre's *Critique of Dialectical Reason* of 1960, written in response to Merleau-Ponty's criticisms of the 1950s, was followed by Lévi-Strauss's *The Savage Mind* (1962), which contained a direct attack on Sartre. Lacan (1966), who like Lévi-Strauss had been influenced by Saussure's structural linguistics, brought Freud back into the debate which by then had been joined by Barthes (1967), but especially by Foucault, who, in *The Order of Things* (1970), outdid both Durkheim and Lévi-Strauss in unearthing the underlying 'code' of civilization. At the same time, and in response to Sartre, came Louis Althusser's *For Marx* and, with

Balibar, *Reading Capital,* 'a counter-signature of the structuralist claim' (Anderson, 1983, p. 37). Poulantzas (1969) and Colletti (1969) enlarged the debate, and since then, we have had the polemic of E. P. Thompson (1978) against Althusser, Anderson's 1980 effort – successful in my view – to mediate this, and, of course, the influential work of the 'post-structuralists', in particular Derrida (1974). This is surely a mixed collection of figures, and no effort will be made here to clarify the many differences or issues. My brief characterization is designed only to focus what follows.

It is fair to say, I believe, that 'structuralism' was motivated mostly by a recognition that the mainstream tradition of social science is methodologically individualist and voluntarist, key features, as I have argued, of the tradition deriving from Hobbes, Locke, Adam Smith, J. S. Mill, Spencer, Pareto, and, on most contemporary readings, to Max Weber. The background of the critique of this tradition, unsurprisingly, is the French tradition of Comte and especially Durkheim and the tradition of Hegel, especially in versions of Marxist historical materialism. The problem, already noted in our accounts of Hegel and Durkheim, is the evaporation of agents who become, in effect, but manifestations or, in Althusserian terminology, 'bearers' of autonomous 'structures' which exist quite independently of them. One form of this, that found in Lévi-Strauss, involves an escape from history via a form of Platonism in which 'ethnographic analysis tries to arrive at invariants beyond the empirical diversity of human societies', and where 'the ultimate goal of the human sciences is not to constitute [persons] but to dissolve them' (Lévi-Strauss, 1966, p. 247). On the Althusserian variant, history is 'a process without a subject'. Social change is but the gradual and discontinuous 'bricolage' of structures which have no human bricoleur, structures which in complex systems of autonomy, dependence, and contradiction offer 'conjunctures' like the one in 1917 which became the Bolshevik Revolution' (Kurzweil, 1980). Insofar as these views are correctives to methodological individualism and voluntarism, they are to be welcomed. On the other hand, they do not, in my view, resolve the root difficulty. This requires a form of realism in social theory, but it cannot adopt either of the historical poles which are the legacy of the nineteenth century, either 'absolute idealism' (Neoplatonism) or 'materialism'.

Post-structuralism is a descendent of structuralism. Influenced by Heidegger, as well as by Saussure and Lévi-Strauss, Anderson (1983) would seem to be correct in arguing that post-structuralism represents a dissolution of 'structures'; thus, in the battle-cry 'there is nothing outside the text', we have not merely a relativism, tolerable enough in itself, but an epistemological nihilism in which truth is an illusion. On this view, the pretense to it reflects metaphysical prejudice (the Western philosophical quest for 'presence').[2] What results, then, is 'a subjectivism without a subject' (Anderson, 1983, p. 54). Undoubtedly there are insights for the social sciences in the writings of Derrida and Foucault, including, for example, the critique of subjectivity as never transparent and the knowledge/power relations analysed by Foucault in his more specifically 'historical' writings. This is not the place, however, to review the difficult, but interesting, questions involved. Instead, I turn to what seems to me to be the most pressing problem for a viable philosophy of social science, that of formulating in a clear and adequate way the 'object' of theory in social science, what social-scientific theory is about. We need to be clear, that is, about the 'ontology' of society.

THE ONTOLOGY OF SOCIETY

It would be more than merely convenient if we could say without qualification that, just as physical theory is about theorized natural structures – quarks, molecules, viruses, mammals, galazies, space–time cones and so on – so social theory is about social structures; that in both cases, theory aims at knowledge of the dispositional properties (laws) of abstracted objects which together help us to explain what happens in the world; and that in both cases, the theorized 'strata' of reality are the *raison d'être* of the different explanatory 'sciences'. To be sure, we would need to notice differences in the kinds of structures theorized; but this in itself constitutes no problem. It has been presupposed right along that the various theorized 'mechanisms' of physical science are very different; accordingly, social structures need not be 'like' natural structures in all relevant respects. Moreover, despite the ease of talking about 'mechanisms', it is not intended by such talk that the very different structures theorized by the sciences are like those theorized in the classical science of mechanics; that, as the corpuscularists had it, 'matter' and mechanical causality, vectors of 'forces', give us the whole story. Plainly this will not

---

[2] Rorty has defended these ideas in his *Consequences of Pragmatism* (1982). In the essay 'Method, social science, social hope', he argues that the old argument between 'behaviorese' and 'hermeneutics' are differences between different 'jargons' – not to be resolved but lived with. 'There is no connection between "explanation" and "understanding" – between being able to predict and control people in a certain way and being able to sympathize and associate with them, to view them as fellow citizens' (p. 198). It is plain that Rorty believes that social science is aimed at 'prediction and control' and as such, is 'useful'. Perhaps a consequence of Rorty's dismissal of the idea that social science can and ought to aim at an understanding of how things stand and why, is his belief that 'we should be more willing than we are to celebrate bourgeois capitalist society as the best polity actualized so far, while regretting that it is irrelevant to most of the problems of most of the population of the planet' (p. 210). See also Rorty, 1986.

do, not even for physical theory. Indeed, despite the continuing attract-
iveness of these crude ideas in some quarters, they have been defunct in
science for well over a hundred years now. One need not look at
quantum mechanics or classical field theory, but only to the more
familiar ideas of molecular chemistry or biochemistry.

'Social structures' and causality in society need not, then, be the same
as any of these. But exactly how these are to be conceptualized is a
matter of contention. For example, 'racism' surely *affects* opportunities
for individuals, and there are social *mechanisms* by virtue of which what
occurs does occur; but what exactly does this mean? Is such talk merely
metaphorical? I think not. On the contrary, and despite some fundamental differences which we will consider, this way of talking about
'social structures' is more than metaphorical or just plain convenient.
After making some critical qualifications, we can continue to use the
language of social structure so as to deliberately reinforce the analogy
between the theoretical physical sciences and theoretical social science.

Individuals and persons surely exist. Social structures do not exist in
the sense of either of these. Yet, as suggested in chapter 8, without the
concept of social structure (or something like it), we cannot make sense
of persons, since all the predicates which apply to individuals and mark
them uniquely as persons are social. We can, for example, predicate a
shape, size, color, or position of a person, just as we can of a stone or a
tree. We can say that a person is hungry or in pain, just as we can say
that a lower animal is hungry or in pain. But the moment we say that the
person is a tribesman or a revolutionary, cashed a check, or wrote a
sonnet, we are presupposing tribes (a social order), a banking system,
and a literary form (Bhaskar, 1979, pp. 34f.).

If, then, methodological individualism is construed as holding that
facts about society or human action are to be explained solely in terms
of facts about individuals, and if facts about persons requires predicates
which presuppose a social context which cannot be reduced (translated)
to predicates having no reference to social context, then methodological
individualism must be false.

Both historically (see chapters 2 and 3) and in its contemporary forms
(Popper, 1962; Watkins, 1963; Brodbeck, 1968), methodological individualism has an anti-metaphysical motivation. And opponents of it –
Rousseau, Herder, Hegel, Marx, Durkheim, and others – are accused,
often rightly, of being 'metaphysicians'. In its modern form, it was a
critical part of the logical empiricist program of eliminating inferred
entities in favor of logical constructions. Thus, just as 'magnetic field'
was to be 'translated' into witnessable conditions and consequences and
thereby incorporated into the language of science, so society was a
logical construction and social predicates were to be translated into

witnessable conditions and 'behaviors'. That nobody today gives credence to the possibility of such a translation is critical, for its means that,
although methodological individualism has been shown to be false, we
nevertheless lack a consensus on what this means.[3]

THE CONCEPT OF SOCIAL STRUCTURE

The problem, then, is just this. We need the idea of social structure, but
social structure does not exist in the way that a magnetic field exists.
And the reason would seem to be this: that *society is incarnate in the
practices and products of its members*. It doesn't exist apart from the
practices of individuals; it is not witnessable; only its activities and
products are. As Giddens writes, 'structure enters simultaneously into
the constitution of the agent and social practices, and "exists" in the
generating moments of this constitution' (Giddens, 1979, p. 5). It is both
medium and product, enabling as well as contraining.

It is 'medium' in being what one uses when one acts as a person. It is
thus also that it is enabling and constraining. For example, a person has
a language, and thus *can* speak. Evidently, to be understood, that
person *must* conform, more or less, to the 'rules' of that language. A
person has 'knowledge' and a range of skills. That person can use these
only because other individuals possess particular skills, are related in
particular ways, and have available to them particular 'materials', all of
which at the same time constrains them.

Social structure is 'product' in the sense that speaking reproduces the

---

[3] The connectedness of so many of the themes in the recent debate has tended to go
unnoticed, a point to be emphasized in the next chapter. We will re-emphasize here,
however, that as Margolis (1984) has pointed out, the assumption that the language of
science must be an extensional language has fuelled an immense amount of discussion in
recent accounts of a proper science. Thus, the 'translation' program (reduction-sentence,
operational definition, and so on) of empiricism presupposed that scientific sentences
expressed in a natural language could be re-expressed in a wholly extensionalist language.
A language is said to be extensional if (to quote Margolis):
1 In its sentences, the substitution of codesignative expressions does not alter the truth-
   value of the resultant sentence. [That is, synonomy, an intensional (meaning) relation,
   gives way to extensional equivalence, identity of reference] . . .
2 For its compound and complex sentences, truth-values are a function only of the truth-
   values of its constitutive clauses [the connectives of *Principia Mathematica* are the only
   ones to be employed; thus causality must be rendered as of the form $(x)(Fx \rightarrow Gx)$].
3 For those clauses, the substitution criterion is satisfied.
It is easy to show, unsurprisingly, that so-called 'intentional contexts', for example, 'Tom
believes that Cicero denounced Catiline', resist this treatment; thus, it was not unexpected
that behaviorist efforts at 'translations of 'psychological predicates also fail. But the
problem was not merely the 'intentionality' of the mental, but the fact that the problem of
meaning, of the intensional, takes one to the *social*. See below for a sketch of language (as
a social structure) depending upon practices, and the next chapter for the bearing of this
on psychology.

language, going to work reproduces the system of capitalism, and voting reproduces electoral politics. Without people speaking English, English ceases to be 'a living language'. As with all social structures, its continuing existence requires continuing speech-practices. On the other hand, the continuing practices may be comprehended in terms of the structures. That is, structures need not be 'independent' of practices for it to be said that practices are structured in such and such a way. Thus, while they do not 'exist' in the same way that natural structures exist, they can be, as in physical science, the objects of *theory*.

Since social structures do not exist independently of activities, they are not simply reproduced but are, as Bhaskar notes, reproduced *and* transformed. Because the language is 'living', it is continually changing. If only a small minority of people were to take the trouble to vote, elections would become transformed into rituals which lack the meaning they now have (Edelman, 1964); and eventually, like the 'hearths' of the ancient *polis,* they would then probably disappear altogether.[4]

Because society is incarnate in the practices of its members, it is easy to lapse into methodological individualism, in which society disappears and only individuals exist. Of course, society has *not* disappeared, since these individuals are *persons* and their acts are *situated,* not simply in a 'natural' world but in a world constituted by past and ongoing human activity, a humanized natural and social world. Farmland and forestland, the city streets, neighborhoods, the buildings which house machines, icons, and lawbooks; violins and folios of music, all both enable and constrain the members who use them. *Per impossibile,* were we to find non-socialized persons interacting with none of these 'artifacts' of humanity, we would not lapse into supposing that only individuals exist, and not society – as, of course, Rousseau and Herder saw.

Because individuals become persons only in society, it is easy to fall into the Platonizing trap of Ranke (see chapter 5) or Durkheim (see chapter 8), to suppose that society has to be something *more than* the organized social practices which embody social structures. Social structures, including language, do pre-exist for *some* individuals, but never for all. When it is said that someone appropriates language from 'society', this means that they 'appropriate it from existing speakers of the language, who, of course, also appropriated it from 'society', that is, from previous speakers, and so on back into *pre*-history.

We move in the direction of Platonism (as does recent French structuralism, for example) by supposing that the language does not simply pre-exist for some individuals, which must be the case, but that it is absolutely prior to activity. 'The language' then 'accounts for' the

---

[4] We might keep the word, of course, and have it identify a *different* practice. Compare 'democracy' ancient and modern. See Barnes, 1982, pp. 27–35.

activity in the sense that the abstract 'forms' account for their concrete manifestations (see chapter 4). When we say that 'the language is "possessed" by speakers', we reinforce this error. 'The language' (like any other structure) is whatever the continued reproduction/transformation by speakers makes it. Elections, nurturing practices, and so on are what they are only by virtue of the activities which constitute them.[5]

To talk about *the* language or *the* structure of a language or, more generally, the structures which are the properties of some concrete society is heuristic in the sense that because activity constitutes them and not conversely, social structures can and do undergo relatively rapid change. Talk about *the* structure is a static idealization, even if indispensable. This makes for an important difference between social science and physical science. Theorizing is never finished in any science, but in the social sciences, theory is continually revisable not merely in the sense that new theories replace or amend older theories, but in the sense that *reality* is changing. The 'rules' – of language or other forms of social activity – are but normative abstractions drawn from shifting uniformities, incapable of being formulated as a closed system (Barnes, 1982; Margolis, 1984).

Accordingly, social science is *inevitably* historical. History is not merely 'the past', but *a sedimented past which, as transformed, is still present.* As Marx and Engels wrote in *The German Ideology*, 'history is nothing but the succession of separate generations, each of which exploits the materials, the capital funds, the productive resources handed down to it by all preceding generations.' By this we must understand that what is 'handed down' is not merely the legacy of material goods but also includes 'knowledge' and the 'handed down' social forms themselves. Moreover, this whole legacy is continually being exploited by each succeeding generation. It is not merely window-dressing or deference to 'context' which demands that an attempt to explain, for example, the emergence of martial law in the Philippines must engage the question of the Philippine colonial past (Lallana, 1986). On the contrary, present forms have their particular nature *by virtue of* their past, and thus present understanding requires an understanding of their genesis.

On this conception, discriminable starting-points or breaks will be signalled by events which made for what, to us, are significant ruptures or transformations in the theorized inherited forms. Periods, epochs, eras will span thse. On this view, we expect continuity with change, both of which are always 'more or less'.

[5] Kurzweil (1980) remarks that 'Foucault's archeology must reject subjectivity. Authors, works, and language are said to be objects in search of a logic independent of grammars, vocabularies, synthetic forms, and words' (p. 207), an excellent example of the trap just noted.

Because social structures are incarnate in the practices of persons, this means that they do not exist independently of the *conceptions* of the persons whose activities constitute (reproduce, transform) them. It is because persons have beliefs, interests, goals, and practical knowledge acquired in their epigenesis as members of society that they do what they do and thus sustain (transform) the structures. That is, there is no question here that persons are the ultimate causal agents as regards everything that makes society what it is; nor is it the case that individuals are 'dupes' of culture (Parsons) or structure (Althusser), that everything that happens goes on 'behind their backs'.

This does not imply a regression to methodological individualism, for two reasons. First, as noted, a person/society dichotomy is spurious; for there is a duality in the sense that society always pre-exists for individuals.[6] Second, while it is true that, as Giddens writes (in criticism of both Parsons and Althusser), all agents have practical knowledge (not necessarily cognitively available) and some degree of understanding of the real nature of social structure which their activities sustain, unintended consequences, unacknowledged conditions, and tacit rules limit the individual's understanding of his or her social world. For example, one works at Los Alamos to earn one's living; one does not work there *in order to* encourage the arms race, still less to bring the world closer to a nuclear holocaust. Nevertheless, these may well be unintended consequences of such work.[7]

Moreover, it may be that the structures which are reproduced by one's voluntary activity are rightly understood as oppressive, and thus that one becomes party to one's continued oppression – quite voluntarily. Indeed, in contrast to methodological individualisms, because social structure is both constraining *and* enabling, what one can and cannot do is determined both by existing social resources and, more particularly, by the nature of the social relations defined by the structures and by one's place in them. Had they even conceived the possibility, neither Louis XIV nor all the peasants in his kingdom could have destroyed the world. But Louis XIV could, of course, do many things that his peasant subjects could not do – from dine regularly on white bread to call for the execution of a traitor. *Versus* methodological individualism, then, 'voluntary acts' are just those done by a person *given*

---

[6] This was a key theme in the writings of John Dewey and George Herbert Mead, especially in *Human Nature and Conduct* (1922) and those writings of Mead's collected as *Mind, Self and Society* (1934). But strange as it may seem, the full force of these writings *never* had an impact on social science. Instead, what one got was a 'social psychology' with a pervasive misconstrual of 'the social'. See chapter 14.
[7] The example is deliberately provocative. The 'may' in 'may be an unintended consequence' is all the argument needs. Such is the nature of the social reality currently sustained by *all* our activities.

alternatives not chosen by that person (whose faculties are in tack and who is unconstrained by force).[8]

Recognizing that social structure does not exist independently of an agent's conceptions and that persons are the causal agents of existing social reality may seem to lead to a voluntarism in which society is the creation of (rational) individuals (see chapter 3). But such is not the case. Such 'creation' is only with materials at hand (see above); it is never *ex nihilo* and never unconditioned. Second, even if the acts of individuals are more or less 'rational', related to definite interests, and so on, their (structured) practices and the changes in them are not generally, if ever, *intended*; still less are these changes 'rational'. As historically sedimented unintended consequences of intentional activities, they appear as 'natural' (Marx), but there is *no* reason to suppose that their 'development' is telic, that change is under the governance of some grand design (see chapter 4).

But changes in activity *do* change society. This suggests that social science is potentially *liberating*. For Marx, social science was *revolutionary,* and while he put considerable emphasis on the problem of ideology construed as 'false consciousness', he saw that this was not the whole story. On his view, capitalist organization would bring workers to understand that their own activities sustained oppressive relations and would, at the same time, make them organizationally *able* to act *collectively* to reconstitute society. This is hardly the place to evaluate Marx's views on revolutionary social change or on the changes in conditions which altered the problem of revolutionary change, changes which, after all, Marx could not have foreseen. Still, it cannot be denied that his most fundamental insights regarding history and society, insights preserved, I hope, in the foregoing, stand in distinct contrast to the prevailing practices of academic social science. Indeed, though only part of the story has been outlined in part II, one must conclude that the modern social sciences have been, unwittingly or not, defenders of the *status quo.* As Veblen put it, rather than 'disturb the habitual convictions and preconceptions' on which present institutions rest, social science has 'enlarged on the commonplace' and offered 'complaisant interpretations, apologies, and projected remedies' – none of which have been dangerous to the *status quo.* Most fundamentally, this was a result of failure on the part of mainstream social scientists to acknowledge that, while social reality is real enough, it is not like unchanging nature, but is just that which is sustained by human activities, activities regarding which humans have the *only* say.

[8] Structure and freedom are not counterposed, as in radical existentialisms. For an emphatic individualist explication of 'the voluntary', see Nozick, 1974. This is almost a *reductio ad absurdum* of the position. On this view, involuntary acts are 'coerced', 'coercion' is physical force, and that is all that needs to be said.

If people are causal agents, they are capable of re-fashioning society in the direction of greater humanity, freedom, and justice. To do this, of course, they must see that they have this power; they must acknowledge that present arrangements can be improved; and they must have some clarity about how they can be improved. It is a simplification to hold that only 'false consciousness' stands in the way of progressive social change, for, as noted earlier, people are not dupes of society. But even if they have some grasp of the reality of society, then, if the foregoing is correct, the solitary individual cannot make change. For change to come about, *practices* must be altered, which means that most of those engaged in reproducing the practices must together alter their activity (Manicas, 1982). This is not the place to develop an account of the causal complexities whose understanding would help us grasp why this has not happened; but I believe it is fair to say that not least of these is our structured incapacity, promoted by technocratic social science, to constitute any sort of adequate social mechanism for unconstrained social inquiry (Dewey, 1927; Mills, 1956; Poulantzas, 1969; Habermas, 1975; Manicas, 1982).

In sum, then, as Bhaskar writes, the foregoing allows us to undercut reification and voluntarism, social determinism and methodological individualism, and the connected errors of the substantive traditions of structuralism and functionalism, on the one hand, and the action-oriented and interpretative sociologies on the other. Thus:

> Society is not the unconditioned creation of human agency (voluntarism), but neither does it exist independently of it (reification). And individual action neither completely determines (individualism) nor is completely determined by (determinism) social forms. In [this conception], unintended consequences, unacknowledged conditions and tacit skills . . . limit the actor's understanding of the social world, while unacknowledged (unconscious) motivation limits one's understanding of oneself. (Bhaskar, 1982, p. 286)

UNDERSTANDING SOCIETY AND
HISTORICAL EXPLANATION

The aim of social science is an understanding of society and social process, where 'understanding' does not have any special sense – for example, involving empathy or some intuition of subjectivity. To be sure, action is meaningful, and understanding society involves understanding what acts *mean* to actors, but while this is part of the story, it is not the whole of it. As Weber argued, understanding society involves *causal understanding,* an understanding of how it is what happens in society happens. On the present view, understanding society involves hermeneutic social science – having a member's knowledge of society – for otherwise one cannot know what one is explaining; but it also involves, as Marx saw, a knowledge of how definite practices are structured, the relations between structured practices, and the tendencies of such practices towards transformation or disintegration.[9]

This is not a functionalism, we should add, if by that one means that we explain when we know how what some 'institution' does contributes to 'the needs of the system' or to 'system-maintenance' (Giddens, 1979, pp. 111ff.). It is one thing to discover how an institution came to be, how it works, what it does, and what its effects are; it is quite another to import into this an unwarranted teleology, an assumption that society, like an organism, has a *telos* (see chapter 8) or that what is 'needed' will somehow get provided. Nor should one suppose that the availability of a system-hypothesis completes the social scientific task. For example, it may be that the reproduction of capitalist relations of production requires that profit be available for reinvestment, but this has not been explained until an account can be given of the particular social mechanisms constituting the causal loop (Giddens, 1979, p. 113). In this regard, of course, social science differs not at all from any of the theoretical sciences, even if we are used to thinking of the biological sciences as particularly concerned with 'systems' notions.

As noted in chapter 7, Weber employed an extremely useful distinction between the abstract and concrete sciences, conceiving of physics as 'abstract' and social science as 'concrete'. On the present view, however, any science which restricts itself to the theorizing of structure is abstract, and any science which aims at the explanation of concrete events is concrete. And since all concrete outcomes are the result of a plurality of causes, operating at different strata of reality, we can make a distinction between *understanding structure* and *explaining events,* between having a grasp of the nomic dispositions of the structures and providing an account of how particular 'mechanisms' and events came together to produce some outcome. Each of the theoretical sciences offers theories of particular strata of reality, and any of them might be involved in the explanation of an event. This is as true of social phenomena as any other.

That is, we can think of social theory as aimed at the theorization of social reality, a non-reducible stratum of reality. But the explanation of

[9] Marx's *Capital,* despite its problems, is the best historical example of social theory as conceived here. 'Things', of course, are 'commodities' which are exchanged at the market price – everybody knows this. But we can explain why things, including labor-power, are commodities and the implications of this. Once accomplished, we can *understand* capitalism.

a social event, the Great Crash of 1929, the Bolshevik Revolution, the emergence of martial law in the Philippines, the election of an American president, and so on, involves knowledge of the 'social mechanisms' of existing structures and whatever else causally contributed to the particular outcome. That the scope of this effort is global was seen by Herder, Montesquieu, and Marx. It is also the grist of much sound historical writing. Indeed, it is not implausible to argue, here with our account of Weber in mind, that in the last analysis, a theoretically informed, multi-causal history is the human science which has the most significance for us.[10]

We do social theory because we want to understand what happens in society; but concrete happenings require a multi-causal account. We need to have an understanding of social structures and their tendencies, to know how they are related and their effects; and we need to relate this sometimes to geography, sometimes to a natural event, such as the eruption of Pompeii or the consequences of a long drought. Finally, if we are to provide an explanation of the event in question, we need to relate the whole business to the acts of people working with and in response to these things. To explain, for example, the Bolshevik Revolution, we need at the very least a grasp of the complicated social relations of Imperial Russia and a knowledge of the inter-state relations obtaining prior to and during World War I; we need to know how the long winter of 1916 affected what happened, and, within the nexus of these complicated structures and events, we need to grasp the particular sequence of steps taken by both individuals and groups – for example, the decision of the provisional government to pursue the war and the ride to the Finland station.

As with the broken water pipes (see chapter 12), the event to be explained is unique, even if we have reason to believe that it could not have happened otherwise, given the particular configuration of causes. Of course, the explanation of a particular historical event, even events of less monumental historical consequence – the more typical task of social scientists – is not likely to be as satisfying as an explanation depending more fundamentally on natural scientific understanding. The reasons are clear. Not only do we have much less confidence in the social theory which gives us insight into the relevant structures but the dominating presence of human agency increases the causal complexity enormously. On the other hand, this is not sufficient reason to abandon

---

[10] There is nothing precious in the label 'social science' as here conceived, especially since distinct alternative 'genres', particularly literature, may quite successfully offer us knowledge of persons and society. See Kenneth Burke, 1971, and Clifford Geertz, 1973. The analogue to theoretical physical science is a social science which seeks causal knowledge. But plainly, not only are there many other important things to know about persons and society, but we sometimes get causal knowledge from alternative genres.

the search for causes, or, as with Weber, to try to simplify the problem with the artificial and misleading device of 'ideal types'.

Nothing in the foregoing implies that history is an immanent process (see chapter 4) or, accordingly, that there are *laws of history*, even if on the present view, there are social laws. But this must mean that we can discover tendencies (again, realistically understood) in the structured practices. It clearly does not commit us to the implausible idea that these are universal. Not every society was or will be 'capitalist', even if at some level of abstraction, all societies generate relations of production. However, we can say that between any two capitalist societies, there will be specific capitalist social mechanisms involved in its reproduction. But we cannot say that for this reason everything that happens in one will happen in the other. Particular contingent events, as well as the irreducible embeddedness of mechanisms in a historically sedimented social reality which has not lost its historicity or particularity, will make for differences of all sorts.

Accordingly, capitalist societies were not 'inevitable'; nor is it inevitable that capitalist societies will be replaced by this or that form of society. If there are laws of capitalism (as I believe there are), we *can* say that some forms will be *likely* and others *unlikely*. Not only do the existing social processes have tendencies, but the materials at hand, the social materials 'exploitable' by the existing generation, make some transformations of these more likely than others. Yet, as before, how agents exploit what is given and how currently unforeseen structural conjunctures will affect action in the future are unknown and at present unknowable. And, as before, this is exactly the same situation, logically, as in physical science.

As Giddens has emphasized, there is no eliminating time from social science, which means, as the foregoing has suggested, that a distinction between social science and history is an abstract distinction, which in the final analysis is not sustainable. At the same time, the interests (and abilities) of inquirers vary. Some will concentrate on 'ethnography', focusing on how members understand their social world (Geertz, Garfinkel); others will emphasize abstract structure (de Saussure, much neo-Marxism). Some will write 'sociological' history (Fustel de Coulange, Weber, Marc Bloch, Braudel, Perry Anderson, Eric Wolf); some will write historically oriented social science (Barrington Moore, C. W. Mills, Arendt, Beer, Bendix, Galbraith, Tilly, Sahlins); and some will concentrate on historical narrative, taking for granted the underlying structural considerations or calling our attention to them only as needed (Hobsbawm, Christopher Hill, E. P. Thompson, Gordon Wood, LeFebvre, Hexter, Avrich, Genovese).

THE DISCIPLINES OF THE SOCIAL SCIENCES

The divorce of history from social science was in some ways the most devastating development in the Americanization of social science. This and the arbitrary branching of the social sciences led to institutionalized impoverishment. The problem here is different from that in physical science, since, whereas a physical science can develop a theory of a stratum of physical reality – for example, molecular chemistry – and thereby produce genuine knowledge, it is not clear that social reality is stratified in the appropriate way. That is, because individuals are socialized into society, and not into specific, discrete, and isolable practices; because the materials for the constitution of practices – beliefs, skills, and so on – often overlap; and because society exists only as incarnate in practices, efforts to 'decompose' society into its 'parts' and then analyse these will inevitably be problematic. Indeed, although we can think of society as a 'whole' comprised of connected structured practices, it is not, for the foregoing reasons, like an organism or some complicated physical system. These metaphors, useful up to a point, simply break down. Thus, while there are different practices (even different kinds of practices) and an inevitably connectedness between them, they are not 'parts' nor 'pieces'. There are, of course, 'households', and people raise families; and there are schools and places of worship, play, and work, but it is the same people who raise families, go to work, pray, and play.

We do, of course, identify practices as 'political', 'economic', 'familial', and so on, but from the present point of view, these are but 'theoretical' distinctions, subject to critique by more refined and more powerful theory; and in any case, this fact is perfectly consistent with the foregoing. The upshot is that that any division of labor as regards the attempt to theorize structures and their relations can, ultimately, be defended as no more than a convenience. Indeed, as I argued in part I, the division of labor in the social sciences was not a consequence of any independent 'givenness of social reality' (even in physical science, there is no such), but of circumstances and events whose outcome had very little to do with the disinterested pursuit of 'truth'.

On the other hand, even after distinguishing between the explanatory sciences and 'sciences' with other concerns, such as 'applied science' and 'social research', there may still be a justification for some sort of division of labor *within* explanatory social science. The idea that the special interests of the inquirer and the need for special skills and training leads an inquirer to develop ideas about but one aspect (the word is chosen carefully) of a society seems plausible enough. Thus, for the purposes of construction of theory, some restricted ensemble of practices may be the focus of inquiry. One might then have, to use Poulantzas's useful terminology, 'regional theories' – for example, of the contemporary democratic state of the United States, of 'the world-economy', the health-care system of Great Britain, or the New York City school system.

But there are dangers. One is the temptation to leap to an illicit universalizing generalization and to assume that what is true of the particular practices under study is true of all such practices (Manicas, 1985). Language gets in our way. After all, schools are schools, agricultural work is agricultural work. On the present view, however, as concrete historical forms, they cannot lose their historicity and particularity. Another danger is the temptation to forget the embeddedness of practices in the ensemble, so that these become one-sidedly severed from their connections. The result is explanatory reductionism in which one causal factor pretends to explain everything.[11]

Finally, if, as Montesquieu, Marx, and Weber insisted, society is a 'totality', there still might be practices which are theorized as *primary* in the sense that they are causally fundamental. This is, of course, the locus of the Marxist concept of 'historical materialism' and the critical role of 'mode of production'. But, as I argued in chapter 6, this will not do as a theory of history. It also has problems as a theory of society, whether in the familiar 'base/superstructure' formulation or in the more recent versions of Althusser and others. While I believe that the idea can be rescued and is important, this is not the place to attempt a defense (but see Manicas, 1985; Giddens, 1985, pp. 135f.).

THE PROGRAM OF BEHAVIORAL SOCIAL SCIENCE

I want to round out this chapter with a more specific comparison between the dominating mainstream paradigm and the realist alternative just sketched. This will bring into sharper focus the contrast between the definition of the task and nature of explanatory social science as conceived here and the mainstream conception. My point of departure is a recent text in behavioral research by Kerlinger (1979) and an actual study described therein.

The study is Marjoribanks's 'competent and imaginative study of influences on mental ability'. The dependent variable was 'mental

[11] An excellent recent example is world-systems theory. Wallerstein and his colleagues have done a genuine service in insisting that there is a global dynamic which has interconnected effects on 'economies'. But instead of making this one of the causally relevant factors, world-systems theory has tended to displace or reduce to marginality all other causes. See Giddens, 1985, pp. 161–70.

TABLE 13.1 Variances accounted for by environment and ethnicity,
Marjoribanks (1972) study[a]

Dependent variable	Independent variable	R^2	
Verbal ability	Environment + ethnicity (A)	0.61	
	Environment (B)	0.50	
	Ethnicity (C)	0.45	
	Effect of ethnicity alone = A − B =		0.11
	Effect of environment alone = A − C =		0.16
Reasoning ability	Environment + ethnicity (A)	0.22	
	Environment (B)	0.16	
	Ethnicity (C)	0.08	
	Effect of ethnicity alone = A − B =		0.06
	Effect of environment alone = A − C =		0.14

[a] This table was derived from Marjoribanks tables 5 and 6. It is in a somewhat different form from his tables.

development', which was measured by four subtests of a standard test, the SRA Primary Abilities Test: verbal, number, spatial, and reasoning. There were two independent variables, 'environmental press' and ethnic group membership, or 'ethnicity'. 'Environmental press' was measured in terms of eight 'environmental forces': 'press for achievement', 'press for intellectuality', and so on. Each in turn was specified by several indices. Marjoribanks's sample consisted of 37 families. From the quantified data derived therefrom, Marjoribanks did several multiple regressions, which are partially summarized in table 13.1.

Quoting Kerlinger's conclusions regarding this study:

Taking the values of table 13.1 at face value, we can reach two or three conclusions. Both environment and ethnicity seem to have considerable 'influence' on verbal ability, especially when they 'work together' (34 per cent). Their contributions alone, while not large, are appreciable (11 per cent and 16 per cent). The 'influence' of environment independent of ethnicity appears to be larger than the 'influence' of ethnicity independent of environment (16 per cent versus 11 per cent). A similar analysis can be applied to reasoning ability. We note especially that environment and ethnicity are not nearly as strongly related to reasoning ability as verbal ability. It is not hard to understand this rather important [sic] finding. The reason is left to the reader to deduce. (p. 176)

Kerlinger is conscientious in warning his readers that, with more than two independent variables, 'analysis and interpretation become much more complex, difficult and even elusive'. Worse, like all methods of statistical analysis, this method (multiple regression) yields only estimates of the values of the R^2s (p. 177). Finally, and 'perhaps above all, researchers will be extremely cautious about making causal statements'.

> Even though we used expressions like 'accounted for' and 'effects', causal implications, while perhaps inescapable because of language connotations, were not intended. . . . When we talk about the influence of ethnicity on verbal ability, for example, we certainly intend the meaning that the ethnic group to which a child belongs influences his verbal ability – for obvious reasons. The more accurate research statement is that there are differences in verbal ability between say, Anglo-Saxon Canadians and French Canadians. But this is a functional difference in ability in the English language. We do not mean that being Anglo-Saxon, in and of itself, somehow 'causes' better verbal ability in general than being French Canadian. The safest way to reason is probably the conditional statement emphasized through this book: If *p*, then *q*, with a relative absence of causal implication. (p. 177)

The foregoing suggests a number of important points. It shows, first, that methodologists in the social sciences are aware that a host of ordinary language expressions have, as Kerlinger says, 'causal implications', that 'influences' (notice the scare quotes in the foregoing), 'effects', 'is due to', 'accounted for', and others ordinarily connote causal efficacy in exactly the realist sense that causes *bring about their* effects.

This is the second point. On the standard (Humean) view, Kerlinger should not be uncomfortable since, on this view, 'if *p*, then *q*' is sufficient for causality. And if so, then, as the Marjoribanks study shows, since 'being Anglo-Saxon' is regularly associated with superior verbal ability, we have the causal expression 'If someone is Anglo-Saxon, then there is a probability K that this person will have verbal ability superior to. . . .' As Paul Lazarsfeld, an eminent methodologist, long ago pointed out:

> If we have a relationship between 'x' and 'y' and if for any antecedent test factor the partial relationships between 'x' and 'y' do not disappear, then the original relationship should be called a causal one. It makes no difference here whether the necessary operations are actually carried through or made possible by general reasoning. (Lazarsfeld, 1955, p. 125)

Lazarsfeld, a theorist of social science, is here consistently Humean. A matter-of-fact connection warrants the imputation of causality, for that is all that causality can mean. But Kerlinger, a pedagogue of social scientists, is not a consistent Humean. While, for him, *in the ordinary sense,* 'the ethnic group to which a child belongs influences his verbal ability – for obvious reasons', the 'more accurate' research statement is that there is a measurable difference in verbal ability between Anglo-Saxon Canadians and French Canadians. What could 'influence' here mean except that there is something about *being* Anglo-Saxon or French Canadian which *brings about* this difference? And while Kerlinger is baffled by how simply 'being Anglo-Saxon' could be a cause, it is for him, nonetheless, 'obvious' that being such 'influences' verbal ability.

In terms of the foregoing account there is no mystery here, of course. 'Ethnicity' is incarnate in speakers. The causality is complicated, but the idea is clear. If one is reared in an Anglo-Saxon household, one *learns* English as one learns the styles, customs, and rules of Anglo-Saxons!

Moreover, on the standard empiricist account of explanation, law-like statements can function in explanatory and predictive contexts. The explanation (or prediction) takes the form of *modus ponens*: If *p*, then *q* (covering law); *p*, therefore *q* (event to explained or predicted). To be sure, as Kerlinger notes, 'such explanations are necessarily only partial and incomplete', and, equivalently, predictions are not certain. This is because there are many variables, and their relationships will be complex. There are 'influences' on verbal ability other than 'ethnicity', and no one pretends that they have all been identified in their exact relation to the dependent variable. Nevertheless, this is not disheartening, since it merely sets the agenda for further research. As a psychologist faced with the same problem recently pointed out: 'The only way psychologists will ever come to understand complex psychological causation is to analyse variables, one by one, sub-set by sub-set, until whole systems of variables are understood' (Stroud, 1984, p. 92). Before concluding this chapter, I want to show that this research program is futile. But first we need to see how 'theory' relates to the foregoing.

THEORY AND EXPLANATION

Kerlinger says, 'A *theory* . . . is a set of interrelated constructs (variables), definitions, and propositions that presents a systematic view of phenomena by specifying relations among the variables, with the purpose of explaining the phenomena' (Kerlinger, 1979, p. 64). As far as I know, no one has ever given a very clear example of a real social-scientific theory spelled out so as to fit Kerlinger's definition. Presumably, everyone has the general idea, and that is sufficient. In his book, Kerlinger 'represents' a theory (of his own contrivance) by a picture (see figure 13.1).

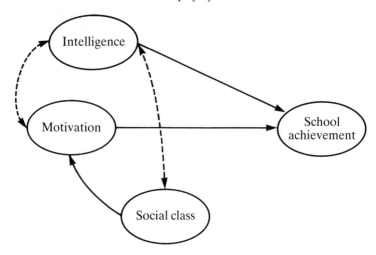

Figure 13.1   Kerlinger's 'small theory'

This 'small theory' seems close to the one Marjoribanks employed in his study. It will suffice in any case. Presumably, a researcher recognizes a pattern and generates some hypotheses regarding the relationships involved. He or she then seeks to specify quantitatively the variables involved and to discover, through analytic techniques, their precise relationships. Theory will serve to 'interpret' the results.

Consider then the relation between 'intelligence' and 'school achieve-ment'. We may guess that the correlation here will be quite high and positive. But is it merely a correlation? Consider the statements: (1) If a person scores well on standard intelligence tests, then there is a prob-ability K that he or she will be a high achiever in school, and (2) If salt is put in water, then there is a probability K that it will dissolve. *Formally*, these are identical. As regards the second there is surely a causal relationship. Indeed, it is an implication of a third statement, that salt is water-soluble, where 'water-soluble' refers to a causal power of salt (see chapter 12). In this case, moreover, we have theoretical knowledge of that causal power, of why it is that salt tends to dissolve in water.

Can similar things be said about the first statement? Plainly, there is some sort of real (non-spurious) relationship between school achieve-ment and intelligence. It is not like a high correlation, say, between the price of eggs in China and sales of the *Wall Street Journal*. But is there anything in the statement corresponding to 'water-soluble' in the third statement?

Now I do not for a moment doubt that there is, and that, therefore, one can, anti-naturalisms in the philosophy of social science notwith-standing, pursue the idea that social science searches for causes. But it will be a fundamental point of the following that the behavioral researcher, following the empiricist methodology set out by Kerlinger (and count-less others!) forbids one to do exactly what is necessary in order to advance our knowledge about what it is that corresponds to 'water-soluble'.

The point involves a tangle which takes some unravelling. It takes us back to the critique of Durkheim and involves much of what was said in this chapter and the last. In a nutshell, Kerlinger, grasps that under-standing is what science is all about, but at the same time, his empiricist commitments to methodological individualism, Humean causality, and theory as an 'interpreted' system of axioms leads him to misconstrue 'understanding' and identify it with prediction and control.

In the preceding example, 'water-soluble' refers to a causal power of salt, made intelligible by means of a grasp of theorized natural struc-tures and their dispositional properties, to $NaCl$, H_2O, and their nomic relations. A moment's reflection will lead one to see that in the first statement what corresponds to 'water-soluble' is *a social mechanism which depends on a set of structured practices,* including for example, the system of intelligence testing, the measures it employs, the nature of the tests and quizzes which are used to grade students for 'achievement', and so on. Just as a theory of the chemical properties of things gives us an understanding of the pattern 'salt tends to dissolve in water', we need a (regional) theory about schools, the structuring of their practices, and the relation of these to other causally relevant structures – those of class, the state, and so forth.

The 'small theory' represented in Kerlinger's picture (figure 13.1) is not wrong so much as seriously misleading, because it *seems* to explain but in fact does not do so. It does this exactly because we take for granted exactly what is needed to do the job of explaining. We 'know', however unreliably, something about the practices of schools. This, in fact, is 'the general reasoning' referred to by Lazarsfeld in the text quoted above. Such 'general reasoning' does indeed make it plausible that sometimes relationships among 'variables' are causal. *It is the real theory in the background of such analyses,* a real, but unstated theory, which fools us into believing that the theory which is up front, the 'partial relationships' among 'dependent' and 'independent variables', is in any way explanatory.

Behavioral researchers are misled in part because they think of their equations as being on a par with the mathematical representations familiar to physical theorists, or at least with the familiar construction of them in textbooks and standard accounts in the philosophy of science.

But, as was argued in the last chapter, one must consider what in physics or chemistry these representations represent, what they do, and how they function.

In these physical sciences, the meanings of the key concepts, symbols, and principles are not part of the explicit representation; in marked contrast to the situation with 'theories' of behavioral research, the meanings are part of a *well-established theory into which scientists are socialized* – not as in behavioral research, *the unarticulated meanings of what is taken for grtanted*. The point is central, for it is precisely here that ideology enters and wreaks its damage. This, indeed, is Veblen's point about 'the vulgar commonplace convictions' – racism, sexism, nationalism, and the 'prepossessions prevalent among those well-to-do classes'.

It is easy to forget that training to be a physicist or a biologist involves learning an enormous amount which is *unspoken,* but without which the continuing practice of science is impossible. Moreover, the implications of the genuine revolution in the received view of theory, the centrality of iconic models, of non-propositional ideas, non-deductive relationships, and intentional meanings, seem not to have made an impact on behavioral researchers. 'Theory' remains for them 'a set of interrelated constructs', innocently void of a host of meanings and assumptions which never get articulated. Physical scientists acquire the 'surplus meaning' of well-established theories in learning their craft; we are all socialized into society. Hence, it would be amazing if commonsensical 'knowledge' did not play a vital role in providing the background meaning of 'hypotheses' in social science. Indeed, it is, *unavoidable.* What is avoidable, however, is the *uncritical appropriation* of this stock of ideas. Plainly this cannot be done if, as is the case, it is not even acknowledged that 'general reasoning' is playing this explanatory role. Doesn't everyone know that women are loving and non-aggressive, that Polynesians are not ambitious, and that in a free society, if you try hard enough, you will succeed?

There is also the question of the goals of science. Kerlinger wrote that 'science is an enterprise exclusively concerned with knowledge and understanding of natural phenomena. Scientists want to understand things' (1979, p. 3). If Kerlinger is talking about the ideal of what we have called 'theoretical science' (the classical ideal of science), then this formulation is exactly correct, and it is a main point of this book to defend such a conception. Science is not one thing, however; nor – and this is more important for the present point – is behavioral research as it is practiced as interested in understanding as it is in prediction and control. Kerlinger would argue, perhaps, that to say this is to cavil; that unless the word 'understanding' is being used in some special sense, as in the way that *verstehen* sociologists use it, for example, then understanding, prediction, and control are *inherently* related. As we know, on the standard covering law model of explanation, explanation and prediction are perfectly symmetrical.

It is surely true that advances in our understanding of the properties which lie behind the manifest phenomena of the world have given us a greatly increased ability to generate technologies. Examples abound, from the biochemical knowledge of growth which has yielded improved fertilizers to the physical knowledge of the atom which has yielded weapons of horrifying destructive power. And in this sense, we increasingly make 'nature' subject to our wills. Understanding is thus connected to 'control', if control is the capacity to put natural processes to use; but 'control' in this sense is not prediction.

We can, in fact, often predict very well without having the slightest understanding; and, conversely, we can understand very well and be utterly unable to predict. We can predict when we have a reliable regularity, one that exists independently of our intervention or because of it. But in neither case, do we need to understand why the pattern occurs, what its causes are, or, in the case where we bring about some effect through some act, why our action has the predictable effect it has. Humans can predict rain by observing that, in general, ominous clouds of a characteristic sort precede it. They do not need an understanding of temperature, dewpoint, the physics of condensation, and so on. Similarly, people knew how to make a fire long before they had any understanding of combustion.

On the other hand, we can understand very well the mechanisms of combustion and fail to predict a catastrophic hotel fire. This is both typical and unsurprising. As was argued in the last chapter, what happens in the world is always the result of complex causation, so that even patterns are often and easily upset. That is, radical contingency is consistent with the lawfulness of the structures of reality. Perhaps this is obvious enough. But if it is, then why does Kerlinger assert, immediately after saying that 'science is . . . exclusively concerned with knowledge and understanding', that scientists 'want to be able to say: If we do such-and-such, then so-and-so will happen' (1979, p. 17). *Understanding has suddenly collapsed into instrumental control.*

It is clear why. If 'theory' is nothing more than 'relations of variables', and variables 'must be observable or potentially measurable or manipulable' (p. 62), then understanding necessarily becomes synonymous with prediction or instrumental control. For purposes of methodological incantations, at least, there is no surplus meaning in theory, and theory does not offer a representation of the structures of reality, structures and processes which, when cognized, would give an understanding but not, by themselves, the ability to predict or control. Theoretical science has been collapsed into its twentieth-century industrialized counterpart, technocratic science.

There is an analog to theoretical physical science in current social science. To go back to our example, if one is interested in understanding differential school achievement, then one is advised to consider the writings of Paul Goodman, John Holt, Jonathan Kozol, Charles Silberman, Stephen Steinberg, and Samuel Bowles and Herbert Gintis. Their 'theories' are not 'sets of interrelated variables', and they do not look much like the mathematical models of textbook 'theories'. Nevertheless, the writers are interested in explaining the patterns which the practices of schools generate, and they see that to do this, one must have an understanding of the underlying, connected social mechanisms. That such analyses raise the hackles of the establishment would not have surprised Veblen – or Marx.

CAUSAL ANALYSIS AND THE ANALYSIS OF VARIATION

Readers may not yet be persuaded that the realist alternative *is* an alternative; that, on the one hand, the works of the writers just cited seem hardly 'scientific', and on the other, that theory in behavioral research is aimed at discovering the causes of phenomena and that quantitative methods remain the best means to that end. I want now to argue that, if the search for causes is the aim of the standard research program, that program is futile. The reason for this is straightforward: causes are not additive, and all the quantitative methods in current use must assume that they are.

Let us return for a moment to Marjoribanks's study. The basic question was 'How do environmental force and ethnicity affect mental development?' (Kerlinger, 1979, p. 173). As seems clear, mental development is the causal outcome of a complex epigenetic process which begins with conception and ends with the death of the organism. A particular genome, itself the product of the conjunction of haploid sex cells is, in embryogenesis, the locus of continuous transactions both in itself and in relation to its 'environment'. It subsequently emerges from the womb and is then in continuous transaction with a human environment. Through both of these conditions, as biologist Paul Weiss says, 'the latitude for epigenetic vagaries of the component elements on all levels . . . is immense'.

Marjoribanks aims to tackle a piece of these complicated problems and to do this by discovering how each of the independent variables separately affects mental development and how they affect it in concert

(1979, p. 173). It is not denied, of course, that heredity influences mental development. The aim, presumably, is to better understand the role of social factors. I earlier summarized the sources of the data. What is now needed is to calculate several regression equations. These are of the form: $Y = a + b_1X_1 + b_2X_2$, where Y is the dependent variable (for example, mental development); a is a constant which is irrelevant for present purposes; X_1 and X_2 are independent variables (for example, 'environmental force' and 'ethnicity'); and b_1 and b_2 are regression coefficients, which, as multipliers of the independent variables, weight them, as is obvious. Moreover, as is also obvious, the independent variables are taken to have additive features.

Determining the regression coefficients is not easy, but the details need not trouble us here. All that is necessary here is to emphasize that 'regression equations give the best possible prediction given sets of data. No other equation will give us as good a prediction' (p. 170). That is, the test of the adequacy of any particular equation will be its predictive success, given the set of data.

The upshot then will be the determination of R, the coefficient of multiple correlation. This is determined by correlating two sets of scores, the Ys calculated ('predicted') from the regression equations and the actual Ys, as specified by independent measures of Y. Given R, we can then calculate R^2, which expresses the variance of the dependent variable accounted for by the regression combination of the independent variables.

To recur to the study (see table 13.1 above), the correlation between verbal ability, a measure of mental development, and the combination of environment and ethnicity (as measured by Marjoribanks's various measures), R, was 0.78, and thus R^2 was 0.61. This means that '61% of the variance of verbal ability was accounted for by environment and ethnicity in combination'. Separate regressions between verbal ability and environment and between verbal ability and ethnicity yielded 0.50 and 0.45, respectively. By substracting these from 0.61 we get 'the separate effects' of environment and ethnicity; thus 16 per cent of the variance in verbal ability is 'accounted for' by environment alone.

This perhaps unduly detailed summary, unnecessary for those familiar with the technique, has at least made clear that if this is causal analysis, causes must be additive. But of course, except for mechanical causation, represented by vectors of forces, causes are not additive. In consequence, the foregoing 'analysis' is almost totally *meaningless*.

The near meaninglessness of this 'competent and imaginative study' is perhaps most convincingly demonstrated by comparing it to typical studies in biology which study the relationship of 'heredity' to 'environment'.

If we take a particular genotype – for example, seeds replicated by inbreeding or cloning (this minimizes genotypic individuality, a dominant feature of human genotypes) – and place specimens in various controlled environments, it is possible to establish rough tables of correspondence between phenotype on the one hand, and genotype-environmental combinations on the other. The results, *never predictable in advance,* give what is called 'the norm of reaction' of that genotype, its 'range of reaction' to environmental variations. Now, it is not possible to predict these norms because – and this is crucial – 'genetic' and 'environmental' factors are not additive. They are *causes in transaction,* which are not independent and which do not interact like vectors of force. That is, because 'genes' cause different outcomes in different transactions, and because the developmental process is mediated and transactional, the latitude for vagaries, as Weiss noted, is immense. Of course, it is not unlimited, and thus one can arrive empirically at norms of reaction in such cases.

Multiple regression techniques are *not* meaningless *given* that such norms *have been established experimentally.* Across a range of environments in which independent variables have been specified and controlled, one can relate the variability in outcome with changes in the independent variables. In a word, one can produce meaningful R^2s. This will not, it should be emphasized, show what proportion of the causation is attributable to what component, since causation does not suddenly become additive. One will have, however, a satisfactory analysis of the variations.

There is a parallel here to Marjoribanks's study, yet there is a gigantic difference. As regards Marjoribanks's project, there is no experimental way to establish norms of reaction. In the first place, we are limited morally. We cannot clone fetuses and establish them in strictly controlled environments. But were this permissible, there would still be no way to specify all the relevant environmental variables, precisely because they are not independent. The social world is real enough, but the mere fact that, *necessarily,* the social world is mediated by consciousness makes it impossible to say how controlled changes are related to what stays the same and how the new condition is then *experienced* by agents. Compare here a change in the amount of nitrogen in the soil as it bears on the development of a cloned seed of grain and a change in the physical environment of an infant on development. Clearly, causes are profoundly mediated in the course of an organism's development, and even the language of transaction – as opposed to interaction – is a radical oversimplication of the causal reality.

Of course, social scientists, including here psychologists, have always known this, and we may assume that this *a* reason why prediction becomes the sole test of the adequacy of the measures and equations. We simply rework the specifications and relations, from 'predicted' to actual, until we get a good fit. But the justification in terms of 'good prediction' is profoundly reinforced by Humean assumptions about causality and by technocratic assumptions about 'explanation'.

On the covering law model, explanation and prediction are symmetrical, and with this conception of explanation, it is necessary only that there is a constant relation between the independent and the dependent variable. Given the extraordinary limits on experimentation in the social sciences, it is no wonder, then, that regression techniques, path analyses, and so on are so attractive. Given all these assumptions, one can be a real scientist without having a theory and without ever doing a real experiment. All we need is data – and plenty of it!

14

Psychology:
Theoretical and Applied

Perhaps 10,000 of the more than 60,000 accredited psychologists in the English-speaking world are engaged in what might be called basic research in cognition and learning, perception, memory, and motivation. The others have primary interests in other areas, although, of course, their work may draw on advances made in basic research. For example, educational psychology concerns itself with learning, motivation, and the rest, but seeks to apply such knowledge to specific problems in school settings. While there are a host of 'specialties' in psychology, there would be widespread agreement among the 60,000 that their interest as psychologists is in 'behavior'. This does not mean, of course, that most of them are 'behaviorists', for the trajectory of behaviorism in psychology, in its 'classical' form in Watson, in the forms it took in the 1940s with the work of Tolman, Hull, and Guthrie, and in the still later Skinnerian form, while it left definite marks and still has enthusiastic supporters, would seem to have run its course (Koch, 1964; Margolis, 1984). On the other hand, not only has the many-roomed mansion of psychology not found a way to integrate its concerns (Staats, 1983), but there is considerable disagreement among basic researchers about how to proceed.

I will argue in this chapter that there is a program of basic psychological research which defines psychology as an autonomous science, neither biology on the one hand nor social science on the other. Spelling this out is not easy, for there are some deep conceptual issues at stake. On the present view, the problem of an autonomous scientific psychology has been intractable because of a series of historically engendered false notions: mistaken ideas about epistemology and the very idea of science (see chapter 12), mistaken notions about the goals of a scientific psychology (see chapter 9), and, finally, a failure to be clear on the relationship of the biological to the psychological, and of the psychological to the social. The first is the legacy of Cartesian dualism; the last of an epistemological individualism in which social processes, while acknowledged, are substantially ignored. These failures can be corrected with an alternative realist understanding.

STRATIFICATION AND EMERGENCE
IN THE HUMAN SCIENCES

If we look at a person from the point of view of biology (including biochemistry), we can speak of an organism which is an ordered complex of orderly complex systems. Roughly, biochemistry starts from the level of atoms and molecules and works upward through the larger and more complex molecules to complicated systems which we normally identify as biological – organelles, cells, tissues, and organs – and finally to the organism itself. As I have already argued, these systems are not givens, but emerge as inquiry proceeds. Further, each of the theories, aiming to explain processes at some level taken by itself, has an impoverished view of the whole, and, while it is sometimes convenient to speak of the 'building blocks' of nature or life, the metaphor is misleading insofar as it leads us to imagine that 'whole/part' relations are additive or conjunctive. On such a view, hierarchies can be 'decomposed' without doing violence to theoretically individuated systems which are 'parts' of larger unities. The whole, however, *is* greater than the sum of its parts. What is required is an appropriately healthy notion of causality in which causes in cooperation produce effects. We can then say that processes affect processes at higher *and* at lower levels of functioning. Activities within some system may have, as the outcome of their causal transactions with other processes, properties at more inclusive higher levels, properties not predicable of the structures at the lower levels. Proteins functioning in larger systems are capable of at least eight major activities of which the amino acids from which they are polymerized are not capable. Complete information about all the atomic positions of an unknown protein does not allow us to infer even that the protein is an enzyme, for example, still less what, in a specific system, its specific causal properties or 'functions' might be.

It is critical here to emphasize that higher-level activities have effects on lower-level structures and activities. Thus, from the most elementary levels – for example, the action of the DNA molecule – to the actions of whole organisms, there are principles of control, setting 'boundary conditions', as it were, and 'ruling' finer-grained processes and activities. Pattee (1976) writes: 'Coordination in biological organisms takes the form of hierarchical controls which at each level provide greater and greater freedom or adaptability for the whole organism by selectively adding more and more constraints to its component parts' (p. 154).[1] The coordinated movements of an organism are paradigmatic. The act of grasping a limb, for example, imposes fantastic constraints on the pertinent systems: perceptual, muscular, and so on. Indeed, Pribram (1971) has offered substantial evidence for the hypothesis that 'acts' – not mere 'movements' – are represented in the cerebral cortex.

Sometimes the emergent properties and 'control' mechanisms are those which our ordinary experience singles out as fundamental. These insure the pertinence of the operative distinctions between the living and the non-living, the sentient and the non-sentient, the minded and the unminded. Life and mind, however, are activities, just like magnetism or oxidation – even if from the point of view of our human interests, there are enormous differences between the activities, 'functional properties', or causal powers, of the inorganic by contrast with the living, and as regards the minded by contrast with the unminded.

The picture is not yet complete, however. Persons are surely minded, but they are best conceived as culturally emergent in exactly the sense that they have capacities (properties, causal powers) – for example, linguistic abilities – predicable of them only by virtue of the causal outcomes of the development of their biological complexity in a social environment. Our problem, then, is to see if this stratified picture of the person allows for a distinctly psychological science and, if so, what its nature and problems are.

'NATURE' AND 'NURTURE'

No one denies that human beings are both biological and cultural, and, accordingly, that how they behave is 'determined' by both biology and culture. But haunting human studies from antiquity has been the problem of how to study this complexity. The problem is tractable, however, once we see that the explanation of behavior is not the proper goal of a theoretical psychology.

We need to notice first that, because causation is not additive (excepting mechanical causation), there is no way, in the epigenetic develop-

---

[1] Even at the level of cells, there is 'control', Polanyi (1968) writes: 'In each embryonic cell there is present the duplicate of a DNA molecule which, being independent of the chemical forces within the DNA molecules, conveys a rich amount of meaningful information. As we see that when this information is shaping the growing embryo, it produces boundary conditions which, themselves being independent of the physical-chemical forces in which they are rooted, control the mechanism of life in the developed organism' p. 133).

ment of an individual, to specify the proportion of causation which can be attributed to 'nature' (heredity/biology) versus the proportion which can be attributed to the 'environment', and, critically, to the *sui generis* real social environment (see chapter 13). This means that it is simply false to say (as some textbooks do) that heredity sets the limits but environment determines the extent of development within those limits (see Hirsch, 1976; Lewontin, 1976). The problem is exactly that there is no specifiable limit independent of some particular transaction with some particular environment, and that differences in the environment make for differences in the limits.

The debate over sociobiology is pertinent here. As Gould (1981) has argued, this debate is often misconceived as a debate over the breadth of ranges. For sociobiologists, 'ranges are narrow enough to program a specific behavior as the predictable result of possessing certain genes. Critics argue that the ranges permitted by these genetic factors are wide enough to include all behaviors that sociobiologists atomize into distinct traits coded by separate genes' (p. 329). But, as Gould points out, there is no 'smooth continuum' here. Rather, at issue are two different theories about the *role* of biological factors in human behavior. 'The sociobiologists have made a fundamental mistake in categories. They are seeking the genetic basis of human behavior *at the wrong level*' (p. 329; my emphasis). More generally, for the biological determinist, the strata have effectively collapsed; instead of seeing that the psychological is the real and causally efficacious part-product of lower-level processes, he ignores the psychological level altogether.

To clarify this fundamental point, we will suggest a plausible sense for the expression 'biologically (or genetically) determined'. Let us say that some capacity, trait, or difference true of humans is biologically determined only if, in realizing that trait, the developing conceptus undergoes a characteristic human development such that it is substantially irrelevant where or when that process occurs. Of course, there is no 'characteristic human development' since 'normal human development' is consistent with a fantastic range of very different environments. Nevertheless, the idea is familiar enough.[2] What is intended has three aspects. First, I want to put aside all the biological questions regarding how DNA, the 'genetic code', and so forth, in cooperation with some environment, give rise to traits through the genotype to the phenotype. Second, I want (at least for the moment) to rule out environmental

---

[2] The foregoing is a way to clarify what Barnes (1976) called 'natural rationality'. We should notice that, strictly speaking, nothing is genetically determined if this means that a sufficient causal condition is the gene arrangement. DNA and RNA, of course, are causally efficacious, but organisms are always products of complex mediations within and without the genome. This explains, of course, the enormous variability in the bounded processes.

'accidents', such as thalidomide babies. Third, and most crucially, I want to acknowledge that humans need a human environment in order to develop, but to make social and cultural differences ideally irrelevant.

Are there traits which are biologically determined in this weakened sense. Of course there are. Humanness is one of them. But this suggests a role for a psychological science. Humanness is an abstraction, but knowledge of *human* powers is genuine, important knowledge. Indeed, it seems hard to deny that there are *psychological* processes which can be explained solely in terms that include the biological and at the same time exclude whatever pertains to acquiring the skills and habits of a particular human culture (Margolis, 1984, p. 68). After all, at least the *potentialities* for human perception, learning, affective response, and so on must be more or less available as conditions for the realization of these processes in the developing organism.

Traits which we have by virtue of our humanness are aptly sum-marized under the rubric 'human nature', since all humans have them simply by virtue of being human. We can see here the connections between *strong* theories of human nature, methodological individualism in social theory (see chapter 3), epistemological individualism in psy-chology (see below), *and* the failure to define a role for psychology. If human nature is ascribed specific contents, specific inclinations, desires, cognitive styles, and beliefs even, we can *deduce* a social theory (Hobbes or Kropotkin!). On the other hand, if 'human nature' is an entirely *empty* idea, then there is *no* science between biology and sociology.

Of course, while we share a human nature, there are differences between us; some of these are biologically determined (in the special weakened sense defined above). Sexual dimorphism would seem to be one. I say 'would seem' here because, although some writers insist that an individual is 'either definitely male or female' (Dawkins, 1976), this may not be so. Thus, even within the obviously biological realm, the idea of a characteristic human development is not innocent. The presence of a Y-chromosome would seem to be necessary for the development of a male, since this is a crucial causal factor in the production of male testes, which in turn secrete androgens that virilize the developing organism. Moreover, it has been speculated that appropriate amounts of androgen must be present at certain times, otherwise 'feminization' may result. The possibility, then, of a set of intersecting variables, rather than an absolute sexual dichotomy, is not at all implausible.

Other biologically determined differences include manifest traits which mark family resemblances, such as facial features, coloration, and body-type. Some of these (or these taken together) allow us to distin-guish larger groupings of people, so that 'family' gets extended to 'people' and to 'race'. One can, of course, raise some very serious questions about the concept 'race', especially from the point of view of biology. It is possible to define races as 'populations which differ in the relative commonness of some of their genes' or as 'populations which differ in the frequencies of some gene or genes'. The point is that the idea of race is highly relative. Indeed, Lewontin has demonstrated that 85.4 per cent of the variation in 17 genes coded with differences in blood occurred within local populations *within* a 'race'. He provides a dramatic illustration: 'If the holocaust comes and a small tribe in the New Guinea forests are the only survivors, *almost all* of the genetic variation now expressed among the innumerable groups of our four billion people will be preserved (quoted in Gould, 1981, p. 323).

Finally, in addition to these more or less evident differences among persons and groups of persons, we must include as biologically determined the not so manifest differences which fall under various biological descriptions; for example, blood type, a host related to sex, such as levels of testosterone, and differences in the brains and central nervous systems of individuals and perhaps, as well, of groups or sexes.

THE CONFUSION OF LEVELS

But what needs to be noticed here is that these neurophysiological (and other biologically determined) characteristics (and differences) constitute only potentialities at the level of realized competences and behaviors; that, while at the neurophysiological level, they are actual, because they are but part-causes of the competences and acts of developing (and developed) persons, their effects at the level of these competences and acts will, in general, be *highly various and unpredictable*.

Consider here athletic ability, with its manifest relation to physiological characteristics. Julius Erving has to have the body he has in order to be the marvellous athlete he is; but he is the marvellous athlete he is because of a great deal more. His quickness, his remarkable leaping ability, and his height do not make him a great athlete, still less a great basketball player. Had he not spent many hours learning to play, he might simply have been another tall man. Even his quickness and leaping ability might have gone unnoticed until they atrophied as potentialities. Athletic ability, like music ability and many others as well, does require particular inherited potentialities; but they become concrete actualities only because of some specific process of social learning, where, as noted the transactional mix is indeterminate.

It was useful to begin with athletic ability because the prerequisite potentialities are more or less on the surface. A person has the right sort of body for basketball or he does not; and similarly as regards musical ability, a person has a good acoustical sense, can 'carry a tune', or he can not. Consider, then, less obviously biologically determined characteristics, the laterality of the brain, for example. Brain scientists tell us that the two hemispheres of the brain are 'functionally distinct, developmentally different and perhaps programmed for asymmetry along a left-right gradient'. Moreover, while neither half functions even relatively independently of the other, there are, it seems, definite, but contestably described differences in *psychologically* characterized processes. Bradshaw writes that 'in the search for a more fundamental mode of hemispheric specialization, several versions of an *analytic* (serial, focal, difference-detecting, time-dependent, sequential) versus *holistic* (parallel, diffuse, similarity-detecting, time-independent, spatial, global, synthetic or gestalt) dichotomy have independently surfaced' (Bradshaw and Nettleton, 1981). Presumably, then, a 'bias' toward the left hemisphere would be a bias toward 'language skills'.

Since it can hardly be doubted that brain function is causally pertinent to psychologically characterized functions and powers, including linguistic competence, it will be useful to pursue this example and to apply our analysis to recent arguments over putative sex-related differences. Thus, it might be argued that the relative superiority of (a fictitious) Philip over his fraternal twin Margaret in mathematical skills is adequately explained by recognizing that male brains tend toward greater lateralization, which makes for a distinct advantage in mathematical ability. It is of some interest to note that a number of feminist writers have in effect agreed with this line of argument in maintaining that women, by virtue of being women, tend to more holistic modes of thought (see Fox Keller, 1985).[3]

No claim need be made on this view that *all* males will be relatively advantaged (disadvantaged); nor should it be forgotten that a host of complicated factors enter in outcomes in particular cases. Nevertheless, so the argument goes, given the empirically established sex-related modal differences in mathematical ability, especially in the case of fraternal twins reared in the same family, the account seems adequate. Indeed, it seems to approximate satisfaction of Mill's Method of Difference. Since sex is the most obvious factor with regard to the differences in this particular competence, it would seem to be sex-linked.

---

[3] Some accounts are sufficiently vague on the critical points at issue to be vulnerable to needless criticism of reverse sexism, in which all the 'good' human qualities are 'female'. Ferguson's excellent *The Feminist Case against Bureaucracy* is perhaps a case in point. She writes, for example, 'that the gender-defined worlds of women and men are created in part by the developmental consequences of our culture's parenting practices' (p. 161). Does the 'in part' here leave space for subsequent social training or prior constraints? The thrust of her account is that the whole business can be accounted for in strictly social terms.

This is, I believe, a best case, but, accordingly, it is critical to see why ultimately it fails as an explanation. On the positive side, it is a best case because not only are there empirical studies which show that males and females rate differently in mathematical ability, but, critically, we have here a theoretically vindicable *mechanism,* differential functions in brain laterality which could *explain* the generalization. This mechanism is far more relevant to the competence at issue than a great many others which might be invoked, especially those at a deeper, more basic level – for example, hormonal differences or differences in terms of cellular microprocesses. To argue from 'genes' to behavior is extraordinary, since genes result in complexly structured whole organisms which are multi-caused; to argue from brain function to behavior does not require an extraordinary leap, even if, as I shall argue, it is illicit.

There are a number of significant points to be made. First, the causal mechanism involves a sex-linked tendency or 'bias', as regards laterality. But tendencies are not in themselves probabilities (see chapter 12). We can say, however, that a tendency will, *ceteris paribus,* he realized, meaning by this that if the causal conditions defined by the *ceteris paribus* are satisfied, the tendency is realized. As regards the tendency towards, say, right laterality, we are at present in no position to specify the relevant *ceteris paribus* clauses. This would require detailed knowledge of the originating androgen-mediated neurohumoral interactions and of the complicated ways in which they interact with other causally relevant mechanisms, including those in the environment of the developing child. In the absence of such knowledge, we cannot say what would account for a failure of the tendency to be realized. We assume in the case of Margaret and Philip that hypothesized differential tendencies in laterality explain the disparity in mathematical competence; but, in the absence of any direct evidence, this remains speculative.

But even if sex-linked biases as regards laterality are realized in the cases of Philip and Margaret – something which cannot establish (at least now) – there remains a considerable causal gap between such neurophysiological facts and manifest global traits and competences. There are three points to be made here. First, it is clear that highly variable social learning is involved in achieving whatever degree of competence is achieved, and that the specific expression of this competence in action will be profoundly influenced by the social environment in which it is exercized. Indeed, it is fair to say that, because the human brain is the primary organ of *human* potentiality, it will be the causal transaction with culture that will be most pertinent in 'determining' the specific desires, beliefs, attitudes, even cognitive and emotive styles possessed and displayed by people. This, of course, is the dominant theme of psychological theories which emphasize the social in the construction of human psychology (Harré and Secord, 1973). Indeed, insofar as their concern is 'behavior' (broadly construed), they are correct in so doing. In this sense, different cultures determine different *forms of humanness* (Herder), and differences in micro-social processes in development – for example, differences in child-rearing practices – are critical in generating differences in our personal powers, desires, attitudes, and liabilities (Dewey, 1922; Shotter, 1984). These differences, of course, are of interest to us. But on the present view, inquiry into them is *not* part of an autonomous psychological science, precisely because these are socially determined. Rather, such inquiry is part of the subject-matter of the social sciences, including social psychology.

On the other hand, a scientific psychology can plausibly direct its attention toward an understanding of the powers *shared* by humans – how we think, learn, desire and so on – precisely because within an extraordinary range of variation in the social environment, *all* humans acquire cognitive and affective competences, all learn, and all develop distinctly human capacities.

Moreover, not only is the social environment critical in determining the specific content of the psychological, but it may well be that the neurological mechanisms are themselves alterable as a consequence of differences in the social environment (Blackmore and Cooper, 1970). Either way, just as we can think of a culturally indifferent environment in order to identify humanness as biologically determined, so we can think of a biologically indifferent *human* nature but where realized human forms and differences are socially determined. Margaret's lag behind her brother in mathematics (and her greater capacity for holistic thought) may be *entirely* due to social factors which affect their expression *or* their realization, either because the neural mechanisms have themselves been affected or merely because inappropriate social learning has taken place, a possibility exploited by much sound and some unsound current rhetoric.

The foregoing considerations, it should be emphasized, throw into chaos ideological interests in grounding claims to 'natural' eminences of competences and traits – of individuals, sexes, or populations. But they constitute no obstacle to achieving a more adequate understanding of the mechanisms which define our *human* nature. Father may be concerned as to why Johnny is a quicker learner than Billy, but, lacking any sort of adequate account of how either of them learn *anything,* we are unlikely to get much help from psychology. The American institutionalization of psychology as a science, motivated by technocratic interests and influenced by Galton and nineteenth-century biological racism, led to an emphasis on 'the psychology of individual differences'. When this was added to the prevailing sexism, inquiry into the generalized normal human adult mind took second place. The question 'How do we learn?' is scientifically tractable, but countless research projects have been funded to discover 'why we are all different' – even if, as noted, an adequate account of our human powers would seem to be a prerequisite for other concerns, whether these interests be well- or ill-motivated.

A second problem over levels is this: whereas global competences, mathematical or linguistic skills, say, stand in some relation to the abstractly (and contestably) characterized attributes which brain research has revealed, attributes labelled as 'focal', 'diffuse', 'time-dependent', and so on, how these are related to global competences is by no means clear. At least, it is considerably less clear than how manifest physical traits – for example, leaping ability or height – are related to basketball ability. The causal relationships among human competences, abstractly characterized functions, and the neuro-anatomical description of laterality are, to say the least, complex. We have, at present, only the most tenuous knowledge of the *mechanisms* which relate cognition to 'analytic' cognitive processes (psychologically characterized!) to brain function. Indeed, this would seem to be exactly the point of psychology as a science!

One final observation is suggested by our example. We must not confuse the two sentences 'Female brains are left-biased,' and 'The female brain is left-biased,' since not only are tendencies sometimes not realized or are realized in highly various ways, but it seems that males can have 'female brains' and conversely. This well illustrates the role of laws in a properly understood conception of science and the world. We may take the best case and assume that there is a well-established biological law relating sex and brain-laterality. We might also assume a *psychological* law relating brain laterality with cognitive function. But these laws will have the form 'A tends to L-ness by virtue of being female,' and 'A tends to C-ness (a cognitive function) by virtue of lateralization L of the brain,' laws which are perfectly consistent with the empirical fact that some females will not manifest C-ness and that some males may. 'A tends to be water-soluble by virtue of being sugar' is sufficiently law-like, but, of course, samples of sugar do *not* always dissolve in water, and there are other compounds which sometimes do.[4]

---

[4] It was argued in chapter 12 that generalizations – for example, 'Females have more holistic cognitive styles' – do not explain specific instances. It will be admitted that when it is *known* that there is no causal relation, direct or mediated, connecting correlated phenomena, appeal to a generalization is patently non-explanatory (even if it remains predictive). But the same considerations apply where the factor is causally implicated but where further information is needed to know exactly the role played by that causal mechanism in the outcome. As was said, this is especially problematic when the factor is a deep-level and complexly mediated factor; where, for example, the reference is to genes, hormones, or brain function. More generally, it is easy to diagnose the objection that an

THE LIMITS OF A SCIENTIFIC PSYCHOLOGY

The limits of a scientific psychology can now be seen more clearly. As humans, we are interested in explanations of why particular people have the particular traits, competences, personalities, attitudes, beliefs, and disabilities which they have. If the foregoing is correct, however, we should not expect a Copernican Revolution in our ability to provide answers to these questions. No two human genotypes are the same, a fact of considerable relevance to the problem. From the moment of conception, the developmental process is epigenetic. Well before the fetus emerges into a social world, the latitude for epigenetic vagaries is immense. After that, everything that happens is an indiscriminable mix of nature and nurture, biology and culture. When, then, our concern is the distinctly *psychological* – the personality, competences and disabilities, beliefs, attitudes, styles, and dispositions – isolating the pertinent causal factors which make for our fantastic human diversity will be profoundly difficult. As William James rightly observed, human individuality is absurd, ultimately inexplicable.

We can, of course, hope to know more than we do – for example, about schizophrenia or learning disabilities – but, as suggested, this knowledge presupposes improved knowledge of the mechanisms of minded beings, of learning, of how individuals appropriate the social mind and make it their own, and more. We may hope to do better in generating ameliorative technologies, both social and psychiatric, *even in the absence* of much improvement in our knowledge of the causal mechanisms which together make for our incompetences and disabilities. Indeed, in this context, it is more than remarkable that we do not put to work what we do know – for example, that we do not eliminate unhealthy conditions of work and housing, that we allow poverty and malnutrition to exist, knowing that it maims and destroys human potentialities.

Finally, we should not expect a Copernican Revolution in our ability to explain the behavior of persons. By and large, we do very well in this (as Weber insisted). For the most part, our appeal to an agent's conscious motives, beliefs, intentions, and attitudes serves to give an

---

explanation is racist or sexist. In isolating one causal factor, the sex or race of a person, without being clear as to how – or indeed, if – it is causally implicated, such explanations make that factor, in essence, the differentiating causal factor. It is thus an error to 'explain' black poverty in the fashion of the Moynihan report by appeal to statistics regarding the differential family structures of white and black Americans. It is an error to explain, in the fashion of Jensen and co-workers, modal differences in IQ scores between races on the basis of inheritance.

adequate explanation of what the agent in question does. If it did not, human life would be impossible. 'Folk psychology' is not 'scientific psychology', but, contrary to the claims of some (for example, Stitch, 1983), if the foregoing is correct, scientific psychology is not a *replacement* for it either.

This is not to say that the acts of persons are uncaused or that the complicated processes in transaction at various levels do not participate in behavioral outcomes. Some of these micro-processes are necessary if there is to be any behavior at all, and some of them have obvious effects on behavior as they are mediated through the various levels. Too much alcohol acting on one's nerve cells obviously affects one's behavior. Nevertheless, what a person does is ultimately 'under the control' of what that person *decides* to do. Of course, what a person decides to do is 'determined' by that person's attitudes, beliefs, motives, and so on, and these too are complicated causal products. The bogey of determinism, however, is only a bogey, in part the product of the pervasive Kantian view which was motivated to save God, Freedom, and Immortality from the mechanical materialists of the eighteenth century. In this view, if the human 'will' is caused, then no efficacy is to be granted to human initiative. But, as noted, behind this is the block universe of the regularity determinists with a conception of law, causality, and system closure which allows for no contingency *anywhere,* neither in nature nor in history.[5]

FUNCTIONALISM IN PSYCHOLOGY

In this part, I turn more directly to the mind/body problem and try to sharpen the account developed in the foregoing. Recent 'functionalism' is a convenient point of departure. We should first notice that the sense of 'functionalism' in this context, though related to some uses of the term in the social sciences, must be distinguished from these. It must also be sharply distinguished from the sense put forward by Skinner (1953), who, appealing to the mathematical use of 'function', held that his explanations were functional. For Skinner, one 'explains' by showing that some 'variable' is a function of some other variable.

In the present context, 'functionalism' refers to the idea that one can distinguish between the physical properties and the functional properties of a system, between its 'structure' and its 'activities'. All physical systems, automobile engines, computers, biochemical systems, and so

---

[5] The reader may be reminded that while it is the problem characteristic of reductive materialism (as noted below), all regularity theories of scientific law share it. (See Bhaskar, 1978, ch. 2; compare also the account of Pareto, above, in chapter 8.)

on have physical properties, but what they do, their activities or 'functions', cannot be described exclusively in terms of their physical structure and organization. For example, enzyme activity is not describable in terms of molecular structure alone. In the philosophy of psychology, functionalism offers a way to distinguish between psychological properties and physical properties. Thus, psychological properties – for example, the abstract characterization of brain laterality as 'difference detecting', 'focal', and so forth – are functional characterizations or activities of the physical states and processes of hemispheres of the brain.

This approach had hoped to dodge the mind/body problem, since it could be held that one need not be concerned with the ontological issues in order to concede the usefulness of descriptions which employ 'mental terms'. We need not ascribe a mental life to a computer programmed for chess to be able to say intelligibly that it 'castled' its king. Moreover, as Margolis (1984) points out, in its usual forms, ontic *dualism* is compatible with functionalism. Margolis went to the heart of the matter by noting that there are two fundamental questions which can be asked. First, are the functional properties heuristically or realistically ascribed? Second, are functional properties abstract properties, or are they merely abstracted from complex properties?

If we say that the computer castled, it is clear that the ascription is heuristic. Similarly, saying that a plant is 'searching for nutrients' is heuristic. As Margolis notes, employed in this way, we would seem to be bound to the reductionist move that these ascriptions are eliminable. Functional properties are *replaced* by causal mechanisms. As computers do not really 'castle', and plants do not really 'search', these locutions could be eliminated in favor of scientifically respectable causal language. Indeed, for the physicalist, they could be eliminated from a science of psychology. As Rorty (1979) put the matter, 'every speech, thought, theory, poem, composition, and philosophy will turn out to be completely predictable in purely naturalistic terms. Some atoms-and-the-void account of micro-processes within individual human beings will permit the prediction of every sound or inscription which will ever be uttered. There are no ghosts' (p. 387).

Between this extremely radical claim and the innocuous claim that the central nervous system is the 'basis' of psychological phenomena is the question of whether neural and biochemical processes and relations can *explain* psychological phenomena. But this question is ambiguous, since those who ask it vacillate between holding that the psychological phenomena to be explained are real and they are not real. In the former case, we have 'stratified monism'; in the latter, a reductive monism (usually a reductive materialism or physicalism). On the latter view, higher-level principles and activities become otiose: once explained, they become unnecessary for the explanation of the phenomena at that level. Indeed, the 'level' has disappeared! In this sense, the 'explanation' of life processes in terms of chemistry makes biology otiose as a science.

It is quite clear that biochemical investigations of the life processes are not committed to reductive materialism. No biochemist denies the reality of emergent life processes. Indeed, it seems that biology as an autonomous science is here to stay. What of psychology? Bhaskar has provided an ingenious argument which shows that reductive materialism as regards psychology leads to bizarre conclusions. The argument is as follows. Suppose B says to A 'Pass the salt,' and A does so. Call this action Xa. Then, either Xa is the unique causal consequence of neurophysiological states, N_1, N_2 ... N_n, such that Xa would have been performed without B's action; or B's action is a causal element in bringing about Xa. Now if the first, reductionist materialism implies 'a form of Leibnitzian pre-established harmony of monads, in which each person's neurophysiology is so synchronized with every other's that it appears as if they were talking and laughing, smiling and winking' (Bhaskar, 1979, p. 135). But if the second, since the relation between A and B is hermeneutic and involves more than a physical relation between A and B, the psychological states of A and B are irreducibly real and yet have causal efficacy. As Bhaskar points out, it was not, strictly speaking, necessary to introduce two people for this sort of argument, since we need only acknowledge that the neurophysiological closure is broken when a person, responding to a sudden shower, for example, opens her umbrella to keep from getting wet! Indeed, it is not even necessary to have *people* in the account, since *neural* closure is broken when an animal *sees* a *threatening* object and takes evasive action. One might try to cling to reductive materialism while admitting this. The price to be paid is the block universe of Laplacean determinism – universal system closure – in which *nothing* is contingent.

On the other hand, if functional properties are realistically ascribed, then they are either abstract properties *or* properties abstracted from more complex properties. The difference is critical, but it does not relate to the potential eliminability of functional properties. On both views, functional properties are not eliminable in favor of (purely) physical properties.

Consider the second alternative. In this case, the properties are real only when physically realized *in some particular way*. They are, as Margolis says 'not (merely) functional ... but *incarnate*' (Margolis, 1984, p. 52). We have already used this idea in talking about society, and we used it in that context to assent to the methodological individualist point that society is made up only of people and the products of their activity; that one need not postulate an independent 'thing' or things to make sense of the *sui generis* reality of the social. The move here is analogous. We need not move to ontic dualism to make sense of the *sui generis* reality (and hence, causal efficacy) of the mental. The 'emergent realist functionalism' of the present view thus holds that:

1   A given system has physical properties; it includes such and such components and is structured so and so.
2   Its activities ('functions') may not be described solely in terms of (1).
3   It has whatever 'functions' it has *by virtue* (at least) *of* (1).

What discriminates between the emergent realism defended here and ontic dualism is the third item, which commits us to the incarnate character of the second.

It is important to see that the third item does not merely say that the activities of which the system is capable need *some* incarnation (or other). For then, what that incarnation is, is psychologically irrelevant. The classic formulation is found in the work of Putnam (1967, 1975). If we consider a Turing machine (an abstract computer with a finite number of internal configurations each of which involves the machine being in one of a finite number of states), then it is clear that it can be *described completely* in terms of these states and the ordered sequences of which it is capable – its 'machine table'. But since such a machine can be realized in an infinite number of ways, mechanical, electronic, and biological, it is clear that we can comprehend its activities *without* concerning ourselves with any particular physical realization. In parallel fashion, psychology can proceed independently of neurophysiology.

We can now see how this version implies an ontic dualism. The properties are real and abstract – not *merely abstracted from* more complex physical properties. If so, they are not *merely sui generis* real, but *independently* real. Put another way, since they are only contingently linked to their realizations, they are ontically distinct.

For the ontic dualist, mind/body interaction remains causally intractable. For the emergent realist, we *explain* functions (activities) precisely by showing that they are the (causal) consequences of the particular physical processes which incarnate them. Indeed, the point holds generally with regard to all systems characterized by the items in our list. Thus, enzymes are constituted of particular organizations of atomic structures (1), but the activities of an enzyme cannot be described solely in terms of the atomic structure of the molecule which constitutes it (2). Yet, according to (3), enzymes do what they do *by virtue of* (at least) their particular structures. The causal explanation of activities (functions, causal powers) in terms of the 'mechanisms' in which they are incarnate is *just what counts as explanation.*

These last considerations suggest that to the three characteristics of emergent realist functionalism identified above, we should add a fourth:

4 At the level of functioning as a system, system properties may causally affect the structure and functioning of the system's component processes.

This allows us to acknowledge, for example, that as in control systems theory, 'feedback' plays a role in system functioning (Dewan, 1976); that the properties of the molecule 'constrain' nuclear forces in chemical transactions (Polanyi, 1968); and finally, as Sperry (1969) puts it, 'conscious properties are seen to supercede the more elemental physicochemical forces'.

The point is critical – on the one hand, perfectly obvious; on the other, seemingly consistent only within an ontic dualism. When Sperry argued for this view in 1965, he noted that 'one had to search a long way in philosophy and especially in science' for defense of a view in which, *without* an implication of dualism, 'mental forces and events are capable of causing physical changes in an organism's behavior or its neurophysiology'. The problem is not, plainly, whether conscious properties 'supercede the more elemental physicochemical forces', for it is not only common psychosomatic phenomena which attest to this – every human (and animal) *action* does. As already noted, hand–eye coordination requires some very high-level 'control' over muscles, tendons, and so on. But if these psychological processes are not ontically over and above their physical incarnation, then their causal efficacy is not either. Their efficacy *is* their efficacy as emergent, but incarnate, properties. Indeed, the argument for psychology is no different in principle from that for biology. While we *can* postulate an independent *vis via* or *res cogitans,* we need not. Indeed, there are good reasons not to.

We noted that there was a radical difference between saying that functional properties are abstract (that is, that they need some realization, but it is irrelevant what that realization is) and holding that the properties are abstracted from more complex properties which incarnate and explain them. In this regard two final points should be made. Most psychologists, I suspect, would not hold that brain processes are irrelevant to the explanation of psychological phenomena. Nevertheless, and even apart from current cognitive psychology, much experimental psychology, including studies of discrimination and reaction studies, is aimed at testing functional hypotheses without regard to the mechanisms which incarnate and explain them. It is as if an ingested neuroleptic alters the psychological outcome without the brain playing a role in *producing* that outcome. The assumption is frequently made that psychologists cannot and need not wait for the results of current neuroscience. Fodor was correct in saying, however, that while we can think of theory construction in psychology as having two phases which may be distinguished 'in point of logic', they are and must be 'simultaneous in point of history' (Fodor, 1968). As the brief account of brain laterality suggested, because 'functions', such as 'focal', 'time-dependent', and so on, are incarnate in specific neural mechanisms, there is no way to consider 'function' apart from its incarnation.

Second, on the emergent realist view, it does not follow that there is only one physical realization of psychological properties, even if, as Margolis writes, 'psychologically endowed systems must be incarnated in some ways judged suitably similar to the incarnation of the psychological properties ascribed to our paradigms – ourselves' (Margolis, 1984, p. 53). That is, while no particular incarnation may be necessary – we could predicate psychological characteristics of beings different from ourselves – there are physical, biological, and behavioral constraints on such predication (Manicas, 1966). There may be considerable disagreement as to what 'suitably similar' means. On the other hand, it would seem to require more than that the non-human be both 'weakly' or 'strongly' equivalent to our paradigm – ourselves. That is, it must not only 'behave' like us (weak equivalence) and realize suitable cognitive procedures leading to such behavior (strong equivalence), but the latter must also be causally linked to the entity's own incarnate states and processes in ways which correspond to the way these work in us (Fodor, 1968; Block, 1978; Margolis, 1984; Leiber, 1985).

PROBLEMS IN COGNITIVE PSYCHOLOGY

Additional substance can be given to the argument by considering how the present view stands with regard to a range of work in current cognitive psychology. On the present view, that work remains tied to an unwarranted epistemological individualism and is, accordingly, incapable of solving the fundamental problems of a scientific psychology: how organisms learn.

Consider that all action requires some ability to classify particulars as instances of abstract categories or kinds. This is the problem of 'tacit knowledge' or, in *Gestalt* terms, the problem of the 'Höffding function'. Philosophers speak of it as the problem of abstraction. Artificial Intelligence theorists label is the problem of 'character recognition'. Traditionally and more generally, it has been called the problem of concept formation.

In a recent review, Kelly and Krueger (1984) argue that the 'classical paradigm' for experiments on concept-formation were largely irrelevant for, as Jerome Bruner noted, they examine 'conceptual attainment with the perceptual-abstraction phase bypassed' (p. 44). The standard theories, which feature the logical notions of intension and extension, and the more recent 'cluster' and 'prototype' theories either presuppose genuine abstraction at some stage in their argument or render it a total mystery. Plato and Kant notwithstanding, we continue to be saddled with the following dilemma: 'If "imputs" require concepts to be meaningful, then concepts must precede "imputs" as in nativism; but if concepts (to be at all useful in the real world) require "imput" for their content, then "imputs" must precede concepts as in empiricism (either of the ontogenetic or phylogenetic variety)' (Turvey *et al.*, 1981, p. 285).

If, as Weimer has argued (1975, p. 278), the mechanisms of abstraction can be neither 'subtractive' nor 'associative', then we have but two choices: either to adopt some sort of innatist theory or to hold that 'all concept formation is creative or productive'. The first option was most clearly advanced by Fodor:

> If learning a language is literally a matter of making and confirming hypotheses about the truth conditions associated with predicates, then [it] presupposes ability to use expressions coextensive with each of the elementary predicates of the language being learned. But . . . the truth conditions associated with *any* predicate of L [some natural language] can be expressed in terms of the truth conditions associated with the elementary predicates of L. [Hence] one can learn what the semantic properties of a term are only if one already knows the language [i.e., a language not learned naturally] which contains a term having the same semantic properties. (Fodor, 1975, p. 80)

As Fodor himself makes clear, the theory entails that it is impossible to learn a genuinely new concept: 'One can't learn [that is, acquire by a cognitive process] a conceptual system richer than the conceptual system that one starts with, where learning is a process of hypothesis formation and confirmation.' This is, *prima facie,* a sufficiently startling conclusion to force a re-examination of its presuppositions. Two are critical. First, words and sentences are not explained as produced and sustained by social activities but by a verificationist theory of meaning in which meanings are 'in one's head' and language is capable of being fully analysed in terms of the dispositions of individuals. Second, Fodor, along with his 'empiricist' opponents, the 'abstractionists' and 'associationists', assumes that 'the only relations between contents of cognitive states which make a process involving those states a cognitive process are the sorts of logical functions used in classical experiments. Logical functions hold between abstract predicates' (Kelly and Krueger, 1984, p. 64). Lest the point be missed, this too is an assumption deriving from logical empiricist quarters. It is the skeleton in the closet of positivism, that a purely syntactic inductive logic modelled on the extensionalist logic of *Principia Mathematica* is possible (Hempel, 1943).

Now, not only are these assumptions in themselves more than dubious, but, when put to work in psychology, they imply a dualism in which organisms, by virtue of their physical makeup, are linked nomically to physical properties in the world *and* are *also* linked *non-nomically* – epistemologically – to behaviorally significant properties of the surrounding world (Turvey *et al.*, 1981, pp. 245f.). On this view, evolution equipped organisms with not merely perceptual and cognitive mechanisms adequate for learning, but with a *conceptual* basis for making correct inferences from the basic energy descriptions to relevant survival properties of their environments. Indeed, as Turvey, Shaw, Reed, and Mace conclude, the view 'takes out a loan on intelligence that science can never repay' (1981, p. 248).

The problem is not that organisms are not inductive learning machines of some sort, but that, instead of proceeding empirically, traditionalists, both innatist and empiricist, have modelled induction on assumptions of empiricist philosophies of science (Weimer, 1975, p. 474; Hess, 1974; Barnes, 1981). To put it more crudely, Hume was not in error in relegating non-demonstrative inference to 'animal belief'. But if so, we would then be far nearer the truth if we modelled 'scientific method' not on 'logic' but on 'animal belief'.

One way to flesh this out, fully in the spirit, if not the letter, of Helmholtz, would have us consider the possibility that 'abstraction is a preconceptual process, involving nonpropositional modes of cognition such as perception' (Kelly and Krueger, 1984, p. 93). We then shed the logician's sense of 'inference' and the philosopher's sense of 'cognitive'. Evidently, Kelly and Krueger's suggestion requires that we also shed information-processing models of *perception*. Thus, the influential theoretical work of Ulric Neisser, Ralph Norman Haber, Lachman and Lachman, Sperling, Sternberg, and others needs to be rejected or radically revised. In fact, Neisser and Haber have changed their minds, strong evidence in itself of the demise of a research program (Neisser, 1976; Haber, 1983).

One thing that seems plain is the revived pertinence of animal learning, not, of course, as the behaviorist sees it, but as Weimer, Campbell, Pribram, and Kandell have seen it. The difference must be emphasized. Characteristically, the behaviorist definition of learning as a change of behavior simply rejected *learning* as the problem (Chomsky,

1959). But with an adequate non-reductionist theory of mind which acknowledges evolutionary continuity, learning, comprehended as the acquisition of knowledge and skills, can be restored to its primary place in psychological science.

I have argued for a convergence between some widely different criticisms of current psychological science and have sought a resolution which preserves psychology as an autonomous science. Nevertheless, it may be insisted that, because humans are social, linguistic creatures the foregoing is not a defense of a limited program for scientific psychology, but a defense of either a non-psychology or at best, an animal psychology.

I have no interest in reserving the word 'psychology' for the inquiry defended in the foregoing. Although on the present view, most people called psychologists are social or human scientists, it is critical from this perspective only that they acknowledge that their interests are inescapably in social processes and their effects on individuals and individual behavior. That is, such 'psychology' must reject its epistemological individualism.[6]

I hope further that it is clear that, I am not claiming that psychology as here conceived can explain either the full-blown conscious life of a human or the behavior of that human. This is no effort to make an end-run around that 'folk psychology' which couches its explanations in terms of desire, beliefs, and motives. There are insuperable obstacles in making these part of a cognitive science (Stitch, 1983); but I have not argued, in physicalist fashion, that folk psychology can be converted into a scientific psychology, nor have I argued, with Stitch and his 'syntactic theory of mind' that folk psychology is a false 'theory'. On the present view, there is no hope that intentionalist explanations can be replaced by a psychology which can explain behavior 'under an appropriate autonomous description', for such a description is not in sight, not does it seem possible (Williams, 1985).

Finally, there may still be a lingering doubt that psychology can in any sense be distinguished from the social sciences, since human cognition is inextricably intertwined with language, and language is inherently social. Indeed, since psychological states are inherently intentional, it may be that psychological states are best modelled on the propositional character of language (Margolis, 1984). Thus, it may be insisted, even if there

---

[6] This has not, I think, been seen by most practicing inquirers, in part because their epistemologies are, at best, but half-heartedly naturalistic. That is, even those who have rejected an empiricist epistemology have not yet seen the full force of the view that knowledge is a social product.

To their credit, Fodor, in his most recent work (1983), and Stitch (1983) see what is at stake, though on the present view, both are firmly tried to untenable assumptions in the philosophy of science.

are 'infrapsychological' pre-conditions for human powers, the investigation of these does not make a psychology (Scriven, 1964).

One suspects in this argument some lingering quibbling, even while it raises a genuine problem. First, it is surely the case that psychological states are intentional. But even assuming that these must be modelled on the propositional character of language, it does not follow that all the mechanisms that produce states so characterized are intentional or 'homuncular' (Dennett, 1983). As argued in the foregoing, what is required of a scientific psychology is causal knowledge of the human powers – not the capacity to explain particular beliefs, desires, or behaviors. Second, insofar as we identify psychological states thus, it will be true that animal psychology cannot fail to be anthropomorphized. We begin with ourselves – *our* paradigm of a psychological being. Theory proceeds by constructing theories of incarnate functional properties and draws hypotheses and evidence wherever it can – including, significantly, other kinds of organisms which display similar and related capacities. Evidently, we may expect discontinuities *and* continuities.

Third, there is an enormous difference, easily missed, between holding that intentional states may best be characterized in terms of a linguistic model and holding that 'where there is cognition, there is also linguistic representation, no matter how far phylogenetically or ontogenetically, the creature is from overt language' (Churchland, 1980, p. 189). The first view is non-committal as regards the nature of the 'representation' or modelling achieved by the organism; the second holds, in effect, that all cognition satisfies the constraints of a sentential automaton whose 'processing' can be analysed in terms of the semantic and syntactic properties of content-specifying sentences; on this view, 'to give an intentional description to an organism is to ascribe the concept of the embedded property or properties to the organism' (Turvey *et al.*, 1981, p. 285).

We have already noted the disastrous consequences of this move for cognitive psychology: that it presupposes a dualism and requires a verificationist conception of meaning and an extensionalist conception of sentences. All these need to be rejected if psychology is to proceed as a science. This is not the place to advocate some particular theory of the processes involved in ecological transactions between organism and environment – except perhaps to remark that no one thinks that the question is child's play – more difficult than determining the categorical basis of familiar dispositions in physical theory, for example, solvency (Turvey *et al.*, 1981, p. 266).

Recent psychology has consecutively embraced two ambitious programs, both motivated by the idea that psychology can *by itself* explain the molar behavior of humans, including, for example the utterance

'Mozart' in response to a piece of music. The first was the program which pretended that there is some sort of univocal invariance between 'stimulus' and 'response' (Taylor, 1964); the second involved the idea that 'information' comes prepackaged for use by a sentential automaton. Once these programs are firmly rejected, however, we can see the potential pertinence of papers with such titles as 'Command Neurons in Pleurobranchaea Receive Synaptic Feedback from the Motor Network They Excite'. Of course, such inquiry will not give us the whole story of human cognition, but at least it promises real beginnings. Neuropsychology needs the tools of any science – nothing more and nothing less. Biology rejected the need for a *vis visa,* and biochemistry did not put biology out of business. I have tried to clarify the reasons for this in terms of emergent functionalist realism and to define, accordingly, a role for scientific psychology. My defense of such a psychology has sharply restricted its aspirations, of course. Yet this should be unsurprising, given a proper understanding of the nature of theoretical science.

THE SOCIAL-PSYCHOLOGICAL SCIENCES AND APPLIED PSYCHOLOGY

I do not wish to leave the impression, however, that I take all psychological inquiry which is not neuropsychological to be either misguided or useless. There is, in the first place, a great deal of experimental work, suggested by physiological concerns, which can and has shed light on the questions of psychology. Examples range from the early work of Wundt to work in *Gestalt* psychology to recent work which shows, for example, that exemplar-based abstraction does not work. There is also that 'psychology' which rejects epistemological individualism and the 'autonomy of cognitive life' in favor of a full-blown social conception of mind and action (Secord, 1986; Harré, 1986). It would be convenient here if we could simply identify this with what is usually called 'social psychology'. But, a great deal of social psychology is fully committed to the autonomy of the cognitive life. Floyd Allport (1924) set the pattern for this style of inquiry. As he insisted:

> There is no psychology of groups which is not essentially and entirely a psychology of individuals. Social psychology must not be placed in contradistinction to the psychology of the individual; it is part of the psychology of the individual, whose behavior it studies in relation to that sector of the environment comprised by his fellows. (p. 4)

The view is surprisingly prominent even if disguised. It is at the basis of a great deal of work designed around the laboratory experiment, work which, even if it recognizes that social processes are critical causal elements in the constitution of individual minds, nonetheless focuses almost entirely on processes that are mental in the sense of 'inner' (Secord, 1986). Indeed, even Mead's (1934) view that 'social psychology presupposes an approach to experience from the standpoint of the individual, but undertakes to determine in particular that which belongs to this experience because the individual himself belong to a social structure' is lop-sided in favor of the socialization process. By focusing on experience, the ongoing effects of social structures on social inter-action have often been relegated to a secondary position. The upshot has been an easy accommodation between 'symbolic interactionism' and Parsonian sociology, between 'micro-sociology' and 'macro-sociology' (Giddens, 1979, p. 50). Against this, one might contrast here the work of Luria and Vygotsky or, in American psychology, the work of Kurt Lewin, Solomon Asch, and Muzafer Sherif.

But the professional activities of perhaps most psychologists have still not been mentioned. Their fields of concern include development, personality, and the abnormal along with many related psychological specialities which are sometimes referred to as applied psychologies, such as clinical, industrial, educational, and medical psychology. In general, all these fields make the effort to engage particular persons and their behavioral patterns as they occur in the concrete social world; hence, they are inevitably multi-disciplinary, concrete sciences.

On the view of science sketched earlier (in chapter 12), the theoretical (abstract) sciences which aim at discovering the structures and mechanisms at work in the world were distinguished from those (concrete) sciences that apply this knowledge to explain, predict, and diagnose what happens in the world. Just as meteorology or geology are concrete sciences drawing on knowledge derived from physics, chemistry, and so on, so history is a concrete human science which seeks to explain historical events as concrete episodes involving particular persons acting in particular structured societies. As a social science, history, of course, is also a 'hermeneutic science' in that, as Giddens argues, there is a double-hermeneutic at work, the hermeneutic between inquirers in establishing the account as veridical and the hermeneutic demanded by the fact that the 'object' of theory is not the natural world, but the meaningful world of agents.

The parallel 'psychological' science is 'biography', the effort to under-stand the concrete person and his or her life history and particular patterns of behavior, including as reflexively applied, self-understanding (Sartre, 1971). As explanatory sciences, the parallels between history and 'biography' are very close. Both offer an account that traces and connects acts and their intended and unintended consequences within a structurally limited area of space of time. The account generally takes the form of a narrative, and the explanation requires that the historian like the biographer be able to enter the situation and communicate to an audience not only what happened, but what it was like (Hexter, 1971). Both may show how the people involved misunderstood their situation and why plans and projects misfired. The clinical psychologist is a 'biographer' in this sense, even if, of course, there may be no written narrative and the 'audience' is titled 'a patient'.

The relationship between common sense and hermeneutic psychological science parallels the relationship between every person as historian versus the professional historian. Hexter points out that in writing history, the historian appeals to two 'records': the record of the past in concrete evidence and 'everything that historians bring to their confrontation with the record of the past' (p. 79). This second 'record', of course, is what every inquirer brings to every inquiry. For Hexter, however, a key difference between every person and the professional concerns the treatment of the first record, 'a difference in grounds on which they expect and receive credence'. This, as was noted in chapter 12, is a key defining feature of those practices we call 'scientific'. But a second feature must also be emphasized. We obviously expect that the historian has a knowledge of the particular society which is the concern of the narrative, that, in other words, the historian brings an understanding of the society to the treatment of the first record. And so it is with laypersons and their professional analogs in psychology. They latter must not only be far more critical with respect to what is taken as fact or evidence, but must also be in a position to employ current theoretical knowledge derived from both psychology *and* the social sciences.

Similar considerations apply to the diagnostic aspect, except that emphasis shifts to what is wrong or amiss. Diagnoses are called for when, from an ordinary point of view, others are enigmatic, and their behavior (beliefs, and so on) is anomalous, bizarre, or unintelligible, or when they seek or need help. It is thus that therapy enters.

It may be that we shall not be in a position to achieve a significantly better grasp of the psychological structures implicated in such cases; or, more optimistically, that as we learn more about the general mechanisms which are implicated, our therapeutic techniques are measurably improved. In any case, the diagnostic and therapeutic sciences, like medicine, require knowledge both of the concrete individual and of the relevant causal mechanisms: neurophysical, psychological, *and* social.

This suggests a final point. The same history that explains why experimental psychology took the turn it did also serve to explain the present emphasis on psychology as an applied family of disciplines; and critically, it also explains why these disciplines, like the parent, experimental psychology, are epistemologically, methodologically, and politically individualistic. The evidence is everywhere: in the primary appeal to personal factors, rather than structural and social factors, in explaining psychological disorder; in its implicit and sometimes explicit definition of amelioration in terms of adaptation – instead of looking at the social causes of normatively unacceptable behavior; and in its promotion of policies which take for granted prevailing social relations, reinforce and in part constitute power in the hands of some, and, more generally, make it easier for the holders of power to exercise their power over others. When, for example, the school psychologist becomes the agent of the disciplinary officer, when the industrial psychologist becomes the agent of the managers, we can be sure that this turn is destructive of just those values of human freedom and human integrity which ought to be the ultimate goal of the human sciences.

Bibliography

Abrams, P. 1968: *The Origins of British Sociology: 1834–1914*. Chicago: University of Chicago Press.

Achinstein, Peter and Barker, Stephen F. (eds) 1969. *The Legacy of Logical Positivism*. Baltimore: Johns Hopkins University Press.

Allport, F. H. 1924: *Social Psychology*. Boston: Houghton Mifflin.

Althusser, L. and Balibar, E. 1970: *Reading Capital*. London: NLB.

Anschutz, R. P. 1953: *The Philosophy of J. S. Mill*. New York: Oxford University Press.

Anderson, Benedict 1983: *The Imagined Community*. London: Verso.

Anderson, Perry 1974: *Lineages of the Absolutist State*. London: NLB.

—— 1976: *Considerations of Western Marxism*. London: NLB.

—— 1980: *Arguments within English Marxism*. London: NLB.

—— 1983: *In the Tracts of Historical Materialism*. London: NLB.

Andreski, Stanislav (ed.) 1974: *The Essential Comte*. London: Croom Helm.

Anscombe, E. M. and Geach, P. T. 1961: *Three Philosophers*. Ithaca: Cornell University Press.

Antoni, Carlo 1959: *From History to Sociology: the transition in German historical thinking*, trans. H. White. Detroit: Wayne State University Press.

Arato, A. and Brienes, P. 1979: *The Young Lukàcs and the Origins of Western Marxism*. New York: Seabury.

Arendt, H. 1958: *The Human Condition*. Chicago: University of Chicago Press.

Aronson, Jerrold L. 1984: *A Realist Philosophy of Science*. New York: St Martin's.

Ashton, T. S. 1964: *The Industrial Revolution, 1760–1830*. New York: Oxford University Press.

Avineri, Schlomo 1972: *Hegel's Theory of the Modern State*. Cambridge: Cambridge University Press.

Avrich, Paul 1984: *The Haymarket Tragedy*. Princeton: Princeton University Press.

Ayer, A. J. 1936: *Language, Truth and Logic*. London: Gollancz. 2nd edn, 1946, New York: Dover.

Ayers, Michael 1984: Berkeley and Hume: a question of influence. In R. Rorty, J. B. Schneewind and Q. Skinner (eds), *Philosophy in History*. Cambridge: Cambridge University Press.

Barnard, F. M. 1965: *Herder's Social and Political Thought: from enlightenment to nationalism*. Oxford: Clarendon Press.

Barnes, Barry 1976: Natural rationality: a neglected concept in the social sciences. *Philosophy of Social Sciences*, 9.

—— 1981: On the conventional character of knowledge and cognition. *Philosophy of Social Sciences*, 11.

—— 1982: *T. S. Kuhn and Social Science*. New York: Columbia University Press.

Barnes, Harry Elmer 1925: *The New History and the Social Studies*. New York: Century.

Barraclough, G. 1962: *The Origins of Modern Germany*. Oxford: Basil Blackwell.

Barthes, R. 1967: *Eléments de semiologie*. Paris, Seuil.

Becker, Ernest 1971: *The Lost Science of Man*. New York: Braziller.

Ben-David, Joseph 1971: *The Scientist's Role in Society*. Englewood Cliffs, N.J.: Prentice-Hall.

Bender, F. 1983: Marx, materialism and the limits of philosophy. *Studies in Soviet Thought*, 25.

Berkeley, George 1964: *The Works of George Berkeley, Bishop of Cloyne*, ed. T. E. Jessop. London: Nelson.

Berlin, Isaiah 1976: *Vico and Herder*. New York: Viking.

Bernstein, Richard 1971: *Praxis and Action*. Philadelphia: University of Pennsylvania Press.

—— 1976: *The Restructuring of Social and Political Theory*. New York: Harcourt, Brace, Javanovich.

Bhaskar, R. 1975: *A Realist Theory of Science*. 2nd edn, 1978. Atlantic Highlands, N.J.: Humanities Press.

—— 1979: *The Possibility of Naturalism*. Brighton: Harvester and Atlantic Highlands, N.J.: Humanities Press.

—— 1982: Emergence, explanation, and emancipation. In Paul F. Secord (ed.), *Explaining Human Behavior*. Beverly Hills, Calif.: Sage.

—— 1983: Dialectics. In T. Bottomore (ed.) *A Dictionary of Marxist Thought*. Cambridge, Mass.: Harvard University Press.

Bilmes, Jack 1986: *Discourse and Behavior*. New York: Plenum.

Blakemore, C. and Cooper, G. F. 1970: Development of the brain depends upon the visual environment. *Nature*, 228.

Bledstein, Burton 1976: *The Culture of Professionalism: the middle class and the development of higher education in America*. New York: W. W. Norton.

Bloch, Ned 1978: Troubles with functionalism. In C. W. Savage (ed.), *Perception and Cognition: issues in foundations of psychology*. Minnesota Studies in the Philosophy of Science, vol. 9. Minneapolis: University of Minnesota Press.

Bloor, David 1976: *Knowledge of Social Imagery*. London: Routledge and Kegan Paul.

—— 1981: The strengths of the strong programme. *Philosophy of Social Science*, 11, 199–213.

—— 1982: A reply to Gerd Buchdahl. *Studies in History and Philosophy of Science*, 13, no. 4.

—— 1983: *Wittgenstein: a social theory of knowledge*. New York: Columbia University Press.

Boas, George 1924: *French Philosophies of the Romantic Period*. Baltimore: Johns Hopkins University Press.

Bodin, J. 1962: *Six Books of a Commonweale*, ed. with introduction by K. D. McRae. Cambridge, Mass.: Harvard University Press. A facsimile reprint of the English translation of 1606.

Bohm, David 1957: *Causality and Chance in Modern Physics*. London: Routledge and Kegan Paul.

Boring, E. G. 1929: *A History of Experimental Psychology*. 2nd edn, 1950. New York: Appleton-Century-Crofts.

Bottomore, T. B. 1964: *Elites and Society*. London: Watts and Co.

Bourdieu, Pierre 1977: *Outline of a Theory of Practice*. Cambridge: Cambridge University Press.

Bradshaw, J. L. and Nettleton, N. C. 1981: The nature of hemisphere specialization in man. *The Behavioral and Brain Sciences*, 4. (See also the extensive discussion which follows their review.)

Brecht, A. 1959: *Political Theory: the foundations of twentieth-century political thought*. Princeton: Princeton University Press.

Brodbeck, May 1968: Methodological individualism: definition and reduction. In Brodbeck (ed.), *Readings in the Philosophy of Science*. New York: Macmillan.

Brown, Harold I. 1977: *Perception, Theory and Commitment: the new philosophy of science*. Chicago: Precedent Publishing.

Brown, Robert 1984: *The Nature of Social Laws: Machiavelli to Mill*. Cambridge: Cambridge University Press.

Bryant, C. G. A. 1985: *Positivism in Social Theory and Research*. London: Macmillan.

Buck-Morss, Susan 1977: *The Origin of Negative Dialectics*. New York: Free Press.

Bunge, Mario 1959: *Causality: the place of the causal principle in modern science*. Cambridge, Mass.: Harvard University Press.

—— 1964: *The Critical Approach to Science and Philosophy*. New York: Free Press.

—— 1967: Technology as applied science. *Technology and Culture*, 8, 329–47.

Burke, K. 1971: *The Philosophy of Literary Form*. Baton Rouge: Louisiana State University Press.

Burnyeat, M. F. 1984: The sceptic in his place and time. In Rorty et al., *Philosophy in History*. Cambridge. Cambridge University Press.

Camfield, T. M. 1973: The professionalization of American psychology, 1870–1917. *Journal of the History of the Behavioral Sciences*, 9, no. 1.

Campbell, Norman H. 1920: *Physics: the elements*. Cambridge: Cambridge University Press. Reprinted as *Foundations of Science*, 1957. New York: Dover.

Carnap, Rudolf 1928: *Der Logische Aufbau der Welt*. Berlin: Welkreis.

—— 1932–3: Psychology in physical language. In A. J. Ayer (ed.), *Logical Positivism*, 1959. Glencoe, Ill.: Free Press.

—— 1936–7: Testability and meaning. *Philosophy of Science*, 3, 420–68; 4, 1–40. Excerpts in Feigl and Brodbeck, 1953.

—— 1938: Logical foundations of the unity of science. Reprinted in Feigl and Sellars, 1949.

—— 1945: On inductive logic. *Philosophy of Science*, 12, 72–97.

—— 1956: The methodological character of theoretical concepts. In Feigl and Scriven, 1956.

Chisholm, Roderick M. 1946: The contrary-to-fact conditional. *Mind*, 55, no. 220. Reprinted in Manicas, 1971.

Chomsky, Noam 1959: A review of B. F. Skinner's *Verbal Behavior*. *Language*, 35.

Churchland, Patricia Smith 1980: A perspective on mind–brain research. *The Journal of Philosophy*, 57.

Clark, Robert T. Jr 1955: *Herder: his life and thought*. Berkeley and Los Angeles: University of California Press.

Cohen, G. A. 1978: *Karl Marx's Theory of History: a defense*. Princeton: Princeton University Press.

Cohen, I. B. 1956: *Franklin and Newton*. Philadelphia: American Philosophical Society.

Cohen, R. S. 1970: Physics, perception and philosophy of science. In R. S. Cohen and R. J. Seeger (eds), *Ernest Mach, Physicist and Philosopher*. Dordrecht: Reidel.

Cohen, S. F. 1984: *Bukharin and the Bolshevik Revolution: a political biography 1889–1938*. New York: Knopf.

Colletti, L. 1973. *Marxism and Hegel*. London: NLB.

Comte, August 1875: *The Positive Philosophy of August Comte*. Freely translated and condensed by Harriet Martineau. 2 vols. 2nd edn. London: Trubner and Co. This edition was 'highly approved by the author'. It was retranslated into French 'for the sake of its diffusion among the author's own countrymen'.

Crick, Bernard 1959: *The American Science of Politics: its origins and conditions*. Berkeley and Los Angeles: University of California Press.

Dahrendorf, Ralf 1971: *Society and Democracy in Germany*. New York: Anchor.

Danziger, K. 1979a: The positive repudiation of Wundt. *Journal of the History of the Behavioral Sciences*, 15.

—— 1979b: The social origins of modern psychology: positive sociology and positive sociology of knowledge. In A. R. Buss (ed.), *The Social Context of Psychological Theory*. New York: Irvington.

—— 1980a: The history of introspection reconsidered. *Journal of the Theory of the Behavioral Sciences*, 16.

—— 1980b: Wundt and the two traditions in psychology. In R. W. Reiber (ed.), *Wilhelm Wundt and the Making of a Scientific Psychology*. New York: Plenum.

—— 1982: Mid-nineteenth-century British psycho-physiology: a neglected chapter in the history of psychology. In W. R. Woodward and M. G. Ash (eds), *The Problematic Science*. New York: Praeger.

Davidson, Donald 1974: Psychology as philosophy. In *Essays on Actions and Events*. Oxford: Clarendon Press, 1980.

Davis, David Brion 1966: *The Problem of Slavery in Western Culture*. Ithaca: Cornell University Press.

—— 1984: *Slavery and Human Progress*. New York: Oxford University Press.

Dawkins, Richard 1976: *The Selfish Gene*. New York: Oxford University Press.

Dennett, D. C. 1983: Intentional systems in cognitive ethology: the Panglossian paradigm defended. *Behavioral and Brain Sciences*, 6.

Derrida, J. 1974: *Of Grammatology*. Baltimore: Johns Hopkins University Press.

de Solla Price, Derek J. 1982: The parallel structures of science and technology. In B. Barnes and D. Edge (eds), *Science in Context*. Cambridge, Mass.: MIT Press.

de Ste Croix, G. E. M. 1981: *The Class Struggle in the Ancient World*. Ithaca: Cornell University Press.

Dewan, M. 1976: Consciousness as an emergent causal agent in the context of control systems theory. In G. G. Globus, G. Maxwell, and I. Savodnik (eds), *Consciousness and the Brain: a scientific and philosophical inquiry*. New York: Plenum.

Dewey, John 1922: *Human Nature and Conduct*. New York: Holt.

—— 1927: *The Public and its Problems*. Chicago: Swallow.

—— 1938: *Logic: the theory of inquiry*. New York: Holt.

—— 1916: *Essays in Experimental Logic*. Chicago: University of Chicago Press; New York: Dover.

Diamond, S. 1980: Wundt before Leipzig. In R. E. Reiber (ed.).

Dilthey, W. 1976: *Selected Writings*, ed., trans., and introduced by H. P. Rickman. Cambridge: Cambridge University Press.

Dorfman, Joseph 1949: *The Economic Mind in American Civilization: 1865–1918*, vol. 3. New York: Viking.

Dretske, F. I. 1977: Laws of nature. *Philosophy of Science*, 44.

Duhem, Pierre 1954: *The Aim and Structure of Physical Theory*, trans. from the French by P. P. Weiner. Princeton: Princeton University Press. First published in 1906.

Durkheim, E. 1938: *The Rules of Sociological Method*. New York: Free Press. First published in 1895.

—— 1947: *The Division of Labor in Society*. New York: Free Press. First published in 1893.

—— 1951: *Suicide*. New York: Free Press. First published in 1897.

—— 1958: *Socialism and Saint-Simon*. Yellow Springs: Antioch Press. Lectures given at Bordeaux from November 1895 to May 1896.

—— 1960: *Montesquieu and Rousseau: forerunners of sociology*. Foreword by H. Peyre, trans. G. Davy. Ann Arbor: University of Michigan. First published in 1892.

Easton, L. D. and Guddat, K. H. (eds) 1967: *Writings of the Young Marx on Philosophy and Society*. Garden City, N.Y.: Doubleday.

Edelman, Murray 1964: *The Symbolic Uses of Politics*. Urbana: University of Illinois Press.

Engels, F. 1935: *Ludwig Feuerbach and the Outcome of Classical German Philosophy*. New York: International Publishers. First published in 1888.

—— 1939: *Herr Eugen Dühring's Revolution in Science*. New York: International Publishers. First published in 1885.

—— 1940: *The Dialectics of Nature*. New York: International Publishers. First published in 1927.

Farber, Marvin 1943: *The Foundations of Phenomenology*. Cambridge, Mass.: Harvard University Press.

Feigl, H. 1969: The origin and spirit of logical positivism. In P. Achinstein and S. F. Barker (eds).

—— 1970: The orthodox view of theories: remarks in defense as well as critique. In M. Radner and S. Winokur (eds).

—— and Sellars, W. (eds) 1949: *Readings in Philosophical Analysis*. New York: Appleton-Century-Crofts.

—— and Brodbeck, M. (eds) 1953: *Readings in the Philosophy of Science*. New York: Appleton-Century-Crofts.

—— and Scriven, M. (eds) 1956: *Minnesota Studies in the Philosophy of Science*, vol. 1. Minneapolis: University of Minnesota Press.

—— and Maxwell, G. (eds) 1962: *Minnesota Studies in the Philosophy of Science*, vol. 3. Minneapolis: University of Minnesota Press.

Ferguson, K. 1984: *The Feminist Case against Bureaucracy*. Philadelphia: Temple University Press.

Feyerabend, Paul 1958: An attempt at a realistic interpretation of experience. *Proceedings of the Aristotelian Society*, new series, 58.

—— 1962: Explanation, reduction and empiricism. In H. Feigl and G. Maxwell (eds).

Fine, Arthur 1984: Einstein's realism. In J. T. Cushing, C. F. Delaney, and Gary M. Gutting (eds), *Science and Reality*. Notre Dame, Ind.: University of Notre Dame Press.

Finer, Samuel E. 1975: State- and nation-building in Europe: the role of the military. In Charles Tilley (ed.), *The Formation of National States in Western Europe*. Princeton: Princeton University Press.

Finley, M. I. 1973: *The Ancient Economy*. Berkeley: University of California Press.

Flexner, Abraham 1930: *Universities, American, English and German*. New York: Oxford University Press.

Flower, Elizabeth and Murphey, Murray G. 1977: *A History of American Philosophy*, vol. 2. New York: Putnams.

Fodor, J. A. 1968: *Psychological Explanation*. New York: Random House.

—— 1975: *The Language of Thought*. New York: Crowell.

—— 1983: *The Modularity of Mind*. Cambridge, Mass.: MIT Press.

Foucault, M. 1970: *The Order of Things*. New York: Pantheon.

Fox Keller, Evelyn 1985: *Reflections on Gender and Science*. New Haven: Yale University Press.

Friedman, Michael 1983: *Foundations of Space–Time Theories*. Princeton: Princeton University Press.

Friedman, Milton 1973: The methodology of positive economics. In *Essays in Positive Economics*. Chicago: University of Chicago Press.

Gadamer, Hans-Georg 1975: *Truth and Method*. New York: Seabury. Originally published in German in 1960.

Garfinkel, H. 1967, *Studies in Ethnomethodology*. Englewood Cliffs, N.J.: Prentice-Hall.

Geertz, Clifford 1973: *The Interpretation of Cultures*. New York: Basic Books.

Gellner, Ernest 1970: *Concepts and society*. In B. R. Wilson (ed.), *Rationality*. New York: Harper.

Genovese, Eugene D. 1965: *The Political Economy of Slavery*. New York: Vintage.

Giddens, A. 1971: *Capitalism and Modern Social Theory*. Cambridge: Cambridge University Press.

—— 1976: *New Rules in Sociological Method*. London: Hutchinson.

—— 1978: *Durkheim*. Hassocks: Harvester.

—— 1979: *Central Problems in Social Theory*. London: Macmillan.

—— 1985: *The Nation-state and Violence*. Berkeley: University of California Press.

Gilbert, Felix 1965: European and American historiography. In J. Higham et al., *History*. Princeton: Princeton University Press.

Goodman, Madeleine J. and Goodman, Lenn E. n.d.: Particularly amongst the sun burnt nations . . .: the persistence of sexual stereotypes of race in bioscience. MS. University of Hawaii.

Goodman, Nelson 1946: A query on confirmation. *Journal of Philosophy*, 43.

—— 1954: *Fact, Fiction and Forecast*. London: Althone.

Gould, Stephen Jay 1981: *The Mismeasure of Man*. New York: W. W. Norton.

Gouldner, Alvin 1970: *The Coming Crisis in American Sociology*. New York: Basic Books.

Grene, M. and Mendelssohn, E. 1976: *Topics in the Philosophy of Biology. Boston Studies in the Philosophy of Science*, 27. Dordrecht: Reidel.

Grobstein, C. 1976: Organizational levels and explanation. In M. Grene and E. Mendelssohn, 1976.

Haber, R. N. 1983: The impending demise of the icon: a critique of the concept of iconic storage in visual information processing. *Behavioral and Brain Sciences*, 6.

Habermas, Jürgen 1971: *Knowledge and Human Interests*. Boston: Beacon Press. Originally published in German in 1968.

—— 1973: *Legitimation Crisis*. Boston: Beacon Press.

Handy, Rollo and Kurtz, Paul 1964: *A Current Appraisal of the Behavioral Sciences*. Great Barrington, Mass.: Behavioral Research Council.

—— and Harwood, E. C. 1973: *A Current Appraisal of the Behavioral Sciences*. Rev. edn. Great Barrington, Mass.: Behavioral Research Council.

Hanson, N. 1958: *Patterns of Discovery*. Cambridge: Cambridge University Press.

—— 1970: Hypotheses Fingo. In R. E. Butts and J. W. Davis (eds), *The Methodological Heritage of Newton*. Toronto: University of Toronto Press.

Harré, R. 1964: *Matter and Method*. London: Macmillan.

—— 1970: *The Principles of Scientific Thinking*. Chicago: University of Chicago Press.

—— 1984: *Personal being*. Oxford: Basil Blackwell.

—— 1986: Personal being. In Margolis et al. *Psychology: designing the discipline*. Oxford: Basil Blackwell.

—— and Secord, P. 1973: *The Explanation of Social Behavior*. Oxford: Basil Blackwell.

—— and Madden, E. H. 1975: *Causal Powers*. Oxford: Basil Blackwell.

Harrington, M. 1972: *Socialism*. New York: Saturday Review.

Hartley, David 1966: *Observations on Man, His Frame, His Duty and His Expectations*. Facsimile edn with an introduction by T. L. Huguelet. Gainsville, Fla.: Scholars Facsimiles. First published in 1749.

Hartz, Louis 1955. *The Liberal Tradition in America*. New York: Harcourt.

Hegel, G. W. F. 1952: *Hegel's Philosophy of Right*, trans. with notes by T. M. Knox. London: Oxford University Press.

—— 1956: *The Philosophy of History*, New York: Dover, trans. J. Sibree with prefaces by Charles Hegel and an introduction by C. J. Friedrich.

Helmholtz, H. 1971: *Selected Writings*, ed. Russell Kahn. Middleton, Conn.: Wesleyan University Press.

Hempel, Carl G. 1943: A purely syntactical definition of confirmation. *Journal of Symbolic Logic*, 8.

—— 1945: Studies in the logic of confirmation. Reprinted in Hempel, 1965.

—— 1950: Empiricist criteria of cognitive significance: problems and changes. Reprinted in Hempel, 1965.

—— 1958: The theoretician's dilemma. Reprinted in Hempel, 1965.

—— 1965: *Aspects of Scientific Explanation*. New York: Free Press.

—— and Oppenheim, Paul 1948: Studies in the logic of explanation. *Philosophy of Science*, 15.

Herbst, Jürgen 1965: *The German Historical School in American Scholarship*. Ithaca: Cornell University Press.

Herder, J. G. 1969: *J. G. Herder on Social and Political Culture*, trans. ed., and with an introduction by, F. M. Barnard. Cambridge: Cambridge University Press. This includes selections from Herder's travel diary, his essay on the origin of language, 'yet another philosopher of history', the dissertation on the reciprocal influences of government and the sciences and the *Ideas for a Philosophy of History of Mankind*.

Herskovits, Melville J. 1953: *Franz Boas*. New York: Scribner.

Hesse, Mary 1962: *Forces and Fields*. New York: Philosophical Library.

—— 1966: *Models and Analogies in Science*. Notre Dame, Ind.: University of Notre Dame Press.

—— 1974: *The Structure of Scientific Inference*. Berkeley: University of California Press.

—— 1980: *Revolutions and Reconstructions in the Philosophy of Science*. Bloomington: University of Indiana Press.

Hexter, J. H. 1971: *The History Primer*. New York: Basic Books.

—— 1973: *The Vision of Politics on the Eve of the Reformation: More, Machiavelli and Seysel*. New York: Basic Books.

Higham, John, Krieger, L. and Gilbert, F. 1965: *History*. Princeton: Princeton University Press.

Hill, Christopher 1972: The radical critics of Oxford and Cambridge in the 1650s. In J. W. Baldwin and R. A. Goldthwaite (eds), *Universities in Politics*. Baltimore: Johns Hopkins University Press.

Hirsch, J. 1976: Behavior-genetic analysis and its biosocial consequences. In N. Bloch and G. Dworkin (eds), *The IQ Controversy*. New York: Pantheon.

Hobbes, Thomas, n.d.: *Leviathan*. New York: E. P. Dutton. First published in 1651.

Hobsbawm, E. J. 1962: *The Age of Revolution: Europe 1789–1848*. London: Weidenfeld and Nicolson.

—— 1968: *Industry and Empire*. Baltimore: Penguin.

—— 1975: *The Age of Capital 1848–1875*. New York: Scribner.

Hofstadter, Richard 1955: *The Age of Reform*. New York: Knopf.

Hollis, Martin and Lukes, Stephen (eds) 1982: *Rationality and Relativism*. Cambridge Mass.: MIT Press.

Holton, G. 1970: Mach, Einstein and the search for reality. In R. S. Cohen and R. J. Seeger (eds), *Ernst Mach, Physicist and Philosopher*. Dordrecht: Reidel. Originally in *Daedalus*, 1968.

Hughes, H. S. 1958: *Consciousness and Society: the reorientation of European Social thought, 1890–1930*. New York: Knopf.

Hull, David 1974: *Philosophy of Biology*. Englewood Cliffs, N.J.: Prentice-Hall.

Hume, D. 1978: *Treatise of Human Nature*, ed. L. A. Selby-Bigge, 2nd edn, rev. P. H. Nidditch. Oxford: Oxford University Press. First published in 1739–40.

—— 1955: *An Inquiry Concerning Human Understanding*, ed. Charles Hendel. Indianapolis: Bobbs-Merrill. First published in 1748.

Iggers, George G. (ed.) 1973: *Von Ranke: the theory and practice of history*. Indianapolis: Bobbs-Merrill.

—— 1983: *The German Conception of History: the national tradition of historical thought from Herder to the present*. Middleton, Conn: Wesleyan University Press.

James, S. 1984: *The Content of Social Explanation*. Cambridge: Cambridge University Press.

James, William 1950: *The Principles of Psychology*, 2 vols. New York: Dover: First published in 1890.

Janik, A. and Toulmin, S. 1973: *Wittgenstein's Vienna*. New York: Simon and Schuster.

Jay, Martin 1973: *The Dialectical Imagination: a history of the Frankfurt School and the Institute of Social Research, 1923–1950*. Boston: Little, Brown.

Jordan, Z. A. 1967: *The Evolution of Dialectic Materialism*. New York: St Martin's.

Kandel, E. 1976: *The Cellular Basis of Behavior*. San Francisco: Freeman.

Kapsis, R. E. 1977: Weber, Durkhem and the comparative method. *Journal of the History of the Behavioral Sciences*, 13.

Keat, Russell 1981: *The Politics of Social Theory*. Chicago: University of Chicago Press.

Kelly, David and Krueger, Janet 1984: The psychology of abstraction. *Journal for the Theory of Social Behavior*, 14.

Kerlinger, Fred B. 1979: *Behavioral Research: a conceptual approach*. New York: Holt, Rinehart and Winston.

Klein, Phillip A. 1983: The neglected institutionalism of Wesley Clair Mitchell: the theoretical basis for business cycle indicators. *Journal of Economic Issues*, 17, no. 4.

Kneale, William and Martha 1962: *The Development of Logic*. Oxford: Clarendon Press.

Koch, Sigmund 1964: Psychology and emerging conceptions of knowledge as unitary. In W. T. Wann (ed.) *Behaviorism* and *Phenomenology*. Chicago: University of Chicago Press.

Koyré, Alexander 1965: The significance of the Newtonian Synthesis. In *Newtonian Studies*, Cambridge, Mass.: Harvard University Press.

Krieger, L. 1975: *An Essay on the Theory of Enlightened Despotism*. Chicago: University of Chicago Press.

Kuhn, T. S. 1957: *The Copernican Revolution*. New York: Vintage.

—— 1962: *The Structure of Scientific Revolutions*. Chicago: University of Chicago Press. Enlarged edn, 1970.

—— 1977: *The Essential Tension*. Chicago: University of Chicago Press.

Kuklick, Henrika 1980: Boundary maintenance in American sociology: limitations to academic professionalization. *Journal of the History of the Behavioral Sciences*, 16, no. 3.

Kurzweil, Edith 1980: *The Age of Structuralism: Lévi-Strauss to Foucault*. New York: Columbia University Press.

Lacan, J. 1966: *Ecrits*. Paris: Seuil.

Laclau, E. 1971: Feudalism and capitalism in Latin America. Reprinted in *Politics and Ideology in Marxist Thought*. London: NLB.

Lakatos, T. and Musgrave, A. (eds) 1970: *Criticism and the Growth of Knowledge*. Cambridge: Cambridge University Press.

Lallana, Emanuel 1986: Marital law in the Philippines. MS. University of Hawaii.

Landes, David S. 1969: *The Unbound Prometheus: technological change and industrial development in Western Europe from 1750 to the present*. Cambridge: Cambridge University Press.

Lazarsfeld, Paul F. 1955: Interpretation of statistical relations as a research operation. In Paul F. Lazarsfeld and M. Rosenberg (eds).

—— and Rosenberg, M. (eds) 1955: *The Language of Social Research*. New York: Free Press.

Leary, D. 1979: Wundt and after: psychology's shifting relations with the natural sciences, social sciences and philosophy. *Journal of the History of the Behavioral Sciences*, 13.

—— 1982: Immanuel Kant and the development of modern psychology. In W. R. Woodward and M. G. Ash (eds).

Leiber, Justin 1985: *Can Animals and Machines be Persons?* Indianapolis: Hackett.

Lenzer, Gertrude (ed.) 1975: *Auguste Comte and Positivism: the essential writings*. New York: Harper.

Lévi-Strauss, Claude (1962) 1966: *The Savage Mind*. Chicago: University of Chicago Press.

Levine, A. and Wright, E. O. 1980: Rationality and class struggle. *New Left Review*, 123.

Levins, Richard and Lewontin, Richard 1985: *The Dialectical Biologist*. Cambridge, Mass.: Harvard University Press.

Lewontin, Richard 1976: The analysis of variance and the analysis of causes. In Bloch and Dworkin (eds) *The IQ Controversy*. New York: Pantheon.

Lieberson, Jonathan 1982: The romantic rationalist. *New York Review of Books*, December 1982. See also Lieberson's reply to critics, New York Review of 13 vols, 12 April, 1983.

Locke, J. 1975: *An Essay Concerning Human Understanding*, ed. P. H. Nidditch. Oxford: Clarendon Press. First published in 1690.

—— 1967: *Two Treatises of Government*. A critical edition, with introduction and *apparatus criticus* by Peter Laslett, 2nd edn. Cambridge: Cambridge University Press.

Lowie, Robert H. 1937: *The History of Ethnological Theory*. New York: Holt, Rinehart and Winston.

Löwith, K. 1982: *Max Weber and Karl Marx*. London: Allen and Unwin.

Lukes, Stephen 1972: *Emile Durkheim: his life and work*. New York: Harper.

—— 1982: Relativism in its place. In M. Hollis and S. Lukes (eds).

Lynd, R. S. 1939: *Knowledge for What? The place of social science in American culture*. Princeton: Princeton University Press.

McCarthy, Thomas 1981: *The Critical Theory of Jürgen Habermas*. Cambridge, Mass.: MIT Press.

McClelland, Charles E. 1980: *State, Society and the University in Germany, 1700–1914*. Cambridge: Cambridge University Press.

McDermott, J. J. (ed.) 1967: *The Writings of William James*. New York: Random House.

Mach, Ernest 1959: *The Analysis of Sensations*. New York: Dover. First published in 1883.

—— 1945: *Popular Scientific Lectures*. 5th edn. Lasalle, Ill.: Open Court.

Machiavelli, Niccolò 1950: *The Prince and the Discourses*. New York: Modern Library.

MacIntyre, Alasdair 1970: The ideal of a social science. In B. R. Wilson (ed.), *Rationality*. New York: Harper.

Macpherson, C. B. 1962: *The Political Theory of Possessive Individualism*. New York: Oxford University Press.

Madden, E. H. and Hare, P. 1976: A critical appraisal of James's view of causality. In W. R. Corti (ed.), *The Philosophy of William James*. Hamburg: Felix Meiner.

Mandelbaum, M. 1964: *Philosophy, Science and Sense Perception: historical and critical studies*. Baltimore: Johns Hopkins University Press.

—— 1971: *History, Man and Reason*. Baltimore: Johns Hopkins University Press.

Manicas, P. T. 1965: Aristotle, dispositions and occult powers. *Review of Metaphysics*, 18.

—— 1966: Minds, machines, materialism and morality. *Philosophy and Phenomenological Research*, 24.

—— (ed.) 1971: *Logic as Philosophy*. New York: Van Nostrand.

—— 1974: *The Death of the State*. New York: Putnams.

—— 1981a: Montesquieu and the eighteenth-century vision of the state. *History of Political Thought*, 2, no. 2.

—— 1981b: Review of Theda Skocpol's *States and Social Revolutions*. *History and Theory*, 10.

—— 1982: John Dewey: anarchism and the political state. *Transactions of the Charles S. Pierce Society*, 18.

—— 1985: Explanation and generalization in Marxist theory. In D. Banerjee (ed.), *Marxian Theory and the Third World*. New Delhi and Beverley Hills, Calif.: Sage.

—— 1986: The legitimacy of the modern state. In J. Toland and R. Cohen (eds), *Legitimacy and State Formations*. Institute for the Study of Human Issues, forthcoming.

—— The foreclosure of democracy in America. *History of Political Thought*, forthcoming.

—— and Rosenberg, A. 1985: Naturalism, epistemological individualism and 'The Strong Programme' in the sociology of knowledge. *Journal for the Theory of Social Behavior*, 15.

Manuel, F. 1956: *The New World of Henri Saint-Simon*. Cambridge, Mass.: Harvard University Press.

—— 1962: *The Prophets of Paris*. Cambridge, Mass.: Harvard University Press.

Marcuse, Herbert 1954: *Reason and Revolution*. 2nd edn. New York: Humanities Press.

Margolis, Joseph 1984: *Philosophy of Psychology*. Englewood Cliffs, N. J.: Prentice-Hall.

Marx, K. 1970a: *A Contribution to the Critique of Political Economy*. New York: International Publishers.

—— 1970b: *Capital*. London: Lawrence and Wishart. First published in German in 1867.

—— 1973: *Grundrisse*. Harmondsworth: Penguin.

—— and Engels, F. 1942: *The Selected Correspondence, 1846–95*. New York: International Publishers.

Masur, G. 1961: *Prophets of Yesterday: studies in European culture, 1890–1914*. New York: Macmillan.

Mayr, Otto 1982: The science-technology relationship. In B. Barnes and D. Edge (eds), *Science in Context*. Cambridge, Mass.: MIT Press.

Mead, George Herbert 1934: *Mind, Self and Society*. Chicago: University of Chicago Press.

Meek, Ronald L. 1976: *Social Science and the Ignoble Savage*. Cambridge: Cambridge University Press.

—— 1977: *Smith, Marx and After*. London: Chapman and Hall.

Meinecke, Friedrich 1970: *Cosmopolitanism and the National State*, trans. R. B. Kimber. Princeton: Princeton University Press. First published in 1907.

Mill, J. S. n.d.: *Auguste Comte and Positivism*. London: Routledge and Co. First published in 1850.

—— 1930: *Logic*. London: Longman. First published in 1843.

—— 1974: *Essays on Some Unsettled Questions of Political Economy*. 2nd edn. Clifton, N.J.: Augustus Kelly. First published in 1844.

Mills, C. W. 1956: *The Power Elite*. New York: Oxford University Press.

—— 1959: *The Sociological Imagination*. Harmondsworth: Penguin.

Mitchell, Wesley Clair 1969: *Types of Economic Theory: from mercantilism to institutionalism*, ed. Joseph Dorfman. Reprint. New York: Augustus Kelley.

Montesquieu, Baron de 1962: *The Spirit of the Laws*, trans. Thomas Nugent. New York: Hafner.

Moore, Barrington, Jr 1966: *Social Origins of Dictatorship and Democracy*. Boston: Beacon Press.

Mulkay, Michael J. 1981: Knowledge and utility: implications for the sociology of knowledge. In N. Stehr and V. Meja (eds), *Society and Knowledge*. New Brunswick: Transaction Books.

Myers, Gerald 1986: *William James: his life and thought*. New Haven: Yale University Press.

Nagel, Ernest 1961: *The Structure of Science*. New York: Harcourt, Brace.

Natanson, Maurice 1963: A study in philosophy and the social sciences. In Natanson (ed.), *Philosophy of the Social Sciences*. New York: Random House.

Neisser, U. 1976: *Cognition and Reality*. San Francisco: Freeman.

Newton, Isaac 1934: *Sir Isaac Newton's Mathematical Principles of Natural Philosophy, and His System of the World*, trans. by Andrew Motte; trans. rev. F. C. Cajori. Chicago: Encyclopaedia Britannica.

Nietzsche, Friedrich 1957: *The Use and Abuse of History*. Indianapolis: Bobbs-Merrill. First published in 1874.

Noone, John B. 1980: *Rousseau's Social Contract*. Athens: University of Georgia Press.

Nozick, Robert 1974: *Anarchy, State and Utopia*. New York: Basic Books.

Oakeshott, Michael 1975: *On Human Conduct*. Oxford: Clarendon Press.

Oberschall, A. 1965: *Social Research in Germany, 1848–1914*. New York: Basic Books.

Okin, Susan Moller 1979: *Women in Western Political Thought*. Princeton: Princeton University Press.

Pareto, V. 1935: *Mind and Society*. 4 vols. New York: Harcourt. First published 1915–19.

—— 1971: *Manual of Political Economy*. New York: Augustus Kelley. First published in 1906.

Passmore, J. 1966: *A Hundred Years of Philosophy*. Rev. edn. New York: Basic Books. First published in 1957.

Pastore, N. 1974: Re-evaluation of Boring on Kantian influence, nineteenth-century nativism, Gestalt psychology and Helmholtz. *Journal of the History of the Behavioral Sciences*, 10.

Pattee, H. H. 1976: Physical theories of biological coordination. In M. Grene and E. Mendelssohn (eds).

Pettit, Philip 1977: *The Concept of Structuralism: a critical analysis*. Berkeley: University of California Press.

Plumb, J. H. 1967: *The Origins of Political Stability: England 1675–1725*. Boston: Houghton Mifflin.

Polanyi, Michael 1958: *Personal Knowledge*. Chicago: University of Chicago Press.

—— 1968: Life's irreducible nature. *Science*, 160.

Polkinghorne, J. C. 1984: *The Quantum World*. London: Longman.

Popper, Karl 1934: *Logik der Forschung*. Vienna: J. Springer. English edn, London: Hutchinson, 1959.

—— 1962: *The Open Society and Its Enemies*, vol. 2. London: Routledge and Kegan Paul.

—— 1963: *Conjectures and Refutations*. London: Routledge and Kegan Paul.

Poster, M. 1975: *Existential Marxism in Postwar France*. Princeton: Princeton University Press.

Poulantzas, Nicos 1969: *Political Power and Social Classes*. London: Verso.

Pribram, K. H. 1971: *Languages of the Brain*. Englewood Cliffs, N. J. Prentice-Hall.

—— 1982: Reflections on the place of the brain in the ecology of mind. In W. B. Weimer and D. S. Palermo (eds), *Cognition and the Symbolic Processes*, vol. 2. Hillsdale, N.J.: Lawrence Erbaum.

Putnam, H. 1962: The analytic and the synthetic. In H. Feigl and G. Maxwell (eds).

—— 1967: The mental life of some machines. Reprinted *Philosophical Papers*, vol. 2 (1975). Cambridge: Cambridge University Press.

Quesnay, François 1972: *Tableau Economique*, ed. with new material, translations, and notes by M. Kuczynski and R. L. Meek. London: Macmillan. First published in 1758–9.

Quine, V. W. O. 1951: Two dogmas of empiricism. *Philosophical Review*, 60.

—— 1968: Ontological relativity. *Journal of Philosophy*, 65, no. 7.

—— 1969: Epistemology naturalized. In Quine (ed.), *Ontological Relativity and Other Essays*. New York: Columbia University Press.

Radner, M. and Winokur, S. (eds) 1970: *Minnesota Studies in the Philosophy of Science*, vol. 4. Minneapolis: University of Minnesota Press.

Randall, J. H. 1940: *The Making of the Modern Mind*. Cambridge, Mass.: Riverside Press.

—— 1962: *The Career of Philosophy*. New York: Columbia University Press.

Ravetz, Jerome R. 1971: *Scientific Knowledge and Its Social Problems*. New York: Oxford University Press.

Reiber, R. E. (ed.) 1980: *Wilhelm Wundt and the Making of a Scientific Psychology*. New York: Plenum.

Reiman, Jeffrey H. 1984: *The Rich Get Richer and the Poor Get Prison*. 2nd edn. New York: Wiley.

Ricardo, David 1972: *The Principles of Political Economy and Taxation*. Introduction by Michael Fogarty. London: J. M. Dent. First published in 1817.

Ricoeur, Paul 1970: *Freud and Philosophy*. New Haven: Yale University Press. First published in Paris in 1965 under the title *De l'interpretation. Essai sur Freud*.

Ringer, Fritz 1969: *The Decline of the German Mandarins: the German academic community, 1890–1933*. Cambridge, Mass.: Harvard University Press.

Robinson, James Harvey 1912: *The New History*. New York: Macmillan.

Rorty, Richard 1970: In defense of eliminative materialism. *Review of Metaphysics*, 24.

—— 1979: *Philosophy and the Mirror of Nature*. Princeton: Princeton University Press.

—— 1982: *Consequences of Pragmatism*. Minneapolis: University of Minnesota Press.

—— 1986: From logic to language to play: a plenary address to the Inter-American Congress, Guadalajara, Mexico. *Proceedings and Addresses of The American Philosophical Association*, 59.

Rousseau, Jean-Jacques 1950: *The Social Contract and Discourses*, trans. G. P. H. Cole. New York: E. P. Dutton. *The Social Contract* was first published in 1762.

Rudner, Richard 1966: *Philosophy of Social Science*. Englewood Cliffs, N.J.: Prentice-Hall.

Russell, Bertrand 1903: *Principles of Mathematics*. Cambridge: Cambridge University Press.

—— 1905: On denoting. In H. Feigl and W. Sellars (eds).

—— 1910–11: Knowledge by acquaintance and knowledge by description. In *Mysticism and Logic*. New York: Doubleday, 1957.

—— 1914: The relation of sense-data to physics. In *Mysticism and Logic*.

—— 1927: *The Analysis of Matter*. London: Kegan Paul.

—— 1948: *Human Knowledge: its scope and limits*. London: Allen and Unwin.

Ryan, Alan 1970: *John Stuart Mill*. New York: Pantheon.

Samelson, Franz 1979: Putting psychology on the map: ideology and intelligence testing. In A. R. Buss (ed.), *Psychology in a Social Context*. New York: Irvington.

Samuelson, P. 1938: A note on the pure theory of consumer's behavior. *Economica*.

Sartre, Jean-Paul 1971: *L'idiot de la famille: Gustave Flaubert*. Paris: Gallimard.

Saveth, Edward N. 1964: *American History and the Social Sciences*. New York: Free Press.

Sayer, D. 1979: *Marx's Method*. Brighton: Harvester.

Schaffner, K. F. 1967: Approaches to reduction. *Philosophy of Science*, 34.

Schaikh, A. 1981: The poverty of algebra. In Steedman et al., *The Value Controversy*. London: NLB.

Schlick, Moritz 1959: Positivism and realism. Reprinted in A. J. Ayer (ed.) *Logical Positivism*. New York: Free Press. Originally published in German in 1932.

Schlipp, P. A. (ed.) 1951: *The Philosophy of Bertrand Russell*. New York: Tudor.

Schorske, Carl E. 1955: *German Social Democracy: 1905–17*. Cambridge, Mass.: Harvard University Press.

Schumpeter, J. A. 1954: *History of Economic Analysis*. New York: Oxford University Press.

Schutz, Alfred 1966: *The Collected Papers*. 3 vols. The Hague: Niijhoff.

Scriven, Michael 1962: Explanations, predictions and laws. In Feigl and Maxwell (eds).

—— 1964: Views of human nature. In T. W. Wann (ed.), *Behaviorism and Phenomenology*. Chicago: University of Chicago Press.

Secord, Paul F. 1986: Social psychology as a science: philosophical, psychological and sociological perspectives. In Margolis et al., *Psychology: designing the discipline*. Oxford: Basil Blackwell.

Sellars, Wilfred 1949: Realism and the new way of words. In Feigl and Sellars (eds).

—— 1956: Empiricism and the philosophy of mind. In H. Feigl and M. Scriven (eds).

—— 1961: The language of theories. Reprinted in W. Sellars *Science, Perception and Reality*. London: Routledge and Kegan Paul, 1963.

Shapere, D. 1969: Notes towards a post-positivist interpretation of science. In Peter Achinstein and Stephen F. Barker (eds).

Shotter, John 1984: *Social Accountability and Self*. Oxford: Basil Blackwell.

Skinner, B. F. 1953: *Science and Human Behavior*. New York: Macmillan.

Skinner, Quentin 1978: *The Foundations of Modern Political Thought*. 2 vols. Cambridge: Cambridge University Press.

—— (ed.) 1985: *The Return of Grand Theory in the Human Sciences*. Cambridge: Cambridge University Press.

Sleeper, Ralph W. 1986: *The Necessity of Pragmatism: John Dewey's conception of philosophy*. New Haven: Yale University Press.

Small, Albion 1924: *Origins of Sociology*. New York: Russell and Russell.

Smart, J. J. C. 1956: The reality of theoretical entities. *Australasian Journal of Philosophy*, 34.

Smith, Adam 1976: *An Inquiry into the Nature and Causes of the Wealth of Nations*; general eds, R. H. Campbell and A. S. Skinner; textual ed., W. B. Todd, 2 vols. Oxford: Clarendon Press. First published in 1776.

—— 1980: *Essays on Philosophical Subjects*; general eds, D. P. Raphael and A. S. Skinner; textual eds, W. P. P. Wightman and J. C. Bryce. Oxford: Clarendon Press.

Somit, Albert and Tanenhaus, Joseph 1967: *The Development of American Political Science: from Burgess to behavioralism*. Boston: Allyn and Bacon.

Spencer, Herbert 1876–97: *Principles of Sociology*. New York: Appleton.

—— 1897: *Social Statics*. New York: Appleton. First published in 1850.

—— 1901: *Essays, Scientific, Political and Speculative*, vol 1. New York: Appleton.

—— 1902: *The Principles of Psychology*. 3rd edn. 2 vols. New York: Appleton. First published in 1855; second edition in 1870.

—— 1976: *First Principles*. Westport: Greenwood Press. First published in 1862.

Sperry, R. W. 1969: A modified concept of consciousness. *Psychological Review*, 76.

—— 1976: Mental phenomena as causal determinants in brain functions. In Globus et al. (eds), *Consciousness and the Brain*. New York: Plenum.

Spitz, Lewis W. 1955: Natural law and history in Herder. *Journal of the History of Ideas*, 16.

Staats, Arthur 1983: *Psychology's Crisis of Disunity*. New York: Praeger.

Stedman-Jones, G. 1973: Engels and the end of classical German philosophy. *New Left Review*, 79.

Steinberg, Stephen 1981: *The Ethnic Myth*. New York: Athenaeum.

Stinchcombe, A. L. 1968: *Constructing Social Theories*. New York: Harcourt.

Stitch, Stephen 1983: *From Folk Psychology to Cognitive Science: the case against belief*. Cambridge, Mass.: MIT Press.

Stroud, Walter L., Jr 1984: Biographical explanation is low-powered science. *American Psychologist*, 39, no. 8.

Sumner, William Graham 1883: *What the Social Classes Owe to Each Other*. New York: Harper.

Suppe, Frederick 1977: *The Structure of Scientific Theories*. Urbana: University of Illinois Press.

Taylor, Charles 1964: *The Explanation of Behavior*. London: Routledge and Kegan Paul.

—— 1971: Interpretation and the sciences of man. *Review of Metaphysics*, 25, no. 1.

—— 1975: *Hegel*. Cambridge: Cambridge University Press.
—— 1982: Rationality. In M. Hollis and S. Lukes (eds).
Therborn, G. 1976: *Science, Class and Society: on the formation of sociology and historical materialism*. London: NLB.
Thompson, E. P. 1963: *The Making of the English Working Class*. New York: Pantheon.
—— 1978: *The Poverty of Theory and Other Essays*. London: Merlin.
Toulmin, Stephen 1961: *Foresight and Understanding*. London: Hutchinson.
—— 1969: From logical analysis to conceptual history. In Peter Achinstein and Stephen F. Barker (eds).
—— 1972: *Human Understanding*, vol. 1. Princeton: Princeton University Press.
Turner, R. S.: Helmholtz, sensory physiology and the disciplinary development of German psychology. in W. R. Woodward and M. G. Ash (eds).
Turvey, M. T., Shaw, R. E., Reed, E. S. and Mace, W. M. 1981: Ecological laws of perceiving and acting: in reply to Fodor and Pylyshyn. *Cognition*, 9.
Veblen, Thorstein 1957: *The Higher Learning in America: a memorandum on the conduct of universities by business men*. New York: Sagamore. First published in 1918.
Vesey, Lawrence 1965: *The Emergence of the American University*. Chicago: University of Chicago Press.
Wallace, William A. 1972: *Causality and Scientific Explanation*. Ann Arbor: University of Michigan Press.
Watkins, J. W. N. 1963: Methodological individualism and social tendencies. In Brodbeck (ed.), *Readings in the Philosophy of the Social Sciences*. New York: Macmillan.
Watson, J. B. 1963: Psychology as the behaviorist sees it. In W. Dennis (ed.), *Readings in the History of Psychology*. New York: Appleton-Century-Crofts.
Weber, M. 1949: Objectivity in social science and social policy. In *The Methodology of the Social Sciences*. New York: Free Press.
—— 1973: *Gesammelte Aufsatze zur Wissenschaftslehre*. Tübingen: J. C. B. Mohr.
—— 1975: *Roscher and Kneis: the logical problems of historical economics*, trans. with an introduction by Guy Oakes. New York: Free Press.
—— 1978: *Economy and Society*. Berkeley: University of California Press.
Weimer, W. B. 1975: The psychology of inference and expectations: some preliminary remarks. In G. Maxwell and A. R. Anderson (eds), *Minnesota Studies in the Philosophy of Science*, vol. 6. Minneapolis: University of Minnesota Press.
—— 1976: Manifestations of mind: some conceptual and empirical issues. In Globus et al. (eds), *Consciousness and the Brain*. New York: Plenum.
—— 1977: A conceptual framework of cognitive psychology. In R. Shaw and J. Bransford (eds), *Perceiving, Acting and Knowing: towards an ecological psychology*. Hillsdale, N.J.: Lawrence Erbaum.
Weininger, S. J. 1984: The molecular structure conundrum: can classical chemistry be reduced to quantum chemistry. *Journal of Chemical Education*, 61.
Weiss, Paul A. 1971: *Hierarchical organized systems in theory and practice*. New York: Hafner.
Wells, G. A. 1959: *Herder and After: a study in the development of sociology*. The Hague: Mouton.
White, Hayden 1973: *Metahistory: the historical imagination in nineteenth-century Europe*. Baltimore: Johns Hopkins University Press.

Wightman, W. P. D. 1976: Adam Smith and the history of ideas. In A. S. Skinner and T. Wilson (eds), *Essays on Adam Smith*. Oxford: Oxford University Press.

Williams, Meredith 1985: Wittgenstein's rejection of scientific psychology. *Journal for the Theory of Social Behavior*, 15.

Wimsatt, W. C. 1976: Reductionism, levels of organization, and the mind-body problem. In Globus et al. (eds), *Consciousness and the Brain*. New York: Plenum.

Winch, Donald 1978: *Adam Smith's Politics: an essay in historiographic revision*. Cambridge: Cambridge University Press.

Winch, Peter 1958: *The Idea of a Social Scheme*. New York: Humanities Press.

Wittgenstein, Ludwig 1961: *Tractatus Logico-Philosophicus*. London: Routledge and Kegan Paul. First published in Germany in 1921.

Wood, Gordon S. 1969: *The Creation of the American Republic, 1776–89*. New York: W. W. Norton.

Woodward, W. R. and Ash, M. G. (eds) 1982: *The Problematic Science: psychology in nineteenth-century thought*. New York: Praeger.

Woolley, R. G. 1978: Must a molecule have shape? *American Chemical Society*, 100.

Wundt, W. 1897: *Outlines of Psychology*, trans. C. H. Judd. Leipzig: W. Engelman.

Zinn, Howard 1980: *A People's History of the United States*. New York: Harper.

Index